BUILDING SUSTAINABLE LEGACIES

THE NEW FRONTIER OF SOCIETAL VALUE CO-CREATION

T0326217

WRITING F

Breaking with academic tradition, this journal offers a unique selection of articles that are written by looking at the future challenges first and then translating these into present times. The right-aligned layout is a material way of reminding us of the fact that "no problem can be solved from the same level of consciousness that created it" (A. Einstein).

PAST ←——————————————————————————→ **FUTURE**

OUR FOCUS

We provide hands-on, pragmatic and user-friendly research, suggestions and case studies as a resource for organisations that are committed to implementing sustainability. It is high time to build bridges between business and academia, with the clear purpose of helping business become truly sustainable.

There are four dimensions to the journal:

1. Understand sustainability challenges
2. Specific dimensions of business sustainability
3. Exciting new solutions to implement
4. Case studies of leading business examples

In addition, we will produce a special issue annually dedicated to an important theme.

UNDERSTANDING CHALLENGES
NEW SOLUTIONS
DIFFERENT DIMENSIONS
BUSINESS EXAMPLES

FEATURING THOUGHT LEADERS OF THE FUTURE

We are featuring professionals from around the world who are at the forefront of knowledge creation: they are pursuing a part-time doctoral sustainable business degree while working actively in various industries worldwide.

Routledge
Taylor & Francis Group

LONDON AND NEW YORK

BUILDING SUSTAINABLE LEGACIES
THE NEW FRONTIER OF SOCIETAL VALUE CO-CREATION

General Editor Katrin Muff,
Business School Lausanne, Switzerland

Illustrator Klaus Elle   *Designer* Yasmina Volet

Illustrations throughout *Building Sustainable Legacies* are supplied by and reproduced with the kind permission of Klaus Elle. Illustrations are an integral part of the journal's design and may not be representative of a contributor's article where it appears on the same page. For more information please contact General Editor Katrin Muff at katrin.muff@bsl-lausanne.ch

First published in 2015 by Greenleaf Publishing

Published in 2017 by Routledge
4 Park Square, Milton Park, Abingdon Oxon OX14 4RN
605 Third Avenue, New York, NY 10017

Routledge is an imprint of the Taylor & Francis Group, an informa business.

ISBN: 9781783533695 (pbk)

BUILDING
SUSTAINABLE LEGACIES

THE NEW FRONTIER OF SOCIETAL VALUE CO-CREATION

ISSUE 7 - DECEMBER 2015

Theme Issue: **Award-winning Case Studies 2015**
A Special Issue of Building Sustainable Legacies

Editor:

Katrin Muff, Dean, Business School Lausanne, Switzerland

ISBN: 978-1-78353-369-5

print ISSN 2053-8898   *online* ISSN 2053-8901

About Business School Lausanne

Business School Lausanne (BSL) is a leading innovator in business education and ranks 3rd in Switzerland (QS 2012-13 Top 200 Global Business Schools). The school's ACBSP accredited degree programs include BBA, Masters, full-time modular MBA, Executive MBA and DBA programs. BSL also provides Executive Training in General Management, Corporate Finance (with preparation for the CFA Level I examination), and Sustainable Business (in collaboration with the University of St Gallen). BSL takes a pragmatic approach to learning by applying theory to practice and is backed by a multidisciplinary faculty of business professionals. BSL attracts students from around the world, creating a multicultural environment of more than 60 nationalities. Established in 1987, BSL is the co-founder of the 50+20 initiative on Management Education for the World (www.50plus20.org) in partnership with the Global Responsible Leadership Initiative (www.grli.org) and the Principles of Responsible Management Education (UN backed PRME).

For more information visit www.bsl-lausanne.ch.

THOUGHT LEADERS OF THE FUTURE

FREDERIC NARBEL

WHO AM I?

Frederic Narbel started his career in Kazakhstan in 2006 after earning his Bachelor of Business Administration from BSL. He then joined Alcoa in Russia as Strategic Marketing Manager and was nominated to Alcoa's talent acquisition programme. After completing his EMBA, he returned to Switzerland and worked in the dental and orthopaedic industries holding the positions of Director of Sales and Operations with a Swiss company. He now works in Geneva, Shanghai and Singapore for a US Dairy company as Director International Sales. Frederic holds a Bachelor in Business Administration, an Executive MBA and is currently completing his Doctorate in Business Administration from Business School Lausanne.

MY INSPIRATION:

My inspiration is to understand how to structure the capital of corporations for it to foster the adoption of sustainable business practices.

DREAMS & AMBITION:

- To understand what makes corporations sustainable.
- To propose a capital structure model fostering the adoption of sustainable business practices.
- To transition from theory to practice.

GULEN HASHMI

WHO AM I?

I am a hospitality professional with over 18 years' experience in the hotel industry. My work experience in the various Hilton International hotels provided me invaluable insights and experience in the management of hotel chains. Then it made sense to move on to the management of small hotels where as a hotel manager, I have been able to apply my know-how at a smaller scale, yet with more flexibility and a higher degree of adaptivity. Moreover, this very decision helped me to maintain a balance between my work life and my family life. Having harnessed this balance for a couple of years, I deeply started feeling the need for self-actualization which led to doing an Executive MBA, a second master's in Environmental Governance and a DBA at the BSL. Since May 2015, I have been working as a senior consultant for the Geneva-based international NGO, WaterLex, leading the "Human Right to Water in the Hotel Industry" project. I am happy juggling through various tenets of life to serve and benefit others, which help me create significance rather than success.

MY INSPIRATION:

My inspiration and life motto is **LIFE itself**, which consists of the following:

L: Love for the Universe
I: Imagination
F: Focus on Significance
E: Effectiveness

DREAMS & AMBITION:

My passion in life is to contribute to the creation of a life that feels good on the inside and serves a common good at the same time. I also believe that organizations can sustainably go beyond success to become significant and contribute to the benefit of others. This pursuit of significance involves addressing social issues in corporate missions while pursuing economic success simultaneously. In this context, my focal research point is helping companies enhance their employee engagement and well-being at the workplace, which would lead to higher business performance at the same time. I strongly believe that the unique DBA programme at the Business School Lausanne, which serves as a bridge between business and academia, will enable me to pursue my passion.

SYEDA NAZISH ZAHRA BUKHARI

Who Am I? A question I am sometimes scared to ask even myself, because of the overpowering stream of countless answers I will get. Nazish Bukhari is simultaneously a teacher and a student; she is a mom and a daughter; she is a supportive life partner and a demanding wife; a friend, a listener, a care provider, an achiever, a gold medallist in academics, and so much more. But *Who Am I?* is not what I think about; for me the burning question is "What Do I Want To Be?" This is the thought that gives me the strength and courage to handle all of the challenges life throws at me each and every day. Nazish Bukhari wants to be "The Best" in every role she takes. I want to be a positive contributor to all the lives that I touch. I want to be a ray of change, hope, and inspiration for my students and for my nation. I want to be *complete* and all this is possible just through *knowledge*.

MY INSPIRATION:

My inspiration, very briefly stated, is "**My Family**".

DREAMS & AMBITION:

I want to be remembered for my positive contributions towards the body of knowledge and the development of my nation. My doctoral research, specifically being conducted and tailored according to my geographic region, will take me closer to my goal.

I want to continuously augment my knowledge and skill set and Business School Lausanne has been the source of knowledge, skill development and strength since the day I applied for its doctoral programme.

SHAMAILA GULL

WHO AM I?

Shamaila Gull is working as a lecturer at the Institute of Business and Information Technology, University of the Punjab, Lahore, Pakistan since 2005. She is a teacher as well as a researcher. She has several research articles on her credit. She is also an elected member of Syndicate (Board of Governors) at her university. Currently, she is enrolled in a Doctoral program (DBA) at Business School of Lausanne, Switzerland. Her area of doctoral research is Corporate Sustainability.

MY INSPIRATION:

My inspiration has always been my "RELATIONSHIPS" with my family and friends.

DREAMS & AMBITION:

My dream has always been to contribute something positive by improving the quality of life of others. Now my area of doctoral program research, Corporate Sustainability, has turned my dream into a reality. By doing research in this specific area in the developing geographical region of the world, I hope to create some research-based knowledge which could play a significant role in improving the lives of common people.

- To contribute something positive by improving the quality of life of others.

- To create research-based knowledge which could play a significant role in improving the lives of common people in a developing country such as Pakistan.

- To make my country proud of me.

Editorial

Issue 7 *December 2015*

Katrin Muff

Dean, Business School Lausanne, Switzerland

IT IS MY GREAT PLEASURE TO PREFACE THE current issue of *Building Sustainable Legacies* featuring seven case studies of advanced sustainability firms from around the world.

The case studies have been conducted by doctoral research consultants in our DBA in Sustainable Business programme and feature a select number of exceptional organizations which have all received our 2015 BSL Sustainability Innovation Award.

The featured companies have been selected based on the Business Sustainability Typology (BST),[1] attempting to identify advanced sustainability types 2.0 and 3.0 companies in the countries in which our doctoral research consultants are active. Of the initial eight company candidates, we are featuring here seven organizations which have successfully passed the evaluation process that accompanied the case study

writing. One organization revealed itself as insufficiently advanced in how it has embedded sustainability and has thus not been recognized with an award.

The initial purely external company analysis had placed two of the seven award companies as BST 3.0 "truly sustainable" organizations and five as BST 2.0 "triple bottom line management" organizations. Further research with and within the organizations has slightly shifted this initial assessment resulting in three organizations typed as BST 3.0, two as BST 2.0 and two as a BST 1.0. Despite the BST 1.0 "refined shareholder management" model, the company results have nonetheless demonstrated important progress in embedding sustainability, particularly as compared to business-as-usual companies, which are especially prominent in its region (Pakistan). We have thus agreed to include the company in this selection as it demonstrates—as all other case studies—valuable and relevant lessons for anybody interested in how to embed sustainability in business, students and practitioners alike. Here is the overview of the featured organizations, alphabetically organized within each BST section:

---

1 Dyllick, Thomas and Muff, Katrin: "Clarifying the Meaning of Sustainable Business: Introducing a Typology from Business-as-Usual to True Business Sustainability", *Organization & Environment*, Online, 23 March 2015 (http://oae.sagepub.com/).

BST 3.0 organizations:

- ▶ Alternative Bank Schweiz (ABS), Switzerland, compiled and written by Frederic Narbel

- ▶ Lancaster London Hotel, United Kingdom, compiled and written by Gülen Hashmi

- ▶ Pebbles PVT Ltd, Pakistan, compiled and written by Nazish Bukhari

BST 2.0 organizations:

- ▶ Beechenhill Farm Hotel, United Kingdom, compiled and written by Gülen Hashmi

- ▶ Interloop Limited, Pakistan, compiled and written by Shamaila Gull

BST 1.0 organizations:

- ▶ Dynamic Sportswear Ltd, Pakistan, compiled and written by Shamaila Gull

- ▶ ICI Pakistan Ltd, Pakistan, compiled and written by Nazish Bukhari

Understanding that organizational sustainability cultures represent an integral and important element of our case study analyses, we have used the SCALA survey of Miller Consultants in the US for this purpose. The pioneering work of Kathy Miller and her team has allowed SCALA to become an emergent reference for companies around the world that attempt to understand their current position in embedding sustainability. Such an analysis serves as a most useful input when defining future sustainability and related change strategies as it has become clear that embedding sustainability is closely connected to a company's cultural profile with regard to key elements pertaining to sustainability. Such elements include the degree of trust in leadership, of employee engagement, of innovation and cooperation across the organization, the degree to which the leader is considered supporting sustainability, and to which degree compensation of management includes non-financial performance factors, as well as the type of previous change (e.g. incremental vs. quantum leap). The growing SCALA database allows comparisons within industries, regions or similar sized companies, some of which may provide interesting insight to an organizational transformation process.

The four authors are presenting their first case studies in this issue. Each of them has a particular interest in business sustainability which they are pursuing in action research projects with four of these companies in a next phase. This coming experience will further deepen their competences in accompanying organizations in their sustainability journeys both as consultants and future-relevant action researchers. Each author is portrayed individually as a thought leader in their own right and we look forward to receiving your comments about the cases that we are presenting here.

Last but not least, it is important to point out that these cases are not written to showcase these companies but to describe as accurately as possible their often very impressive journey in embedding sustainability in their organizations. It goes without saying that such journeys are full of challenges, obstacles, opportunities and successes and we have considered these mostly as learning journeys that we hope are of interest to our practitioner and academic readers.

Katrin Muff

Alternative Bank Schweiz AG
A banking model for the future*

Frederic Narbel
Alternative Bank Schweiz AG, Switzerland

Introduction

This paper is a contribution to a larger research aiming to compare sustainable companies to their more traditional counterparts. The goal is to identify core characteristics of sustainable companies and share them with organizations aspiring to become sustainable. As such, the aim of our research is to develop three comparable case studies which illustrate how an organization came to the notable results it has accomplished when critiqued from a sustainability perspective.

This paper is an attempt to produce a case study which is not only a contribution to the overall effort of the current and future Business School Lausanne research cohorts, but also provides an insightful tool to working professionals who are in managerial positions and have an interest in sustainable business practices. As such, the case study is written in a style that allows the reader to learn from other carefully screened companies' experiences so the lessons can be applied in a meaningful manner. The technical aspects linked to this case study are discussed in the appendix section in order to improve the reader's experience. The companies analysed in our case studies are recognized for their achievements in the field of sustainability. The reader has to keep in mind that this paper is part of a doctoral thesis and as such has been written in order to comply with the need for more formal criteria including clarity, precision and stringency of argumentation.

* The author would like to acknowledge the active contribution and support of Christian Arnsperger (external research analyst and scientific adviser to Alternative Bank Schweiz), Martin Rohner (CEO of Alternative Bank Schweiz) for granting access to his organization and for providing the necessary support to conduct the case study and Markus Mühlbacher (Head of Sustainability).

Alternative Bank Schweiz AG

A survey conducted in 1982 demonstrated that there was an interest in Switzerland for an alternative bank whose purpose would be to promote societal and environmental values. At the same time the Swiss population rejected an initiative of the Swiss Socialist Party aiming at suppressing Swiss bank secrecy with 73% of the votes (de Montmollin, 2001). These results created a turning point for those involved in ABS's creation as it was considered an opportunity given that 464,000 Swiss citizens expressed discomfort with the development of the Swiss financial centre and its practices to which ABS wanted to offer an alternative. Today and over 30 years later, ABS's CEO Martin Rohner and his team face a very similar discussion. This time the bank wants to develop an alternative model to the current asset management practices in the banking sector. Rohner and Markus Mühlbacher (Head of Sustainability) are looking at their bank's future and are asking themselves what these practices could look like to keep in line with ABS's very special mission and purpose.

> interest in Switzerland for an alternative bank whose purpose would be to promote societal and environmental values

Alternative Bank Schweiz AG is a joint stock company headquartered in Olten, Switzerland, and was incorporated in 1990. It had a balance sheet of CHF1.4 billion on 31 December 2013. It is the leading provider of ethical banking services and a pioneer in the implementation of social and environmental standards in Switzerland. What makes the bank special is that it generated value in 2013 not just for its owners, but also for the common good with 82% of its financial products. A good example illustrating the creation of value for the common good is ABS's value-added loan category labelled as "Efficient buildings". It is assessed by applying an internal rating method looking at the impact on the environment, the well-being of the people living in the building as well as the financial sustainability of the project for its owners (Alternative Bank Schweiz, 2014c). The second assessment is conducted by using the Swiss Minergie standard for energy efficient and environmental construction.

ABS is recognized as a sustainability leader as illustrated by the prize it was awarded in 2012 by the Cantonal Bank of Zürich for "putting into practice transparency, sustainability and ethics as its first principles of business strategy" (Alternative Bank Schweiz, 2012). ABS is also a member of Öbu, the Swiss Association for Sustainable Business (Öbu, 2014f). The bank emphasizes "the pursuit of ethical principles over profit maximization" (Alternative Bank Schweiz, 2014a) and pursues significant initiatives in the field of sustainability as illustrated for example by its loan issuance policy: "loans are issued principally in the area of social or ecological housing, organic agriculture, renewable energy, as well as SMEs" (Alternative Bank Schweiz, 2014a). ABS ranks highest on the Business Sustainably Typology Matrix proposed by Dyllick and Muff, as will be shown in this case study.

The four phases of organization development: 1980–2014

ABS's history will be reviewed in this section of the case study in order to understand how the bank reached its very advanced business sustainability position and how it became the recognized sustainability leader it is today. The review is divided into four distinct time periods and is based primarily on information available in the bank's *Moneta* quarterly publication.

Phase I: reflection, value protection and company creation

A survey conducted in 1982 demonstrated that there was an interest in Switzerland for an alternative bank whose purpose would be to promote societal and environmental values. As a result the bank established a list of positive and negative criteria aiming to describe the areas in which it wanted to be active and those it did not want to fund in any case (König & Wespe, 2006, pp. 45-47).[1] The list of negative criteria covered forces affecting humans and the environment in many sectors of the economy. It included nuclear energy, transportation and addictive products such as alcohol, tobacco and drugs. As a result and since then, projects funded by ABS are required to be decentralized, self-determined, in favour of gender equality[2] and demonstrate respect to the environment.

The working group for an alternative bank (GTBA) created in 1987 rapidly comprised 1,600 members and 120 organizations and companies. The first general assembly took place in 1988 during which it was decided that the name of the bank would be Alternative Bank Schweiz and that the legal form of the organization would be a joint stock company. During the same year, the association started raising capital in order to create the company and two branch offices in the Swiss states of Geneva and Ticino. It is interesting to refer to König and Wespe's work (2006, p. 15) which states, "the constitution of ABS on paper was not just a program; it also ensured compliance with its core values". This will for compliance is materialized in the company's Articles of Association with a very explicit description of the goals in article 2:

---

1 Mario König and Aglaia Wespe have published a review of ABS's history in a 70 page document titled "L'histoire d'une banque extraordinaire: L'alternative". The document was ordered by the bank for its 15th anniversary in 2006. The researchers will refer to the document throughout the case study as it includes a very comprehensive review of the various questions ABS and its founders were asking themselves in the early stages as well as within its first 15 years of operations.

2 Gender equality is one of ABS's core values. In all the documents reviewed by the researcher written in French, ABS made use of both the masculine and feminine subject pronouns which is not common. We see this as an affirmative action taken by ABS to be in compliance with its values.

the company aims to help support alternative economic, ecological, socio-political and cultural projects through the grant and management of funds and capital as well as other related activities in accordance to its guidelines, by the exploitation of a bank ... the bank will not work to maximize its profits (Alternative Bank Schweiz, 2014d, p. 3).

While article 2 clearly establishes the purpose of the organization, article 5 creates a safeguard by regulating the ownership structure of the company: "each shareholder may hold a maximum of 3% of all shares registered in the share register, including shares issued from authorized capital" (Alternative Bank Schweiz, 2014d, p. 5). It is interesting to note that ABS has included a further protection of its values in this article:

> **each shareholder may hold a maximum of 3% of all shares registered in the share register**

only corporations and public entities supporting the goals and ideals of the company are allowed to acquire registered Class A shares with privileged voting rights ... the company may buy the shares back for its own account or for the account of third parties at fair value if certain conditions relative to their acquisition are no longer met (Alternative Bank Schweiz, 2014d, p. 5).

König and Wespe (2006, p. 48) comment that "there was the fear of uncontrolled concentration of power to a minority which would divert ABS from its original goals" when writing the Articles of Association. They argue that it is a common fear in alternative and independent companies. Markus Mühlbacher confirms that today the board of directors has to review and accept every application to the share register (M. Mühlbacher, personal communication, 28 August 2014).

In 1989 the working group conditionally approved ABS's Articles of Association, the bank's policy in terms of investment and credit guidelines and the internal regulations of the organization (Alternative Bank Schweiz, 2013c, p. 40). Egger (1989, p. 5) states that ABS perceived at the time that the dominant economic system was primarily responsible for the intensification of environmental problems as well as for increasing social and economic inequalities worldwide. To Egger, ABS had to be opposed to continuous development and its business model had to be an alternative concentrating on the resolution of ecological and societal problems, providing equal rights to men and women, the satisfaction of basic human needs, the preservation of life, creativity and innovation.

The bank submitted its application to request the authorization to exercise its banking activities to the Swiss Federal Banking Commission in 1990. At that time 2,700 individuals, organizations and companies had subscribed to a share capital of CHF9.5 million which was CHF4.5 million more than what was required by Swiss law. The Federal Banking Commission granted its authorization and ABS opened its office in Olten, Switzerland (Alternative Bank Schweiz, 2013, p. 40). At the time, ABS's vision was comprehensive and focused. Primarily it was: not to engage in stock trading activities, international financial transactions, no involvement with funds of doubtful origin, limit its operations to classical banking operations of savings and credit, and to observe clear ethical and ecological guidelines in terms of financing activities, all of it with a partial suppression of Swiss bank secrecy and in total equality of genders (König & Wespe, 2006, p. 8).

Of note is an interesting article written by Raschle (1992, p. 3) in which he explains that the establishment of an alternative bank requires as much effort as the creation of a conventional financial establishment if not more. He states that there are specific features to an alternative bank such as the different needs of individuals in the field of human relations, the democratic decision-making process and the practice of greater transparency to customers which make the process even more complex. The difficulty of applying democracy to ABS's decision making process is well described by König and Wespe (2006, p. 21) who argue that due to the Swiss Federal Banking Commission being the one granting the rights to a bank to operate, a large assembly or foundation which would have been asked to vote a particular change to the proposal made to the Banking Commission would not have been practically feasible. In this case, a smaller group representing ABS's interests had to speak on behalf of all of its stakeholders. This is an interesting example illustrating the limitations of the founders' ideology when faced with practical realities.

In the SCALA survey, ABS's employees identified four reasons which they believe have led the bank to address sustainability issues:

▶ The first reason with 85.7% agreement is the awareness of the bank's responsibility to the environment.

▶ The second reason with 76.2% agreement is because of ABS's organizational purpose.

▶ In third place and with 61.9% agreement is the recognition of how ABS could address societal needs.

▶ In fourth place and with 42.9% agreement is the desire to create long-term value for its stakeholders.

Phase II: the early days

ABS ended 1991 with a balance sheet value of CHF57 million and a loss of CHF756,000. It had 3,750 clients and had granted 103 loans. The publication of these results was followed by the first audit of ABS's finances as imposed by Swiss law. The audit report acknowledged ABS's successful start but was not free of blame. According to König and Wespe (2006, p. 32) the report stated that utmost attention should be paid to ABS's profitability as it was a key point for the future of the bank. They continue by stating that in comparison to other regional banks, costs at ABS were very high. As a result, ABS concluded that costs had to be reduced in all sectors (König &

Wespe, 2006, p. 30). The fact that the Swiss Federal Banking Commission had insight on the profitability of the organization caused great nervousness to ABS's management. König and Wespe (2006, p. 30) quote Andreas P. Ragaz[3] saying in May 1992 that "ABS is financially weak. With the situation today, the bank should focus in priority on its own survival and therefore cannot even use a small part of its capabilities for other purposes". This is an important event because when ABS was founded, its main objective was essentially to make the bank viable not profitable. It was considered as being feasible once the total balance sheet value was of approximately CHF100 to CHF120 million (König & Wespe, 2006, p. 33).

At the same time and to add to the complexity of the situation, the accumulated frustrations among female employees resulted in the women's strike of 14 June 1991. Raschle (1992, p. 3) states that it was difficult to find required trained bank specialists and women were under-represented in the profession. He states that it was most likely one of the reasons why women were granted less interesting tasks and roles within the organization. König and Wespe (2006, p. 25) state that:

> both genders want alternative forms of working and operating. On the other hand, they want a clear hierarchy in the company and want nothing or almost nothing to do with the decision making process as it is perceived as being very complex.

Raschle (1992, p. 3) argues that at the same time, every team member mentioned problems associated with co-management. At first, most employees imagined they were part of a self-managed organization when they joined ABS. However, they realized rapidly that they were obliged to observe the daily life of a bank which does not always respect the principle of direct democracy. Very strict legislation governing the industry made changes almost impossible. The economic reality played a role in the way the company had been managed since then and in setting its future strategy.

In 1993, the deferred loss of the bank was fully compensated and a first capital increase was initiated. At the time and even with the financial metrics looking promising, ABS still faced significant challenges. Raschle (1992, p. 3) captures some of the frustrations and issues the bank faced in its early days very well in his article. He states that "like any other financial institution, ABS did not develop in a vacuum, but quite the opposite, in a highly regulated universe populated by a large competition. Compromise, even renouncing to certain initial objectives was therefore inevitable". 1994 ended with a net profit of CHF291,000. For the first time, CHF100,000 could be allocated to the incentive fund defined in the Articles of Association (Alternative Bank Schweiz, 2014d, pp. 2-3). In 1995, the bank celebrated its 5th anniversary and its balance sheet amounted to CHF185 million. At that time, the bank had

---

3 Andreas P. Ragaz has been part of ABS's project from the very beginning holding different roles within the organization.

BUILDING SUSTAINABLE LEGACIES

THE NEW FRONTIER OF SOCIETAL VALUE CO-CREATION

WRITING FROM THE FUTURE

Breaking with academic tradition, this journal offers a unique selection of articles that are written by looking at the future challenges first and then translating these into present times. The right-aligned layout is a material way of reminding us of the fact that "no problem can be solved from the same level of consciousness that created it" (A. Einstein).

PAST   **FUTURE**

OUR FOCUS

We provide hands-on, pragmatic and user-friendly research, suggestions and case studies as a resource for organisations that are committed to implementing sustainability. It is high time to build bridges between business and academia, with the clear purpose of helping business become truly sustainable.

There are four dimensions to the journal:

1. Understand sustainability challenges
2. Specific dimensions of business sustainability
3. Exciting new solutions to implement
4. Case studies of leading business examples

UNDERSTANDING CHALLENGES
NEW SOLUTIONS
DIFFERENT DIMENSIONS
BUSINESS EXAMPLES

In addition, we will produce a special issue annually dedicated to an important theme.

FEATURING THOUGHT LEADERS OF THE FUTURE

We are featuring professionals from around the world who are at the forefront of knowledge creation: they are pursuing a part-time doctoral sustainable business degree while working actively in various industries worldwide.

consistent application of its guidelines in its daily activities (Alternative Bank Schweiz, 2013c, p. 40).

The 3% cap on share ownership was increased to 5% during the General Assembly of May 2014 (M. Mühlbacher, personal communication, 28 August 2014). Martin Rohner explains that the increase in the cap on share ownership was necessary because of ABS's rapid growth which resulted in the bank being challenged by its equity ratio. ABS's capital monetization strategy is based on three pillars. The first one is to generate its own reserves through its own profits. The second and most important pillar is to raise new capital and deepen the level of investment of the existing shareholders (at the moment there are approximately 4,600 shareholders). The third pillar is relatively new. The bank is trying to mobilize large scale value-based investors that are willing to invest more money into ABS. This is the reason why ABS had to raise the cap on share ownership from 3 to 5% (M. Rohner, personal communication, 5 November 2014). Martin Rohner argues that this process was not simple and that it generated a lot of discussions during the General Assembly as it was feared that larger shareholders would dominate future General Assemblies. As a result, the board of directors was asked by the shareholders to present possible measures to reduce that risk. One of the solutions currently being explored is to disclose the name of the large shareholders present in the audience during the General Assembly for example. Another alternative is to become more specific on the decisions which need a qualified or unqualified majority. Martin Rohner states that he is currently working on it together with the board and that the proposed solution will be presented to the shareholders during the next General Assembly (M. Rohner, personal communication, 25 September 2014).

> the increase in the cap on share ownership was necessary because of ABS's rapid growth

ABS's position on the Business Sustainability Typology Matrix

The discussion taking place earlier in this case study enables the reader to become familiar with ABS's history and the various triggers at the level of the initiative, organization-culture and organization as a whole. The next part of the case study will assess ABS's positioning against the Business Sustainability Typology Matrix as proposed by Dyllick and Muff (2015, p. 13).

ABS's position will be assessed in the following paragraphs based on three criteria which are concerns, organizational perspective and values created. The reader will be taken first through a brief theoretical definition of the factors looked at and then the assessment will be presented.

Dyllick and Muff (2015) state that concerns are issues that businesses choose to consider and address (Dyllick & Muff, 2015, p. 4). ABS covers the three-dimensional concerns (economic, ecological and societal). This fact is materialized in reality by looking at ABS's annual reports in which one can see that the bank assesses its performance using financial, societal and environmental performance metrics. In its societal metrics, the bank considers the ratio between the lowest and the highest salary (1 to 3.69 in 2013) and the percentage of female employees among the company management (48% in 2013) for instance. In terms of environmental metrics the bank measures its emissions of greenhouse gases and the average energy consumption per employee (Alternative Bank Schweiz, 2013c, p. 2). The assumption is further confirmed by the SCALA survey results in which 65% of the respondents believe that ABS is trying to create social, environmental and economic value by addressing sustainability issues while 30% of the respondents believe that the bank is making a positive contribution solving critical societal challenges. This covers the prerequisites for a company to qualify as a Business Sustainability 2.0 organization.

The assumption is further confirmed by the fact that 73% of the respondents to SCALA strongly agreed that ABS's management integrates sustainability practices into its decision-making. With a mean of 1.27, ABS has a better rating than the benchmark which has a mean of 2.57. This comparison is of interest as it highlights one of ABS's key differentiating factors, namely its focus on sustainability. Moreover, 40% of the respondents to SCALA strongly agreed that ABS's management has a clear business case for pursuing sustainability goals. With a mean of 1.7 ABS has a significantly better rating than the benchmark which has a mean of 2.1, which means that the bank has a clearer vision on sustainability when compared to its counterparts.

Dyllick and Hockerts (2002) and Dyllick and Muff (2015, p. 5) add an additional dimension which "requires business to live off the income and preserve the capital base". Christian Arnsperger states in ABS's annual report (Alternative Bank Schweiz, 2013b, pp. 6-8) that in today's economy, growth is generally considered as very positive from an economic perspective but when looked at from an environmental perspective, it has a huge impact. If Switzerland's consumption habits were to be extended to the rest of the world, it would mean that humanity would consume the equivalent of the output of three planets per year. ABS does not endorse continuous growth. It proactively seeks not to be a neutral intermediary and aims to fulfil its social responsibility. The bank does not pursue the maximization of profit which gives it more freedom than other banks to focus on achieving broader values.

Christian Arnsperger (Alternative Bank Schweiz, 2013b, pp. 6-8) argues that the bank's objective is to contribute to building an economy which is more durable. The bank is convinced that economic growth can be selective and finely adjusted. It supports sectors consuming less energy, emitting fewer greenhouse gases, waste, and resulting in less poverty and inequality. The bank is targeting selective growth which is more socially responsible and environmentally friendly. He argues that Switzerland needs a larger ABS (a larger bank which could have a broader impact due to its size). The bank's balance sheet value is growing, so are the deposits made to the bank and the funds it invests. This strategy enables the bank to increase its impact and contribution to society. This strategy does not mean that the bank can live without being profitable. It is important for the bank to generate a sufficient margin in order to guarantee the long-term sustainability of its business model which will allow ABS to continue to be an alternative to the existing banks. The long-term perspective is confirmed by the SCALA survey results in which 45% of the respondents strongly agreed and a further 45% agreed that the leaders of the company take a long-term view when making decisions.

Organizational perspectives

Dyllick and Muff (2015, p. 5) explain that "other approaches for integrating sustainability into business focus not on the concerns, but on the organizational perspectives used by business. These include managing risks and opportunities and embedding sustainability throughout the organization".

Egger (1989, p. 5) states that ABS perceived in 1989 that the dominant economic system was primarily responsible for the intensification of environmental problems as well as for increasing social and economic inequalities worldwide. She further comments that ABS's business model is an alternative concentrating on the resolution of the ecological and societal problems, providing equal rights to men and women, the satisfaction of basic human needs, the preservation of life, creativity and innovation (Egger, 1989, p. 5). Article 2 of ABS's Articles of Association further confirms this point of view very explicitly:

the company aims to help support alternative economic, ecological, socio-political and cultural projects through the grant and management of funds and capital as well as other related activities in accordance to its guidelines, by the exploitation of a bank ... the bank will not work to maximize its profits (Alternative Bank Schweiz, 2014d, p. 3).

ABS has five fundamental values which are:

▶ To place ethics before profits

▶ To be a credible and transparent partner investing in the protection of natural resources

▶ To innovate and attain financial yields allowing for social development

▶ To inspire discussion on the role of capital and interests in the society in general

▶ To value the active participation of its stakeholders (Alternative Bank Schweiz, 2011, p. 3)

What defines a truly sustainable company is an outside-in versus an inside-out approach. In ABS's case the company was the means to reach an objective and not the end goal in itself. Article 2 of ABS's Articles of Association is the strongest possible confirmation of this assumption. It is clearly stated that the bank has goals it wants to reach and values it wants to protect. The bank is in itself the solution ABS's founders have found to solve the sustainability issues they had identified and wanted to address. As such ABS is a truly sustainable company when judged by the organizational perspective taken.

Values created

Dyllick and Muff (2015, p. 6) argue that there is a…

…third type of approach focusing neither on concerns nor on organizational perspectives, but on the particular values created or preserved by a business. They look at the output of the business process for defining BST, not on the input or the process. Different outputs discussed in the literature are integrating economic, ecological and social value creation, creating shared value, and the reemergence of social purpose.

> **Since its creation, ABS wanted to contribute to the creation of added-value as a direct outcome of the projects it funded**

Since its creation, ABS wanted to contribute to the creation of added-value as a direct outcome of the projects it funded and be very transparent about its results (whether positive or negative). Initially, ABS did this by publishing each loan including the name of the borrower, the amount lent and the purpose of the project in its *Moneta* publication. Over time and given the growth of the bank, this became more difficult. In order to allow for transparency on its loans, ABS developed a new system in 2013 that displayed the segmentation and allocation of its loans. The new system now enables ABS to demonstrate the positive impact a certain loan category has either in societal or ecological terms. ABS calls the added-value the "impact value". All of the loans granted are in compliance with ABS's standards and do not infringe any of the bank's exclusion criteria. ABS argues in its 2013 annual report (Alternative Bank Schweiz, 2013c, p. 21) that it was the first Swiss bank able to prove through its loan portfolio how it contributes to the common good. The new system does not only help the bank illustrate what it does but it also demonstrates how the bank invests its money in a more focused way. In 2013, nearly 82% of the loans generated either societal or environmental value (Alternative Bank Schweiz, 2013c, p. 21). The bank states "it is our responsibility as socially and ecologically responsible bank not to lose sight of the social and ecological impacts our funding activities have and to report them transparently" (Alternative Bank Schweiz, 2013c, p. 19).

ABS proposes seven value-added loan categories which are:

1. **Efficient buildings.** This loan category represented 20% of all loans in 2013. ABS assesses the value created by looking at two factors:

   ▶ An internal rating method which includes the impact on the environment, the well-being of the people living in the building as well as the financial sustainability of the project for its owners

   ▶ By taking a Swiss construction standard called Minergie into consideration

2. **Affordable housing** which has to be rented at the cost of capital with no profit for its owners representing 19% of all loans in 2013.

3. **Buildings with other social purposes** which have to show evidence that the project generates value to society for example through the creation of a habitat, as an innovative neighbourhood rehabilitation project or the protection of a monument representing 6% of the loans in 2013.

4. **Renewable energies** which have to be projects based on almost limitless sources of energy when looked at from a time perspective or which is renewed rapidly (sun, biomass, wind, etc.) representing 12% of the loans in 2013.

5. **Cultural and social benefits**. The organizations and institutions which are funded by ABS have to address a societal need for culture, training, health and people integration representing 10% of the loans in 2013.

6. **Sustainable farming**. The farming, marketing or processing of agricultural products with at least one of the following certifications: Bio Suisse, Demeter or Fair Trade representing 4% of the loans in 2013.

7. **Sustainable economies** which have to either be a provider of products supporting a sustainable economy, work methods which are perceived as particularly sustainable or a project which is very similar to ABS's endeavour representing 3% of the loans in 2013.

There is an eighth category discussed in ABS's results which is a combination of two loan categories resulting in affordable housing meeting ecological standards, representing 8% of the loans in 2013. Christian Arnsperger confirms that:

> the new tool used to evaluate ABS's loan portfolio helps the bank to better illustrate what it does as an organization and its goal which is to maintain a level of at least 80% of all loans having an added value created at any given time (C. Arnsperger, personal communication, 21 June 2014).

ABS also provides interesting results in terms of stakeholder engagement which is a key factor in the sustainability assessment of the company; 60% of the respondents to SCALA agreed that ABS has a clear strategy for engaging all internal stakeholders in its sustainability efforts, while 55% of the respondents to SCALA agreed that ABS has mechanisms in place to actively engage with external stakeholders about its sustainability efforts. With a mean of 2.20 ABS ranks better than the benchmark which has a mean of 2.50. This comparison is of interest as it means that ABS is more likely to take the broader interest into consideration while making a decision by including external stakeholders in the discussion when compared to its traditional counterparts. Fifty-two per cent of the respondents to SCALA strongly agreed and 42% agreed that ABS sends a clear and consistent message to external stakeholders about its commitment to sustainability.

When assessed from a value creation perspective, ABS is a company qualifying as truly sustainable as its ultimate goal goes beyond the triple bottom line value creation. ABS is aiming at creating value for the common good and therefore qualifies as a Business Sustainability 3.0 organization.

Key features of ABS's approach to business sustainability

This section identifies approaches to doing business that differentiate ABS from companies which are not as developed when looked at from a sustainability perspective. Two key features have been identified, transparency and the creation of a board of ethics. These two aspects are very different and not something ABS's more traditional counterparts engage in.

Transparency about customers

ABS has strived for its activities and their impact to be as transparent as possible whether they are related to the inside or the outside of the bank. From the very beginning it expected its customers to make an effort in the form of providing the bank with honest information on the origin of their money and for it to be declared to the tax authorities. A key element in fostering transparency was the partial removal of Swiss bank secrecy. The loans granted by the bank had to be published in *Moneta* and in the bank's activity report. This was only possible with the consent of the customer. This is a characteristic that worked without problems for many years even though it was a risky experiment. König and Wespe (2006, p. 50) state that *Moneta* never aimed to just be a journal for customers. Vieili (1992, p. 3) argues that because of ABS's desire for transparency and publication of its thought-process, *Moneta* echoed debates on the expansion and evolution of ABS since the beginning. He states that divergent views and interests were able to be expressed freely. He further adds that many questions, such

> **A key element in fostering transparency was the partial removal of Swiss bank secrecy**

as ABS's positioning within the Swiss financial centre and the direction to take will have to be answered or will need to be discussed in the future. He concludes by saying that the publication has to offer the right platform for a transparent discussion. This approach is a key differentiating factor as ultimately customers agreeing to the bank's transparency requirements were forced to comply with its values and therefore were expecting the bank to protect them and act accordingly creating a self-reinforcing relationship. As success was confirmed, this focus on transparency reinforced the confidence that the public had in ABS. König and Wespe (2006, p. 51) argue that it was also a demonstration to conventional banks that transparency was achievable in the Swiss banking industry and therefore made it more difficult for them to argue that banking activity could not survive without secrecy. This statement is essential as it truly confirms ABS's achievement of becoming a credible alternative to the traditional banking sector.

König and Wespe (2006, pp. 51-53) argue that transparency on and discussions of differences (when in the general public's interest) belonged to ABS's business culture. They state that *Moneta* allowed ABS to apply the principle of trust through transparency. ABS's desire to be a bank "made of glass" (Raschle, 1992, p. 3) was not limited to accounts and loans: it covered the entire project for an alternative bank. It is interesting to note that the principle of transparency reached unexpected limits in its implementation. Improving search engines on the internet with access to the names and loan details included in the digital version of the reports made the dissemination of the information possible resulting in a major problem when considered from a privacy and data protection perspective. As a result the publication of names in an electronic format was discontinued (König & Wespe, 2006, p. 51).

ABS's focus on transparency resulted in today's very high level of trust within the organization; 70% of the respondents to SCALA agreed and 15% strongly agreed that the overall level of trust within ABS is high. With a mean of 2.05 ABS's employees have a stronger level of trust when compared to the benchmark which has a mean of 2.17. The 2.05 score means that ABS's employees are more likely to trust their colleagues when compared to other traditional financial organizations. It is argued that the higher level of trust comes from ABS's more democratic decision-making process.

Board of ethics

Wicki (1991, p. 1) states in *Moneta* that at the foundation of the bank in 1990, the board of ethics had been designed as a signal to the financial world in which few businesses cared about environmental or social issues. The board of ethics was tasked to think about the overall importance of banking, the role of money in society and aspects of power related to financial and credit operations among others. It is interesting to note that the founders of the bank made sure the existence of the board of ethics was protected with article 20 of ABS's Articles of Association. Article 20 states that "the General Assembly elects a Board of Ethics for 3 years on the proposal of the Board of Directors. It is an independent ethics control entity in charge of controlling the implementation and supervision of ABS's ethics principles" (Alternative Bank Schweiz, 2014d, p. 11). Wicki (1991, p. 11) argues that the board of ethics, by the fact that it does not intend to intervene directly, must fulfil the role of supreme body of control. Its seven members personify the moral and political motivations which led to the creation and startup of ABS. ABS's business must obey social criteria and environmental policies that offer a real alternative to the commercial practice of most other banks (Wicki, 1991, p. 1).

In 2005, the board of ethics came to the conclusion that it was no longer the adequate tool to protect ABS's values. As explained by Bühler in her article (2005, p. 13) "despite the promising model of the Board of Ethics, it concluded that a new form of ethical review was required". König and Wespe (2006, p. 53) state that the board of ethics had the highest possible position on the organizational chart, even above the board of directors. The intention of the founders was to protect ABS and its board of directors from making choices leading them to become yet another bank similar to the very banks to which they aimed to propose an alternative. According to Bühler (2005, p. 11), the board of ethics in its original format had resulted in a structural conflict between two bodies elected by the General Assembly namely the board of directors and the board of ethics. The problem came from the fact that the scopes of responsibility between the two boards were somewhat blurred. She states that the board of directors assumed the responsibility for the business and therefore had decision-making powers. On the other hand, the board of ethics had control over the entire business; a responsibility which is also important but which had no decision-making power. In her article Wicki (2005, p. 11) explains that the new model proposed to the board of directors in 2005 aimed to strengthen and separate the roles of the two boards within the bank. To her, it was necessary because the mission of the board of ethics was not very well understood outside of the organization. She states that the board of ethics was seen from time to time by external stakeholders as being in charge of setting ABS's strategy or vision which was false. These two tasks were the sole responsibility of the board of directors.

The new model aims at strengthening the role of the board of directors which must be free to act within the framework of the implementation of ethical strategic objectives of the bank. As a result and since 2005, the Institute of Business Ethics at the University of St-Gallen controls the implementation of the ethical orientation of ABS and publishes its own independent report in the bank's annual report. (The institute is referred to as the ethics control body in this case study). The benefit of outsourcing the responsibility to a third party helps eliminate the recurrent difficulty of determining the position of the board of ethics within the organization and the possible conflicts of interest arising from it (König & Wespe, 2006). Finally, working with a third party enables a clear separation of the decision-making power of the board of directors and an independent and impartial monitoring of ABS's activities by an independent body. In today's format the board of directors steers the bank including its ethical direction and the external ethics control body controls how the bank deals with ethical questions, just like external auditors control the use of ABS's funds (M. Rohner, personal communication, 5 November 2014).

ABS today and tomorrow

Christian Arnsperger sees ABS today as being a microcosm defined as a stable sustainable alternative ecosystem (C. Arnsperger, personal communication, 21 June 2014); 72% of the respondents to SCALA strongly agreed and 19% agreed that a commitment to sustainability is essential to the company's success in the long term. With a mean of 1.95 ABS's employees have stronger perceptions of this value compared to the benchmark which has a mean of 2.33. Forty-two per cent of the respondents to SCALA agreed and 29% strongly agreed that they were engaged in work that is connected to sustainability goals. With a mean of 2.05 ABS ranks much better than the benchmark which has a mean of 3.00. This result means that ABS's employees feel that they are contributing more to achieving sustainability targets than their counterparts in traditional financial organizations.

Understanding the employees' assessment of their management and company is also critical; 57% of the respondents to SCALA identified ABS's management as being significantly better with regards to its commitment to sustainability while 38% thought it was better when compared to other Swiss banks. Of the respondents, 47.6% identified ABS as being proactive and 52.3% identified the bank as being active in its approach to sustainability. Seventy per cent of the respondents to SCALA identified ABS as being very engaged with sustainability, 36% of the respondents strongly agreed that ABS's management is able to inspire both its internal and external stakeholders about sustainability-focused issues and initiatives, and 59% agreed. ABS's mean of 2.18 is comparable to the benchmark which has a mean of 2.20. Forty-eight per cent of the respondents to SCALA strongly agreed and 52% agreed that ABS's management is knowledgeable of the issues pertaining to sustainability. With a mean of 1.52 ABS is significantly better than the benchmark which has a mean of 2.43. Forty-three per cent of the respondents to SCALA strongly agreed and 48% agreed that ABS has embedded sustainability into the operating procedures and policies. With a mean of 1.76 ABS is much better than the benchmark which has a mean of 2.67. Sixty-two per cent of the respondents to SCALA agreed that ABS has a company-wide management system for sustainability and 62% of the respondents agreed that ABS has integrated sustainability-related goals into the performance management system of the company. With a mean of 2.57 ABS is better than the benchmark which has a mean of 3.17. This paragraph is important as it illustrates that ABS's employees trust their management when it comes to implementing the bank's vision of offering a credible alternative to the existing banking system in Switzerland. It also illustrates that sustainability is well understood within the organization and that it is a topic of critical importance to ABS.

A surprising result from the SCALA survey is that ABS's employees do not believe that their company rewards innovation. This result can be substantiated by the fact that ABS as an organization does not provide its employees with financial rewards. In case of an outstanding achievement an employee may be rewarded for example with a team dinner or a share of the company but a cash bonus is never offered (M. Rohner, personal communication, 5 November 2014). With a mean of 2.81, ABS ranks behind traditional banks which have a mean of 1.83. This confirms the assumption that the word "reward" is understood as a monetary reward which is a standard practice in traditional financial organizations. Sixty-two per cent of the respondents to SCALA agreed that ABS has a strong track record of implementing large-scale change successfully. With a mean of 2.38 ABS ranks better than the benchmark which is at 2.67. This result is further confirmed with 76% of the respondents to SCALA agreeing that ABS has a strong track record for implementing incremental (small, continuous) change successfully. The employees' perception of ABS being a company not rewarding innovation is to be compared against the fact that 42% of the respondents to SCALA agreed that ABS employees actively challenge the status quo. Seventy-six per cent of the respondents to SCALA believe that ABS values them as employees and their contributions. With a mean of 2.05 ABS ranks better than the benchmark which has a mean of 2.33. This is an interesting fact as it can be understood that ABS's employees feel freer than their counterparts at traditional organizations to speak up and challenge the decisions made within the organization. Nineteen per cent of the respondents to SCALA strongly agreed that ABS's management is willing to take measured risks in pursuit of sustainability and 66% agreed. ABS's mean of 2.00 is better than the benchmark which has a mean of 2.86. These results are an illustration of ABS's collaborative and democratic decision-making culture discussed earlier in this case study. Overall, they also highlight the organization's commitment to pursuing sustainability goals.

To Christian Arnsperger a good example of the bank's financial sustainability is its capacity to smooth costs and benefits over time as shown in Figure 1. The three curves representing the bank's total assets (blue), customer holdings (red) and loans (green) show a linear evolution with no jolt. ABS's business model enables the bank to grow at its own rhythm. To him, the steady sustainable growth is primarily attributed to the bank's long-term approach to business (C. Arnsperger, personal communication, 21 June 2014). This perspective is confirmed by the SCALA survey results in which 45% of the respondents strongly agreed and 45% agreed that the leaders of the company take a long-term view when making decisions.

Figure 1 Continuous and steady growth
Source: Alternative Bank Schweiz - Rapport de gestion 2013

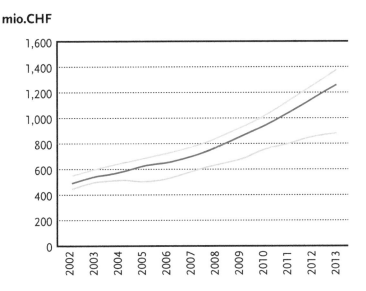

Interestingly, some problems faced by ABS in its early days remain an issue limiting ABS's impact today. König and Wespe (2006, p. 37) argue that it became rapidly difficult for ABS to provide all the funds available to finance women's projects in its early days. The problem came either because of the lack of availability of projects meeting all the necessary safety guarantees requested by the bank or because women were not seeking *loans* under the name "women's project". In 2014 the lack of projects to be financed meeting ABS's requirements was still an issue (C. Arnsperger, personal communication, 21 June 2014). Another illustration is its difficulty to find the right types of candidates. As discussed earlier in in this case study, Raschle (1992, p. 3) states in his article in *Moneta* that at the beginning of the bank, it was difficult to find enough trained bank specialists and that women were underrepresented in the profession. Christian Arnsperger confirms that it is still a problem currently faced by the bank. He states that it is difficult to find candidates for vacant positions within the bank who possess the necessary knowledge of the regulatory framework and who are not influenced by their past experience in other financial institutions (in terms of bonuses, ethics and general code of conduct) (C. Arnsperger, personal communication, 21 June 2014). An interesting insight from the SCALA survey is that when it comes to rewards and compensation, 14% of the respondents to SCALA strongly agreed, 19% agreed and 33% had a neutral opinion on whether rewards and compensation are clearly linked to ABS's sustainability goals. The remaining 30% of the respondents to SCALA disagreed and only 4% strongly disagreed on the compensation being linked to the bank's sustainability goals. An assumption can be made that ABS's employees are driven by the values of the banks and that their behaviour is not guided by monetary rewards. This can

BUILDING
SUSTAINABLE LEGACIES
THE NEW FRONTIER OF SOCIETAL VALUE CO-CREATION

WRITING FROM THE FUTURE

Breaking with academic tradition, this journal offers a unique selection of articles that are written by looking at the future challenges first and then translating these into present times. The right-aligned layout is a material way of reminding us of the fact that "no problem can be solved from the same level of consciousness that created it" (A. Einstein).

PAST   **FUTURE**

OUR FOCUS

We provide hands-on, pragmatic and user-friendly research, suggestions and case studies as a resource for organisations that are committed to implementing sustainability. It is high time to build bridges between business and academia, with the clear purpose of helping business become truly sustainable.

There are four dimensions to the journal:

1. Understand sustainability challenges
2. Specific dimensions of business sustainability
3. Exciting new solutions to implement
4. Case studies of leading business examples

In addition, we will produce a special issue annually dedicated to an important theme.

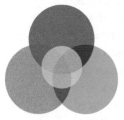

UNDERSTANDING CHALLENGES
NEW SOLUTIONS
DIFFERENT DIMENSIONS
BUSINESS EXAMPLES

FEATURING THOUGHT LEADERS OF THE FUTURE

We are featuring professionals from around the world who are at the forefront of knowledge creation: they are pursuing a part-time doctoral sustainable business degree while working actively in various industries worldwide.

Routledge
Taylor & Francis Group

LONDON AND NEW YORK

laws are: 1) Basel III asking banks to increase their capital; 2) Swiss Finish which are Swiss directives exceeding the minimum requirements of Basel III; 3) Dodd-Frank Act enacted in 2010, this American law largely affects all financial transactions and their regulation; 4) MiFID (Markets in Financial Instruments Directive) which is a European directive aiming at harmonizing national financial markets and which is also applicable to Swiss banks either because they have cross-border activities with European citizens or in order to anticipate applicable rules which will be implemented by the FINMA (Swiss Financial Market Supervisory Authority) in 2018; 5) FATCA (Foreign Account Tax Compliance Act) which is a US law requiring US tax payers to declare and pay taxes also on all accounts held abroad; 6) Act on Collective Investment, which is a Swiss law revised in March 2013 regulating assets held in funds. It now includes cross-border cases and improves investor protection. Böhr and Zuleta (2013, pp. 14-15) argue that the supervisory authorities will cease adding to the complexity when regulation and ethics become complementary.

This ever more complex regulatory environment will definitely have an impact on ABS and its future course of action and sheds an interesting light on the following paragraphs. ABS as a bank is less likely to face less problems moving forward than traditional banks because of its conservative business model reducing the overall level of risk faced by the bank.

Christian Arnsperger brings up a critical and interesting evolution taking place at ABS with the addition of an asset management wing to its product portfolio. The bank's General Assembly adopted new guidelines in 2011 on the basis of which the board developed a new strategy positioning the bank as the "leading credible provider of banking services exclusively geared towards ethics". This is seen as a major change as the bank was concentrating until then on traditional management of deposits and loans and it is in conflict with the initial vision and mission the founders of the bank had. One of the problems linked to asset management is the fact that these types of services make it more difficult for ABS to assess the impact of the value creation of its investments. ABS needs to finalize an investment concept which is in line with the bank's values and philosophy (C. Arnsperger, personal communication, 21 June 2014). In the 2013 annual report (Alternative Bank Schweiz, 2013c, p. 23), the ethics control body states that the development of asset management activities is primarily driven by economic motivations as numerous customers would like to benefit from higher yields. On the other hand, the bank wants to create a second pillar of activity in order to reduce its exposure to financial operations relying primarily on interest rate differentials during extended phases of low interest rates. The ethics control body raised the question whether this would reinforce or eventually weaken the alternative bank model proposed by ABS. The board states that it observed tensions between ABS's traditional business model and the newly proposed asset management wing as its impact is more difficult to assess when compared to the more traditional services offered by ABS. Moreover, it is perceived that engaging in this new type of activity may result in contributing to speculative bubbles.

The ethics control body states that the resulting problem of engaging in asset management activities is the fact that the money invested when buying shares for example is not used to support ethical companies but third party investors. As such, the resulting impact on the economy is indirect in a best case scenario. The ethics control body states that the rating proposed by ABS enables it to target companies having a high societal and environmental impact and that it is a useful tool because when ABS negotiates shares on the secondary market, the rating gives a good understanding of what can and cannot be considered as a sustainable company. The ethics control body therefore concluded that the investment activities will have to be reinforced by direct investments made into appropriate companies on the primary market. It also recommended investigating whether ABS can play a role through shareholder-activism and engagement strategies. It states that these two courses of action are currently being investigated by the bank (Alternative Bank Schweiz, 2013b, p. 23). ABS published an article on the subject in *Moneta* (Alternative Bank Schweiz, 2013c, p. 20) stating that an investment committee consisting of internal and external stakeholders will make the final selection of securities which will be offered and recommended to ABS's customers for investment. Their decisions will be based on societal, environmental and economic factors. Earlier in this case study König and Wespe's work (König & Wespe, 2006, p. 8) was referred to in which they stated that ABS's initial vision was not to engage in stock trading activities, not to engage in international financial transactions, not to engage with funds of doubtful origin, limit its operations to classical banking operations of savings and credit, and to observe clear ethical and ecological guidelines in terms of financing activities, all of it with a partial suppression of Swiss banking secrecy and in total equality of genders. Martin Rohner agrees that ABS is at a crossroads. To him asset management is a logical evolution as ABS has a responsibility to lead the way. He states that ABS wants to show that things can be done differently when looked at from an ethical standpoint in the field of sustainable investments (M. Rohner, personal communication, 25 September 2014). The Asset Management Team has developed an investment concept that builds on four pillars: balance, focus on client needs, selectivity and impact (Alternative Bank Schweiz, 2013a, c). Currently, it is in the process of developing guidelines for implementation with the support of Christian Arnsperger. The issue of how to reconcile asset management with value based banking is also discussed in the context of the Sustainable Banking Scorecard currently under development by the Global Alliance for Banking on Values (M. Rohner, personal communication, 25 September 2014). The Global Alliance for Banking on Values is a foundation made up of the world's leading sustainable banks. Its members include microfinance banks, credit unions, community banks and sustainable banks using finance to deliver sustainable development (Global Alliance for Banking on Values, 2014).

Conclusion and new questions

The purpose of this case study was to identify a recognized sustainability leader and understand what makes it different from its more traditional counterparts. A manager looking at transforming the purpose of his or her organization and seeking to make it evolve along the Business Sustainability Typology Matrix as proposed by Dyllick and Muff (2015) could apply some of the key learnings presented in this section.

Takeaways

The first key takeaway is the process followed by the founders of the bank to identify the sustainability problems they wanted to address and offer an alternative to. The democratic decision making process undertaken fostered discussion and the exchange of ideas. This approach starting by identifying a sustainability problem and then designing a solution to address it is very uncommon. (It is even less common when looking at banks as their primary purpose usually is to generate a profit.)

The second key takeaway is to look at the approach taken to define the purpose and values of the organization. Very early in the process it was decided to include stakeholders in the discussion. This is an interesting insight when looking at Narbel and Muff's paper (2013, p. 58) arguing that "one of the options to ensure the incorporation of broader societal interest … is to add stakeholders". ABS did not specifically express it that way, however the interests of stakeholders were considered in the early discussions. The assumption is based on the fact that the association for the creation of the bank had 1,600 members and 120 organizations and companies whose interests were represented during the General Assembly in 1987 (2 years before the legal creation of the bank).

Once the values were agreed upon, the founders worked on protecting them. This is the third key takeaway. The purpose was to make sure that neither the bank nor its future management or its shareholders would be able to change its course of action and purpose. To that effect, stringent Articles of Association were established. It is interesting to note that they do not only set the values and purpose of the organization in stone but also regulate the type of shareholders the company wants to attract. It also gives the bank the possibility of buying shares back from shareholders who no longer share its values. König and Wespe (2006, p. 48) comment that "there was the fear of an uncontrolled concentration of power by a minority which would divert ABS from its original goals" when writing the Articles of Association. They argue that it is a common fear in alternative and independent companies. The 5% limitation imposed to shareholders limiting the concentration of power is of particular interest and something believed to be of potential interest to other companies.

The fourth key takeaway is the creation of the board of ethics whose purpose is to ensure compliance of the day-to-day activities of the bank to its original values and purpose. The board of ethics was eventually disbanded and replaced by an independent ethics control body in 2005, since this was better suited for the purpose of monitoring ethical behaviour (M. Rohner, personal communication, 25 September 2014). When looked at from a tripartite guardianship angle, its function is of high interest. Narbel and Muff (2013, p. 59) argue that "in order to create a working tripartite guardianship system … it is critical to ensure that the guardianship has statutory powers" which enable the ethics control body to influence the decision-making process. It is a remarkable example of tripartite guardianship implementation on a voluntary basis.

Questions for the future

ABS's strategy of offering asset management services may be considered as a risk for the bank to move away from "real economy" activities and thus to disconnect from its original values. ABS is working together with an external ethics and sustainability adviser in order to define the operational rules for ABS's asset management arm. Even if this evolution is not in line with the founders' original strategy, it is unlikely that ABS's positioning on the Business Sustainability Typology Matrix will be affected. The bank positions this evolution in a new realm seeking to offer an alternative to the more traditional asset management activities of its counterparts. This is in line with the bank's new positioning adopted during the 2011 General Assembly positioning the bank as the "leading credible provider of banking services exclusively geared towards ethics". Therefore, this evolution can be seen as being in line with the purpose of the organization. It will be interesting to learn more from ABS in the future on the framing of its asset management activities as this is a challenge faced by any organization currently offering sustainable investment products.

Bibliography

Alternative Bank Schweiz. (2011). Lignes directrices de la Banque Alternative Suisse SA.

Alternative Bank Schweiz. (2012). In *Banque Alternative Suisse - Actualités*. Retrieved from http://www.bas.ch/fr/a-propos-de-la-bas/la-bas-aujourdhui/actualites/news/2012/01/30/alternative-bank-schweiz-gewinnt-zweiten-platz-beim-zkb-nachhaltigkeitspreis-fuer-kmu-2012.

Alternative Bank Schweiz. (2013a). ABS Anlagekonzept. Retrieved from https://www.abs.ch/en.

Alternative Bank Schweiz. (2013b). La gestion d'actifs: une étape vers le mandat de gestion de fortune. *Moneta - Journal pour un usage différent de l'argent*, p. 20.

Alternative Bank Schweiz. (2013c). *Rapport de gestion 2013*. Zürich: Ropress Genossenschaft.

Alternative Bank Schweiz. (2014a). In *Alternative Bank Schweiz - A brief outline*. Retrieved from http://www.abs.ch/en.

Alternative Bank Schweiz. (2014b). In *Archives de Moneta*. Retrieved from http://www.bas.ch/fr/la-bas-agit/journal-moneta/archives-de-moneta

Alternative Bank Schweiz. (2014c, October 16). In *Triple utilité*. Retrieved from http://www.bas.ch/fr/entreprises-et-institutions/prendre-un-credit/projets-immobiliers

Alternative Bank Schweiz. (2014d). Status du 21 août 1990 (version du 27 janvier 2014).

Bohr, B., & Zuleta, A. (2013). *Contraintes ou confiance?* Olten: Moneta. pp. 14-15.

Bühler, M. (2005). *Rendre le contrôle éthique plus efficace*. Olten: Moneta p. 11.

de Montmollin, D. (2001). In *Offshore Services - Switzerland / International Cooperation and Swiss Banking Secrecy*. Retrieved from http://www.internationallawoffice.com/newsletters/detail.aspx?g=025690fc-1fb7-4ed3-932e-c0373889ca82.

Dyllick, T., & Hockerts, K. (2002). Beyond the business case for corporate sustainability. *Business, Strategy and the Environment*, 11(2), 130-141.

Dyllick, T., & Muff, K. (2015). Clarifying the meaning of sustainable business: introducing a typology from business-as-usual to true business sustainability. *Organization & Environment*, 1-19.

Egger, M. (1989). *Affaires et convivialité*. Olten: Moneta, p. 5.

Global Alliance for Banking on Values. (2014). In *About us*. Retrieved from http://www.gabv.org/about-us.

König, M., & Wespe, A. (2006). *L'histoire d'une banque extraordinaire: L'alternative*. Zurich: Ropress.

Miller Consultants. (2013). In *SCALA; the Sustainability Culture and Leadership Assessment Pilot*. Retrieved from ww.millerconsultants.com: http://millerconsultants.com/sustainability-culture-and-leadership-assessment-pilot.

Narbel, F., & Muff, K. (2013, October). Driving Sustainable Business Implementation through Tripartite Guardianship. *Building Sustainable Legacies - The New Frontier of Societal Value Co-creation*. 46-67

Öbu (2014e). In *Le réseau pour une économie durable*. Retrieved from http://www.oebu.ch/fr/oebu/le-reseau-pour-une-economie-durable.

Öbu. (2014f).In *Tous les membres d'Öbu*. Retrieved from http://www.oebu.ch/fr/membres/entreprises-membres

Raschle, I. (1992, June 25). *Moins de tutelle, plus de confiance*. Olten: Moneta, 3.

Rindlisbacher, S. (2014). *Fonds propres, les règles changent mais pas les problèmes*. Olten: Moneta, 19.

Savitz, A. W., & Weber, K. (2006). *The Triple Bottom Line: How Today's Best-run Company Are Achieving Economic, Social and Environmental Success - And How You Can Too*. New York: John Wiley & Sons.

The Federal Authorities of the Swiss Confederation. (2014). *Federal Act on the Amendment of the Swiss Civil Code - Part Five: The Code of Obligations*. Bern, Switzerland.

Vieli, H. (1992). *Le coût de la croissance*. Olten: Moneta, 3.

Wicki, M. (1991, June 20). *La "banque éthique" à l'épreuve de la pratique*. Olten: Moneta, 1.

Appendix 1: case study research protocol

Sample selection

Six validity criteria were used in order to screen the three companies for the case studies. The companies had to be recognized and verified as sustainability leaders with criteria including proofs of third-party screening. They had to be pursuing significant initiatives in addressing and contributing to resolve important societal and/or environmental issues and, among the three of them, they had to share similar characteristics allowing for a comparison.

The researcher first defined Switzerland as being the limiting geographical boundary for the sample. The second filter applied to the sample was to check whether the targeted company was a member of Öbu. Öbu is a Swiss Sustainable Business Network of 401 member companies (Öbu, 2014), which encourages private companies to become more sustainable. The Öbu affiliation is perceived as a valid filter as its member companies want "to foster the development of the Swiss economy in accordance to the principles of sustainable development. Thus, they not only act in an environmentally and socially responsible way, they also improve their long-term competitiveness" (Öbu, 2014). The third filter applied to the sample was to check whether the target company was recognized as a sustainable company. In order to do so, the researchers looked at whether the target company had been nominated for, or whether it had received an award for its work or engagement for sustainable business practices. The fourth filter was to rank the company on a scale of Business Sustainability 1.0 to 3.0 as defined by Dyllick and Muff in their paper (2015). Only companies qualifying as Business Sustainability 2.0 defined by Savitz and Weber (2006) as taking the triple bottom line into consideration or Business Sustainability 3.0 defined as truly sustainable business were selected. The fifth filter was to identify companies active in the financial industry and the sixth and final filter was to look for companies which either were joint stock companies[5] as defined under title 26, article 620 of the Swiss code of obligations (The Federal Authorities of the Swiss Confederation, 2014, p. 206) or cooperatives as defined under title 29, article 828 of the Swiss code of obligations (The Federal Authorities of the Swiss Confederation, 2014, p. 299).

SCALA survey

Once the three companies were identified and agreed to participate in the research, the researcher used the SCALA™ (Sustainability Culture and Leadership Assessment) survey in order to assess the company's current capacity for executing its sustainability strategy.[6] The SCALA™ survey...

> ...is an assessment instrument composed of items pertaining to culture and leadership. The assessment contains both sustainability-specific content as well as more general organizational climate content that has been demonstrated or asserted in other research to impact the execution of sustainability strategy (Miller Consultants, 2013).

The SCALA™ survey used here is a questionnaire consisting of 30 questions to which the Business School Lausanne and the research cohort added ten additional questions specifically aimed at gaining more insight for the specific research needs. The original version of the questionnaire was available in English only. For the needs of the research, the questionnaire has been translated into French by the researcher and into German by a native German speaker. Both were reviewed by Business School Lausanne for quality control purposes.

The assessment was conducted in the form of an online survey among the employees of ABS. The employees were identified by Alternative Bank Schweiz (ABS) as being relevant and representing the organization as a whole and not only a specific organizational level. The case study is based on 24 responses out of 29 surveys sent representing a response rate of 83%. As a comparison, the average response rate to the general SCALA survey is approximately 40% (K. Miller Perkins, personal communication, 23 July 2014). The ABS respondents were: one C-level executive, two senior

---

5 Joint stock company is the business term used to describe a company limited by shares.
6 The SCALA™ survey and its results have been administered by the researcher and processed by Miller Consultants in Kentucky, USA.

managers, four middle managers, one first line manager and 21 from other positions; 71% were male and 29% were female; 41% were aged 41–50 and 22% were aged 20–30. The survey was completed by a total of 24 ABS employees (4 in French and 20 in German). The survey was conducted over a 2-week period from 25 June until 9 July 2014.

ABS's results are compared against an international benchmark composed of 11 financial institutions other than insurance. About half are retail banks. All have more than 1,000 employees. They are located in Germany, United Kingdom, Australia, USA, Spain, France, Canada and Switzerland. The group is mixed in terms of leadership. About half show leadership in some aspect of sustainability. Some are leaders in environmental sustainability, some are leaders in social sustainability and only two show leadership in both. The two that are leaders in both are large retail banks. The benchmark data is averaged over all 11 financial institutions (K. Miller Perkins, personal communication, 23 July 2014). The benchmark is used in this case study as a comparison with ABS's results and for discussion purposes, although it is to be expected that ABS rates above the benchmark.

Qualitative research

In this paper, the researcher used three data gathering techniques which were the study of archives available to the public, interviews of internal and external stakeholders as well as a survey (see SCALA™ methodology). ABS documented its thinking process in a thorough and transparent manner in its quarterly publication titled *Moneta*. *Moneta*'s purpose is to foster transparency. The first edition was published in 1989 (Alternative Bank Schweiz, 2014). The researchers also had access to ABS's Articles of Association, a document identifying the bank's guiding principles and a historic review published in 2006.

Appendix 2: Business Sustainability Typology Matrix

In their paper, Dyllick and Muff (2015) propose a Business Sustainability Typology Matrix. The matrix is the summary of "the different approaches to business sustainability" allowing for the differentiation between different types and their particular contributions to solving sustainability challenges. The three types of business sustainability models developed in their paper and the principal characteristics are summarized in Figure 2.

Figure 2 Typology of business sustainability and their key characteristics
Source: Dyllick and Muff, 2015

BUSINESS SUSTAINABILITY TYPOLOGY (BST)	Concerns (What?)	Values created (What for?)	Organizational perspective (How?)
Business-as-usual	Economic concerns	Shareholder value	Inside-out
Business Sustainability 1.0	Three-dimensional concerns	Refined shareholder value	Inside-out
Business Sustainability 2.0	Three-dimensional concerns	Triple bottom line	Inside-out
Business Sustainability 3.0	Starting with sustainability challenges	Creating value for the common good	Outside-in
The key shifts involved:	1st shift: broadening the business concern	2nd shift: expanding the value created	3rd shift: changing the perspective

The following paragraphs provide the reader with a brief explanation on Dyllick and Muff's (2015) business sustainability vision applied to banking. They create the necessary background to understand our assessment of ABS's position.

Business Sustainability 1.0

Dyllick and Muff (2015, p. 9) argue that when applied to banking...

...and looking at issues of governance first, BST 1.0 means introducing new rules for compliance in areas like corruption or money laundering, in dealing with politically exposed persons or regimes, ethical codes, compensation schemes for management in the long-term or pursuing stakeholder dialogues. New or integrated banking processes may be introduced for energy and climate management, sustainable purchasing, green IT, building and infrastructure, diversity, old age employment, or home office solutions. In the area of products and services sustainability concerns may be integrated into project finance, asset and credit management, into increasing fee transparency or by introducing new products in areas like microfinance or student loans.

Business Sustainability 2.0

Dyllick and Muff (2015, p. 10) argue that when...

...applied to banking BST 2.0 means contributing sustainability values through programs and actions taken in the areas of governance, processes, and products/services. Instead of positive side-effects resulting from actions addressed at specific concerns in these fields, results are the outcomes of purposeful action. Not only fighting corruption, money laundering, or tax evasion but also stakeholder dialogues are pursued deliberately with the goal of making measurable contributions in these areas. Objectives are defined and their achievements are managed, measured, and reported. Programs and activities with regard to banking processes are pursued not only with the goal of making measurable contributions, for example, to reduce the CO_2-footprint or to improve diversity across all levels of employees but also by voluntarily limiting top management compensation as well as the variable part of the compensation of hedge-fund managers. The activities are typically embedded into the organizational and management structures. Banking products and services are created and offered around specific objectives in areas such as financing sustainable construction, healthy living, regional and urban development, or financing business projects for markets and entrepreneurs where new forms of collaboration and financing (e.g., microfinance) are needed. Also, responsible investment products are not only developed but also actively marketed and promoted by trained customer service representatives to achieve defined market objectives.

Business Sustainability 3.0

Dyllick and Muff (2015, p. 12) argue that:

Banks need to address the enormous challenges to finance sustainable infrastructures for a world populated by 9 billion people of which an ever-increasing number live in mega-cities. They will have to shift funding from unsustainable investments to strategic projects of regional relevance (securing of water, food, etc.). According to the outside-in logic, banks start out evaluating relevant sustainability challenges in their societal contexts. They then evaluate and decide what challenges they can and want to contribute to. The choice will be among such issues as wealth and income inequalities, youth unemployment, old age assurance, climate change, energy efficiency and renewable energies, sustainable construction and living, new models of sustainable tourism, old-age provisions, assisted living, financing public health, education, or integrating of foreigners and migrant workers. Products and services will include packages of information and consultation, new forms of collaboration, public–private partnerships, new forms of financing and collaterals like microfinance, crowd financing, or people funds. Also, banks will have to address the challenges of systemic risks created by their collective behaviour for societal groups and whole countries. The effectiveness of their strategies is measured by the contributions they make and the values thereby created for the different stakeholders and for the business itself.

✉ Route de l'Oche 17, 1195 Dully, Switzerland

☏ +41 79 349 85 02

🖥 frederic.narbel@bsl-lausanne.ch

Lancaster London Hotel

Glamour and sustainability: thriving on a strong sustainability culture as a pioneer in hospitality

Gulen Hashmi

Business School Lausanne, Switzerland

The challenge

Sally Beck, the recently appointed General Manager of the iconic, mid-century Lancaster London hotel, was driving from her home towards the peaceful and tranquil Hyde Park neighbourhood where the Lancaster London is located. It was an early Monday morning in typical rainy London weather when she realized that quite a number of Londoners were happily walking and exercising in the beautiful Hyde Park despite the rain, which prompted her to reflect on her next steps in this leading role she had been dreaming of. As a new GM of this famous Hyde Park hotel where the Beatles opened the Yellow Submarine nightclub and where *The Italian Job* was filmed, she could well lead the Lancaster London to become the happiest as well as the most caring sustainable hotel ever in London by 2017 when the hotel would turn 50.

On the verge of a huge sustainability refurbishment worth £50 million, Sally realized that there was an awful lot of work to be done to bring this 1960s hotel back to its former glory. Many features needed to be adapted or changed to be the most sustainable deluxe hotel with the least environmental impact and the most positive contribution to society. She wanted to change some of the industry notions and show that glamour and sustainability could actually go hand in hand in the hotel business. This set an ongoing challenge for the team.

Under the previous GM's guidance and in her previous positions as Director of Marketing & Sales and Hotel Manager at the Lancaster, respectively, sustainability had firmly been taking ground in the form of environmental initiatives. The hotel had been recognized for a number of environmental awards, in which the hotel's Director of Procurement, Environment and Sustainability and a recent sustainability champion, Clare Wright, had played a key role in successfully coordinating the sustainability activities and their implementation.

Sustainability had, to a large extent, been established in the hotel's vision and values deriving from the slogan "We always care", yet she didn't believe that the Lancaster London was taking the opportunity to be as flexible and engaged as it could be to solve societal challenges and be happy at the same time. She knew that the hospitality industry, out of so many other industries, could do this work better than most. So how could the Lancaster London build on the momentum of its current sustainability endeavours and realize its vision to be the happiest, the most caring and the most sustainable hotel in the capital? How could the Lancaster London accomplish this during the upcoming three-year refurbishment project? An inclusive corporate culture was one of the Lancaster London's most valuable assets, and yet as a role model, how could she turn this soon-to-start challenging refurbishment period into a smooth and inspiring one whereby all her team members would feel more engaged, happy and committed to the care of everyone, now and in the future? If the hotel team achieves even a fraction of the harmony that the hotel bees in the hotel's rooftop honey farm appear to manage—in terms of an incredibly developed sense of output and teamwork—then the entire team would be proud and happy indeed.

While walking towards her office at this historic hotel, she also knew deep in her heart that if she ever were to leave a legacy as an hotelier, it would be the message that an efficient system of flexibility, teamwork and collaboration would change the rules of the game and was the secret to no one having to sacrifice his or her entire life in the undeniably labour intensive hotel industry. Maybe the hotel's recent nomination for the Business School Lausanne's Business Sustainability Innovation Award and the academic Lancaster London case study would shed light on her *how* questions.

As Sally eased herself into the chair in her office with a cup of freshly brewed tea, she grabbed the Lancaster case study that had been lying on her table for some time, and delved into it with curiosity. This is what she read:

Introduction

In recent years, corporate sustainability has gained momentum in boardrooms across the world through a convergence of pressures from investors, customers, employees, citizens, governments and non-governmental organizations. Hotels, in particular, are squeezed between the push of legislation, the pull of consumer pressure groups and economic concerns related to cost savings (Goodno, 1994). As expectations from these stakeholders are shaped by current and future environmental and social challenges such as climate change, the effects of pollution on public health, scarce energy resources, water availability, social inequities and eroding trust in institutions, an increasing number of hotels have started engaging in some form of sustainability activity over the past few years. However, most hotels' approach to sustainability tends to focus on projects that impact the bottom line: minimizing waste, gaining resource efficiencies, incorporating energy alternatives or developing environmentally friendly products, services or processes (Chong and Verma, 2013). Only recently, some forward-thinking hotel companies have become aware of new opportunities inherent in social and environmental issues to create new corporate strategies and reshape their business models around what is called the "triple bottom line" values in sustainability. These companies have been measuring success not only by profit, but in balance with environmental stewardship and social equity as well.

Although these sustainable companies develop new strategies and programmes, or adapt existing products or services to address specific sustainability issues or stakeholders with improved triple bottom line value creation, they still seem to possess an "inside-out" organizational perspective (Dyllick and Muff, 2013). Yet, in today's business context of increasing economic, social and environmental uncertainty, almost every organization is unable to solve societal challenges alone. In this light, Dyllick and Muff (2013) make the case for a more meaningful purpose of business sustainability: to act as positive change agents of an interconnected ecosystem and start off with societal challenges through an *outside-in* perspective.

Although such an ambitious systems building approach, "Doing good by doing new things with others", may look like a utopian idea, recent research findings suggest that companies can start with societal challenges, adapt to them, profit from them, and improve societal well-being (Network for Business Sustainability, 2012). In a recent report for the UN Global Compact, 84% of the 1,000 global CEOs surveyed agreed that business "should lead efforts to define and deliver new goals on global priority issues". But only a third said, "that business is doing enough to address global sustainability challenges" (United Nations Global Compact, 2013). In today's business environment, sustainability is something that many companies are striving toward, but few (if any) have yet fully achieved.

Such a gap between the pursuit of corporate sustainability principles and actual sustainability performance may be due to the presence of varying definitions and understandings of sustainability, which have emerged in relation to organizations. These definitions vary on the extent to which they classify business sustainability as either mainly ecological concern (Shrivastava, 1995), or as social responsibility of a company (Carroll, 1999), or broaden the concept of business sustainability to integrate corporate economic activities with organizational concern about the natural and the social environment (Dyllick and Hockerts, 2002; Dunphy *et al.*, 2003). Sustainability typically addresses social, environmental and economic issues. However, sometimes governance issues or culture are added as further dimensions (Dyllick and Muff, 2013). Such a variety of definitions are likely to have created confusion and impediments in the pursuit and implementation of business sustainability, as corporate leaders and members find it difficult to interpret and operationalize the term (Faber *et al.*, 2005). Similarly in the hospitality industry, hotels may have differing understanding, concerns and motivations for sustainability and thus, may exhibit different levels of business sustainability in their sustainability journey with regards to the interests of the common good.

While there are not only different levels of business sustainability, there is also a lack of clarity on how to best implement corporate sustainability in organizational practice (Daily and Huang, 2001). Several scholars posit that in order to fully respond to environmental and social challenges, companies will have to undergo significant cultural change and transformation (Post and Altman, 1994; Welford, 1995). The overarching idea is that companies will have to develop a strong culture of sustainability when moving towards business sustainability (Crane, 1995). Past research has mainly focused on the overall adoption of sustainability practices by companies and related classification schemes (Dunphy *et al.*, 2003), with focus on external factors such as environmental regulation or pressures from customer groups and the community (Howard-Grenville, 2006). Several studies have identified internal organizational factors such as leadership commitment, employee/managers' values and beliefs, employee empowerment or reward systems, as crucial aspects for achieving corporate sustainability (Daily and Huang, 2001; Wilkinson *et al.*, 2001). However, several recent studies have found links between top management support for sustainability and sustainability implementation or cultures of sustainability (Holton *et al.*, 2010; Adriana, 2009; Angel del Brio *et al.*, 2008; Dixon and Clifford, 2007).

In these studies, organizational culture is often cited as the primary reason for the failure of implementing organizational change programmes. An organization's culture (and its underlying values and ideology of management) plays a vital role in fostering or hindering the implementation of sustainability initiatives. Different aspects of organizational culture may indeed suggest a parallel to the different levels of business sustainability. Thus, this case study not only sheds light on the Lancaster London's business sustainability level as a successful and significant hotel that strives to serve the common good, but also assesses its organizational culture as an important enabler of its successful sustainability implementation. In this case study, we pursue the following four research objectives:

1. Assess the business sustainability position of the Lancaster London hotel best practice policy in the hospitality industry

2. Understand how the Lancaster London got to its current business sustainability position through transformational shifts in the organization and in its organizational culture

3. Identify the organizational perspective/approach through which the Lancaster London addresses and resolves sustainability issues (inside-out vs. outside-in)

4. Contribute to a multiple-case analysis of a wider pool of sustainable companies from various industries, to facilitate an exchange of know-how among practitioners as well as between academia and the business world

While exploring the above-mentioned issues, we harness Dyllick and Muff's (2013) Business Sustainability Typology (BST) (Appendix I) as the overarching framework to guide the case. Dyllick and Muff's (2013) typology is particularly helpful as it guides companies to define their vision and mission inspired by today's and tomorrow's sustainability challenges and helps to understand business sustainability in terms of concerns, processes (approach) and value creation, all of which have so far remained an under-explored issue in the sustainability literature.

Thus, in preparing this case study, we begin by conducting a review of the literature on the phases of change towards sustainability in the hospitality industry. We refer to theories from institutional and sustainability research to understand the drivers that lead hotels to move beyond compliance into more complex and strategic stages that ultimately address sustainability challenges. Further on in the literature review, we channel our focus to the role of the organizational culture in order to better understand the transformational shifts at the level of sustainability initiatives and the organization as a whole. The literature study, coupled with our own interview and survey findings, serves as a tool to understand the different sustainability phases in the Lancaster London's sustainability timeline and the leverage points of its current sustainability strategy—its holistic vision and its focus on educational hospitality. Our own interview and survey findings are further assessed to describe Lancaster London's business sustainability position under the relevant criteria of the Dyllick/Muff Business Sustainability Typology. In addition, to complement our findings, we describe certain aspects of the Lancaster London's sustainability culture, which are assumed to support their current vision and sustainability implementation. Finally, to ensure sustainability of effort for the hotel's future sustainability endeavours, we conclude by analysing the importance of aligning strategy with culture, followed by a summary of the relationship of our findings to the broader field of sustainability research and organizational culture.

While the findings do not allow us to make any definitive claims about how the organizational culture affects the financial performance of the Lancaster London, the survey and interview data are used to reinforce recent research about the significantly important role of the organizational culture in leading to Lancaster London's current sustainability achievements. Our first main finding suggests that the Lancaster London's overarching hotel vision starts with a societal concern, which is embedded in an *outside-in* organizational perspective. The Lancaster London appears to create value for the common good through leading various sector-specific and cross-sectoral collaborations and relationships aimed at educational hospitality and increased capacity building in the hospitality industry—a critical societal challenge that needs to be resolved. This can be considered as the Lancaster London's positive contribution to society. Our second main finding relates to why this is the case. We find that the Lancaster London has a unique asset, which is its strong organizational culture of sustainability that has significantly contributed to its reputation as a sustainable hotel.

Our analyses suggest that in terms of its sustainability timeline, the Lancaster London's sustainability strategy has, over the years, evolved from a fairly generic, compliance-oriented strategy towards a more customized one that is driven by the demands of the markets where the hotel has a presence or plans to expand in the future. Complying with laws and regulations as well as with voluntary third party accreditation criteria, the hotel has successfully gained recognition as a sustainability landmark in the hotel industry. However, more recently over the past couple of years, the Lancaster London appears to have gone further to focus on not only decreasing negative environmental impacts and increasing stakeholder happiness, but also on increasing the hotel's positive contribution to society at large. This is a novel approach to translate sustainability challenges into business opportunities, making "business sense" of environmental and social issues.

As far as the Lancaster London's current business sustainability level is concerned, it is interesting to highlight that although the Lancaster London appears to have been aligning its social, environmental and economic concerns with the triple bottom line (people, planet, profit) values of sustainability in an integrated approach with a broadened stakeholder perspective, it has gone beyond this phase to formulate a vision to serve society at large. Its vision statement, "We always care", emerges from a holistic societal concern, which replaces the industry's traditional focus on guests. The value proposition clearly goes beyond the three dimensions of the triple bottom line to include a broader societal issue rather than pure three-dimensional concerns. The Lancaster London's primary sustainability concern is on delivering educational hospitality. Some of the hotel practices related to educational hospitality involve engaging guests in eco-friendly or sustainable practices such as sustainable transportation and sustainable leaving, as well as forming sectoral/cross-sectoral level engagements. The latter further serves to increase capacity building that is much needed in the hospitality industry. The Lancaster London's holistic vision and pursuit of educational hospitality certainly make a positive contribution to society, which makes it a truly sustainable and distinguished hotel in the industry.

> The value proposition clearly goes beyond the three dimensions of the triple bottom line to include a broader societal issue rather than pure three-dimensional concerns

In terms of organizational culture, the Lancaster London's sustainability goals, initiatives and achievements appear to have come from values which each and every staff member truly believe in. Such a value-driven sustainability orientation justifies the hotel's strong culture of sustainability. However, it is interesting to note that while a strong culture of sustainability prevails, in

> a value-driven sustainability orientation justifies the hotel's strong culture of sustainability

general, executive/senior managers are more positive than middle managers who, in turn, are more positive than the front-line staff. This may indicate that top-level managers are likely to have the strongest sense of ownership of sustainability initiatives and commitment to sustainability because they are responsible for making the most critical decisions (including corporate social responsibility [CSR] decisions) and therefore would be likely to have a positive view of the policies they helped create. In addition, although the team members and their contribution *are* valued, this feeling of *being valued* is more dominant among the males than among the females. This may be due to the relationship between perceptions of CSR/sustainability and how *feeling valued* differs for women and men, as extant research on employee perceptions of CSR show.

This case study draws attention to these differences in perceptions of the Lancaster London's organizational culture and raises critical questions on how the Lancaster London can further synergize these perceived differences to align its strong culture of sustainability with its state-of-the-art vision. The case study contributes to one of several produced by the Business School Lausanne that aim to provide the best practice research evidence for practical problems. Extant research found instances where practitioner knowledge leads theory (NBS, 2010). Thus, this study is intended to form a piece of the puzzle that will help move Lancaster London as well as other sustainability-oriented hotels forward on the path toward becoming truly sustainable. On the academic side, this case study serves the need for more comparison studies of best practice companies involved in various "levels" of sustainability implementation.

Literature review

Phases of change towards sustainability

In the face of troubling scientific facts and figures about the diminishing planetary resources and increasing societal challenges such as social equity, gender equality or poverty, an accelerating number of hotels have started to engage in some sort of sustainability-related hotel practices over the past few years. A sustainable hotel operation, according to the American Association, Green Hotels, is the following: "Green Hotels are environmentally sustainable properties whose managers are eager to institute programmes that save energy, save water and reduce solid waste while saving money to help protect our one and only earth". Sloan *et al.* (2013), on the other hand, define a sustainable hospitality operation as "a hospitality operation that manages its resources in such a way that economic, social and environmental benefits are maximized to meet the need of the present generation while protecting and enhancing opportunities for future generations". While Green Hotels' definition highlights the business case for hotels based on environmental friendliness, Sloan *et al.* (2013) refer to a broader meaning of sustainable business that sees sustainability as managing for the triple bottom line values of sustainability—a process by which firms manage their financial, social and environmental risks and opportunities (Network for Business Sustainability, 2012).

Indeed, corporate leaders are feeling pressure to address environmental and social concerns along with financial performance (Holliday, 2001; Livesey and Kearins, 2002). Goodno (1994) argues that hotels are situated in a context squeezed between the push of legislation, the pull of consumer pressure groups and economic concerns related to cost savings. Hotels have focused primarily on cost savings as the initial step in their multifaceted sustainability journey (Chong and Verma, 2013). As cost savings are largely associated with "green" practices, several authors have long criticized the tourism industry, particularly the hotel industry, for their intense focus on the environmental dimension to become "sustainable" (Font and Harris, 2004; Roberts and Tribe, 2008). Yet, environmental initiatives can be the stepping-stone towards sustainability and hotels could evolve to include social and ethical aspects as well as integrate in the community (Kernel, 2005).

A review of literature, in fact, suggests that companies often go through phases starting with simple, easy-to-implement strategies and progressing towards more complex and potentially rewarding approaches (Mirvins and Googins, 2009; Hoffman and Bansal, 2012). As companies evolve through the phases, they assume more complex responsibilities, increase their interactions with stakeholders, and strive to align their business model or corporate culture with sustainability goals. (Miller and Serafeim, 2014). Nidumolu *et al.* (2009) posit that the first steps most companies take in the long sustainability journey usually arise from the law. Similarly, a 2009 BCG Report "The Business of Sustainability" found that the biggest drivers of corporate sustainability investments were government legislation, consumer concerns and employee interest in sustainability; of which, government legislation was the principal driver of sustainability efforts by nearly all the industries analysed. While the nature and number of phases differ, nearly all hotels first engage with sustainability by focusing on legal compliance, for the purpose of managing economic risks and opportunities, saving costs and increasing shareholder value.

However, a more recent study found that only 9% of survey respondents who said they adopted sustainability strategies as a result of legislation reported that their sustainability practices added to their profitability (MIT and BCG Report, 2012). Thus, smart companies comply with the most stringent rules and do so before they are enforced, simply to harness substantial first-mover advantages in terms of fostering innovation (Nidumolu *et al.* 2009). As Bronn and Vidaver-Cohen (2009) assert, it is actually more desirable for businesses to have less regulation in order to have more freedom in decision-making to be able to meet market and social factors. Yet, a 2012 Gram Green Paper[1] on the UK hospitality industry's attitudes towards sustainability, for instance, shows that although 83% of hoteliers want their business to be greener than it is now, the majority of hoteliers (53%) actually believe that they do not have the financial resources to realize this ambition, largely citing budget restrictions as the main barrier (William Reed Business Media, 2014).

In addition to legal standards, hotels also feel compelled to abide by voluntary codes—general ones, such as the Greenhouse Gas Protocol, or sector-specific ones, such as the Green Tourism Business Scheme (GTBS)—to exhibit socially responsible behaviour. Once hotels have learnt to manage risks and efficiencies through compliance, many of them further evolve to engage in some sort of CSR activity such as charity projects and community involvement that reflect deeply held values. Some even go further and become proactive about environmental issues to make their value chains sustainable. Although the initial aim of making value chains sustainable is usually to create a socially responsible corporate image, most companies capitalize on reduced costs or creating new businesses as well (Nidumolu et al. 2009). Deale (2013) asserts that hotels aim to increase efficiencies throughout the value chain with separate CSR activities in the form of donations of goods, services and more recently volunteer hours. In the hotel industry, CSR projects are believed to lead to guilt-free hotel operations, enhanced corporate reputation in the eyes of eco-minded hotel guests and even attraction of new guests (Euromonitor International, 2012).

Hitchcock and Willard (2009) assert that CSR leads to positive public relations, legitimacy and improved corporate image with shareholders and community; and thus can be a differentiating factor and a source of competitive advantage for businesses. Legitimization can be a valid driver of sustainability by both large and small hotels although methods and motivations for societal legitimization would differ between small and medium hotels (Font et al. 2014). A previous study shows that large hotels, hotels with a classification between three and five stars and chain hotels were more likely to experience positive CSR benefits than small, two star classified and independent hotels (Kirk, 1998). Interestingly, this search for competitiveness is based on the assumption that CSR and corporate financial performance (CFP) are positively related (Carroll and Shabana, 2010). Yet,

---

1 Gram is the UK's leading refrigeration supplier with over 35 energy efficient products listed and takes its commitment very seriously with its strong presence on the Energy Technology List (ETL). For 2012, Gram teamed up with the leading channel associations within the industry including: Considerate Hoteliers Association, LACA (Local Authority Caterers Association), NACC (National Association of Care Catering), Sustainable Restaurant Association and TUCO (The University Caterers Organization), to produce a third Green Paper to add to its legacy.

extant research finds positive, neutral and negative relationships between CSR and CFP, making this relationship debatable (Griffin and Mahon, 1997; Margolis and Walsh, 2001). Furthermore, there are two pitfalls associated with traditional CSR strategies: first, business is pitted against society rather than recognizing their interdependence; and, second, CSR is relatively a defensive concept rather than a strategic lens (Porter and Kramer, 2011).

Once hotels have enjoyed the benefits of managing legal compliance coupled with voluntary CSR practices, they see themselves integral to society. It may well be this relatively recent concept of CSR that provides an understanding of evolution in the meaning of sustainability from *green* to *sustainable*. They tend to easily recognize the relevance and the need to respond to social and environmental concerns along with economic concerns. This is often the outcome of a radical shift in mind-set from doing things better to doing new things. They simply move from operational optimization and *defensive* CSR activities towards a strategically focused organizational transformation phase (Antonis *et al.*, 2011; Visser, 2010). This shift is argued to be the result of recognition that current models of CSR have largely been ineffective at solving societal challenges (Visser, 2010; Moore and Westley, 2011; Porter and Kramer, 2011). While traditional CSR programmes comprise activities such as employee volunteer programmes or charitable giving and philanthropy, "strategic" CSR reframes sustainability and social benefits as a driver of business innovation, value creation and competitive advantage (Hoivik and Shankar, 2011; Porter and Kramer 2007, p. 2).

Thus, in this phase, three-dimensional concerns of people, planet and profit take precedence with a broadened focus on stakeholders. Businesses in this phase of sustainability relate economic, environmental and social concerns to the triple bottom line values of sustainability (Dyllick and Muff, 2013). The concept of triple bottom line (TBL) measures the multi-dimensional business contributions to sustainability (Elkington, 1997). It is a synergistic search for creating economic, environmental and social value through the adoption of sustainability efforts (Hart and Milstein, 2003). Hotel sustainability strategies entail new programmes and initiatives that are developed and implemented with the aim of addressing specific sustainability issues or stakeholders.

Developing sustainable offerings or redesigning existing ones to become eco-friendly leads to "becoming sustainable" (Nidumolu *et al.*, 2009). This is in line with Orsato's (2006) eco-branding strategy which asserts that environmental product differentiation would create greater environmental benefits or impose smaller environmental costs, compared to similar products. Although this may lead to increased operating costs, such differentiation would simply satisfy the green market niche willing to pay a premium for environmentally friendly products (Blanco *et al.*, 2009), which would, in turn, enable the hotel to command a price premium or increase market share (Reinhardt, 1998). A main pitfall of managing for the TBL is the confusion created with regard to measuring and comparing the trade-offs between economic, social and environmental values. While environmental initiatives are easily measurable in the short-term with objective data, social initiatives require a longer time span and subjective data that is harder to measure (Sasidharan *et al.*, 2002). Different social dimensions such as health and education cannot be summed or aggregated since their outcomes are not additive.

A more recent development of TBL is the concept of "creating shared value" (CSV), which argues for economic value creation in a way that simultaneously creates societal value. In this sense, it represents one particular model of implementing strategic CSR in larger organizations. CSV can be defined as creation of meaningful economic and social value whereby new benefits exceed the costs for the business and society simultaneously (Porter and Kramer, 2011). In other terms, it is a business strategy for companies to create measurable shareholder value by identifying and addressing social problems that intersect with their business. This creates new opportunities for companies, civil society organizations, and governments to leverage the power of market-based competition in addressing social problems (Shared Value Initiative website).

InterContinental Hotels Group (IHG), the largest hotel company in the world, for example, identified water and waste as environmental and social issues with significant shared value potential and launched its group-wide online environmental management system, Green Engage, in 2009 by testing various options for reducing water, waste and energy to lower its environmental footprint while also driving down hotel operating costs. In 2011, Green Engage further became aligned to LEED, making IHG the first hotel company to have an existing hotel programme aligned. This way, IHG transparently communicates to its customers the true value of how they are "saving the planet" by quantitatively measuring environmental performance. Furthermore, the hotel group recognized the need for increased capacity building in the industry and thus set up the IHG Academy to ally with community and educational institutions to give people real-world hospitality knowledge. The IHG Academy raises job skills and creates economic opportunity around the IHG hotels while creating a pipeline of prepared and engaged potential recruits.

A major limitation of CSV is that it overlaps with CSR; thus it is not always clear what builds a "core" business approach to shared value (SV). Furthermore, there is still the need for practical drivers for companies that seek SV, which makes it difficult to make a business case. The "how" of measuring SV is still not completely clear considering the overlapping areas of "defensive" CSR and CSV. For example, while IHG's Green Engage programme aggregates the total cost savings generated by resource use reductions (e.g. water, energy and waste), it cannot compare resource reductions with the workforce development outcomes of its IHG Academy programme, although the company could compare the two programmes' financial returns. This may be due to the infancy of the concept in the sense that operational tools and measurement of SV have only recently started to be developed (Bockstette and Stamp, 2011). Finally, time lags between improving the competitive context and profit maximization are not deeply explored, partly due to the fact that investments in societal value creation are likely to bring about up-front costs.

Although the concept of shared value creation is a state-of-the-art contribution towards linking corporations to society at large, and thus a progressive leap from the opposing views of shareholder value management (Rappaport, 1988; Friedman, 1970) and stakeholder value management (Freeman, 1984), it is limited to those issues and concerns that emphasize the "business case" for sustainability and thus economic value for business (Dyllick and Muff, 2013).

In these times of escalating societal challenges, however, there is great need for businesses to move forward and become eco-effective or socio-effective by solving sustainability issues of societies (Dyllick and Hockerts, 2002). Social businesses promise a higher effectiveness in addressing sustainability challenges than commercial businesses as the social mission supersedes financial benefits as their primary objective. Felber (2010)'s Economy for the Common Good movement and Sukhdev's (2012) Corporation 2020 are examples of new business models that support social businesses and social entrepreneurs. Sabeti *et al.* (2009) highlight a "fourth sector" of organizations oriented towards social benefits, like government agencies and NGOs, yet unlike them, who are able to earn their income themselves. Similarly, B-Corporation in the US and community interest companies in the UK are some examples of privately owned organizations that prioritize their social mission over economic value creation. Although changing the mind-set from the traditional "business case" to the societal good may be too idealist for commercial businesses including hotels, there is clearly a market for new organizational forms with a clear social purpose (Dyllick and Muff, 2013).

In light of this extant theory and literature, Dyllick and Muff (2013), in their Business Sustainability Typology, posit that a truly sustainable business translates sustainability challenges into business opportunities making *business sense* of societal and environmental issues. By starting out with societal challenges such public health, poverty, climate change, biodiversity or social justice, a truly sustainable business makes a positive contribution to society and the planet rather than reduce its environmental impacts only. The authors draw attention to the prevalent *inside-out* organizational perspective most business approaches derive from, and further highlight the need to frame business sustainability through a different approach—an *outside-in* organizational perspective—which they believe, will lead companies to true sustainability.

Yet, such an *outside-in* organizational perspective requires a radical shift in mind-set from commercial self-interest to societal good. Caring for the well-being of other stakeholders directly creates value for shareholders (Freeman *et al.*, 2010; Porter and Kramer, 2011), as well as drawing attention to the performance implications of a corporate culture of sustainability (Godfrey, 2005; Margolis *et al.*, 2007; Porter and Kramer, 2011). An organization's culture guides the decisions of its members by establishing and reinforcing expectations about what is valued and how things should be done. Thus, culture is often described as "the way we do things around here" (NBS, 2010). Over time, a company builds up its own culture and this culture is continuously reinforced and reshaped through the daily practices of its members. Although there is a lack of consensus regarding a common definition of the term "organizational culture" (Ashkanasy *et al.* 2000), there is a range of definitions from shared values, ideologies and beliefs (e.g. Schwartz and Davis, 1981), to notions of accepted behavioural rules, norms and rituals (e.g. Trice and Beyer, 1984), and most commonly, shared patterns of meaning or understanding (Louis, 1985; Smircich, 1983).

Corporate culture describes and governs the ways a company's owners, management and employees think, feel and act. A company's organizational culture can be founded on beliefs included in its vision or mission statement. Organizational culture can be a useful tool for organizational change programmes as the values and ideological underpinnings of a company's culture affect how sustainability is implemented (Cameron and Quinn, 2006; Jarnagin and Slocum, 2007). Thus, it plays a vital role in the success or failure of sustainability strategies in becoming a truly sustainable business (Miller-Perkins, 2011).

In this case study, a culture of sustainability, thus, is one in which organizational members hold shared assumptions, values and beliefs about the importance of balancing economic efficiency, social equity and environmental accountability (NBS, 2010). It is assumed that a stronger culture of sustainability is attained if values and beliefs underlie the mission or vision of the organization. Furthermore, a culture of sustainability has been found to increase the effectiveness of leadership commitment and external stakeholder engagement, which, in turn, fosters trust, innovation and mechanisms for execution (Eccles *et al.* 2012).

To date, however, the role of leaders' values has been largely overlooked in the discourse on execution of CSR activities and sustainability performance (Orlitzky *et al.*, 2011). Emerging research demonstrates that corporate success depends on leaders' perceptions of and actions on the challenges and demands of CSR and corporate social performance (Waldman, 2011). Indeed, degree of accountability towards others and breadth of stakeholder group focus have been found to determine various responsibility orientations of leaders (Pless *et al.*, 2012).

Pless *et al.* (2012) identified four orientations that leaders may use to exhibit responsibility and implement CSR: "traditional economist", "opportunity seeker", "integrator" and "idealist". While the traditional economist has an orientation of short-term economic value creation aimed at shareholders, the opportunity seeker takes on social responsibility as part of the strategy of longer-term value creation with the aim of realizing competitive advantages such as a better reputation or new market opportunities. These two orientations imply a low degree of accountability towards others and are limited to legal and economic concerns. Orientations of idealistic and integrative leaders, however, derive from a broader degree of accountability to go beyond these two concerns and include business responsibilities that are relevant to society as a whole (e.g. sustainability challenges). While the integrator considers profits to be an outcome that is likely to result from running a purposeful and responsible business for multiple stakeholder groups, the idealist sees leadership as a servant-based responsibility and aims to serve the needs of a specific stakeholder group (Van Dierendonck, 2011).

Understanding cultural elements of organizations fosters successful execution of sustainability strategies. Attitudes towards specific aspects of sustainability such as leaders' values concerning environmental and social issues are certainly relevant as the above-mentioned most recent research highlights. Yet, specific characteristics of culture such as flexibility, external orientation, stability, control and tolerance for ambiguity could be equally significant, to manage challenges in execution even when the organization's sustainability strategy is well set and clear (Miller-Perkins, 2011).

Thus, the Lancaster London case study has been crafted in light of the Dyllick/ Muff Business Sustainability Typology as well as Lancaster London's organizational culture, to better understand the framing of its business sustainability in the sustainability journey.

Methods

Rationale

In this case study, two interrelated methodologies were used to gather data on the Lancaster London. First, a Sustainability Culture and Leadership Assessment (SCALA) survey was conducted both online and as hard copies to understand certain aspects of the Lancaster London's sustainability culture, as well as primary elements of the Dyllick/Muff Business Sustainability Typology in terms of concerns considered (inputs), the organizational perspectives applied (processes and approach) and the type of value created (outputs). Subsequently, the typology was used as the overarching framework to craft semi-structured interview questions that would provide a more detailed and clearer picture of the Lancaster London's business sustainability level in the sustainability journey. The study provides insights into the Lancaster London's business sustainability level and organizational culture and emphasizes the important role culture plays in successful implementation of sustainability strategies.

Methodology

SCALA survey

The Sustainability Culture and Leadership Assessment (SCALA) survey was used as a support tool to assess and describe organizational culture and climate. The SCALA survey was developed by Miller Consultants in 2012. Set up in 2010, Miller Consultants is a US-based consulting company, which specializes in sustainability research that focuses on the sustainability culture and sustainability leadership in corporations. The SCALA instrument is composed of items pertaining to culture and leadership. The items derive from a review of the public literature and interviews with thought leaders. To construct SCALA, data from across many surveys was gathered (Miller-Perkins, 2011). Thus, each item in the assessment is tied to a specific survey item or derived from a characteristic uncovered in previous research reviews. The assessment contains both sustainability-specific content as well as more general organizational climate content that has been found to impact the execution of sustainability strategies.

The SCALA survey serves to contribute to research objective 2 in the "Introduction", which aims to explore the transformational shifts in Lancaster London's timeline as well as in its organizational context. SCALA data helps us to understand the impact of and changes in organizational culture and also serves to elucidate the overall business sustainability level and how it was achieved in research objectives 1 to 3. Collecting descriptive data through the SCALA survey shows how certain aspects of Lancaster London's culture supported or hindered the development of sustainability initiatives, as well as how these initiatives influenced its culture. It further helps us to identify the hotel's capacity for executing progressive sustainability strategies.

The SCALA survey consisted of four sections and a total of 43 questions, of which the first four in Section I were general questions on location, gender, age group and company position of the interviewees. The next 26 questions in Section II were related to cultural characteristics on sustainability and correspond to research Objective 2, while the following 11 questions in Section III were related to business sustainability positioning of the hotel based on the Dyllick and Muff (2013) typology; and correspond to research objectives 1, 2 and 3. Finally, the two questions in Section IV explored an understanding of the hotel's health and well-being focus and do not correspond to any specific research objective, yet aim to identify a potential area of concern for the hotel, on which the researcher and the hotel could work together for a mutual learning opportunity as the next step. The questions in Section II were further sub-categorized under organizational leadership (eight questions), organizational systems (four questions), organizational climate (five questions), change readiness (three questions), and internal (three questions) and external stakeholders (three questions), respectively. As such, Section II questions serve to assess levels of change readiness to support sustainability initiatives, measure similar or varying perceptions across stakeholder groups, identify company strengths that can be leveraged to meet sustainability goals, and improve on areas of possible concern regarding sustainability goals. The survey used a mixture of semi-open, open and mainly Likert scale questions.

The sample was chosen from the entire 465 hotel staff that included both permanent and casual staff (temporary) members. The response rate was 104 (22%), of which 13 were covered online and 91 were hard copies. This is more than the expected 20% average response rate for similar surveys. The survey was administered online for the management team and as hard copies for supervisors and front-line staff for ease of following up the survey turnarounds by the marketing manager. The survey was conducted in April 2014.

The SCALA survey yielded quantitative data that complemented the qualitative data from semi-structured interviews and the literature review. The statistical analysis was done through SPSS. The findings served to characterize the hotel's sustainability culture and leadership profile, and were also analysed with regard to differences in position. The three different position levels identified were: executive/senior managers, middle managers (department heads) and front-line staff. Understanding organizational culture by position level was essential; previous research shows that those at the highest levels in the organization have the most positive impressions of their companies' CSR or sustainability initiatives (Stawiski *et al.* 2010).

Interviews

The interviews aimed to explore research aims 1 to 3 to shed light on the business sustainability position of the Lancaster London in detail. The sample for the interviews was chosen from lead hotel staff employed at the Lancaster London and the hotel's external stakeholders, who appeared to have extensive knowledge of and engagement in the hotel's sustainability initiatives. The interviews were preceded by an initial phone interview with the general manager of the hotel as the key informant. The researcher further worked in collaboration with the marketing manager in choosing interviewees, based on their level of experience and engagement in the sustainability initiatives.

The total number of interviewees listed was 13. Of these, ten participated in the study. Some of the potential interviewees were not available as they were off duty or unavailable. The interviews were ultimately conducted with eight organizational leaders (hotel manager, department heads, CSR committee members) and two external stakeholders. Table 1 provides a detailed list of the interviewees.

Table 1 Interviewees and their engagement with the Lancaster London

Name	Title	Years of engagement with Lancaster London's sustainability initiatives
Clare Wright	Director of Procurement, Environment and Sustainability	More than 5 years (24 years)
Oliver Darwin	Risk and Procurement Manager	3–5 years
Jo Hemesley	Senior Corporate Sales Manager	More than 5 years
Louise Pitcher	Marketing Manager	1–3 years
Aideen Whelehan	HR Manager	1–3 years
John Firrell (external stakeholder)	Director of Considerate Hoteliers Association	More than 5 years
Alex Debebe	Assistant Chief Engineer	3–5 years
Sally Beck	General Manager	More than 5 years
John Sweet (external stakeholder)	Renovation Project Manager	3–5 years
Margo van der Werf	Executive Housekeeper	3–5 years

As can be seen from Table 1, eight of the ten interviewees have a minimum three to five years of engagement with the hotel's sustainability initiatives and thus were able to easily provide invaluable insights into the hotel's sustainability orientation towards addressing societal challenges over the past few years. The interviews were conducted in a pre-assigned meeting room on the hotel premises. They were administered in person from 5 May to 7 May 2014. Prior to the interviews, interviewees were contacted by the marketing manager in charge of the case study and were provided with an outline of the interview question topics. Each interview lasted approximately 50 minutes.

During the interviews, detailed notes were taken on the interview guide, which entailed categorized second-guessed responses that derived from the literature study. The interview questions in the interview guide were based on the Dyllick/Muff Business Sustainability Typology and were divided into four general themes, as identified from the literature review and expert faculty review. The first part of the interview covered the general attitudes towards sustainability such as the understanding of sustainability and sustainable business practices. The second part attempted to identify the type of business sustainability in terms of concerns and the type of value created. The third part of the interview explored the current sustainability practices and future plans in resolving sustainability issues. Finally, the fourth part expanded on the hotel's approach (inside-out vs. outside-in) to address and resolve sustainability challenges, with regard to strategic focus and implementation. For a smooth read, the interview and the SCALA survey findings are presented in a dispersed rather than concentrated manner (listed) throughout the case study.

A sustainability landmark: the Lancaster London hotel

It is the sustainability of effort that counts in sustainability (Sally Beck, General Manager, Lancaster London, 2014).

Opened in 1967, the Lancaster London is one of three prestigious London hotels in the Thai hotel management company, the Lancaster Landmark Hotel Company Limited, which specializes in the luxury hotel market sector. The Lancaster Landmark Hotel Company Ltd is both the owner and the operator of the Lancaster London, as well as its two sister hotels, the Landmark London and the K West Hotel & Spa. The group prides itself in offering outstanding facilities along with a high level of service, and being one of UK's leading sustainable hotels. The Lancaster London is officially the AA's[2] most sustainable hotel in London. In 2013, Lancaster London turned over £28.4 million and employed over 400 people.

Conveniently situated in the centre of London directly overlooking the Italian Gardens in Hyde Park and within walking distance from Marble Arch, Oxford Street and Paddington Station, the Lancaster London is within easy access of the Heathrow Express, enabling guests to be at Heathrow Airport in just 15 minutes. In addition to its central location, the four-star-deluxe Lancaster London has been a well-known feature of the London skyline. Its 416 bedrooms have superb views over the park and the London townscape and feature all modern amenities such as beautiful oak furniture, deep pile carpets, exquisite marble bathrooms and high-speed internet access. The rooms offer the ultimate in relaxation and are designed to be the ideal environment for business and leisure travellers. The Lancaster London is

---

2 The AA is the only pan-Britain assessing organization and is the British Hospitality Association's Patron Supplier for quality rating and assessment to the hospitality industry. In collaboration with Visit England, Visit Scotland and Visit Wales, the AA has developed Common Quality Standards for inspecting and rating hotels and guest accommodation through the AA accommodation scheme.

one of Europe's largest and most flexible meeting and banqueting venues. Its 15 conference rooms have the ability to cater for a variety of events, from small business meetings to large receptions for up to 3,000 people. The hotel is best known for its award-winning events rooms: the Nine Kings Suite and the Westbourne Suite. These two principal function suites, each accommodating up to 1,200 guests, are well-known venues for the most prestigious conferences, award ceremonies, meetings and dinners. In addition, the Forest Suite is a collection of contemporary meeting, conference and syndicate spaces, catering for up to 200 guests.

The hotel also boasts two restaurants: Nipa, which serves authentic Thai cuisine, and the award-winning Island Grill, with its Three Star rating by the Sustainable Restaurant Association, which serves contemporary British and European dishes. Nipa Thai combines outstanding traditional cuisine with subtle authentic décor and a warm and welcoming ambience, bringing the soul of Thailand to London. It is one of an elite selection of Thai restaurants in the UK to have received the "Thai Select" award from the Thai Government for restaurants that have achieved the highest standards of quality and cuisine. As for Island Grill, it offers an excellent selection of modern European dishes, cocktails and wines to suit every taste and appetite within its stylish and contemporary interiors that boast superb views across neighbouring Hyde Park.

The Lancaster London has long been aware of the necessity of delicately balancing its guests' well-being with avoidance of perceived hardship and thus has been faced with the challenge of ensuring consistent quality while at the same time innovating through sustainability. The £11.5 million sustainability refurbishment in 2011 is a good example of the Lancaster's sustainability endeavours to innovate and pioneer sustainable development in hospitality. In 2011, the hotel went through a Nine Kings Kitchen Project for the ballrooms, commercial kitchens and loading bay. While the catering capacity of the Nine Kings Suite and the Westbourne Suite was increased to 1,200 people, kitchens were refitted with energy efficient equipment. The kitchens were refitted with the following state-of-the-art "green technology": Meiko dishwashers were fitted with integral reverse osmosis pumps that recycle heat; new coffee makers were put into use to produce coffee on demand without the need to keep water on the boil; storage areas were chilled with flexibility to turn into ambient storage to save power; motion sensor lights were installed and extractor canopies with KSA multi-cyclone grease separator filters were installed, to separate cooking grease from the smoke, allowing it to be collected and recycled. The kitchens were re-made to run only on electricity.

CSR has been an integral part of Lancaster London's vision, "We always care", which derives from hotel values (Lancaster London presentation, 2014). The hotel values are broken down into eight categories:

> **CSR has been an integral part of Lancaster London's vision, 'We always care'**

▷ We care about our happiness, and the happiness of others.

▷ We care about being true to others and ourselves.

▷ We care about facts and facing situations.

▷ We care about engaging hearts and minds.

▷ We care about providing an exceptional hospitality experience at every touch point.

▷ We care about performance and solutions.

▷ We care about praising and acknowledging success.

▷ We care about the environment and the future (sustainability).

As can be seen, all of the eight values embody what CSR represents, which is about caring for guests, employees, community and the planet. The Lancaster London's vision truly highlights the significance of caring for the well-being of everyone on the planet to ensure sustainability for present and future generations. The Lancaster London's values-based sustainability orientation is further reflected in the interviews held with the Lancaster team as well as various external stakeholders. To understand general attitudes towards sustainability, interviewees were asked about what sustainability and sustainable business practices mean to them, as well as what they thought would be the best way to implement sustainable business practices and why.

As the interview findings suggest, almost half of the interviewees (four out of ten) think that sustainability is part of their personal values and lifestyles. While one interviewee mentioned that it is both compliance as well as personal life, another interviewee mentioned that it is part of her professional life. Other personal definitions of sustainability were: "All things green", "Protecting the environment: protecting your own people and developing them", "Harmony between humans and nature; finding a balance between the two", "Being able to continue with less resources", and "Legitimization as well as viability". When asked to describe the meaning of *a sustainable business practice*, three interviewees mentioned resource-efficiency and green practices whereas another three interviewees mentioned making value chains more sustainable and educating customers/employees/suppliers about sustainable practices. Furthermore, while one interviewee described it as "At least being neutral", another description of a sustainable business practice was "being sustainable in the connection and effort level, as well as understanding sustainability of effort", with two others having described it as balancing economic, social and ecological value. As can be inferred from these findings, many of the senior management team buy into sustainability from a values-based personal viewpoint; yet when it comes to understandings of *a sustainable business practice,* the definitions are quite varied.

The Lancaster London believes that is possible to do well by doing good to others, and runs an active and energized CSR committee, both to drive their existing policies and to seek new initiatives. The hotel works together with various stakeholders such as suppliers, business partners, employees and the local community.

The Lancaster London further promotes sustainability and awareness of green issues simply by leading through example. Honey and bees, for instance, are a key part of the Lancaster London's desire to communicate its sensitivity towards the ecosystem issue. The hotel's Rooftop Honey Farm reflects the hotel's concern for the decreasing bee population in the wider ecosystem, and the annual London Honey Show is a very good example of forming a next-practice platform with the bee and food industry to create awareness of this sustainability issue. Similarly, the hotel works with and rewards like-minded sustainable suppliers that also respect their local environment and community. The Lancaster London's vision statement, "We always care", derives from a holistic worldview that sets the stage for the hotel's sustainable business operations and proactive engagement in the hotel industry. The hotel successfully engages in setting CSR standards in the industry and changing the rules of the game, rather than reacting to established industry norms. This is evident in the various interconnections established across its value chain: the new "green product" such as the Bee Green Package, the launch of the Lancaster London Community Consortium, the Lancaster Academy founded in partnership with the Institute of Leadership & Management, and the launch of the Hotel Apprenticeship Scheme in collaboration with other hotels. All these initiatives demonstrate the Lancaster London's pioneering sustainability efforts at the sector-specific as well as cross-sectoral levels.

Thus, the hotel has gained recognition within the industry, along with top sustainability awards including: "Considerate Hotel of the Year",[3] "Hotel CATEYS' Green Hotel of the Year",[4] "Green Tourism for London Gold",[5] and

---

3 Considerate Hotel of the Year award recognizes the best all-rounder in environmental, sustainable and socially responsible performance within the UK's and also for the first time within the international hotel industry. This is the ultimate award presented by Considerate Hoteliers Association to the hotel or guesthouse that engages in a wide range of environmental initiatives from water conservation, waste reduction and support for sustainable food, to CSR.

4 The Caterer and Hotelkeeper awards, or the CATEYS, are a UK award ceremony for the hospitality industry, first held in 1984. They have been described as the hospitality industry's equivalent of the Oscars. Recipients are nominated, selected and awarded by the industry through *Caterer and Hotelkeeper* magazine. Hotel CATEY Green Hotel of the Year award recognizes the greenest hotel as one of its categories.

5 Green Tourism for London is a business development model that is being pursued by the UK Government. The aim of Green Tourism for London is to promote the development of environmentally friendly tourism options and to enhance buildings to meet tightening green standards. It is one of many programmes that have grown out of the Green Tourism Business Scheme. The Gold Award is the highest standard a business can achieve within the GTBS scheme and is only awarded to businesses that have demonstrated excellence in sustainable tourism.

"Sustainable Restaurant Association 3 Stars",[6] to name a few. These notable results, coupled with the leadership commitment of its management team and its central London location that fuelled its business growth over the years, are further believed to have contributed to the hotel's strong sustainability orientation in the hospitality industry. In the interviews held with the Lancaster London's stakeholders, higher company profile and enhanced reputation (cited three times), increased marketing communications such as press releases (cited three times), and increased employee commitment and engagement (cited three times) were cited most often as the contribution of these various awards to the hotel business, followed by improved and broadened stakeholder relationships (cited twice).

The Lancaster London's improving financial performance and business growth over the years was also cited as a contributing factor to its strong sustainability orientation. A majority of the interviewees (cited seven times) mentioned that the hotel's sustainability initiatives did not hinder the hotel's financial performance; further stating that, on the contrary, they favoured the conditions and resources for its sustainability investment. However, the general manager mentioned that although sustainability increased their short-term costs and return on investments (mandatory Carbon Reduction Commitment payments, for instance, averaged £77,000 in 2014–2015, as compared to £41,000 per year during 2011–2014; the payments are further expected to increase in line with inflation afterwards), it started paying off in terms of public relations and cost reductions in the long term.

The Lancaster London's sustainability journey

Investing in "green technology" and "philanthropic" CSR

Given the competitive nature of the hotel industry and the associated difficulty of increasing revenue, the potential for reduction of operating costs provided a compelling first incentive for the Lancaster London to consider investments in environmental technologies.

---

6 Sustainable Restaurant Association (SRA) stars are three potential ratings of the SRA that examine restaurants in 14 key focus areas and provide detailed evidence to support their answers across three main sustainability categories: sourcing, environment and society. The ratings are carried out online and overseen by expert SRA assessors as: One Star, Two Star and Three Star Sustainability Champion. Restaurants that achieve Champion status are flagged up online in the Restaurant Guide and the good news is shared with the press, restaurant guides and critics. The *Sunday Times* calls them "The Michelin Stars of Sustainability" and any business serving food anywhere on the planet can get an independent Sustainability Rating.

Building Sustainable Legacies 7 *December 2015*

As a forward-thinking independent London hotel that sensed first-mover advantages in environmental initiatives, the Lancaster London set sail on the sustainability journey in 2005, with the launch of its Green Team. The Green Team introduced Green Week and started contacting charities. Having realized that the legislative burden for greater sustainability will only increase over time, such as carbon levies on energy bills, mandatory carbon reporting for listed companies and the Carbon Reduction Commitment, the Lancaster London believed it was good business sense to implement sustainability strategies, especially with regards to energy. Thus, in 2005, the hotel voluntarily decided to take part in the Carbon Trust Audit, and consequently started bottle and cardboard recycling.

In 2006, in addition to its ongoing recycling initiatives, the Lancaster London started off with small-scale carbon management practices. In parallel to these environmental practices, the hotel started "philanthropic" CSR such as charity fund-raising with London Air Ambulance, the Passage and St Mary's hospital mainly through the initiative Bring & Buy Sales. Also, the Purchasing Manager's Forum and Green Days were started with environmental guest speakers, which enabled networking with academia.

2007 marked capital expenditures on green initiatives when energy-saving bulbs in all guest bedrooms and inverters on pumps were installed as part of the Inverter Project that was started for the installation of variable speed drives to hotel pumps and motors which were 3 kW and above. All heating and cooling pumps were replaced as well as all tower block windows. In the same year, the Lancaster London also started working with education institutions: the Metropolitan University did an environmental project with the hotel, and relationships with hotel schools such as the Noorderpoort and the Hotel School Lausanne were built.

The Lancaster London is one of the most environmentally friendly hotels in the capital and ensures its actions match its philosophy: "to walk softly on the planet". Under "We always care about our impact on the environment", the hotel successfully redefined productivity in the value chain by engaging in energy monitoring and reduction, water reduction, waste reduction, recycling and reusing products, pollution, sustainable sourcing, honeybees and food mileage. The hotel has taken a very thorough approach to energy saving practices, reducing landfill waste and increasing recycling. Behind the scenes, presently, there are weekly staff meetings to monitor recycling and wastage targets and brainstorm new energy saving measures. The £11 million sustainability refurbishment of the hotel's events spaces and commercial kitchens in 2011 saw the implementation of the latest green technology and created state-of-the-art, energy efficient kitchens and banqueting facilities. For instance, the dishwashers were changed to have integral heat exchange pumps to reheat the water coming into the machines, thereby saving energy.

The following is a categorized overview of the Lancaster London's sustainability-related organizational management and processes that constitute the building blocks of its green technology to date:

Energy efficiency

Regarding energy, the Lancaster London's initiatives include investments in electric metering, use of LED lighting in ballrooms, all electric events kitchens, motion sensors on Salamander grills and installation of inverter units on pumps and motors. The engineering department monitors the hotel's energy consumption weekly and can take appropriate action to achieve energy reduction. The hotel currently has an energy reduction target of 5% on a yearly basis. In an effort to achieve this target, the boilers were changed and the plant replacement project was started in 2013. The hotel now has a sophisticated building management system, which optimizes the efficiency of the hotel's boilers, and monitors controlled temperature settings.

Water reduction

Low flow showers and basin taps, taps and urinal sensors in the guest rooms and public toilets, a water bottling system as well as the replacing of all dishwashers with integral reverse osmosis pumps all demonstrate the Lancaster London's concern over saving water.

Waste reduction, recycling and reusing products

The hotel has achieved zero landfill by collaborating with WRAP (Waste & Resources Action Programme), a company limited by guarantee, through the voluntary Hospitality and Food Service Agreement that aims at the reduction of food and packaging waste, proactive menu management and plate waste in the staff canteen. All glass, paper, plastic, cardboard, cooking oil and food are meticulously separated and recycled in the hotel loading bay.

Pollution

The Lancaster London is mindful to only use water-based paints for all decoration works. Furthermore, the hotel uses the correct disposal procedure for all its electrical and electronic waste under the WEEE directive.[7]

---

7 The Waste Electrical and Electronic Equipment Directive (WEEE Directive) is the European Community directive 2002/96/EC on waste electrical and electronic equipment (WEEE) which, together with the RoHS Directive 2002/95/EC, became European Law in February 2003. The overall aim is for the EU to recycle at least 85% of electrical and electronic equipment waste by 2016.

The purchasing procedures support the hotel's sustainable sourcing strategy, which includes food, beverages and, as far as reasonably possible, all other products. Most food is sourced through local suppliers except where special products are required, as in the case of the traditional Thai restaurant, Nipa Thai. Similarly, the cheese served in the Island Grill restaurant is only bought from producers within a 100-mile radius. The hotel is also mindful of the number of deliveries received each week, and strives to eliminate all packaging waste in favour of reusable packaging—for all deliveries. The hotel cares for the well-being of its employees by providing a well-balanced diet in the canteen, with choices of freshly prepared dishes using local produce.

As can be seen, for the Lancaster London, sustainability does not appear to be limited to water, energy and food waste, which are mainly seen as conventional "green" or environmental practices. In addition to environmental initiatives related to water, energy and food waste in its value chain, the Lancaster London also proactively engages in other sustainable hotel practices such as sustainable sourcing, sustainable purchasing and disposal.

From *green* toward *sustainable* with a broader stakeholder focus

Sustainability is a multifaceted journey and thus requires "cross-pollination" among various stakeholder groups. This involves taking care of stakeholders in the value chain, voluntary partnerships and memberships to third parties such as various accreditation bodies, to achieve productivity as well as to enable and strengthen the infrastructure surrounding business operations. Having realized this, the Lancaster London's drive to be more efficient has been extended from the hotel operations to all components in the value chain. In 2008, the Lancaster London signed up to the Green Tourism Business Scheme (GTBS)[8] and a "bronze" award was achieved. Launched in 1997, GTBS is the only green business certification programme validated by Visit

---

8 The Green Tourism Business Scheme (GTBS) is an outgrowth of an understanding of the UK Government that sustainability is not a trend that is going away. The scheme has led to the development of a number of very popular green tourism initiatives including Green Tourism for London. The GTBS award recognizes places to stay and visit that are taking action to support the local area and the wider environment. It is the largest sustainable (green) scheme to operate globally and assesses hundreds of fantastic places to stay and visit in Britain. Businesses that meet the standard for a GTBS award receive a Bronze, Silver, or Gold award based on their level of achievement. Areas that a business is assessed on include management and marketing, social involvement and communication, energy, water, purchasing, waste, travel, natural and cultural heritage and innovation. The Gold Award is the highest standard a business can achieve within the GTBS scheme and is only awarded to businesses that have demonstrated excellence in sustainable tourism.

Britain, the country's official tourism organization. The mission of the GTBS certification criteria is "to offer guidelines to tourism businesses on how to make their operations more sustainable while still delivering a high quality service". The four levels of certification under GTBS are: Going Green, Bronze, Silver and Gold. The scheme assesses properties every two years based on criteria that are divided into ten areas and hit upon 150 measures. Similarly, the hotel received "bronze" with Visit London Awards 2008 for the Sustainable Tourism Award. Departmental energy use and waste streams have begun to be monitored; the inverter project continued and a sub-metering electrics project was started to measure each outlet and benchmark individual areas.

In 2009, the Green Team was reformed into the Environmental and Energy Task Force and started off with an energy awareness and an energy poster campaign. The hotel started collaborating with Carbon Clear, a leading UK-based carbon management firm, which compiled historic carbon footprints for the years 2005–2006 and 2006–2007 to assess Lancaster London's readiness for the Carbon Trust Standard (CTS). The hotel went Silver with GTBS, installed five hives and set up a honey team mentored by a famous bee expert. Collaboration with the Considerate Hoteliers Association (CHA) also commenced and flow restrictors on guest showers and taps were installed as additional initiatives. Consequently, flow rates were reduced from 12–14 litres per minute to 6–8 litres per minute. This was then extended to public toilets and included urinal sensors.

As the Lancaster London's sustainability timeline suggests so far, the hotel appears to have gone beyond compliance to reduce costs and business risks. Collaborations with the GTBS, Carbon Clear and CHA all are examples of the hotel's voluntary initiatives to align with various stakeholder groups in the sustainability journey. The hotel believes that their awards serve to fuel their energy and passion keeping them focused on their sustainability initiatives and their continuous measurement as voluntary members of sustainability-driven associations (Clare Wright, Lancaster London, 2013).

Pursuing a "triple bottom line" approach

In 2010, the Environmental and Energy Task Force was reformed into the Eco Initiatives Group, which came up with a logo and a guest booklet entitled "Conserving Our Resources". Proactive initiatives such as a jogging map for guests were produced and distributed and a waste audit was initiated. The Lancaster London was further accredited with the Carbon Trust Standard (CTS).[9] The Westbourne kitchen project was started in parallel

---

9 The Carbon Trust Standard for Carbon is a voluntary certification and mark of excellence that enables all organizations to demonstrate their success in cutting their carbon footprint and gain a competitive advantage. Carbon Trust Certification is widely considered as the world's leading certifier of organizational carbon footprint reduction.

to energy-saving initiatives through reduction of the number of corridor lights and the installing of LED lights and motion sensors in public toilets. To enhance employee well-being, a cycle to work scheme and a mentoring programme with Oxford Brookes University were introduced. The Lancaster London received the Investors in People Bronze Award.

In 2011, the hotel went Gold with GTBS. This was an outcome of the £11.5 million investment in the Westbourne and Nine Kings Kitchen projects with an upgrade in modern technology by installing, in cool and hot areas, efficient fridges, cookers and dishwashers. Food packaging was reduced through decanting into the hotel's own containers. In 2011, the hotel had 6 tonnes of waste, equivalent to 51 Routemaster double decker buses, yet by working closely with Veolia on a waste management system, the Lancaster London has had financial savings of almost £13,000 since 2011. Regarding disposal, since 2011, the hotel has had no compactor to separate the waste streams. Currently, the Lancaster London's waste management initiatives completely offset their carbon emissions as the hotel avoids 249% more CO_2 emissions than it would have otherwise generated (2013 Veolia Case Study, Evidence 7.2). Recycling of all food waste was initiated, and nose-to-tail dining[10] aimed at zero food waste was introduced. The Lancaster London organized the 1st London Honey Show on the hotel premises. Five more hives were added and a Kitchen Apprenticeship Scheme was launched under the People Initiatives.[11] The Lancaster London further introduced the eco-project of sustainable table decorations in Island Grill, whereby the traditional freshly cut flowers were replaced with living pea shoots. Pea shoots embody sustainability and waste reduction as they can be harvested in just 2–4 weeks and unlike the flowers, they continue to grow and flourish in front of guests' eyes. On the CSR side, the hotel raised about £1,448 for Hospitality Action by adding a discretionary £1 to guests' bills. Prior to that, the hotel used a similar method to fundraise for the local homeless charity, SleepSmart.

The Lancaster London started working with sustainable suppliers and partners to develop eco-friendly raw materials and other components, as well as reducing waste. The hotel works closely with their suppliers and

---

10 "Nose to Tail Dining", a term seemingly coined by British chef and restaurateur, Fergus Anderson, involves food preparation using as much of the entire animal (or plant) from nose to tail as possible. Chef Anderson, author of the book, *The Whole Beast: Nose to Tail Eating*, owns St. John, a restaurant in London where according to Amazon.com "he serves up the inner organs of beasts and fowls in big exhilarating dishes that combine high sophistication with peasant roughness".

11 The People Initiatives are initiatives of the Lancaster London, which aim at developing the Lancaster London team members as well as colleagues in the hospitality industry. Other initiatives include developing suppliers, setting up the Lancaster London Academy and launching of the Lancaster London Community Consortium.

a preferred supplier list (PSL)[12] to ensure the traceability of all produce purchased. The Lancaster London believes that product traceability is very important to reliability as traceability provides the ability to identify and track a product or an ingredient to its point of origin. As such, the Lancaster London arranges routine visits to farms where it sources its produce, mindful of food miles (number of deliveries), local sourcing and conserving natural resources such as fish. The hotel also strives to generate its own produce as much as possible. The hotel chefs, for instance, make their own jam, compotes and honey, which are used in all the hotel restaurants. Prospective suppliers are scrutinized to see if they too respect their local environment and community. The hotel favours working with suppliers who provide reusable packaging—considered even better than recycling.

In 2012, collaboration with suppliers was initiated to decant return packaging on delivery. While the hotel created awareness of the importance of local sourcing through farm visits that demonstrate how food is produced, it also created awareness of conserving natural resources such as fish through its kitchen apprenticeship programme. Similarly, food miles is a vital concept in the planning and purchasing of the Lancaster London's supplies: the hotel currently ensures that what it buys comes from local and sustainable sources wherever possible—like the cheese served in the Island Grill. The 100-mile radius policy is not the case in the Nipa restaurant where local sourcing is limited due to the Thai concept of the restaurant where ingredients for the menu items require importing all the way from Thailand. Buying seasonal is a top priority and purchasing is taken seriously in the form of careful ordering, bulk buying, and close collaboration with the kitchens.

Having realized that sustainability is more than cost savings and increased corporate reputation through CSR activities, the Lancaster London has proactively taken steps in making sustainability a respected and integrated business issue. The hotel's vast array of stakeholder dialogues from guests to suppliers to the local community plays a significant role in this integration of sustainability. For instance, the Lancaster London has recognized the fact that a sizable number of hotel guests prefer eco-friendly offerings and thus developed new products such as the "Bee Green Package": in addition to the traditional meeting room hire with no overnight stay (09.00–17.00 currently), flipchart and stationery add-ons, the package includes three servings of fair-trade tea/coffee and biscuits, seasonal working buffet lunch,

---

12 The PSL entails suppliers that are preferred in terms of businesses that an organization or a company may wish to work with. The suppliers can become "preferred" in a number of ways: either a company may have used them before, or they may have approached a company with background on their proposition, or a similar company may have recommended them. "Preferred" suppliers are tested through structured appraisal, evaluation and regular benchmarking on price and performance. Although PSL does not in itself guarantee a level of business, it should be thought of as a guide when considering a sourcing strategy.

house bottled water and a carbon offsetting option for all meeting delegates. The hotel's development of this product was a consequence, not just a side effect, of its business activities and its deliberately defined goals and programmes addressing the sustainable living culture of its environmentally conscious guests.

As a forward-thinking hotel that makes *business sense* of sustainability issues, the Lancaster London also took on a proactive and collective approach toward the need for increased capacity-building in the industry, such as employee growth, diversity and inclusion, supplier relations and development, as well as knowledge sharing with the industry. "We Seek to Grow Our Own People" is an example of the hotel's human resources (HR) goals relating to the vision "We always care", which aims to provide a safe and inspiring environment for the Lancaster London staff giving them every opportunity to grow and develop.

> **As a forward-thinking hotel that makes *business sense* of sustainability issues**

The Lancaster London's proactive approach to sustainability implementation is also reflected in the interviews held with various managers, where the majority of the interviewees (eight out of ten) think sustainability implementation is purely a business responsibility rather than the responsibility of the public sector or third parties. They personally see sustainability and CSR as growing in the consumer consciousness and would like to act ahead of new legislation to be able to determine the rules of the game well in advance. As far as their justification for seeing sustainability implementation as a business responsibility was concerned, while six interviewees mentioned the business opportunities inherent in environmental and social issues, four interviewees highlighted the advantages inherent in new business models, facilitated through sector-wide or cross-sectoral collaborations with others.

The Lancaster London team is well aware of the environmental and social issues in "We always care", as well as the future concerns they feel they should address. In the SCALA survey, support for charities, local community engagement, support for youth unemployment and the Apprenticeship Scheme were the most widely mentioned social issues that respondents believed the hotel addresses especially well. Other social issues that were mentioned were diversity, social equity, improving the quality of life and well-being. Furthermore, supporting old people, helping war victims, addressing food shortage and all sorts of volunteering work were mentioned as social issues that the hotel is not currently addressing but that they wished it would address. All these issues mentioned truly relate to the Lancaster London's social concerns.

Regarding the environmental issues that the hotel addresses especially well, recycling was the most widely cited issue in the survey, followed by waste management, sustainable food sourcing and energy, respectively. Furthermore, beehives on the roof as well as the impact of hotel operations on the environment were cited among the environmental issues the hotel also addresses well. When asked about the environmental issues that the hotel is not currently addressing that the respondents wished the hotel would address, making use of natural energy sources (alternative energy, solar energy) was the most widely cited issue. Further suggestions to address other environmental issues were: using the Sustainable Restaurant Association's criteria for the hotel's conference and event business; sustainable furniture purchasing throughout the hotel and consistent reduction in business mileage by sales colleagues and recycling in smaller outlets. All these issues mentioned truly relate to the Lancaster London's environmental concerns.

successfully redefines its 'hospitality' core business around the above-mentioned environmental and social issues

Although the Lancaster London balances economic, social and environmental dimensions of sustainability to a certain extent, and invents, produces and reports measurable results in well-defined sustainable development areas (energy and water saved, carbon emissions avoided in waste management, CSR donations raised) while doing this in an economically sound and profitable way, it goes further than this triple bottom line approach and successfully redefines its "hospitality" core business around the above-mentioned environmental and social issues, as will be elaborated on in the following section.

Transcending into reorganizing around societal issues

In 2012, the Lancaster London made a giant leap and transcended into a phase where its organizational perspective shifted from an "inside-out" organizational perspective to an "outside-in" one. Through this new organizational perspective, the Lancaster London was able to focus on several societal issues within its span of operations. The hotel wanted to increase awareness of the decreasing bee population, the relatively less skilled and qualified labour prevalent in the hospitality industry and sustainable living among its team members and guests. To address and tackle these relevant societal and environmental issues, the hotel preferred to focus on a strategy to deliver educational hospitality through which it could make a positive contribution to society.

As a first step, the Eco Initiatives Group was reformed into the CSR Team to increase the span of sustainable operations and address a wide range of social issues through more industry collaboration and various philanthropic CSR projects. The restructuring of the Green Team to the current CSR Team is a good example of the hotel's reorganizing process as it endeavours to tackle sustainability challenges and, in that sense, requires a mind-set and passion for a holistic sustainability perspective that is more than the "business case for sustainability".

2012 was an amazing year for awards received, which included: a Gold star with GTBS, the Caterer & Hotelkeeper's (CATEY) Green Hotel of the Year 2012, a Green Tourism for London Gold, the Considerate Hotel of the Year 2012, the Sustainable Restaurant Association's three stars for the Island Grill restaurant, an Investors in People Gold Award and CTS Certification. The Preferred Hotel Group's Great Initiatives for Today's (Tomorrow's) Society (GIFTTS) recognition and awards programme recognized the Lancaster London for their work with "Community, Environment and Philanthropy". Despite the multitude of awards received, the hotel continued its sustainability initiatives: hosted the 2nd London Honey Show, installed electric charge points in the car park as well as a water bottling plant. The Hotel Apprenticeship Scheme was also launched in the hotel kitchens.

More recently in 2013, implementation of ISO 14001[13] standards became the Lancaster London's big area in environmental sustainability. Furthermore, as part of the voluntary Hospitality and Food Service (HaFS)[14] Agreement with the UK's Department for Environment, Food and Rural Affairs (Defra) Waste & Resources Action Programme (WRAP),[15] baseline data for the year 2012 were fed into the relevant portal. The Lancaster London has been aware of the UK Government's plan to develop a comprehensive Waste Prevention Programme by the end of 2013 under the Climate Change Act 2008, which targets emissions cuts of at least 34% by 2020, and 80% by 2050—below the 1990 baseline. In England, the Review of Waste Policies, published on 14 June 2013, makes a commitment to rural development for the hospitality sector, to identify those areas with high carbon impact, namely food and packaging waste in the hospitality sector. However, in addition to the various policy measures, the Lancaster London has also been well aware of the fact that dealing with waste sustainably creates opportunities for business growth and cost savings across the UK economy (Lancaster London WRAP Presentation, 2013).

---

13 ISO 14001 is the cornerstone standard of the ISO 14000 series. It specifies a framework of control for an environmental management system against which an organization can be certified by a third party. ISO 14001 is not only the most well-known, but is the only ISO 14000 standard against which it is currently possible to be certified by an external certification authority.

14 The Hospitality and Food Service Agreement is a voluntary agreement to support the sector in reducing waste and recycling more. The agreement is flexible to allow any size of organization to sign up, from multinational companies to smaller businesses, from sector wholesalers/distributors to trade bodies.

15 WRAP works closely with interested and relevant organizations and individuals to determine the targets for the Hospitality and Food Service (HaFS) Agreement. The targets are owned by WRAP and collectively delivered by signatories. WRAP delivers this agreement across the UK through its national programmes, including Zero Waste Scotland.

Thus, the Lancaster London started collaborating with Veolia, an environmental services company, which prepared a greenhouse gas report on the Lancaster London and found that its overall carbon performance ratio was 2.49. This showed that the hotel avoided more than twice as many CO_2 emissions than it generated. As can be seen, the environmental performance of the Lancaster London's waste management is very encouraging as the emissions released are completely offset by the material and energy recovery benefit. A Veolia Case Study was also done on the hotel's recycling and waste management provision. The study demonstrated that the Lancaster London recycles 69% of all its waste, with 31% still going into general waste. The study also showed that of the 31%, some goes further into incineration and the part that does not burn goes to road aggregate, resulting in zero landfill.

On the CSR side, the Lancaster London Community Consortium was launched with local charitable groups to support ongoing projects in the area, ranging from schools to those who are disadvantaged to the elderly. In order to fund these projects, the hotel started collecting £1 per room when the guests check out (with a possibility to opt-out) on a trial basis, and the amount of money collected is then matched by volunteering hours of the Lancaster London team. The Lancaster London truly involves the local community in the creation of deliberate social values. Furthermore, the hotel initiated an ongoing campaign whereby the hotel donates old TVs and disposable items from guest rooms (curtains and pillows) to the Invisible Children's Charity so that unused hotel stuff is recycled and used to raise money. Finally, the first seeds of collaboration were planted with the Institute of Leadership & Management in the launch of the Lancaster Academy, which aimed to provide hospitality diplomas to the young and prepare them for the industry through capacity building.

> The Lancaster London truly involves the local community in the creation of deliberate social values

Furthermore, the Lancaster London introduced the yearly "Supplier of the Year 2012 Awards" for its own suppliers in the categories of large company, small company and highly commended and invited suppliers to attend the annual staff awards dinner. Thus, the hotel has been providing recognition and incentives for those suppliers who have been going the extra mile in developing sustainable business practices. The Lancaster London recognizes its suppliers based on the following set of criteria: environmentally positive farming, local and seasonal, sustainable fish, fair trade, ethical meat and dairy, healthy eating, treating people fairly, community engagement, contribution to waste management, energy efficiency and water saving. Figure 1 provides an overview of Lancaster London's sustainability milestones in a timeline.

Figure 1 Milestones in the Lancaster London's sustainability journey
Source: Developed for the case study

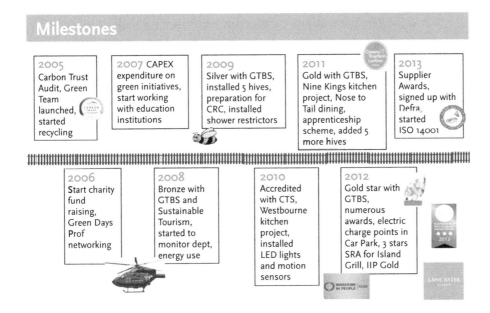

The hotel exhibits proactive leadership in forming next-practice platforms through collaborative partnerships, such as the launch of the Hotel Apprenticeship Scheme in 2012, the launch of the Lancaster London Community Consortium in 2013, and the set-up of the Institute of Leadership & Management in 2014, all of which help the Lancaster London make *business sense* of educational hospitality and generate more space for sustainability initiatives at the company level. The following section will elaborate on the *leverage points* of the Lancaster London's current strategy to better understand its relatively impactful positive contribution to society.

Core elements of the Lancaster London's sustainability strategy

A holistic vision: "we always care"

The Lancaster London's vision of "We always care" and the eight previously mentioned hotel values constitute the heart of their sustainability initiatives. This proactive response is clearly highlighted in the hotel leaflet, as part of "Walking softly on the planet"—the Lancaster London's environmental ethos that derives from the hotel's vision of "We always care": "The world's natural resources are precious and often irreplaceable. Underlying our commitment to everyone, now and in the future, we strive to *walk softly* on our planet".

In parallel to the award-winning environmental initiatives to reduce negative impact on the environment, the hotel strives to act responsibly toward their community and within their industry, thus making a positive contribution to society. The hotel enjoys partnerships with several major organizations involved in sustainability issues such as the Carbon Trust, Carbon Clear, the Green Tourism Business Scheme (GTBS), Defra, WRAP, Sustainable Restaurant Association, Investors in People and the Considerate Hoteliers Association (CHA).

> **the hotel runs apprenticeship schemes to help young people into jobs in the hospitality industry**

Furthermore, the hotel runs apprenticeship schemes to help young people into jobs in the hospitality industry. National Vocational Qualifications (NVQs) are awarded and mentoring is offered throughout their time at Lancaster London. Work placements are offered and created for students from the UK and the rest of the world through the Charity Springboard UK and independently. This clearly shows the Lancaster London's commitment to recruiting and training disadvantaged young people and encouraging in them a sense of purpose and concrete life goals.

Finally, the Lancaster London believes that they can only give their best to others when they are in touch with the best in themselves. Thus, the hotel strives to enact its previously mentioned hotel values through the following culture:

▶ Where all team members have the ability to be the best they can be

▶ Where team members are supported and developed as far as they need and want to be

▶ Where succession planning is available for everyone's career

▶ Where everyone is happy and works proactively in every aspect of the Hotel Vision

▶ Where there is no fear

▶ Where team members are treated fairly

▶ Where every team member learns from mistakes through constructive support and open communication

Educational hospitality: products and services with a purpose

The Lancaster London has long realized the importance of the positive impacts it could make on guests and has chosen to lead by example in offering its guests products and services with a purpose for society at large. In addition, it realized that the hospitality industry had been lagging behind in terms of a skilled workforce and that not everyone who aspired to work in the industry was qualified nor had the resources to get qualified. Thus, to implement its holistic vision 'We always care' and to contribute to the well-being of society at large, the hotel decided to take the lead by focusing specifically on educational hospitality and harnessing its resources and competences to shape and adapt its products and services to address this societal issue. In other words, it made "business sense" of educational hospitality as a societal issue to be improved, which made the hotel stand out in the industry. The Lancaster London's primary focus on educational hospitality is channelled into two avenues:

▶ Engaging guests in eco-friendly and sustainable principles aimed at stimulating sustainable consumer behaviour

▶ Engaging in sectoral and cross-sectoral collaborations

Engaging guests in eco-friendly and sustainable principles

Underlining its commitment to the care of everyone on the planet, the Lancaster London has been proactively engaging with its guests by informing and educating them about unsustainable choices and practices. The Lancaster London aspires to inspire individual guests, businesses and competitors to follow suit. The Lancaster London believes that to change the collective rules of the game, hotel guests ought to act as important agents of change in the hotel's sustainability initiatives. Guests who stay at the Lancaster London are actively encouraged to engage in eco-friendly principles through a variety of means. The hotel contributes to educational hospitality with the following initiatives:

▶ Through the environmental page on the guests' in-room TVs, hotel guests are made aware of small things that can make a big difference such as: reusing towels and bed linen rather than replacing them, keeping windows shut when using the air conditioning, etc.

▶ E-brochures are available to all guests in place of printed collateral

▶ The hotel has compiled a guest leaflet entitled "Conserving Our Resources", which is a summary of the initiatives the hotel has committed itself to, and ensures their guests are informed regarding their green initiatives

▶ The hotel offers guests the option of carbon offsetting. Guests are able to offset their carbon footprint throughout their stay when booking online by opting to contribute to a carbon offsetting project

▶ Guests are offered a meeting package, the "Bee Green Package", which includes room hire, three servings of fair-trade tea/coffee and biscuits, seasonal working buffet lunch, stationery and house bottled water, carbon offsetting for all delegates and flipchart

▶ All bottled water that is offered to the guests in meetings, events and restaurants is bottled on site in reusable bottles, which saves 12 tonnes of glass per year

▶ With Hyde Park on the doorstep, jogging is a popular pastime and guests are provided with maps showing a variety of routes, a copy of which can be obtained at the reception. The hotel offers complimentary parking for green and electric cars as well as two charging points. There is an excellent public transport network in the vicinity of the hotel and guests are encouraged to use it widely

▶ Guests are encouraged to make use of the Barclays cycle hire scheme. Secure bicycle parking is available to both staff and guests in the 2nd floor car park

▶ Concerned with the sharp decline in honeybees, the Lancaster London is the first central London hotel to install beehives. The ten-hive Rooftop Honey Farm was a result of the green team initiative to support the urban honeybee population, and is home to 500,000 bees. The hotel's "Bee Team" collects 100 kg of honey annually, which is then served in the hotel's Island Grill and is also given as gifts to guests and clients alike

▶ There is a "Responsible Visitor Charter" on the hotel's website for guests with seven simple suggestions. Guests are encouraged to follow the hotel's lead in practices such as using greener means of travel, walking or cycling, and using the bike racks installed at the hotel

▶ The hotel works with its guests and colleagues to generate donations for the two charities that aim at the homeless, SleepSmart and the Passage

These initiatives not only engage guests in eco-friendly and sustainable principles but also create awareness of sustainable living, sustainable sourcing and sustainable transportation. New and innovative products such as the Bee Green Package and services are created as a voluntary and proactive contribution to a societal challenge, educational hospitality and the well-being of society and planet at large.

Engaging in sectoral and cross-sectoral collaborations

The Lancaster London has been contributing positively to sectoral as well as cross-sectoral level collaborations

Developing sectoral and/or cross-sectoral cluster development, in other words, forming next-practice platforms, reinforces not only the business itself but also its infrastructure such as its value chain, its suppliers as well as its collaborations with various industry players, third parties and the public sector. The Lancaster London has been contributing positively to sectoral as well as cross-sectoral level collaborations through the following practices:

▶ The Trail Blazer Apprenticeship scheme to help young people find jobs in the hospitality industry. The Trail Blazer is a partnership of six London hotels, which contributes to increasing the human resources capacity of the industry. NVQs are awarded and mentoring is offered throughout the apprentices' time at the Lancaster London. Such a partnership certainly helps to elevate the relatively low skills required by the industry. Furthermore, the partner hotels benefit from a common pool of talent. This certainly has advantages for individual hotels where the tradition of employee mobility or transfer is relatively limited as compared with chain hotels

▶ The Lancaster Academy set up in partnership with the Institute of Hospitality, which aims to qualify young people in or into the hospitality industry through a balanced mix of practice and theory

▶ Work placements for students from the UK and the rest of the world, which are facilitated through the UK charity, the Springboard UK, and independently

▶ The Lancaster London Community Consortium, collaboration with five different charities on five different projects which target contribution to society through volunteering hours. Having long felt the need, the Lancaster London, as one of its newly launched initiatives, has shifted its focus from donating money to educational time. For instance, as one of these projects, the bee team pays regular visits to local schools to create awareness of the importance of bees and their role in the ecosystem. Similarly, other hotel staff spends time with the elderly chatting and enjoying teatime with them, simply to make them happy and integrate them into society.

▶ First ever and free-to-attend London Honey Show, which brings together various "actors" in the bee and food industry. Every year the hotel invites bee-keeping enthusiasts, commercial honey producers, exhibitors and the general public to an event to promote awareness about honeybees. The event also hosts prize giving for a variety of competitions such as "Best School/College Honey", "Best Packaging" and even "Best Colored Honey", in an effort to stimulate a wave of interest in beekeeping.

▶ Supplier awards which are integrated into yearly staff awards: the Lancaster London works with like-minded sustainable suppliers who are scrutinized for their respect to their local environment and community. The hotel's suppliers are recognized under the categories of: supplier of the year, highly commended large company and small company and special recognition award.

All these proactive initiatives help the Lancaster London create transparency, share best practices in the industry and redefine new rules in its current business context, which lead to increasing the impact and outreach of its holistic vision.

Lancaster London as a truly sustainable business

Having assessed the important phases of evolution in the Lancaster London's sustainability timeline, and core elements of its current strategy, this section will assess the Lancaster London's sustainability positioning based on the relevant criteria of the Dyllick/Muff Business Sustainability Typology. The three criteria of the typology reflect elements of a typical business process model: 1) the relevant concerns (drivers, motivations); 2) the organizational perspectives applied (starting with societal challenges (outside-in) vs. starting with existing business, strategy or product-lines (inside-out)); and 3) type of value created.

Focus on societal concerns

Sustainability requires a multifaceted perspective indeed; while the traditional business perspective is one-dimensional with economic concerns, the sustainability perspective typically includes the three concerns of social, environmental and economic issues. Yet, truly sustainable companies go further than starting with well-defined sustainability dimensions and start with the society at large and societal concerns.

The Lancaster London's vision is aimed at society as a whole, highlighting the relevant stakeholders that the hotel feels accountable to. The vision is exemplary as it is not limited to the three well-defined areas of sustainability (social, environmental and economic), but aims at providing care for the well-being of all. Such a holistic societal concern includes various sustainability issues that the hotel believes it can contribute to most effectively by adapting or developing company resources. Below are the elements of this vision that are of major concern to the Lancaster London, as explicitly stated on the hotel website and internal documents:

We always care about our colleagues.

We always care about developing our colleagues.

We always care about Equal Opportunities and Diversity.

We always care about engaging our guests in our initiatives.

We always care about our local community.

We always care about our industry.

We always care about charitable activities.

We always care about fundraising events.

We always care about our impact on the Environment.

The interview findings are indeed aligned with this exemplary hotel vision aimed at society in the sense that when interviewees were asked about the impact of the economic downturn on the hotel's commitment towards sustainability initiatives, half of the respondents cited increased concern with society and the planet, and four interviewees cited concern with company stakeholders. While only one interviewee mentioned a stronger concern with the bottom line, all the rest mentioned that financial performance had not been an issue during the downturn, largely citing the hotel's outstanding location as a central London hotel as well as the quality accommodation and service it provides.

The findings of the interviews held with the Lancaster London team and its external stakeholders further shed light on this concern with society and the planet. More than half of the interviewees (six out of ten) thought that previous GM's personal values (altruistic, feeling socially responsible) and lifestyle largely accounted for the hotel's initial engagement in the vision "We always care" as well as the sustainability initiatives thereof. While two interviewees mentioned cost savings and competitive advantage as the main driver for the hotel's sustainability engagement, another two interviewees mentioned the need to comply with the requirements of the Environment Agency and Carbon Trust as the driving force that led to the hotel's sustainability initiatives. Finally, one senior manager remarked on a desire to contribute to societal well-being through economic activity. These findings not only suggest the importance of company leaders' personal values and lifestyles but also resource-efficiency concerns and compliance, as triggers of the Lancaster London's sustainability initiatives.

SCALA findings also align with the interview findings. In the SCALA survey, both executives/senior managers (87%) and middle managers (71%) chose "Awareness of our responsibility to the environment" as the most widely cited motive that led the hotel to start addressing sustainability issues. On the senior managers' side, other perceived drivers for addressing sustainability issues were the "Desire to improve efficiency and impact the company's bottom line" (53%), "Recognition our company could address societal needs" (47%) and "Desire for innovation and growth" (47%), respectively. On the middle managers' side, other mentioned drivers were the "Desire for innovation and growth" (38%), followed by "Need for reputation building" (33%). These findings support the aforementioned personal values and lifestyle that are perceived to have led to the Lancaster London's noteworthy sustainability performance, and further reflect the management team's concern and awareness of responsibility for the environment and society.

Interestingly, front-line staff (46%) chose the "Desire for innovation and growth" as the primary motive/concern behind the hotel's sustainability initiatives. This was followed by the "Awareness of our responsibility to the environment" (43%) and the "Desire to engage employees" (34%), respectively. This may imply that front-line staff perceive the hotel's sustainability endeavours more as a result of the *business case* than pure *awareness* of responsibility to the environment, although the difference between these two overarching motivations is too minor (3%) to make further judgments. The SCALA survey findings overall support the Lancaster London's vision, which entails the aspects of "We always care about our industry", "We always care about our colleagues" and "We always care about our impact on the environment". It is this awareness of responsibility to the environment that may have led to the Lancaster London's *outside-in* organizational perspective, which will be elaborated in the following section.

When assessed with regard to the *concerns* criteria, the Lancaster London appears to have started off its sustainability journey with societal concerns, which is typical of truly sustainable businesses. "We always care" is a proactive vision, which entails a shift of perspective that not only seeks to minimize negative impacts but also seeks to create a significant positive impact in critical and relevant areas for society and the planet.

Creating value for society

While the purpose of the current economic paradigm is to create economic value, sustainability perspectives are broader and balance economic, environmental and social values aimed at various stakeholder groups that are directly affected by the business activities. Yet, the Lancaster London has an even more ambitious approach and goes beyond direct stakeholders and also includes indirect stakeholders and the "common good" that are only indirectly affected by its business activities. For instance, the hotel cares about not only corporate happiness but also happiness of future generations and environmental health, as stated in the hotel values underlying the vision "We always care". With its primary concern with society and planet, the hotel truly utilizes its resources and competences for collaborative partnerships and projects in educational hospitality. While the hotel's environmental ethos, "Walking softly on the planet" contributes to minimizing the hotel's negative environmental impacts on the planet, its vision "Care for the well-being of all on the planet" contributes to increasing its positive impact on the well-being of society.

Interestingly, in the SCALA survey, 58% of the respondents perceive their vision's primary concern with society and planet as a triple bottom line value, that is, more than half of the respondents think that their company is trying to create economic, social and environmental value by addressing sustainability issues. This is followed by "Making a positive contribution to solving critical societal challenges", as cited by 21.6% of the respondents. While 73% of the executive/senior managers perceive the type of value created as a TBL value, 20% see it as a positive contribution to society. The front-line staff, however, sees no difference between the values of TBL and positive contribution (56% versus 56%, respectively). It is worth drawing attention that although front-line staff perceives "Desire for innovation and growth" as the primary concern behind the hotel's sustainability initiatives, they see no difference in the value created in terms of TBL and positive contribution to society. Thus, it could easily be inferred that the front-line staff sees the positive contribution the hotel delivers in the sustainability journey.

Similarly, the majority of the interviewees think that the Lancaster London, through its strategic focus on sustainability, is trying to create a deliberate TBL value as the outcome of this focus. Six out of ten interviewees mentioned the development and implementation of new strategies and programmes aimed at sustainability issues in a proactive way. The same interviewees also mentioned that stakeholder concerns are considered with environmental and social concerns in a proactive manner. While three interviewees mentioned positive contribution to society as an outcome of the hotel's sustainability efforts, one of the key external stakeholders mentioned the fact that the hotel might be managing risks arising from new environmental and social concerns in the hope of embracing opportunities to please shareholders.

When further asked about "in what aspects the Lancaster London contributes exactly to societal well-being" (positive common good), the most widely cited aspect was educating relevant stakeholders and creating awareness of sustainability through various events and partnerships. The hotel is also believed to have contributed to social equity through collaborations with the local community, apprenticeship schemes and employee diversity, although to a lesser extent. Contribution to quality of life and contribution to health and well-being were among the least cited contributions to the positive common good. Educating guests, suppliers, employees and local community clearly seem to be the Lancaster London's primary contribution to society at large.

Finally, the most widely cited societal challenge the interviewees thought the Lancaster London can solve by capitalizing on its current resources and relationships, was poverty/social justice (cited six times), followed by educating guests and suppliers (cited three times) as well as contributing to the improvement of public health (cited three times). The widely cited social justice issues that the Lancaster London could contribute to involved improving the quality of life and well-being of disadvantaged groups such as the unemployed, the homeless and the sick as well as employee diversity, inclusion and assistance during difficult times. Some other invaluable interviewee insights also included: "homelessness in the Westminster area", "enhancing reuse of food", "improvement of volunteering hours rather than money", "minimizing food waste", "increased communication with guests on sustainability" and finally, "improvement of the apprenticeship scheme to better include the front-line staff".

Although the Lancaster London's vision starts with a societal concern and has an *outside-in* organizational perspective, based on the interview findings with various stakeholders and the SCALA survey, the hotel is perceived to create triple bottom line values in sustainability, with the exception of the front-line staff who see the value created as both a TBL and positive contribution to society. These findings indeed contradict with the hotel's positive contribution to society through the programmes and actions taken in the area of product and services as well as governance. Engaging guests in eco-friendly and sustainable principles and forming next-practice platforms to change the rules of the game in the industry, are novel examples of caring about indirect stakeholders and the *common good* and can be considered as good examples of positive contribution to society, which constitutes one of the criteria for a truly sustainable company.

One possible explanation for this contradiction may be the infancy of *sustainability* as a concept in the hotel industry. As elaborated in the Introduction, the definitions of sustainability prevalent in the industry, to date, have either focused on resource efficiencies and *green* practices, or at best *managing for the triple bottom line*. Perceiving educational hospitality and next-practice platforms as positive contributions to society might seem like a utopian idea. This also seems to be the case with various sustainability-related accreditation bodies whose grading criteria heavily focus on the environmental dimension of sustainability with limited social criteria that largely entail a philanthropic CSR angle (Font and Harris, 2004). The authors' research shows that social standards are ambiguous, the assessment methodologies are inconsistent and open to interpretation and that there is considerable variation on what is understood as sustainable depending on the type of tourism companies targeted (Font and Harris, 2004).

An *outside-in* organizational perspective

Dyllick and Muff (2013), in their typology, posit that companies usually start off with their existing business, strategy or product-lines and work on making them more sustainable (inside-out perspective), with the aim of creating social, environmental and economic values (triple bottom line). Such an inside-out perspective leads to initiatives and actions that are by nature limited in their contributions to solving sustainability challenges. True sustainability, however, works the other way around by starting with sustainability challenges, and questioning how company resources and competences can be used and adapted to make "business sense" of these challenges.

The Lancaster London indeed displays this different strategic approach to business and shifts the traditional *inside-out* business perspective to an *outside-in* perspective by starting out with a societal challenge—educational hospitality. Having started out with a proactive and holistic vision statement, "We always care", that derives from a societal concern, the hotel strives to make a positive contribution to a broad range of stakeholders and the society at large. It engages in developing new strategies towards sectoral or cross-sectoral levels to deliver educational hospitality: the Lancaster London Community Consortium; the Lancaster Academy, which runs in partnership with the Institute of Hospitality; the Trail Blazer in Apprenticeship Scheme that leads the government initiative; and finally, the template programmes for apprentices sharing with industry. Such collaborative partnerships help the hotel proactively change the status quo.

In the SCALA survey, 84.4% of the respondents think that the hotel's current approach to sustainability is proactive or active, although senior managers and middle managers are much more likely than front-line staff to think so. Similarly, 93% of the respondents think that the hotel is either "engaged" or "very engaged" with sustainability, although the data suggests that senior managers are much more likely than middle managers or front-line staff to say that the hotel's sustainability engagement is at the level of "very engaged".

Although the Lancaster London appears to have excelled in employee engagement overall, the findings indeed present an area of improvement for the Lancaster London as they indicate a need for increased staff engagement at the operational level. This would require engaging front-line staff and middle managers more often in the sustainability decision-making process to enhance a stronger sense of ownership of future sustainability initiatives.

It is this proactive *outside-in* organizational perspective that distinguishes the Lancaster London from other hotels that only start off with three-dimensional concerns (social, environmental, economical). Dyllick and Muff (2013) assert that truly sustainable businesses see themselves as responsive citizens of society and this seems to hold true for the Lancaster London. The Lancaster London truly translates a sustainability challenge into a business opportunity making *business sense* of societal and environmental issues. The Lancaster London first looks at the external environment within which it operates and asks itself what it can do to help resolve critical challenges utilizing the resources and competences it has at its disposal. The Trail Blazer Apprenticeship scheme, for instance, is an initiative that not only resolves the issue of youth unemployment but also provides benefits from a common pool of skilled and trained talent for the participating hotels.

The Lancaster London's *outside-in* organizational perspective is further reflected in the restructuring of its Green Team to the current CSR Team. Formed in 2005, the Green Team introduced the Green Week and started contacting the charities—the Passage, Air Ambulance and St. Mary's Hospital. In 2008, the Green Team started using departmental action plans, and a duty managers' environmental checklist was created. In 2009, the Green Team was reformed into the Environmental and Energy Task Force, which made the Energy Awareness and Energy Poster campaigns. In 2010, the Environmental and Energy Task Force was reformed into the Eco Initiatives Group that aimed for a proactive approach in handling environmental issues. The group prepared the guest booklet "Conserving Our Resources" and a jogging map in addition to the waste audit as new initiatives. Finally in 2012, the Eco Initiatives Group was reformed into the current CSR Team to better deal with a broader scope of CSR issues including sustainability. The CSR Team currently has representatives from each department in the hotel. As can be seen, through such organizational restructuring, the Lancaster London has successfully reorganized around "educational hospitality" as its overarching societal concern, and adapted its resources and competences making "business sense" of this challenge.

When judged with regard to the *organizational perspective* criteria, the Lancaster London appears to be a truly sustainable company.

When assessed from the overall three dimensions of a business process model, however, the Lancaster London appears to qualify as a truly sustainable company, as it not only walks softly on the planet but also contributes positively to society. Figure 2 gives an overview of the Lancaster London's business sustainability positioning based on the Dyllick and Muff Business Sustainability Typology, as detailed in terms of concerns, organizational perspective and type of value created.

Figure 2 Lancaster London's business sustainability positioning in the Dyllick/ Muff Business Sustainability Typology
Source: Developed for this case study

Business Sustainability 3.0 – The Lancaster London hotel

From "philanthropic" CSR to "strategic" CSR

- Caring for the well-being of all on the planet, as led by the Hotel Vision Statement: **"We Always Care"**

- This includes: conserving the planet's resources, as led by the Hotel Environmental Ethos: **"Walking softly on the planet"**

- Educational hospitality
- Creating awareness of sustainable living
- Engaging guests in eco-friendly/sustainable principles
- Redefining productivity in the value chain
- Sustainable transportation
- Sustainable sourcing
- Eco-branding (Green Products)
- Forming next practice platforms (sectorial/cross-sectorial level engagements)
- Eco-system awareness (bee population)

- Contributing positively to the care and well-being of everyone on the planet, which include:
- Colleagues
- Guests
- Local community
- Industry
- Disadvantaged groups
- Environment
- Decreasing hotel's negative environmental impacts as part of underlining their commitment to everyone

After having positioned the Lancaster London as a truly sustainable business overall, we now look at the organizational and cultural underpinnings of this strategy. While organizational culture plays an important role in organizational strategies, it matters even more with sustainability strategies due to the unique and challenging context they require. Most sustainability-related research over the past few years showed that culture is important in the success of sustainability strategies (Miller-Perkins, 2011).

Thus, the following section will focus on understanding various aspects of the Lancaster London's sustainability culture, which largely accounts for the hotel's success as a best practice hotel in the field of sustainability, and may also serve as the building block for the hotel's future sustainability strategies.

A strong sustainability culture

Organizational culture includes norms regarding appropriate and desirable interactions with others outside and within the walls of the organization (Miller Perkins, 2011). More positive and constructive organizational cultures are associated with more positive staff morale, improved service quality and outcomes, greater sustainability of existing and future sustainability programmes and reduced staff turnover (Glisson, 2007). Yet, how culture relates to the sustainability implementation remains to be explored further. Knowing more about this relationship would inform efforts to facilitate sustainability transformation. For instance, organizations with less positive organizational cultures, such as cultures with low senior leadership commitment or low tolerance for ambiguity (Miller Perkins, 2011), may require more intensive employee engagement support to develop well-coordinated sustainability implementation plans.

To describe in more detail how the Lancaster London's culture and leadership support the implementation of its sustainability strategy, we rely on the SCALA results, which are presented below.

Organizational leadership

Organizational leadership refers to those who are in formal positions of authority from the executives at the top of the organization down through the ranks of the organization (Miller-Perkins, 2011). Companies whose leaders have a clear vision for sustainability would be in a better position to achieve sustainability-related goals. An excellent management team with a focused approach appears to have made the Lancaster London one of the UK's leading sustainable hotels. According to the SCALA results, 87% of the respondents agreed that their leaders have a clear vision of sustainability, although executives/senior managers (93%) and mid-managers (92%) show a more positive response than front-line staff (82%). Furthermore, 88% of respondents agreed that the leaders of the company take a long-term view when making decisions. Finally, 87% of the respondents agreed that their leaders have a clear business case for pursuing sustainability goals.

Previous research shows that companies that have a sound business case for their sustainability strategies in the first place are likely to find it easier to integrate sustainability into their decision making (Miller-Perkins, 2011). This is also the case with the Lancaster London as 88% of the respondents agreed that the leaders of the company integrate sustainability into their decision-making, although executives/senior managers (93%) were significantly more positive than front-line staff (86%, $p < .04$).

In addition, integration of sustainability goals into management and governance structures includes cross-functional committees, policies and guidelines (Dyllick and Muff, 2013). The Lancaster London's cross-functional CSR team is made up of representatives from all departments who meet on a monthly basis. Through its cross-functional CSR committee, the hotel plans various sustainability initiatives into its business agenda, and keeps monthly track of its progress on those initiatives. While the engineering team measures the results of these initiatives, the Director of Procurement, Environment and Sustainability coordinates the overall sustainability agenda. Sustainability achievements are reported in a transparent and externally verified way through the relevant third parties such as the WRAP, GTBS, CHA and Veolia that monitor the hotel's progress with regard to pre-established criteria. The hotel goes through routine annual accreditation such as those of the GTBS or the CHA. For instance, GTBS assesses the hotel's sustainability performance based on the following generic scoring sections: marketing and management, communication, energy saving, water issues, purchasing, waste minimization, travel and transport, nature and culture and innovation. On the other hand, WRAP, under its the Hospitality and Food Service (HaFS) Agreement, assesses the hotel more specifically based on a prevention target and waste management target in the categories of food, glass, card, mixed recycling and general waste.

Furthermore, the Lancaster London successfully integrates sustainability objectives into the planning and reporting cycles. Sustainability goals and activities are largely embedded in the line functions and in the compensation of management. In the SCALA survey, 82% of the respondents reported that the hotel has integrated sustainability-related goals into the performance management system, with no significant difference between the hotel positions. Similarly, 62% of the respondents reported that rewards and compensation are clearly linked to the organization's sustainability goals, again with no significant difference between the hotel positions. These findings were also supported in the interviews where the majority of the interviewees (eight out of ten) mentioned that sustainability had been integrated into line functions. Yet, four managers highlighted that this integration was either partial or at manager level only. Finally, two interviewees mentioned that there is ongoing restructuring around societal challenges with new alliances or partners.

Another important aspect of effective governance is smooth implementation of strategies and goals. This applies to sustainability as well. It is noteworthy that in the interviews held with the management team and the external stakeholders, enhancement of a more engaged organizational culture was the most widely cited challenge (five out of ten) in the hotel's implementation of sustainability, followed by internal resistance to change due to corporate culture (two out of ten) as well as insufficient resources in terms of time and money (two out of ten). Consumer perception of greenwashing was mentioned only once as a barrier in the sustainability implementation.

Two other indicators regarding the Lancaster London's governance and leadership success are how the team perceives the hotel's as well as their leaders' performance relative to those of other companies in the industry. In the SCALA, 82% of the respondents rated the Lancaster London better than other companies in the industry with regard to sustainability, while 18% of the respondents thought that their company was about the same as other companies in the industry. However, when results by position are considered, executives/senior managers (60%) and mid-managers (58%) were significantly more positive than front-line staff (55%, p< .03). Similarly, 76% of the respondents reported that the hotel's leaders compared better than the leaders of other companies in their region with regard to commitment to sustainability, yet with no significant difference between the hotel positions. This shows that the hotel's relatively better sustainability performance may be linked to the leaders' commitment to sustainability.

Companies with leaders who can inspire others with their visions would be more apt to create momentum for their sustainability initiatives. This appears to hold true for the Lancaster London, as 80% of the respondents agreed that the leaders of their company are able to inspire others about sustainability-focused issues and initiatives, although executives/senior managers (93%) and mid-managers (88%) were significantly more positive than front-line staff (72%, p< .01).

Finally, success with sustainability requires corporate leaders to possess a clear understanding of the issues and the personal commitment to address them. The literature indicates that leadership commitment is critical to successful implementation of sustainability strategies (Eccles *et al.* 2012). Furthermore, courage to take risks plays a crucial role in leading companies to incremental or radical improvements in the journey. The Lancaster London SCALA data show that 68.6% of the respondents agreed that the leaders of the company are willing to take measured risks in pursuit of sustainability; however, the agreement among mid-managers (84%) was significantly more than the agreement among the front-line staff (61%, p< .02). The respondents (77%) further agreed that the leaders of the hotel are knowledgeable of the issues pertaining to sustainability. Finally, 76% of the respondents agreed that their leaders are personally committed to issues pertaining to sustainability, with no significant difference between managers and front-line staff.

Overall, the findings on organizational leadership suggest that, in general, senior managers are more positive than middle managers, who are more positive than the front-line staff. This clearly reinforces previous research, which shows that people at the highest levels in the organization are also the most positive about and committed to the organization (Stawiski, 2010).

Organizational systems

Organizational systems are the mechanisms through which work is regulated and results are measured and communicated (Miller-Perkins, 2011). The author further asserts that in order to meet sustainability goals, organizations need systems for regulating work and measuring and communicating results. The Lancaster London SCALA data show that 87% of the employees agree that the hotel has embedded sustainability into the operating procedures and policies, with 84% having confirmed further the presence of an enterprise-wide management system for sustainability. While 82% of people agreed that the company has integrated sustainability-related goals into the performance management system, only 62% agreed that rewards and compensation are clearly linked to the organization's sustainability goals.

Organizational climate

Miller-Perkins (2011) defines organizational climate as the characteristics of the internal environment as experienced by its members. The long-termism of sustainability entails uncertainty, which can be challenging for organizations. Thus, understanding of the organizational climate can contribute to more predictable corporate behaviour and sustainability implementation. Levels of trust are an important indicator of organizational climate in an environment of uncertainty. In the SCALA, 80% of the Lancaster London team agreed that the level of trust within their organization is high, although executive/senior managers (100%) as a group were significantly more positive than front-line staff (73%, p< .001). Also, most of the staff (74%) reported that most people in the hotel believe that a commitment to sustainability is essential to the company's success in the long term, with no significant difference between positions.

The degree to which an organization supports learning is another aspect of organizational climate as leaders may consider enhancing the organizational climate in order to succeed in an uncertain environment. Eighty-nine per cent of the Lancaster London team agreed that continual learning is a core focus of their organization, although the agreement among executive/senior managers (100%) was significantly higher than front-line staff (85%, p< .02). One way of facilitating organizational learning is to encourage people to learn from external sources. In the SCALA survey, 59% of the respondents agreed that their company encourages people to learn about sustainability from external sources.

Finally, organizational cultures that are willing to take risks and are committed to innovation are highly likely to thrive when faced with ambiguity (Miller-Perkins, 2011). The Lancaster London data show that 77% of the respondents agreed that their company rewards innovation.

Change readiness

Sustainability goals and strategies require organizational change; thus, organizational cultures that excel in the capability of handling change are more likely to thrive with their sustainability initiatives (Miller-Perkins, 2011). Handling change entails both the ability to sense and act on change signals as well as the ability to experiment rapidly and economically to learn new and better ways of coping with change (Reeves et al., 2012). This is reflected in the degree to which people actively challenge the status quo. In the SCALA, 65% of the Lancaster London team thinks that the hotel actively challenges the status quo.

Previous research suggests that the best predictor of future behaviour is often past behaviour; thus, past change efforts are an important indicator in assessing change readiness: 75% of the Lancaster London team reported that the hotel has a strong track record of implementing large-scale change successfully. When small, incremental change was considered, 71% of the team agreed that their company has a strong track record for implementing incremental change successfully, although agreement among the mid-managers (84%) was significantly more than that of the front-line staff (62%, p< .02).

Internal stakeholders

Internal stakeholders are groups or individuals within the bounds of the organization who can affect or are affected by the achievement of the sustainability objectives (Miller-Perkins, 2011). Sustainability efforts are successfully implemented in organizations where employees feel valued by the company, and care about the company and its values. Such organizations further believe that sustainability means more than an added cost to the hotel.

The Lancaster London's internal stakeholders are its employees, both front-line staff and managers, who make up its corporate culture. In the SCALA, 67% of the respondents believe that the hotel has a clear strategy for engaging all internal stakeholders in its sustainability efforts although middle managers (84%) were significantly more positive than front-line staff (57%, p< .02). Regarding perceptions of congruence between sustainability goals and strategies, 73% of the Lancaster team believed that they are engaged in work that is connected to sustainability goals, with no significant difference between perceptions of managers and front-line staff. Furthermore, 75% of the team believes that the hotel values them and their contribution, yet interestingly, males (82%) are significantly more positive about feeling valued than are females (67%, p< .02).

External stakeholders

External stakeholders are groups or individuals outside of the organization who can affect or are affected by the achievement of the sustainability objectives (Miller-Perkins, 2011). External stakeholders play a crucial role in giving organizations a systems advantage as they enable organizations to extend their adaptive capacity beyond their own organizational boundaries to include a network of partners and collaborators in the broader ecosystem (Reeves *et al.*, 2012). The adaptive capacity increases as organizations continuously go through the social interactions that external stakeholders provide as learning platforms. Thornton *et al.* (2012) assert that social exchanges serve as the tool to organizational change and that social interactions provide the key motor that transforms organizational practices.

The Lancaster London indeed has an extensive range of external stakeholders, which include boards of directors, suppliers, external project managers and consultant, customers, NGOs and all of civil society to some degree. This is demonstrated in the SCALA survey whereby 65% of the respondents believe that the hotel has mechanisms in place to actively engage with external stakeholders about its sustainability efforts, although senior managers (80%) were significantly more positive than front-line staff (57%, p< .03) about this external stakeholder engagement.

The Lancaster London further appears to possess a consistent and integrated engagement strategy that deliberately targets key external stakeholders. In the SCALA, 77% of the respondents agreed that their company sends a clear and consistent message about the hotel's commitment to sustainability although senior and middle managers (86% and 92%, respectively) were significantly more positive than front-line staff (67%, p< .04).

Finally, the Lancaster London has successfully managed to shift its focus from *the firm* to *the ecosystem*. This is strikingly evident in the hotel's sustainable sourcing strategy that builds on the capabilities of its suppliers. The Lancaster London is aware of the fact that the hotel does not operate in isolation from its surroundings and that, to compete and thrive, it needs reliable local suppliers that believe in the benefits of sustainable practices. In the SCALA, 87% of the respondents believe that the hotel encourages sustainability in its supply chain although senior and middle managers (100% and 96%, respectively) were significantly more positive than front-line staff (79%, p< .01).

The outcome: aligning strategy with culture

As the SCALA results highlight, the Lancaster London's culture, organization and leadership are well aligned with their sustainability strategy and goals. The hotel has a clear business case for sustainability and thus is able to integrate its sustainability goals well into the sustainability decisions, and into its operating policies, procedures and performance management systems. Rewards and compensation are clearly linked to the organization's sustainability goals. The leaders of the company appear to be knowledgeable, inspiring, risk loving as well as personally committed to sustainability. Regarding the organizational climate, the level of trust, continual learning and focus on innovation are highly prevalent. The hotel has a strong track record for implementing both large-scale and incremental change successfully, which can be a good indicator of progressive sustainability strategies. Finally, the hotel is quite capable of actively challenging the status quo and engaging both internal stakeholders and external stakeholders in its sustainability initiatives. Thus, the Lancaster London appears to possess a good mix of both an externally focused, adaptable and flexible culture as well as an internally focused, stable and durable culture, although as the timeline suggests, the hotel appears to be evolving towards the externally focused end of the continuum with escalating stakeholder relationships and developing next-practice platforms.

Strikingly, although the employees and their contribution are valued, this feeling of "being valued" is more dominant among the males than among the females. This may be due to the differing expectations and personal belief systems of females and males; however, elaborating on this gender difference falls outside the scope of this case study and thus hierarchical level has not been controlled for in the study.

This case study relates more to the differences in perceptions from the top of the organization down through the ranks of the organization. As such, in general, executives/senior managers are more positive than middle managers, who in turn, are more positive than the front-line staff on almost all of the interval scale items. This demonstrates higher self-esteem, confidence and commitment on the management side. Indeed, recent research shows that the higher people are in the organization, the more committed they are in general and the more positive they are about the organization's sustainability or CSR efforts (Stawiski *et al.*, 2010). More positivity on the side of the management team can be rooted in the hotel's clearly set sustainability goals and strategies, as well as leaders' strong sustainability-related values and commitment to sustainability. Yet, some specifically overlooked aspects of the dominant culture may well explain this gap between the perceptions of management and the front-line staff, which may indicate a potential area of improvement. There appears to be potential to bridge this gap in positivity among the levels and embed sustainability further down to line functions. This would help improve and align some specific aspects of the dominant organizational culture with the ambitiously set hotel vision and sustainability strategies thereof.

Discussion points

Through its state-of-the-art vision, the Lancaster London aims to contribute to the *common good/well-being* of various stakeholder groups and society as a whole. The Lancaster London strategy relates its eight core values to six different stakeholder groups to define the relevant space of the *common good*. These stakeholder groups are: colleagues, industry, guests, the local community, disadvantaged groups (the young unemployed, the elderly, the disabled and school children), and the environment itself. While the hotel's environmental ethos "Walking softly on the planet" contributes to minimizing the hotel's negative environmental impacts on the planet, its vision, "We always care", contributes to increasing its positive impact on the well-being of society. This is indeed in line with Dyllick and Hockerts' (2002) research that highlights the need for business to go beyond multidimensional business contribution to sustainability and become eco-effective or socio-effective by solving the sustainability issues of societies.

As the Lancaster London's timeline explicitly demonstrates, the hotel initially started off with *green technology* investments to decrease its negative impacts on the environment in line with its environmental *ethos* "Walking softly on the planet", while achieving resource efficiency gains at the same time. This has further led the Lancaster London to engage in various sustainable practices such as: energy monitoring and reduction, water use reduction, waste reduction, recycling and reusing products, pollution reduction, sustainable sourcing, honeybees and food mileage. Complying with laws and regulations as well as with voluntary third party accreditation criteria, the hotel has successfully gained recognition as a sustainability landmark in the hotel industry. Companies can indeed improve productivity in the value chain by developing the quality, quantity, cost, and reliability of inputs and distribution while simultaneously acting as a steward for essential natural resources and driving economic and social development (Porter and Kramer, 2011).

As the interview findings suggest, the Lancaster London team demonstrates strong and broad concerns for others, which, as the interview findings show, appear to be largely rooted in company leaders' moral values and principles (half of the interviewees mentioned the previous GM's sustainable lifestyle and sustainability related values such as altruism). This supports the theory that one of the three frames that explain pro-sustainability behaviour in tourism enterprises is through lifestyle choices and habits informed by values rather than formalized plans (Matten and Moon, 2008). *Success* for managers/owners of small to medium sized hotels (including independent hotels) is largely rooted in their own circumstances (Carlsen *et al.* 2008), which at times but not always, requires managing a company based on sustainability values (Ateljevic and Doorne, 2000). Sustainability in small to medium sized hotels is explained through the relationship between business and society, as the expectation of being socially responsible increases with the increased perception of success of the company, not just business size (Matten and Crane, 2005). This suggests that more financially successful businesses are highly likely to implement CSR actions to legitimize their status. This may be the case with the Lancaster London team as the team explicitly expresses sustainability as a pure business responsibility rather than that of a non-governmental organization or government.

Furthermore, as the SCALA results show, awareness of the responsibility for the environment is the most widely cited reason to start addressing sustainability issues. This is in contrast with Jones *et al.*'s (2007) argument that if businesses act as good agents in the interests of shareholders, the overall human welfare would be enhanced. The Lancaster London's investments in CSR projects such as the Lancaster London Community Consortium are highly likely to contribute, directly or indirectly, to the hotel's bottom line. This is certainly in line with Waldman and Siegel's (2008) assertion that CSR derives from instrumental thinking to maximize the wealth of the firm. However, the Lancaster London's understanding of responsibility goes beyond social responsiveness and philanthropic CSR, and further entails proactive engagement in a societal challenge—educational hospitality—which is explicitly reflected in the various partnerships and collaborations the hotel has been leading recently, such as the Trail Blazer in Apprenticeship scheme that is run with other industry players and the Lancaster Academy that is run in partnership with the Institute of Hospitality.

Furthermore, the Lancaster London has also successfully recognized the complexity of a global, interconnected business context, which is characterized by a multitude of stakeholder group interests. For example, the hotel cares about human rights issues, such as diversity, contributes actively to resource efficiency through "green" technology, and expresses commitment to care for the interests and needs of all legitimate stakeholders in its vision statement. Such stakeholder orientation is certainly reflected in the hotel's drive towards efficiency, which extends from the hotel premises to the value chain where the hotel works with suppliers to develop eco-friendly raw materials and components and reduce waste. As Nidumolu *et al.* (2009) posit, companies develop sustainable operations by analysing each link in the value chain and first they make changes in obvious areas such as supply chains. The Lancaster London appears to truly possess strategic thinking and a sense of the economic bottom line with a stakeholder perspective and social ideals. In this sense, it has a strategic, proactive, multifaceted as well as an integrative approach towards sustainability (Pless, 2007; Pless and Maak, 2011). This justifies Freeman *et al.*'s (2007) stakeholder theory as well as Porter and Kramer's (2011) proposed concept of "Shared Value Creation" that highlight mutual value creation on the part of both companies and society at large.

Uniquely, the Lancaster London's overarching hotel vision starts with a societal concern, which is embedded in an *outside-in* organizational perspective. To also translate sustainability challenges into business opportunities, making *business sense* of environmental and societal issues is a novel approach. In this regard, the Lancaster London appears to possess an eco-social advantage, which is about turning negative externalities into business opportunities (Reeves *et al.*, 2012). This is also justified by Peter Drucker's (2003) argument, "Every single social and global issue of our day is a business opportunity in disguise" (cited in Cooperrider, 2008). Moreover, understanding sustainable hotel operations through a holistic vision such as "We always care", as change of perspective, may very well bring about an understanding of the various interacting components, systems and different stakeholders, the happiness of whom is the ultimate purpose of being sustainable in the hotel industry. A holistic worldview necessitates system thinking whereby everything is related in some way and each part and each person in the business can contribute towards more sustainability (Landrum and Edwards, 2009). The hotel industry is not only hotels themselves; it is indeed an open, dynamic and complex system with various interacting components and different stakeholders (Mill and Morrison, 1997; Thanh and Bosch, 2010).

Interestingly, as both the SCALA survey and the company interviews demonstrate, the hotel optimizes triple bottom line values across different bottom lines (social value, environmental protection, profit). Rather than maximizing shareholder value or social profits, the management team focuses on what they perceive as a balanced and sustainable value for business and society (Husted and De Jesus Salazar, 2006), although the front-line staff sees this value creation both as TBL and positive contribution to society. The hotel seeks differentiation in terms of products and services such as the Bee Green Package, the London Honey Show and jogging maps for guests. Value is created not just as a side effect of the hotel business activities, but also as the result of deliberately defined goals and programmes addressed at specific sustainability issues (Dyllick and Muff, 2013). The hotel aims to create value for various stakeholders including shareholders, and society at large—regardless of any concern for reputational benefits or enhanced public relations. Furthermore, economic value creation is only seen as an outcome of running a responsible and meaningful business. This is indeed in accordance with the concept of triple bottom line, which measures the multi-dimensional business contributions to sustainability (Elkington, 1997). Coupled with a focus on innovation, this can be considered a synergistic search for creating economic, environmental and social value through sustainability efforts (Hart and Milstein, 2003).

Yet, the Lancaster London appears to also contribute positively to the common good (societal well-being) through the various sector-specific and cross-sectoral collaborations and relationships in the form of next-practice platforms; in other words, through local cluster development. Next-practices change existing paradigms by questioning the status quo, which leads to sustainability-related change. Sustainability can lead to interesting next-practice platforms that originate from innovations (Nidumolu *et al.*, 2009). For instance, the Trail Blazer in Apprenticeship Scheme, led by the Lancaster London, is a formation among six hospitality organizations (hotels and restaurants) that leads a government initiative in the industry, for the purpose of increasing the capacity of the relatively less skilled workforce typical in the industry. Similarly, the Lancaster Academy that was established in partnership with the Institute of Hospitality is an example of a cross-sectoral collaboration with the Ministry of Education to increase the know-how of the skilled, as well as the capacity of the young unemployed.

One of the most important interview findings that present an opportunity for the Lancaster London's development and progressive sustainability strategies was enhancement of a more engaged organizational culture, as the most widely cited challenge the Lancaster London faces in implementing sustainability initiatives. The need for more employee engagement is also reflected in the SCALA survey findings where, in general, executive/senior managers are more positive than middle managers who, in turn, are more positive than the front-line staff on almost all of the interval scale items. There are also differences in nominal scale items such as what led the company to start addressing sustainability issues. Front-line staff chose "to engage employees" more often than did executive/senior managers, and the executive/senior managers chose "desire to improve efficiencies" more often than did the other two groups. Likewise, executive/senior managers and middle managers chose "awareness of our responsibility to the environment" more often than did front-line staff. More positivity on the management side can be considered as a good sign of strong leadership commitment. As previous research shows, organizations that have strong leadership commitment are more likely to succeed in reaching sustainability-related goals (Eccles *et al.*, 2012). Yet, the findings also signal the need for an area of improvement in employee engagement as part of a more inclusive culture.

While leaders may initiate change by creating a new vision, it is the social interactions that create the common understanding and shared vision that predicate action (Demers, 2007). It is at this stage that organizational culture comes into play, as for many organizations the problems seem to be rooted in a mismatch between some specific aspects of the dominant culture and the sustainability goals and strategies (Miller-Perkins, 2011). Company leaders most often feel confused about the big question: "Better to set goals to match the current dominant culture, or better to change the culture to align with the goals they wish to set?" The answer to achieving this crucial alignment lies in the underlying reasons for making the commitment to sustainability in the first place. Finally, regardless of which approach the Lancaster London decides to take, the first step will depend on an understanding of the aspects of the organizational culture that are relevant to the sustainability terrain.

The future

As Sally finished reading the nicely elaborated case study, she thought about the big question that was raised in the paper: "Should the Lancaster London choose to change its sustainability strategy to match its culture, or should it instead choose to change its culture to align with its current strategy?" She poured another cup of tea and started reflecting on the possible answer.

She knew the Lancaster London had the right vision and goals to serve the well-being of its current stakeholders and future generations, yet it seemed to lack a clear path for achieving them in alignment with the cultural aspects of its corporate culture. The hotel indeed had a flexible, adaptable and externally focused culture yet the front-line staff needed to believe in and adopt every aspect of the "We always care" vision to fully engage in the progressive sustainability initiatives. They needed to feel more valued and as positive as the management team itself in the upcoming sustainability refurbishment period.

Just then, another great idea came to mind. What if the Lancaster London should harness its unique cultural strength of being externally focused and collaborate with BSL in a mutual learning project that would facilitate employee engagement. This would indeed set the stage for another invaluable cross-sectoral partnership…but at the international level: a partnership with a leading Swiss innovator in sustainability education! Going the extra mile with employee engagement and overcoming any potential sceptics among the front-line staff would, in turn, foster internal cross-functional integration and an inverted hierarchy that both seemed essential to achieving the Lancaster London's state-of-the-art corporate vision. The setting up of the Lancaster London Well-being Programme seemed to be the ideal starting point! "Happy Together and Forever" sounded like a nice name for it.

As she picked up the phone to call BSL, feeling so grateful for the nomination, she placed the case study securely in her briefcase.

Bibliography

Adriana, B. (2009). Environmental supply chain management in tourism: The case of large tour operators. *Journal of Cleaner Production*, 17(16), 1385-1392.

Angel del Brio, J., Junquera, B. & Ordiz, M. (2008). Human resources in advanced environmental approaches: A case analysis. *International Journal of Production Research*, 46(21), 6029-6053.

Ateljevic, J. & Doorne, S. (2000). Staying within the fence: Lifestyle entrepreneurship in tourism. *Journal of Sustainable Tourism*, 5(8), 378-392.

Carroll, A.B. (1999). Corporate social responsibility. *Business and Society*, 38(3), 268-295.

Carlsen, J., Morrison, A., & Weber, P. (2008). Lifestyle oriented small tourism firms. *Tourism Recreation Research*, 33(3) 255-263.

Chong, H.G. & Verma, R. (2013). Hotel sustainability: Financial analysis shines a cautious green light. *Cornell Hospitality Report*, 13(10), 6-13.

Cooperrider, D. (2008). Social innovation. *BizEd*, July/August 2008, 32-38.

Crane, A. (1995). Rhetoric and reality in the greening of organizational culture. *Greener Management International*, 11(12), 49-62.

Daily, B.F. & Huang, S. (2001). Achieving sustainability through attention to human resource factors in environmental management, *International Journal of Operations and Production Management*, 21(12), 1539-1552.

Demers, C. (2007). *Organizational Change Theories: A Synthesis*. California: Sage Publications, Inc.

Dixon, S.E.A. & Clifford, A. (2007). Eco-preneurship – A new approach to managing the triple bottom line. *Journal of Organizational Change Management*, 20(3), 326-345.

Dunphy, D. Griffiths, A. & Benn, S. (2003). *Organizational Change for Corporate Sustainability*. Routledge: London.

Dyllick, T. & Hockerts, K. (2002). Beyond the business case for corporate sustainability. *Business Strategy and the Environment*, 11, 130-141.

Dyllick, T. & Muff, K. (2013). Clarifying the meaning of sustainable business: Introducing a typology from business-as-usual to true business sustainability. Retrieved from http://ssrn.com/abstract=2368735.

Eccles, R.G., Ioannou, I. & Serafeim, G. (2012a). The impact of a corporate culture of sustainability on corporate behavior and performance. *Working Paper 12-035*, May 9, 2012. Boston: Harvard Business School.

Eccles, G. R., Perkins, M. K., & Serafeim, G. (2012b). How to become a sustainable company. *MIT Sloan Management Review*, 53(4), 43-50.

Elkington, J. (1997). *Cannibals with Forks: The Triple Bottom Line of 21st Century Business*. Oxford: Capstone.

Faber, N., Jorna, R.J. & van Engelen, J. (2005). The Sustainability of sustainability. *Journal of Environmental Assessment Policy and Management*, 7(1), 1-33.

Font, X. & Harris, C. (2004). Rethinking standards from green to sustainable. *Annals of Tourism Research*, 31(4), 986-1007.

Freeman, R.E., Harrison, J.S., & Wicks, A.C. (2007). *Managing for Stakeholders: Survival, Reputation, and Success*. New Haven, CT: Yale University Press.

Glisson, C. (2007). Assessing and changing organizational culture and climate for effective services. *Research on Social Work Practice*, 17, 736-747.

Global Compact. (2013). Global corporate sustainability report. Retrieved from https://www.unglobalcompact.org/AboutTheGC/global_corporate_sustainability_report.html.

Goodno, J.B. (1994). Eco-conference urges more care. *Hotel and Motel Management*, 209: part 1, 3 and 22.

Hart, S.L. & Milstein, M.B. (2003). Creating sustainable value. *Academy of Management Executive*, 17(2), pp. 13.

Holton, I., Glass, J. & Price, A.D.F. (2010). Managing for sustainability: Findings from four company case studies in the UK precast concrete industry. *Journal of Cleaner Production*, 18(2), 152-160.

Howard-Grenville, J. (2006). Inside the black box: How organizational culture informs attention and action on environmental issues. *Organization and Environment*, 19, 46-73.

Husted, B.W. & De Jesus Salazar, J. (2006). Taking Friedman seriously: Maximizing profits and social performance. *Journal of Management Studies*, 43, 75-91.

Jones, T.M., Felps, W., & Bigley, G.A. (2007). Ethical theory and stakeholder-related decisions: The role of stakeholder culture. *Academy of Management Review*, 32, 137-155.

Landrum, N.E. & Edwards, S. (2009). *Sustainable Business: An Executive's Primer*, New York: Business Expert Press.

Matten, D. & Crane, A. (2005). Corporate citizenship: Toward an extended theoretical conceptualization. *The Academy of Management Review*, 30(1), 166-179.

Matten, D. & Moon, J. (2008). Implicit and explicit CSR: A conceptual framework for comparative understanding of corporate social responsibility. *The Academy of Management Review*, 33(2), 404-424.

Mill, R. & Morrison, A. (1997). *The Tourism System: An Introductory Text*. 3rd Edition. Dubuque, IA: Kendall Hunt Publishing Company.

Miller-Perkins, K. (2011). Sustainability culture: Culture and leadership assessment. Miller Consultants Inc. Retrieved from www.millerconsultants.com/sustainability.php.

Network for Business Sustainability (NBS). (2010). Embedding sustainability in organizational culture: A systematic review of the body of knowledge. Retrieved from http://www.nbs.net/wp-content/uploads/dec6_embedding_sustainability.pdf.

Network for Business Sustainability (NBS). (2012). Innovating for sustainability: A guide for executives. Retrieved from www.nbs.net.

Nidumolu, R., Prahalad, C. & Rangaswami, M. (2009). Why sustainability is now the key driver of innovation. *Harvard Business Review*, September, 57-64.

Pless, N.M. (2007). Understanding responsible leadership: Role identity and motivational drivers. *Journal of Business Ethics*, 74, 437-456.

Pless, N.M. & Maak, T. (2011). Responsible leadership: Pathways to the future. *Journal of Business Ethics*, 98(S1), 3-13.

Porter, M. & Kramer, M. (2011). Creating shared value: How to reinvent capitalism and unleash a wave of innovation and growth. In *Harvard Business Review*, Jan-Feb: 62-77.

Post, J.E. & Altman, B.W. (1994). Managing the environmental change process: Barriers and opportunities. *Journal of Organizational Change Management,* 7(4), 64-81.

Reeves, M., Haanaes, K., Love, C. & Levin, S. (2012). Sustainability as adaptability. *Journal of Applied Corporate Finance,* 24(2), 14-22.

Shrivastava, P. (1995). *Greening Business: Profiting the Corporation and the Environment.* Cincinnati: Thompson Executive Press.

Stawiski, S., Deal, J.J. & Gentry, W. (2010). Employee perceptions of Corporate Social Responsibility: The implications for your organization. *Quick View Leadership Series,* Center for Creative Leadership: USA.

Thanh, V.M. & Bosch, O.J.H. (2010). Systems thinking approach as a unique tool for sustainable tourism development: A case study in the Cat Ba biosphere reserve of Vietnam. *International Society for Systems Sciences,* Wilfrid Laurier University, Waterloo, ON, Canada: 18-23.

Thornton, P.H., Ocasio, W. & Lounsbury, M. (2012). *The Institutional Logics Perspective: A New Approach to Culture, Structure and Process.* Oxford: Oxford University Press.

Waldman, D.A. & Siegel, D.S. (2008). Theoretical and practitioner letters: defining the socially responsible leader. *Leadership Quarterly,* 19, 117-131.

Welford, R.J. (1995). *Environmental Strategy and Sustainable Development: The Corporate Challenge of the 21st Century.* Routledge, London.

Wilkinson, A., Hill, M. and Gollan, P. (2001). The sustainability debate. *International Journal of Operations and Productions Management,* 21(2), 1492-1502.

Appendix I: The Dyllick/Muff Business Sustainability Typology

The Dyllick/Muff Business Sustainability Typology uses three elements of a typical business process model: the relevant concerns considered (inputs), the type of value created (outputs), and the organizational perspectives applied (processes) (Dyllick and Muff, 2013). Dyllick and Muff draw attention to the fact that the broader sustainability perspective typically entails social, environmental and economic concerns, in contrast to the traditional business perspective that entails economic concerns only. Regarding the type of value created, Dyllick and Muff highlight the need for businesses to contribute to the positive common good by going beyond triple bottom line value creation. They envisage true business sustainability as one that contributes to resolving environmental, social or economic issues on a regional or global scale. Finally, regarding the organizational perspectives applied, the authors turn around the traditional *inside-out* perspective that aims to invent, produce and measure within the three-dimensional sustainability aspects, to an *outside-in* perspective that starts with sustainability challenges that lie beyond the company boundaries. The typology aims to serve scholars and practitioners by clarifying the drivers and aims of business sustainability (Hashmi and Muff, 2014). As business sustainability (BS) evolves from 1.0 to 2.0 and 3.0 respectively, the relevance and contribution to resolve societal issues increase, with Business Sustainability 3.0 exhibiting "true business sustainability".

Figure 3 Typology of business sustainability and their key characteristics
Source: Dyllick and Muff, 2013

BUSINESS SUSTAINABILITY TYPOLOGY (BST)	Concerns (What?)	Values created (What for?)	Organizational perspective (How?)
Business-as-usual	Economic concerns	Shareholder value	Inside-out
Business Sustainability 1.0	Three-dimensional concerns	Refined shareholder value	Inside-out
Business Sustainability 2.0	Three-dimensional concerns	Triple bottom line	Inside-out
Business Sustainability 3.0	Starting with sustainability challenges	Creating value for the common good	Outside-in
The key shifts involved:	1st shift: broadening the business concern	2nd shift: expanding the value created	3rd shift: changing the perspective

At the level BS.1, a business responds to extra-market business challenges that result from environmental or social concerns that are typically voiced by external stakeholders. Thus, managing economic risks and opportunities takes precedence as a strategy. While the focus is primarily on managing risks, embracing opportunities typically follows later. Existing strategies, outlooks, products and services remain unchanged. There are often no changes in the corporate structure in terms of governance and leadership focuses on seeking opportunities. There is often a central function or unit in charge of or coordinating response to sustainability challenges, and the reporting is mostly on good news and economic benefits. Primary corporate attitude is basically reacting to societal pressures for the purpose of refined shareholder value.

At the more advanced BS.2 level, the stakeholder perspective is broadened with the aim of creating social and environmental values in addition to economic value; in other words, the business manages for the triple bottom line through particular programmes that are consequently measured and reported. The primary focus is on developing and implementing new strategies and programmes that are addressed at specific sustainability issues or stakeholders. The business further reconceives new products and markets. While existing products and services are adapted, new products and services are also developed to improve triple bottom line value creation, yet without questioning their societal value. Sustainability goals are integrated into planning and reporting cycles as well as into management and governance structures, mainly through cross-functional committees, policies and guidelines. Furthermore, sustainability goals and activities are embedded in line functions as part of sustainability implementation. While internal reporting includes differentiated triple bottom line activities and results, external reporting includes reporting on sustainability goals and achievements, which is often externally verified. Primary corporate attitude entails a pattern of active exchange with a broad group of stakeholders for the purpose of social, environmental and economic values (triple bottom line), yet still with an "inside-out" organizational perspective.

Finally, at the BS.3 "true business sustainability" level, there is a shift in mind-set from minimizing negative impacts to creating positive impacts in significant issues relevant to the society and the planet. This derives from an "outside-in" organizational perspective, unlike those prevalent in the lower levels of business sustainability. Capabilities and resources are redefined to resolve societal issues that form the baseline for new strategies, business models, products and services. At this advanced level, companies engage in changing the collective rules of the game through sector-wide or cross-sectoral strategies. The primary focus is on societal concerns that supersede focus on customers. Furthermore, markets and strategies derive from societal challenges. New products and services are created as a voluntary and proactive response to societal challenges, likely in collaboration with new partners. The company governance structure includes relevant societal representatives who contribute to the relevant decision-making processes throughout the organization. The company reorganizes around the societal issues it addresses and includes new players in these open and dynamic structures. Reporting entails societal value creation with different societal stakeholders. Primary corporate attitude entails a pattern of voluntary, proactive as well as interactive collaboration with new players for the purpose of creating value for the common good.

✉ Armand Calinescu street no.19.
Sector 2, Bucharest, Romania.

☎ +90 532 2618027

💻 gulen.hashmi@bsl-lausanne.ch

Pebbles (PVT) Ltd sustainable real estate developers
Building hopes

Syeda Nazish Zahra Bukhari

Business School Lausanne, Switzerland

Context

> Man everywhere is a disturbing agent. Wherever he plants his foot, the
> harmonies of nature are turned to discord (Marsh, 1864).

While driving on the 64 km long, partly broken down road, of the Lahore-Sheikhupura industrial area I suddenly thought I saw a mirage. But as I took a closer look I realized that it was not an illusion; the green walled residential community housed in the middle of the highly polluted Sheikhupura industrial estate was a reality. This residential community, called the "Ecommunity", is a project of Pebbles (Pvt) Ltd, located in Sheikhupura, which is an industrial city of the Punjab province of Pakistan. The city shares one of its borders with Lahore, the provincial capital of Punjab. The Sheikhupura industrial estate was developed in 1969 for the purpose of increasing the industrial development of the surrounding regions. The area houses several industrial units ranging from paper, seed, leather, steel, stainless steel, chemical, pharmaceutical, rice, stone and marble grinding, to textile, poultry and animal feed, flour, soap and many other industries (Gilani *et al.*, 2013). The industrial estate did serve the purpose it was established for, but at what cost, one may wonder. Various researches done on the region's environmental condition, reveal that the ceramics, steel, leather, textile, pharmaceuticals and the fertilizer industry are causing severe pollution in the area. According to the official Environmental Protection Agency (EPA) of the country out of 482 industrial units present in and around this area, only seven are observing the National Environmental Quality Standard (NEQS). Several industrial units have been termed "dangerous" for both human and animal life and a major reason behind the local crop destruction. A growing rate of tuberculosis, chest infection, hepatitis, lungs, eyes, liver, skin and respiratory diseases have been reported among the residents of this area.

However, when the factory owners or management are asked about why they are indulging in such unsustainable practices, they say that the treatment plants for the hazardous wastes are very costly and they cannot afford them (Dawn, 2004). Research conducted in the industrial area of Sheikhupura revealed a positive relationship between the increased rate of hepatitis C among the locals and the heavily growing pollution in the area (Sohail, Mughal, Arshad, & Arshad, 2010). Given the extremely unsustainable condition of the region, it can be understood why an outside observer may believe "Ecommunity" to be a hallucination. The context in which Pebbles (Pvt) Ltd's sustainable housing community is situated was what attracted me to explore this organization more deeply through a case study analysis.

Introduction

Pebbles (Pvt) Ltd is a "sustainable project management and development company", started under the "Dawood Hercules Corporation (DH Corp)" in 2008. It is the first and the only sustainable real estate development company in Pakistan (About DH Corp, 2015). The company was selected for the Business School Lausanne's (BSL) sustainability case study research after measuring its sustainable validity against the following measures.

> ▶ The company is a recognized and verified sustainability leader in its particular industry, having proof of third-party verification.

> ▶ The company has been pursuing significant initiatives in addressing and contributing to resolve important societal and/or environmental issues in its geographical region.

Once it was verified that Pebbles (Pvt) Ltd fulfilled the qualifying criteria for the BSL case study, the company's journey of sustainability and its current position on the continuum of true business sustainability was analysed using a qualitative research approach. Qualitative research is a term used for various investigative methodologies that emphasize the importance of looking at different variables in their natural setting, in which observing and analysing the interaction between the multiple variables is the key to obtaining diverse data patterns (Jacob, 1988). The technique of data triangulation was adopted for the collection of data, which is the convergence of multiple data sources in order to provide a more detailed and balanced picture of a situation, in addition to validating the data involved through cross verification from two or more sources (Denzin, 1978). The following tools of qualitative research were adopted for the collection, analysis, and interpretation of the case study data:

> ▶ Archive (all external and internal company information, including company websites, internal documents, videos, articles, media reports and various other case studies related secondary data)

▶ Interview (with current employees and external stakeholders)

▶ Survey

▶ Personal observation of the company's sustainable housing community. This is a type of observational research in which the researcher personally interacts with the subjects or observes from a distance, thereby obtaining data directly from the source (Kawulich, 2005). The researcher in the case study visited the housing community and interacted with the residents so as to get a true picture about their living experience.

The objective of the case study was to embark on a journey of learning and discovery with the company in such a way that the following research questions are answered:

▶ What is the company's Business Sustainability (BST) position based on the Dyllick/Muff business sustainability typology grid?

▶ How did the company get to their current BST position? What were the major milestones or challenges in the organization's sustainability journey that shaped the company's historical timeline? What are the company's current ambitions, aspiration and plans in the relevant societal/ecological issue and what externalities is the company facing?

▶ How did the company approach and resolve sustainability issues on both organizational and employee levels?

The structure of the case study is as follows: First, the meaning, origin and history of "sustainable real estate" is understood through a review of literature. The concept of sustainable real estate development is studied at both a global and a regional (Pakistan) level in order to gain a better understanding of the context in which Pebbles (Pvt) Ltd is operating. After gaining comprehension about the industry in which our research partner company is operating, the methodology of the case study is explained. Third, the journey of the company, on the path of business sustainability is discussed chronologically. In order to add another perspective about the organization's sustainability performance, the next section describes and analyses the results of the "Sustainability Culture and Leadership Assessment" (SCALA) survey. The survey adds richness to the case study by providing us with the employee's perspective of the company's sustainable culture and the role of leadership in adopting business sustainability within the organization. Building on the data gathered by the previous sections, the next section of the case study will determine the company's business sustainability position in the light of the Dyllick/Muff Business Sustainability Typology. Based on the patterns identified throughout the case study, the sustainability journey of Pebbles (Pvt) Ltd is analysed on the basis of how far the company has travelled upon embracing the spirit of true business sustainability. The data in the case study has been discussed, analysed and explained by reviewing it through a contextual lens, deciphering the data in reference to the specific geographic conditions the company is operating in.

A contextual approach is used while analysing an organization's commitment towards business sustainability and its sustainability performance because research reveals that the business environment of the developing nations itself poses numerous difficulties for the companies in the adoption of business sustainability (Wilfried & Vanhonacker & Pan, 1997). Country-specific studies done by Munoz (2009), Asteriou and Price (2001) and Ahmed and Pulok (2013) concluded that the political instability of a country negatively impacts the economic growth of that country. According to research, this relationship is more evident in the case of developing countries. Developing countries, as classified by the International Statistical Institute (2015) are "countries with a GNI (Gross National Income) per capita of US$11,905 (approx. €10,749.87) or less". Furthermore, Hofstede (1980) stated that countries vary greatly with respect to culture and that culture is one of the major forces impacting the performance of a business. Therefore, if the business environment, the national culture and the political stability of a country is different from other countries, the organizations operating within that country will be facing unique challenges in the adoption and incorporation of corporate sustainability.

> **if the business environment, the national culture and the political stability of a country is different from other countries, the organizations operating within that country will be facing unique challenges in the adoption and incorporation of corporate sustainability**

Pakistan is an example of a developing country (ISI, 2013) which, according to the World Bank (2013a):

> Is facing significant economic, governance and security challenges in achieving durable development outcomes. The persistence of conflict in the border areas and security challenges throughout the country is a reality that affects all aspects of life in Pakistan and impedes development. Pakistan's economy continues to underperform. There is no improvement in the security situation; political tensions have grown; there is no abatement in energy crisis, which continues to dampen the growth prospects and impacts the fiscal situation.

The organizations operating in Pakistan have to face all the above quoted adversities in addition to various other corporate challenges. Therefore, for a business the journey of sustainability is not just a process of internal evolution, it is the story of a battle fought on numerous fronts. The World Resources Institute report (1994–95) on sustainable development states that "the most pressing environmental challenges in developing countries in the next few decades will be health hazards created by lack of access to clean water and sanitation, indoor air pollution from biomass stoves, rapid urbanization, and deforestation" (Bruce, Albalak, & Rachel, 2000). A survey conducted by the United Nations revealed three key challenges to sustainable development in the world: "the

> **for a business the journey of sustainability is not just a process of internal evolution, it is the story of a battle fought on numerous fronts**

absence of sustainable cities, scarcity of food and nutrition security and the lack of energy transformation". Rapid urbanization, in almost all parts of the world, has caused a rise in the real estate sector. This boom has resulted in the development of highly unsustainable living communities. According to research "urbanization causes an increase in the emission of pollutants into the atmosphere, a higher need to clear lands, and a loss of biodiversity in virgin forests on a global scale". Studies reveal that in most cases indoor air of a building may be more polluted than the outside air. Indoor air pollution can be caused by solvents from paints, plywood adhesives, finishes and backing materials, certain construction materials such as asbestos, formaldehyde and lead, and production of excess heat inside the building. Indoor air pollution can cause irritation of the eyes, nose and throat, headaches, dizziness and in worse cases may also be a reason for the development of respiratory diseases or cancer (UN World Economic and Social Survey, 2013).

These challenges highlight the need for sustainable living within developing countries. We will review the concept of sustainable living in more detail in the next section.

Literature review

Human population is growing in terms of both number and need. Researchers as early as Malthus (1798) realized that the growth of human population is of an unsustainable nature. Malthus wrote that "human population grew exponentially while resources grew arithmetically", which will cause the human population to outgrow the resources in a very short interval of time. He concluded that this disequilibrium will lead to famines, wars and plagues. This, however, did not happen as was predicted by Malthus because of the advent and advancement in various technologies, the improvement of health and sanitation facilities and the slowing down of the growth of the human population (Kelly, 2009). In 1968 Garrett Hardin again analysed the unsustainable use of natural resources, in his book *The Tragedy of the Commons*. He wrote that "the tragedy of the commons evolves when individuals use a public good, but do not pay for the full cost of it". Hardin, however, took a moral stance on the resolution of this issue and observed that it has become imperative for societies to educate their citizens about the moral obligation of protecting the natural environment, since modern technology will soon become an inadequate saviour for mankind. Widespread public concern, in the 1960s over the degradation of natural resources has been reported as the main reason behind the 1972 United Nations Conference on the Human Environment in Stockholm. At this

it has become imperative for societies to educate their citizens about the moral obligation of protecting the natural environment, since modern technology will soon become an inadequate saviour for mankind

conference it was agreed that "the capacity of the earth to produce vital renewable resources must be maintained and, wherever practicable, restored or improved". In 1980 the United Nations Environment Programme (UNEP) formulated the "World Conservation Strategy", in which the concept of "development that is sustainable" was discussed formally for the first time. The strategy stated that:

> This is the kind of development that provides real improvements in the quality of human life and at the same time conserves the vitality and diversity of the Earth. The goal is development that will be sustainable. Today it may seem visionary, but it is attainable. To more and more people it also appears our only rational option
> (Kelly, 2009).

The concept of sustainable development was elaborated further, in the Brundtland Report, *Our Common Future*. Sustainable development was defined by the Brundtland Commission of the United Nations on 20 March 1987 as: "development that meets the needs of the present without compromising the ability of future generations to meet their own needs" (WCED, 1987). One of the major objections to the Brundtland Commission report was that it stated sustainable development as a hypothetical goal which still needed to be defined in practical terms. The UK Government stated: "There can be no quarrel with the [Brundtland principles] as a general definition. The key point is how to translate it into practice, how to measure it and to assess progress towards its achievement" (Whitby & Ward, 1994). The 1992 Rio Earth Summit on environment and development provided the basis for the practical application of sustainable development. Following this summit, sustainable development was applied to a diverse range of areas, including sustainable living.

Sustainable living is defined as a "lifestyle that attempts to reduce an individual's or society's use of the Earth's natural resources and personal resources" (Ainoa *et al.*, 2009). Globally the concept of sustainable living started in the 19th century, in geographic regions where rapid industrialization was taking place. In some regions people had started to realize that advancements in technology were causing great harm to the environment and rapid urbanization was adversely impacting both the quantity and quality of various natural resources. In the early 1800s, some of the people in America started developing personal lifestyles or ways of living that took into consideration the protection of the environment in which they were living. Henry David Thoreau, an American author and naturalist, is considered to be the first person to write about sustainable living in 1854 (Sustainable Development, 2012).

Sustainable real estate development can be traced back to the concept of sustainable living. Sustainable real estate is also called "green real estate". The concept of sustainability has gained importance in the real estate and construction sector in the past decade. Real estate developers, all around the world, are facing numerous challenges, including the need to use sustainable energy resources, the need for sustainable urban development within existing neighbourhoods, reduction of pollution, ensuring lower maintenance cost and lowering greenhouse gas emissions (Apanavičienė et al., 2015). Research conducted in the United States states that sustainability is becoming imperative for the real estate market of the country because "buildings, both residential and commercial, consume 40% of the energy used in the US and are responsible for more than one third of the US total carbon dioxide emissions" (Goering, 2009). According to the "green building facts" report by the US Green Building Council (2015), buildings account for 38% of the total carbon dioxide emission, 73% of electricity consumption and 13.6% of water consumption in the country. Similar research done in Singapore reveals that commercial and industrial buildings alone are contributing approximately 15% of the total carbon dioxide emission in the country. It is further observed that despite the government's efforts to promote green buildings, the private sector is not very proactive in these countries (Dapaah et al., 2015). Just a slight overview of the situation reveals that the need for nations to adopt sustainable living practices is becoming more and more pressing, with each passing day.

> the need for nations to adopt sustainable living practices is becoming more and more pressing, with each passing day

Sustainable real estate development provides a solution to many of the above-mentioned problems. According to research, compared to an average commercial building, a certified green building will exhibit 25% less energy consumption, 11% less water consumption, 34% less greenhouse gas emission, 27% higher occupation satisfaction and 19% lower maintenance costs. It has been estimated that in 2015, 40–48% of the new non-residential construction will be green in the US and the figure will reach 84% by 2018. Currently, 83% of the commercial buildings in Brazil, 73% of institutional projects in the UAE and 65% of building renovation projects in the UK are being developed according to green building standards (U.S Green Building Council, 2015).

According to the definition given by the World Green Building Congress, a "green building" has the following features:

A green building uses energy-efficient and eco-friendly equipment, recycled and environmentally friendly building material. It offers quality indoor air for human safety and comfort. The building has a system of generating renewable energy, efficient use of water, effective control and building management system along with effective use of the existing landscape (Dapaah, Hiang, Shi, & Sharon, 2015).

The World Green Building Council (WGBC) was established in 2002, as a network of green building councils from all across the globe. It has more than a hundred member countries. The WGBC provides the member countries with the sustainable tools and strategies through which they can promote local green buildings and address global issues such as climate change, indoor air pollution and sustainable utilization of natural resources (WGBC, 2015). Currently, there are five major national certification formats for green building in the US, which are being followed in other parts of the world as well. These include ASHRAE (American Society of Heating, Refrigeration, and Air-Conditioning Engineers), ENERGY STAR, LEED (Leadership in Energy and Environmental Design), Green Globes and NAHB (Northern Arizona Home Builders) Model Home Building Guidelines. The ASHRAE standards were developed in the 1970s and are considered to be the first and the oldest building sustainability standards. The LEED certification is the most complex and the most recognized and accepted sustainable building or green building certification (Goering, 2009).

Pakistan, like the rest of the world, is also facing the various threats caused by rapid industrialization and unsustainable growth of the real estate sector. In Pakistan, the real estate sector is the second largest employer, contributing over 2% to the GDP (gross domestic product) of the country, having an asset value of approximately $700 billion. One of the main reasons behind the growth of the real estate sector in Pakistan is that the entire 190 million population of the country dream of owning a house. This large population invests heavily in the real estate sector (Pakistan Real Estate News, 2015). This robust, but unsustainable growth has created a severe energy shortage in the country. Pakistan depends almost entirely on fossil fuels for the generation of energy. The burning of fossil fuels causes heavy emission of greenhouse gases (GHG), which trap heat in the atmosphere. In a newspaper interview, Mr Azher Abbas, a member of the Pakistan Council of Architects and Town Planners (PCATP), and Institute of Architects Pakistan (IAP) said:

> The increasing energy demand is not only a result of the population growth, but also a result of the concrete jungle our cities have turned into. Considering the current and future energy forecasts in Pakistan, green buildings offer the only way out. The west has repositioned its strategies towards a green revolution; we also have no other choice (Dawn, 2009).

According to research, the journey of sustainable construction started in Pakistan much later than the rest of the world. In 2005, an earthquake having an intensity of 7.8 on the Richter scale hit the northern areas of the country. It caused great destruction in the area and the government started looking for ways through which it can ensure speedy construction of the destroyed communities without depleting the critical natural resources of the country. At that time various industry experts suggested the use of sustainable building practices, like the use of recycled building material and renewable energy sources (Asghar, 2014). In November 2009, the World Green Building Council accepted the formation of the Pakistan Green Building Council (PGBC) and after three years, in 2012, the PGBC was accepted as a prospective member of the WGBC. The council covered the areas of construction that can affect the environment, including:

> Subsoil water levels, water consumption and usage, climate change, deforestation, carbon footprints, air quality, transportation, agriculture, industry, renewable and alternative energy/fuel, energy/fuel consumption and usage,

design of buildings, living patterns, green product/building certification system and environmental education at grass root level (Rana, 2013).

The chairman of the PGBC states:

> Most of Pakistan's energy, water and air quality problems can be solved if we all make a conscious effort. Sustainable development was a major consideration in many nations. Unfortunately, Pakistan is behind the curve in this area. The problem is that we failed to make good energy bylaws and implement them (Naqvi, 2013).

Pebbles (Pvt) Ltd was the first residential society of Pakistan to gain membership of the US Green Building Council, in 2009. Currently, 14 construction projects have USGBC membership in Pakistan, among which Pebbles (Pvt) Ltd is the only residential housing society project. How did the Dawood Hercules Corporation (DH Corp) come up with the unprecedented concept of sustainable urban development in Pakistan? We will travel upon and analyse the historical timeline of the company in order to better understand its sustainability journey.

Methodology

In addition to secondary data, three primary data gathering instruments were used in the case study: employee survey, employee interviews and customer observation. A Sustainability Culture and Leadership Assessment (SCALA) survey was conducted to gauge how much sustainability is embedded within the leadership and culture of the organization. The research instrument was designed by Miller Consultants in 2012. The survey focuses on various elements of the company's leadership and culture that contribute to the successful implementation of business sustainability within the organization. The purpose of this patented research instrument is to provide "the company, information about their organization's current capacity for executing sustainability strategies" (SCALA, 2014). The questions pertain to the following elements of business sustainability:

- Organizational leadership
- Organizational systems
- Organizational climate
- Change readiness
- Internal stakeholders
- External stakeholders

The survey consisted of four sections and 43 questions. The survey was a blend of open-ended and closed-ended questions. The closed-ended questions generated responses on the Likert scale, with the answer choices ranging from "Strongly Agree" to Strongly Disagree". The first four questions gathered demographic data about the respondents. The next 32 questions were closed-ended, generating data about the organization's culture and leadership, developed by Miller Consultants from the cumulative results of numerous sustainability researches. Five open-ended questions were added to the survey instrument by Business School Lausanne (BSL), in order to assess the true business sustainability position of the company. The last two open-ended questions were included by the researcher, as a filter, to verify the responses to the closed-ended questions of the survey. The questionnaires were provided to the respondents in hard copy form. Pebbles (Pvt) Ltd has a total of 15 managerial and non-managerial employees. Since only the managerial level employees were aware of the concept of business sustainability and the vision of the company, only they were taken as the survey sample. The survey was filled by all the managerial level staff of the organization—eight employees. It was administered by the researcher at the head office of the organization, generating a 100% response rate. The results were analysed and documented by Miller Consultants, Inc. The survey respondents were equally divided between the two genders, i.e. four females and four males. Three respondents belonged to the senior management level, three to the middle management level, and two were first line managers. In terms of age, five respondents fell within the 20–30 years bracket and one respondent from each of the 31–40 years, 41–50 years, and 51–60 years brackets.

Based on various patterns identified through the secondary research and the survey analysis, a series of interviews were conducted with the management of the company. The interviews were semi-structured, in which the interview protocol was shared with the respondents prior to the interview. This was done to ensure maximum generation of relevant information during the interview. The interviewees were selected jointly by the researcher and the CEO of Pebbles (Pvt) Ltd, based upon their involvement in the Ecommunity housing project (see Table 1). The interviews took place in the head office of the company. All the respondents were engaged with the company's first sustainable housing community project, Ecommunity, and were able to provide valuable information regarding the organization's sustainability perspective and the journey it took to transform the dream of Samad Dawood, the CEO of Dawood Hercules Corporation, into a reality. The third data gathering technique used by the researcher was the personal observation of the sustainable housing community, through a series of visits. During the visits the researcher communicated with the residents of the housing community in order to gather data regarding customer satisfaction and the authentication of sustainable living claims made by the organization. Furthermore, the external environment and its impact on the housing community was also observed by the researcher. These techniques combined with the story of the organization's sustainable journey were used to accomplish the research objectives of the case study.

Table 1 Interviewee list and years of association with the company

Name	Title	Years of association with Pebbles (Pvt) Ltd
Mr Abdullah Yousaf	Chief Executive Officer	7 Years
Ms Farida Razzak	Finance Officer	6 Years
Ms Ayesha Bajwa	Manager Finance	3 Years
Ms Zunaira Nadeem	Business Controller	2 Years
Mr Amir Zaidi	Ex-CEO	6 Years

Pebbles (Pvt) Ltd

The Dawood Hercules Corporation traces back its roots to the 1920s, during which the founding member of the company, Ahmed Dawood, opened his first shop of cotton yarn in the subcontinent (the name given to Pakistan and India jointly under British rule, before the two countries separated and became independent nations in 1947). In 1948, Dawood expanded his business interests further and created the Dawood Hercules Group. Today the Dawood Hercules Corporation has the following business divisions:

> Engro Corporation Limited

> The Hub Power Company Limited

> Dawood Lawrencepur Limited

> Tenaga Generasi Limited

> Inbox Business Technologies (Pvt) Limited

> Pebbles (Pvt) Limited

> Cyan Limited

> e2e Business Enterprises (Pvt) Limited

> Bubber Sher (Pvt) Ltd

In 1964, the DH Corp entered the real estate market of Pakistan. The company constructed the Dawood Center in Karachi, Pakistan. It was a commercial project undertaken by the company, on an individual basis. In 2008, the DH Corp decided to formally enter the real estate business through the formation of a separate business entity (DH Corp, 2015). The reason behind entering the real estate sector was the attractive growth patterns of the industry during that time period. Pakistan has one of the highest urbanization rates, 3.2%, in South-East Asia. This provides a lot of opportunities for the real estate companies (Zaheer, 2015). According to a report issued by the World Bank:

The housing demand in urban centers, of Pakistan, is increasing at an annual rate of 8%. The total shortfall, which in 2009 was recorded at 7.57 million units, has now touched the 10-million mark. Market experts say that the total number of houses built every year in Pakistan is somewhere between 0.15 – 0.2 million, whereas the country needs 1 million new houses annually (0.7 million for the population growth and 0.3 million for replacing old houses and to cover the existing shortage) (Haq, 2015).

Samad Dawood, the CEO of DH Corp, was greatly interested in the real estate sector. However, he was aware that the great boom in the country's real estate market was highly unsustainable and contributing to the country's energy and resource scarcity problems. His vision was to offer a solution to the problem rather than adding to it by creating yet another commercially run, profit oriented real estate development company (A. Yousaf, personal communication, 10 December 2014). Aamir Raza, the first CEO of Pebbles, states:

the great boom in the country's real estate market was highly unsustainable and contributing to the country's energy and resource scarcity problems

It is increasingly evident that our present day living structures are being challenged by a host of factors, particularly in relation to the design intent, space optimization, effective energy usage, water wastage, pollution, landscape, parking spaces, ventilation, natural light, fire fighting, garbage disposal and above all safety and security of the occupants. The growing environmental pollution was a painful reality in my younger days. After decades, I feel that it has taken the form of crisis in our country.

As a result of this vision, Pebbles (Pvt) Ltd started in September 2008, as Pakistan's first sustainable project development and management company. The top management at DH Corp realized that in order to become a solution provider, they had to think and act sustainably. The ex-CEO of the company, Amir, says:

It is only the carefully planned ideas and designs that can help save further deterioration of the environment and our lifestyles. Conservation of resources and sustainability is the call of the day and intelligent use of resources needs to be realized as the real pivotal focus of construction

It is only the carefully planned ideas and designs that can help save further deterioration of the environment and our lifestyles. Conservation of resources and sustainability is the call of the day and intelligent use of resources needs to be realized as the real pivotal focus of construction. Conservation of resources and their smart, sensible use is a beauty that's more realistic (Raza, 2014).

At that point in time there was no concept of sustainable construction in Pakistan and therefore, no industry standards or rules for the company to follow. Pebbles started its journey with the following vision: "To penetrate the up-and-coming real estate market by encouraging sustainable business practices, efficient building concepts and to demonstrate a strong awareness about preservation, recycling of resources and reliable energy sources" (Pebbles, 2015). Since Pakistan had no local Green Building Council Pebbles joined the US Green Building Council in 2009. It was the first construction company in Pakistan to have membership of USGBC. The company started functioning under the standards of USGBC. The top management of the company also started working towards the development of the "Pakistan Green Building Council (PGBC)" (A. Bajwa, personal communication, 10 December 2014). In 2009, a number of industry experts applied to the WGBC for the formation of the PGBC. Aqrab Ali Rana, a LEED certified architect, states:

> In Pakistan, the environment is not high in the list of issues. Transforming the vision and mission of a few into a mass movement proved to be a tough job. After three years of dedicated work and meeting strict requirements, in 2012, the World GBC accepted Pakistan GBC membership as a prospective member. In parallel the Security Exchange Commission of Pakistan (SECP) also accepted the Pakistan GBC application. Pakistan GBC was licensed to run as a non-profit organization in November 2012 (Rana, 2013).

Pebbles (Pvt) Ltd was one of the founding members of the Pakistan Green Building Council. In 2010, Pebbles started working on its first sustainable housing community project. It was initially named "Sheikhu Garden Housing Society", but in 2011, the name was changed to "Ecommunity". The name symbolized the sustainable nature of the housing community. The first step was the selection of the location for the housing community. The company had a number of economically and aesthetically attractive options. However, Samad Dawood had the vision of developing a sustainable housing community that would prove the benefits of sustainable development within an unsustainable environment. He wanted the adversities of the location to be the challenge that would be solved through sustainable development and management of the housing community (A. Yousaf, personal communication, 10 December 2014). Ultimately, the top management of the company selected a 222,577 square metre piece of land on the main Lahore- Sheikhupura road. The location, which was in the middle of the highly polluted industrial area, was the first sustainability challenge for the company. It was believed by the company's management that the advantages of sustainable living would be best highlighted against the contrasting unsustainable background and Ecommunity would prove to be the green haven that the adversely affected local population was looking for. The project was designed on the basis of LEED building standards, which continuously measures and monitors how well a building performs across the metrics of: energy savings, water efficiency, CO_2 emissions reduction, improved indoor environmental quality, and sustainable utilization of resources.

Samad Dawood had the vision of developing a sustainable housing community that would prove the benefits of sustainable development within an unsustainable environment

Ecommunity

Ecommunity is the first ever housing scheme of Pakistan that is built on green building practices. Based on the green building guidelines of LEED, the housing community has about 36% of the area for residential purpose,

15% of the community is green (parks and gardens) and 40% of the area is covered by wide and spacious roads, by roads and avenues with tree lined walkways (see Fig. 1). The rest of the space consists of aesthetically and sustainably planned commercial areas and community centres. The housing society offers four types of residential options with varying sizes and features. The houses were designed keeping in mind the individual requirements, preferences and resource availability of various customers. (ecommunity, 2015).

The four types of houses, available for the customer, are:

> A 126.47 m² house with four design options

> A 177.05 m² house with four design options

> A 252.93 m² house with four design options

> A 505.86 m² house with two design options

Figure 1 Aerial blueprint of Ecommunity

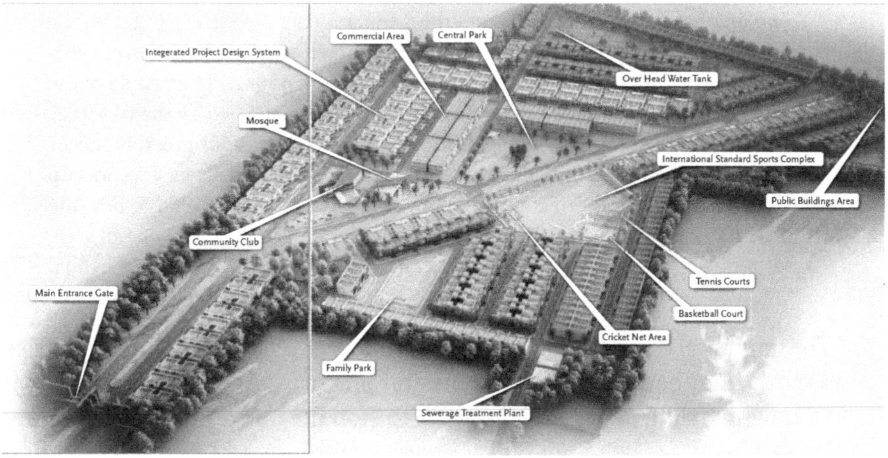

All the houses are built to fulfil the following "green targets":

> Water use reduction up to 40%

> Energy reduction up to 50%

> Renewable energy usage up to 2.5%

> HVAC (heating, ventilation, and air conditioning) requirement reduction up to 30%

> Material reuse, up to 20%

> Usage of construction materials which could be procured within 500 km radius of the site up to 50%

> Usage of rapidly renewable material up to 5%

▶ Improved indoor environmental quality and providing extra ventilation in all living spaces

▶ Reduction in carbon dioxide concentration inside the house

▶ Consideration for healthier neighbourhood and privacy factors

> Ecommunity was being developed on the values of conservation and preservation of nature, which were in contradiction to the practices being followed by the other actors operating in the area

When Pebbles Pvt Ltd started the construction of Ecommunity, one of the biggest challenges faced by the company was the neighbouring industries. As previously discussed, the surrounding area is heavily polluted because of the environmentally unsustainable activities of the various industries. Ecommunity was being developed on the values of conservation and preservation of nature, which were in contradiction to the practices being followed by the other actors operating in the area. However, Pebbles stepped forward to fight the battle for the thousands of lives being threatened and damaged by the greatly rising and uncontrolled pollution in the area. The ex-CEO of the company, Amir, stated during his interview:

We did face some resistance from the neighbouring industries, but with the support of local public and the concerned government bodies, we were able to start and successfully complete the Ecommunity project. The people of the area were sick and tired of environmental pollution created by the factories. The administration was very helpful since they thought that our green practices would not only beautify the general area rather it would act as a wonderful source of learning for other people to follow. You have seen yourself that how the factories have ruined the environment and the natural habitat in the general area. So, where else would we need a project like Ecommunity? (A. Zaidi, personal communication, 13 August 2015).

The company served legal notices to a number of surrounding industries against their hazardous waste emission practices. A legal notice was sent to a neighbouring paper mill, in order to stop the hazardous gas emission. The various gases were not only a severe health hazard to the surrounding areas, but also served as a source of bad smell in the vicinity. Along with taking legal action the company planted numerous fragrance producing trees along the boundary walls of the community to counter the adverse effects of air pollution (A. Bajwa, personal communication, 10 December 2014). The master planning and infrastructure design of Ecommunity were developed by an international consulting firm, Unicorn Consulting Services Pvt Ltd. The construction work was carried out by one of the top ten construction companies of the world, China Metallurgical Group Corporation (MCC). In 2013, MCC ranked 302th among the world's Fortune 500 companies. Since the company was a member of the US Green Building Council the supply chain processes and all the construction procedures were adopted in line with the systems promulgated by the council. In order to bring sustainability within the supply chain the company used local construction materials from sources within 500 km of the site for at least half of the project. This ensured increased earnings for the surrounding communities and businesses (A. Zaidi, personal communication, 13 August 2015). For the designing of sustainable houses, Ecommunity hired a LEED certified architect, Aqrab Ali Rana. He is among the very first architects in Pakistan to gain an internationally recognized certification in sustainable architecture. At the time the Ecommunity project was started, Rana was working in the United Arab Emirates. The CEO personally contacted him and requested him to come to Pakistan and work with Pebbles on the Ecommunity project. The main gate of the society was especially designed by another architect, Atika Waheed. The concept of green walls was used in the designing of the main gate of the society. The whole society is surrounded by walls covered with green creepers (plants), giving the image of a beautiful green walled community (A. Yousaf, personal communication, 10 December 2014; see Fig. 2). Green walls have been identified as a symbol of the green building movement in the US. Research reveals that air that circulates within a green walled building is cleaner. In addition, the green walls offer natural resistance to both hot and cold weather, remove airborne pollutants such as toluene, ethyl benzene, xylene, and other volatile organic compounds, and can also block low frequency noises (Green Walls, 2015). The interior of the houses was designed by Sadia Rasheed, who was also nominated for the "Asia Pacific Property Awards 2014–15" for her designs in the Ecommunity project.

Figure 2 Green walled entrance of Ecommunity

A sewerage treatment plant was built in the housing society which resulted in a 40% reduction of fresh water usage in the community; greatly saving this scarce and vital natural resource. The developers came up with the concept of introducing green roofs on the houses. A green roof is a roof that is partially or completely covered with vegetation along with a maintenance system. According, to the US green roofs organization the benefits of green roofs include thermal insulation for buildings, thereby reducing the energy consumption and hazardous emission of by-products by various temperature regulating devices, capture of airborne pollution and atmospheric deposition, filtering of noxious gases, and a decrease in the amount of carbon dioxide emissions to the atmosphere (Green Roofs, 2015). According to the bylaws of Ecommunity the residents are required to have at least 14.7% green area in their houses. In Pakistan, the government requires only 7% of the residential space to be green and even that is not being actively enforced by the officials or followed by the housing societies. But Pebbles made this a rule in their housing community to promote environmental sustainability. A waterproof roof top material for the houses was specially imported from Italy, which was designed in the shape of small cups that could store water. As the water evaporated from the small cups a cooling effect was created. This greatly reduced the need to use HVAC equipment. The residents were provided with the option of installing solar panels which would result in the decrease of energy usage and cost. The houses were designed to provide extra ventilation, thus reducing the electricity usage and indoor pollution (ecommunity, 2015). Ecommunity is a residential society built for the middle class families earning their livelihood from surrounding areas. It offered the public a chance of sustainable living at affordable rates.

This was evident from the comparative data collected on the prices of the residential plots in Ecommunity and various other housing societies existing within a 5 km radius (Zameen, 2014).

Table 2 Comparative land cost

Size of land in sq. ft (approx.)	Prices of Ecommunity (approx.)	Prices of surrounding housing societies (approx.)
126	€10,982/-	€15,814/-
252	€21,964/-	€48,524/-
505	€43,928/-	€79,403/-

The figures in Table 2 show that the cost of land in Ecommunity is lower than the cost of land in surrounding commercially built residential societies. Research reveals that sustainable houses cost less in the long term as well because of decreased life-cycle costs, lower utility expense, lesser maintenance needs, and improved occupant health (Balogh, 2015). The residential community also offers numerous facilities for residents' well-being:

▷ A central community swimming pool and spa (with steam, jacuzzi and sauna)

▷ Amphitheatre

▷ Squash courts

▶ Tennis courts

▶ A basketball field

▶ Indoor games in the community centre such as snooker, gymnasium

▶ A football stadium distinctively designed on par with international standards

▶ Pollution-free green environs featuring jogging/walking tracks and tree-lined paved walkways for pleasure walks

In 2012, the company formally announced the sale of houses or plots in Ecommunity. Initially, 14 model houses were constructed. By the end of 2014, nine of these model houses were sold along with more than 25 residential plots. In 2014, the company entered the Ecommunity project in the "Asia Pacific Retail Property Awards" and it was the first residential community in Pakistan to win this award. The company was termed as a "Highly Commended Residential Development in Pakistan" by the awarding body. This was the first time, in Pakistan, that a residential community won such an award. Before this a number of real estate developers had won the award, but on individual units only (house/building).

Currently, approximately 80% of the residential plots in the housing society have been sold. This reveals positive sales figures for Ecommunity, depicting an above average occupancy rate in the residential community market. The company's accounts are prepared annually and duly audited by external auditors. However, the financial reports are not shared with the public since Pebbles is a private limited company. A CEO's monthly newsletter is submitted to the corporate office for the parent company's (DH Corp) monitoring and reporting purposes. Quarterly board meetings are held to gauge performance of the management and to take strategic policy decisions to improve performance of the company.

Sustainable culture and leadership

According to Hils and Jones (2012), a culture is "the specific collection of values and norms that are shared by people and groups in an organization and that control the way they interact with each other and with stakeholders outside the organization". A culture of sustainability is one in which the organization's environmental and social performance is given importance along with financial performance. Research reveals that the leadership style and values along with the corporate culture of sustainable organizations differ from their traditional counterparts in various ways (Eccles, Ioannou, &

Serafeim, 2011). In this section the SCALA results are used to describe the cultural and leadership values of Pebbles (Pvt) Ltd.

Organizational leadership

"What standards were to the 1990s, leadership is to the future. This shift depicts awareness that standards and strategies by themselves are not powerful enough to accomplish large-scale, sustainable reforms" (Fullan, 2002). Research reveals that it is not possible for an organization to travel on the path of sustainable development without the vision and active engagement of the leadership (Fullan, 2005). This is supported by the data gathered through SCALA where, five out of eight respondents strongly agreed that the leadership of the company has a clear vision of sustainability and the remaining three respondents agreed with the statement. Three respondents strongly agreed and five agreed that the leaders of the company have a clear business case for pursuing sustainability. Four respondents strongly agreed and four agreed that sustainability is integrated within the decision making of the organization and the leaders inspire others about sustainability. Three respondents strongly agreed and four agreed that the leaders are knowledgeable about sustainability and are personally committed to achieving true business sustainability.

The reason behind the greatly favourable perception of employees about the leadership is the strongly visible commitment of the owners towards sustainability. As discussed earlier, Pebbles was formed with the vision of sustainability and the leaders demonstrated their personal commitment by choosing the sustainable options even if it meant greater challenges. The ex-CEO of the company stated:

> Sheikhupura, the city where Ecommunity is built, is very special to me. Not only has the Dawood Hercules group had an association with the city and its people for over four decades, it is also my hometown. It is an honor for me to be able to contribute to the beauty and quality of life of this historic city (ecommunity, 2015).

> When we started the project "Ecommunity" many of the stakeholders we contacted discouraged us. They said that such a project cannot be economically or commercially viable

The current CEO of the company, who has been a part of Pebbles since the very beginning, says that

> When we started the project "Ecommunity" many of the stakeholders we contacted discouraged us. They said that such a project cannot be economically or commercially viable. Even the industry experts had little awareness of sustainable real estate development. But our leadership was committed to sustainability. Now after the success of our project, people are starting to realize the importance of sustainable development in the construction industry (A. Yousaf, personal communication, 10 December 2014).

Organizational systems

Out of eight respondents, three strongly agreed and four agreed that Pebbles has embedded sustainability into the organization's operating system and policies. All the respondents were aware of the enterprise wide management system for sustainability, showing the integration of sustainability within the working boundaries of the respondents. Two respondents strongly agreed and six agreed that the company has integrated sustainability goals into the performance management system while three strongly agreed and four agreed to the statement that the rewards and compensation are clearly linked to the organization's sustainability goals. These results are supported by the implementation of the "integrated project delivery" (IPD) system during the planning and construction of Ecommunity. The IPD is a methodology in which all stakeholders are involved and integrated in the project life cycle, in order to optimize project results, increase value to the owner, reduce waste, and maximize efficiency. The IPD system developed in Pebbles connected the company to the project engineers, architects, planners, construction professionals, designer and clients and all the stakeholders with each other.

Organizational climate

Pebbles Pvt Ltd is a small company with a small group of people working on similar goals. All the employees are aware of and passionate about the need for sustainable development in Pakistan. This similarity of ideology and coherence of ideas has created a bond within the workforce of this company. This was observed during the interviews and was also evident in the survey findings, in which two respondents strongly agreed and five agreed that the level of trust within the organization is high and continual learning is the core focus of the organization. Five respondents strongly agreed and three agreed that the organization rewards innovation.

Change readiness

The company is the pioneer of sustainable real estate development in Pakistan. It is one of the founding members of the sustainability real estate council in the country. The employees of the company also perceive their organization as an agent of change, with three respondents strongly agreeing and five agreeing to the statement that the company has a strong track record of implementing large and small scale change successfully. One respondent strongly agreed and four agreed that the company actively challenges the status quo.

An employee of the company said:

I had no idea about what sustainable development and sustainable living meant, before I joined Pebbles. Here, I not only learned what true sustainability means, I saw it being implemented practically. Now I try to bring elements of sustainable living, which I learned from my company, in my own home (F. Razzak, personal communication, 10 December 2014).

> **All the respondents in the SCALA survey shared positive experiences of being involved in various sustainable activities and narrated the feelings of being proud and happy about making a difference and a positive contribution to society**

This viewpoint is also supported by the SCALA results, in which four out of eight respondents strongly agreed and three agreed that the company has a clear policy for engaging the internal stakeholder in its sustainability efforts. Four respondents strongly agreed and the remaining four agreed that all the employees are engaged in sustainability related work. One employee strongly agreed and seven agreed that they feel valued by the organization. The positive feedback, regarding the involvement and engagement of internal stakeholders is reinforced by the responses generated through the series of open-ended questions in the survey. The employees were asked about the various sustainability initiatives the company was taking, their involvement and feelings about them. All the respondents in the SCALA survey shared positive experiences of being involved in various sustainable activities and narrated the feelings of being proud and happy about making a difference and a positive contribution to society.

Five out of eight employees surveyed, feel that the company and its leadership are better than the other companies in the industry, with respect to their commitment towards sustainability. Five respondents perceive that the company has a proactive approach to sustainability and the remaining three believed the approach to be active. Three of the internal stakeholders surveyed thought the company to be "very engaged" in sustainability and five believed it to be "engaged".

External stakeholders

> **Pebbles introduced the concept of sustainable real estate development in Pakistan**

Pebbles introduced the concept of sustainable real estate development in Pakistan. Since it was the first mover in the field it had to start from the beginning. First, there was no central body to set the rules or guidelines and no supply chain partners having experience of sustainable construction. The company along with developing the country's first sustainable housing community also laid down the foundation and precedent for others to follow. In the SCALA survey, two of the respondents strongly agreed and six agreed that the company has a mechanism in place to actively engage its external stakeholders in the sustainability initiative; three respondents strongly agreed and five agreed that the company encourages sustainability in its supply chain. Four out of eight respondents strongly agreed and the remaining four agreed that the company sends out a clear and consistent message to its external stakeholders about its commitment to sustainability. During the personal interaction with the residents of Ecommunity, I met with the first resident of the housing community, Mr Shahid, who stated that the company had delivered upon their promise and commitment of a greener, healthier and happier living community. He said that he was given legal possession of his house before the promised time and now he is living a more secure, healthier and happy life with his family in Ecommunity. Most of the families living in this residential colony belong to the middle class. The CEO of the company, Mr Abdullah, stated in his interview that the company discouraged bulk buying of residential plots by various intermediaries because they wanted to make sure that the living environment of the community does not get compromised by unsustainable commercial activity (A. Yousuf, personal communication, 10 December 2014).

The CEO of Unicorn consulting services, Mr Pervaiz feels that:

> Ecommunity is a unique project which was visualized for the first time in Pakistan. Its tree lined avenues, wide roads, underground electricity network, water recycling plant and segregation of pedestrian and vehicular traffic are features that cannot be found in other residential societies in our country and add to the sustainable development of communities.

The overall analysis of the employee survey reveals a positive and supportive leadership and culture with respect to sustainability. The employees feel that their company is working as a solution provider in the real estate industry and making a positive contribution to the current unsustainable environment of the country. The results of the survey reinforce the feedback generated through the interviews, observation and review of literature. All the employees surveyed narrated their personal efforts and contributions to the Ecommunity project and recorded a feeling of being proud of their work and their company.

Synergizing all the information collected and adopting the methodology of data triangulation, we will analyse Pebbles Pvt Ltd's sustainability position through the use of the Dyllick/Muff Business Sustainability Typology in the next section.

Business Sustainability 3.0: truly sustainable business

Dyllick and Muff (2015) have developed a typology of true business sustainability (BST) (see Fig. 3). In this typology an organization is analysed on the basis of a typical business process model, consisting of:

▶ **Inputs**. The relevant concerns considered by the organization (the drivers of sustainability)

▶ **Outputs**. The values created by the organization

▶ **Process**. The organizational perspectives applied (starting with societal challenges (outside-in) vs. starting with an existing business or product-lines (inside-out))

On the basis of the company's performance on the three elements, it is placed in one of the following positions in the business sustainability typology:

▶ Business-as-Usual 0.0 (the current economic paradigm)

▶ Business Sustainability (BST) 1.0 (redefined shareholder value management)

▶ Business Sustainability (BST) 2.0 (managing for the triple bottom line)

▶ Business Sustainability (BST) 3.0 (true sustainability)

On the basis of the information gathered from the various data sources, Pebbles (Pvt) Ltd has been placed at the BST 3.0 level of the Dyllick/Muff business sustainability typology. In the typology BST 3.0 signifies a truly sustainable business. According to Dyllick and Muff (2015), a BST 3.0 company functions by:

Shifting its perspective from seeking to minimize its negative impacts to understanding how it can create a significant positive impact in critical and relevant areas for society and the planet. A Business Sustainability 3.0 firm looks first at the external environment within which it operates and then asks itself what it can do to help overcome critical challenges that demand the resources and competencies it has at its disposal.

We will analyse the BST position of Pebbles using the three elements of the business process model.

Figure 3 Framework for considering different approaches of business sustainability

BUSINESS SUSTAINABILITY TYPOLOGY (BST)	Concerns (What?)	Values created (What for?)	Organizational perspective (How?)
Business-as-usual	Economic concerns	Shareholder value	Inside-out
Business Sustainability 1.0	Three-dimensional concerns	Refined shareholder value	Inside-out
Business Sustainability 2.0	Three-dimensional concerns	Triple bottom line	Inside-out
Business Sustainability 3.0	Starting with sustainability challenges	Creating value for the common good	Outside-in
The key shifts involved:	1st shift: broadening the business concern	2nd shift: expanding the value created	3rd shift: changing the perspective

Organizational perspective

Two organizational perspectives have been discussed in the Dyllick and Muff (2015) typology:

▷ **Inside-out perspective** "in which an organization usually starts off with its existing business, strategy or product-lines and work on making them more sustainable"

▷ **Outside-in perspective** "in which an organization starts out by reviewing pressing sustainability challenges that society faces, and then engages in developing new strategies and business models that overcome these"

A BST 3.0 company follows the outside-in perspective and "the potential for contributing positively will vary largely between companies, their resources, strategies and purposes, and it will vary between different industry sectors and societal contexts". Pebbles Pvt Ltd follows the outside-in organizational perspective of a BST 3.0 level company. The company started with the ideology of working towards a solution to the greatly damaging and unsustainable growth of the country's real estate sector. This is evident from the fact that the company is the first sustainable real estate developer in the country. According to an industry expert:

Pebbles (Pvt) Ltd, is a unique real estate development company providing astute solutions based on the principles of sustainable development. By considering the health and well-being of the residents alongside the long-term sustainability of the environment. Pebbles (Pvt) Ltd has created an outstanding and aptly named community.

The company's ex-CEO, Amir, states:

I take a great deal of pride to be the first to have developed a sustainable housing scheme in the country. Such projects are commercially viable and if handled correctly, could bring lot of commercial success to the developers. The environmental and energy challenges are the main reasons due to which market for such projects is growing faster than before.

> **creating a greener, cleaner and happier living place for the people of Pakistan**

He said that several industry experts said that the Ecommunity project could not succeed commercially. However, the company stuck to its ideology of creating a greener, cleaner and happier living place for the people of Pakistan. A BST 3.0 company "starts out by reviewing pressing sustainability challenges that a society faces, and then engages in developing new strategies and business models to overcome these challenges". The story of the Pebbles sustainability journey starts off in a similar manner. The owners wanted to enter the real estate sector as a solution provider. As discussed in the earlier sections, the real estate sector of Pakistan is rapidly growing, but this growth is causing a severe energy crisis within the country along with an unsustainable burden on the already diminishing natural resource base of the country. Pebbles entered the real estate industry with the following vision of sustainability: "we at Pebbles very consciously shoulder the responsibility about the invaluable (and fast shrinking) natural resources of our country and hence strive to conserve and preserve all that Mother Nature has bestowed upon us". The mission statement of the company is "encouraging sustainable business practices, efficient building concepts and demonstrating a strong awareness about preservation, recycling of resources and reliable energy sources in the real estate market of Pakistan". The mission of the company is well captured in its claim of a "Greener, Cleaner, Happier Pakistan". One of the residents of the company's sustainable housing community stated that: "Ecommunity is one of the best residential communities in Pakistan. Living within the green walls of this society we forget about the adverse external environment and enjoy the pleasures of nature". A respondent in the SCALA survey stated: "we are fighting industrial pollution and providing a cleaner and greener living environment. The company owns the responsibility of creating awareness about energy conservation and the protection of our environment to ensure the sustainable development of our society".

> **Living within the green walls of this society we forget about the adverse external environment and enjoy the pleasures of nature**

In the business sustainability typology (Dyllick and Muff, 2015) the output of a BST 3.0 company is explained as: "the 'values created' change from the triple bottom line to creating value for the common good, defined as that which benefits society and the planet as a whole". The values created at Pebbles have been defined by the CEO:

> Our company is a reflection of our earnest desire for a better quality of life for the people of this country. The fundamental intent behind our concept was to develop a society where the health and happiness of our inhabitants and their families was taken as the key measure of success for community's development.

In the sustainability survey six out of eight respondents termed "awareness of our responsibility to the environment" as the reason behind the adoption of business sustainability and the remaining two respondents termed the main reason as "recognition of how our company could address societal needs". When the employees were asked in a survey what they thought the company was trying to achieve through its sustainability initiatives, five out of eight respondents selected "making a positive contribution to solving critical societal challenges". The sustainable houses in Ecommunity are achieving the following outputs, in comparison to similar sized conventional houses:

Our company is a reflection of our earnest desire for a better quality of life for the people of this country. The fundamental intent behind our concept was to develop a society where the health and happiness of our inhabitants and their families was taken as the key measure of success for community's development.

- ▶ Reduction in the use of fresh water by 40%

- ▶ Reduction in the use of energy by 50%

- ▶ Increase in usage of renewable energy sources by 2.5%

- ▶ Reduction in the usage of HVAC equipment, resulting in lesser indoor and outdoor pollution and efficient energy utilization

- ▶ Increased recycling or reuse of building material

- ▶ Usage of local construction materials from within a 500 mile radius, aimed at promoting economic activity in the surrounding areas and creating earning opportunities for the locals

- ▶ Improved indoor environmental quality and provision of extra ventilation in all living spaces to reduce electricity utilization

- ▶ Reduction in carbon dioxide concentration in the community and houses through the use of green walls and green rooftops

- ▶ Consideration for safety and privacy factor for the residents. This value is being delivered by 24-hour surveillance of the society by an external security agency

All these features have been observed by the researcher in the architectural and interior design of the sustainable houses within the community.

Concerns

In the typology of business sustainability, "concerns" highlight the issues addressed by a company. A truly sustainable business (BST 3.0) moves beyond the triple bottom line concerns (economic, social and environmental) towards solving critical sustainability challenges faced by society.

Economic

A BST 3.0 company is operating to overcome a major sustainability challenge in the country, i.e. unsustainable real estate development, and resolving it through the adoption of green building practices. The company places sustainable concerns before its economic concerns. This is evident through the selection of the company's housing community location. Although the company had a number of financially viable options, the top management chose the environmentally unsustainable industrial estate area for the development of "Ecommunity". The reason behind this was that the owners and the top management wanted to prove that sustainable real estate development is the solution that can make the difference in our country. In comparison to a commercial real estate project the sale rate of the community was slow in the beginning, but has rapidly increased up to almost 80% of the residential plots being sold off by the end of 2014. The reason for this has been attributed to a lack of awareness regarding sustainable living among the customers. However, the management is committed towards creating awareness and acceptance of sustainable living among all the stakeholders as they consider it the only path towards a sustainable nation.

Environmental

Pebbles (Pvt) Ltd is a member of the US Green Building Council and one of the founders of Pakistan Green Building Council. The company has successfully created Pakistan's first sustainable residential housing community, which has been awarded the "Best Urban Development" award by the International Property Award, UK. The Ecommunity project of Pebbles is a solution offered to the residents of an environmentally unsustainable industrial area. The residential community is built according to green building standards, offering sustainability features like green rooftops, green walls, architecture and interior of houses designed to control and decrease indoor air pollution and excessive use of energy dependent appliances for controlling the temperature, water recycling plant and use of renewable building materials. The company's BST 3.0 level concerns are also evident from the company's plan to start the development of two new sustainable housing communities in environmentally unsustainable areas of the country. When the employees were asked about the major concerns that the company was addressing with its business model, most of the respondents stated the preservation and restoration of the environment as the primary concern.

For the greater good of society, the company has taken legal action against a number of polluting industrial units without any legal or social obligation to do so. The company procured most of the building material, for the Ecommunity project, from within a 500 mile radius of the construction site. The purpose behind this company policy was to boost economic activity within the surrounding areas and create earning and employment opportunities for the neighbouring businesses and public.

A green future?

Pebbles (Pvt) Ltd started its sustainable housing project with the slogan, "Towards a Greener Pakistan". The company started off by trying to bring together the apparently contradicting goals of commercial and sustainable success. The Ecommunity project is a success story in terms of sustainability, but can it be termed a commercial success? The occupancy rate of the housing community is increasing, the sales rate has reached almost 80%, but when compared to various commercial real estate projects in the region industry experts think it could have been much greater and faster. So, does the story of Pebbles reveal that sustainable success and economic success are trade-offs in the Pakistani real estate sector? The answer to this question may have been a "yes" five years ago, but today it is a "no". The consumer market is not the same as was available to Pebbles back in 2008, when the company started. Now in 2015, research reveals that "Pakistan has the most eco-friendly homes for sale and for rent among the 30-plus countries in Asia, Africa, the Middle East and Latin America the site examined — for the second year in a row" (Inman, 2015).

> **The company started off by trying to bring together the apparently contradicting goals of commercial and sustainable success**

It shows that:

The supply of sustainable houses in Asia and Latin America is rapidly increasing, which indicates the shift in attitudes towards green living that is occurring in these regions. With the fast-paced economic development now underway in these countries, it is just a matter of time before they outgrow their neighbors in terms of the supply of sustainable homes (Nichols, 2014).

Further studies show that a growth is being observed in the demand for green housing and commercial property in emerging markets such as Pakistan, Mexico and Bangladesh (Naqvi, 2013). Consumers are becoming aware of the benefits of sustainable living. It is now time for business to understand that sustainable development should not be viewed as a trade-off between profits and planet, rather it is "a different market approach that is the perfect synthesis between 'for profit' and 'non-profit' which represents an interest that goes beyond the financial to encompass the environmental as well social benefits, to prove there is a sustainable future" (Rana, 2013).

> **Literally, a pebble is a small stone that has been made smooth by the impact of wind or sand on its surface. Pebbles (Pvt) Ltd has also taken the shape of a truly sustainable business in the face of numerous unsustainable adversities**

Pebbles (Pvt) Ltd is the first building block, put down by the Dawood Hercules Corporation for the development of sustainable living in Pakistan. Literally, a pebble is a small stone that has been made smooth by the impact of wind or sand on its surface. Pebbles (Pvt) Ltd has also taken the shape of a truly sustainable business in the face of numerous unsustainable adversities. The vision of this company is fast becoming a reality, as the people of this country are becoming increasingly aware and appreciative of the concept of sustainable living. The top management is still committed towards the ideology of a "Greener, Cleaner and Happier Pakistan". The company is planning to start two more sustainable housing projects in the near future. They want the people of Pakistan to realize, that: "the Earth has rights, too, to live without pollution. What mankind must know is that human beings cannot live without Mother Earth, but the planet can live without humans" (Morales, 2010).

Bibliography

Ahmed, A. (2014, July 14). Pakistan's urban air pollution off the charts: World Bank. *Dawn*. Retrieved from http://www.dawn.com/news/1119031.

Ainoa, J. K., Lahti, L., Saarikosk, N., Sivunen,A., Storgårds, J., & Zhang, .H (2009). *Future of living*. Helsinki: Helsinki University Print.

Apanavičienė, R., Daugéliené, A., Baltramonaitis, T., & Maliene, V. (2015). Sustainability aspects of real estate development: Lithuanian case study of sports and entertainment arenas. *Sustainability*, 7, 6497-6522.

Asghar, Z. (2014). The need for eco-friendly buildings in Pakistan. Retrieved from http://www.ameradnan.com/blog/the-need-for-eco-friendly-buildings-in-pakistan.

Asteriou, D., & Price, S. (2001). Political instability and economic growth: UK time series evidence. *Scottish Journal of Political Economy*, 48(4), 383-399.

Balogh, A. (2015). Do sustainable homes cost more? Retrieved from http://www.concretenetwork.com/concrete/greenbuildinginformation/do_sustainable.html.

Bruce, N., Albalak, R.P., & Rachel, P. (2000). Indoor air pollution in developing countries: a major environmental and public health challenge. *Bull World Health Organ*, 78(9), 1078-1092.

Brundtland, H. (1987). Report of the World Commission on Environment and Development: Our Common Future. Retrieved from www.un-documents.net/wced-ocf.htm.

Dapaah, K.A., Hiang, L. K., Shi, N.Y., & Sharon (2015). Sustainability of sustainable real property development. The Journal of Sustainable Real Estate, 1(1), 204-225.

Dawn (2004, August 30). *SHEIKHUPURA: 190 industrial units get notices - Environment rules violation.* Retrieved from http://www.dawn.com/news/368907/ sheikhupura-190-industrial-units-get-notices-environment-rules-violation.

Dawn (2009, March 29). *Interview: Green buildings offer the only way out.* Retrieved from http://www.dawn.com/news/860033/interview-green-buildings-offer-the-only-way-out.

Denzin, N.K (1978). *The Research Act: A Theoretical Introduction to Sociological Methods.* New York, USA: McGraw-Hill.

DH Corp. (2015, April 29). Business interests. Retrieved from: http://www. dawoodhercules.com/business-interests_pebbles.php.

DH Corp. (2015, April 10). About DH corp. Retrieved from http://www.dawoodhercules. com/about_our-heritage.php.

Dyllick, T., & Muff, K. (2015). Clarifying the meaning of sustainable business: introducing a typology from business-as-usual to true business sustainability. *Organization & Environment,* 1-9.

Eccles, R.G., Ioannou, I., & Serafeim, G. (2011). *The Impact of a Corporate Culture of Sustainability on Corporate Behavior and Performance.* Working paper. Harvard Business School.

Ecommunity (2015). *Living Options.* Retrieved from http://ecommunity.pk/inside.php.

Fullan, M. (2002). Leadership and sustainability. *Principal Leadership,* 3(4).

Fullan, M. (2005). *Leadership & Sustainability: System Thinkers in Action.* Thousand Oaks: Corwin Press.

Gilani, S.R., Mahmood, Z., Hussain, M., Baig, Y., Abbas, Z., & Batool, S. (2013). A study of drinking water of industrial area of Sheikhupura with special concern to arsenic, manganese and chromium. *Pakistan Journal of Engineering & Applied Science,* 13, 118-126.

Goering, J. (2009). Sustainable real estate development: the dynamics of market penetration. *The Journal of Sustainable Real Estate,* 1(1), 167-201.

Green Roofs (2015). Green roofs benefits. Retrieved from http://www.greenroofs.org/ index.php/about/greenroofbenefits.

Green Walls (2015). Green walls benefits. Retrieved from http://www.green-walls.co.uk.

Haq, S. (2015, March 1). Real estate sector picking up in Punjab. *The Express Tribune.* Retrieved from http://tribune.com.pk/story/845846/real-estate-sector-picking-up-in-punjab.

Hardin, G. (1968). The tragedy of the Commons. *Science,* 162(3859), 1243-1248.

Hills, C.W., & Jones, G.R. (2013). *Strategic Management: An Integrated Approach.* Mason, OH: South-Western, Cengage Learning.

Inman News Feed (2015, April 29). Among emerging markets, Pakistan ranks No. 1 for eco-friendly housing. *Philly Weekly.* Retrieved from http://www.philadelphiaweekly. com/real-estate/among_emerging_markets_pakistan_ranks_no_1_for_eco-friendly_housing-301740371.html.

Jacob, E. (1988). Clarifying qualitative research: A focus on traditions. *Educational Researcher,* 1, 16-24.

Kawulich, B.B. (2005). Participant Observation as a Data Collection Method. *Forum: Qualitative Social Research*, 6(2).

Kelly, C. (2009). *Origins of Sustainability*. Leeds: University of Leeds. Retrieved from http://www.its.leeds.ac.uk/projects/sustainability.

Khwaja, M.A. (2012). Environmental challenges and constraints to policy issues for sustainable industrial development in Pakistan. *Sustainable Development Policy Institute*, p. 31.

Lifshitz, I. (2010). Balancing sustainability with economic development in developing countries – the case study of Indonesia. *Environmental Leader*, pp. 8-9.

Malthus, T.R. (1798). *An Essay on the Principle of Population* (1st ed.). London, England: J. Johnson.

Marsh, G.P. (1864). *Man and Nature*. New York, USA: C. Scribner & co.

Morales, E. (2010, December 11). Bolivia's defiant leader sets radical tone at Cancún climate talks. *The Guardian*. Retrieved from http://www.theguardian.com/environment/2010/dec/11/cancun-talks-evo-morales.

Naqvi, H. (2013, August 22). Go Green: "Pakistan needs sustainable development". *The Express Tribune*. Retrieved from http://tribune.com.pk/story/593460/go-green-pakistan-needs-sustainable-development.

Nichols, W. (2014, August 13). Green buildings spring up in Asia and Latin America. Retrieved from: http://www.businessgreen.com/bg/analysis/2359958/green-buildings-spring-up-in-asia-and-latin-america.

Pakistan Real Estate News. (2015). Magnitude of real estate sector in Pakistan. Retrieved from: http://www.abnamro.com.pk/2015/02/03/magnitude-real-estate-sector-pakistan.

Pebbles (2015). Our vision. Retrieved from http://www.pebbles.com.pk/ourvision.html.

Rana, A.A. (2013, no date). Pakistan green building council launches membership. *Archi Times*. Retrieved from http://archpresspk.com/new-version/Pakistan-green-building-council.html.

Raza, A. (2014). CEO's message. Retrieved from http://www.pebbles.com.pk/pebbles.html.

SCALA. (2014). *The Sustainability Culture and Leadership Assessment Survey Pebbles Pvt. Ltd.* Louisville: Miller Consultants Inc.

Sohail, M.I., Mughal, M.S., Arshad, N., & Arshad, M. (2010). Incidence of Hepatitis B and C in industrial areas of Sheikhupura. *Pakistan Journal of Zoology*, 42(6), 673-677.

Sustainable Development. (2012). What is sustainable living? Retrieved from http://www.sustainabledevelopmentinfo.com/what-is-sustainable-living.

The International Statistical Institute. (2013). Developing countries. Retrieved from http://www.isi-web.org/component/content/article/5-root/root/81-developing.

U.S Green Building Council. (2015). *Green Building Facts*. Washington, DC: Sustainable Green Building Council.

UN World Economic and Social Survey. (2013, July 2). Rapid urbanization threatens sustainable development. Retrieved from http://www.un.org/en/development/desa/news/policy/wess.html.

United Nations General Assembly. (1987). Report of the World Commission on Environment and Development: Our Common Future. *United Nations General Assembly, Chapter Two: Towards Sustainable Development; Paragraph 1"*, p. Transmitted to the General Assembly as an Annex to document A/42/427.

World Green Building Council. (2015). *About WorldGBC*. Retrieved from: http://www.worldgbc.org/worldgbc/about.

Whitby, M., & Ward, N (1994). *The UK Strategy for Sustainable Agriculture: A Critical Analysis*. Newcastle: University of Newcastle.

Wilfried, R., Vanhonacker, & Pan, Y. (1997). The impact of national culture, business scope, and geographic location on joint venture operations in China. *Journal of International Marketing, 5*(3), 11-30.

World Bank. (2013a, April 26). Pakistan: achieving results in a challenging environment. Retrieved from http://www.worldbank.org/en/results/2013/04/26/pakistan-achieving-results-in-a-challenging-environment.

World Bank. (2013b). Pakistan. Retrieved from http://data.worldbank.org/country/pakistan.

World Business Council for Sustainable Development. (2015). 10 key messages. Retrieved from http://www.wbcsd.org/newsroom/key-messages.aspx.

Zaheer, F. (2015, March 27). Real estate - sit ins' effects still being felt. *The Express Tribune*. Retrieved from http://tribune.com.pk/story/849102/real-estate-sit-ins-effect-still-being-felt.

Zameen. (2014, September 18). ECommunity Housing Scheme Sheikhupura – A green dream finally come true. Retrieved from http://www.zameen.com/blog/ecommunity-housing-scheme-sheikhupura-a-green-dream-finally-come-true.html.

Zeeshan, M., & Ahmed, V. (2013). Energy, environment and growth nexus in South Asia. *Environ Dev Sustain*, 1465–1475.

✉ Syeda Nazish Zahra Bukhari, Assistant Professor, Institute of Business & Information Technology (IBIT), Quaid-a-Azam Campus, University of the Punjab, Lahore, Pakistan.

☎ 092-4299230826 (Ext-106)

💻 nazish.bukhari@bsl-lausanne.ch

Beechenhill Farm Hotel's meaningful legacy

Evolving from the sustainability of business towards the business of sustainability in hospitality

Gulen Hashmi

Business School Lausanne, Switzerland

The challenge

While having one of her routine daily walks in the peaceful open moorlands, farmlands, and wooded valleys of the Staffordshire Peak District National Park where Beechenhill is located, Sue Prince, Order of the British Empire (OBE),[1] owner and manager of the Beechenhill Farm Hotel paused along the Dovedale Gorge, to reflect on the sustainability initiatives of her family-run eco-hotel. To Sue, sustainability was not purely compliance to environmental legislation, nor was it a marketing tool; it was something she had threaded into the very core values of her family business. Her experience in the farmlands and her love of the Peak District had led her to create a sustainable hotel business from the ground up.

As a folk artist and OBE, Sue believed her creativity in arts had not only contributed to her decision to diversify into the tourism business, but also to the greening of farming and tourism in the protected environment of the Peak District National Park. Over the years, she had not only been exploring innovative, practical and appropriate ways of addressing rural efficiency, dealing with economic pressures and reducing the carbon footprint of her family's tourism business in this fascinating National Park, but also, and perhaps more importantly, she had been striving to share her sustainability know-how with a broader audience of influencers, planners,

---

1 The Order of the British Empire (OBE) recognizes distinguished service to the arts and sciences, public services outside the Civil Service and work with charitable and welfare organizations of all kinds.

small businesses, government bodies, individuals and holiday guests. *Success for Sue was grounded in her own circumstances, which at times, meant managing the family business based on sustainability values.* Thus, she believed that the secret of Beechenhill's success in sustainability was making the "eco-experience" at Beechenhill celebratory and fun for visitors; and the message she wanted to convey was: "If we can do it in such a protected environment, so can you... and here's how". *Walking the walk and talking the talk* while sharing her successes and hardships had indeed been the building blocks of her *sustainable* hotel business. But she also knew in the depths of her heart that sustainability was—for her daughter Alex, an ex-primary school teacher, and her husband Rob, a technical expert, who had both joined the family business in 2010—still a concept that needed further infusion in their hearts as well as in their minds.

Having successfully linked their farm business with tourism, Sue and her husband took the essential first steps of going *green* and *organic* in Beechenhill's sustainable farm hotel venture. Even though it was evident (after having earned recognition as one of the UK's most sustainable small hotels) that Beechenhill's hospitality business was headed in the right direction, she decided that they ought to, as their "novel next step", pursue perfection in the sustainable hotel business—a target towards which they had already been progressively advancing.

However, she felt the need to have certain aspects of her family's sustainability culture assessed by an objective third party, to ensure Beechenhill's continued success in sustainability, as she was on the verge of handing over a meaningful legacy to her prospective heirs. Maybe Beechenhill's recent nomination for the Business School Lausanne's Sustainability Innovation Award and the academic Beechenhill case study that had been crafted and presented to her therein would shed light on the delicate, thought-provoking link between Beechenhill's current sustainability orientation and the continued success of its future sustainability strategy. In her farmhouse office, that boasted a distinctive view of the magnificent Manifold Valley, after grabbing a cup of freshly brewed fair-trade tea into which she had poured a generous amount of their award-winning organic milk, Sue continued the easy-to-read, coherent case study compiled by the Business School Lausanne. It read...

Introduction

This case study analyses Beechenhill Farm Hotel's business sustainability positioning as a successful and leading sustainable hotel in the hospitality industry. A sustainable hotel, at its best, refers to a hotel that voluntarily implements sustainable practices to reconcile social, environmental and economic concerns, and to create triple bottom line (people, planet, profit) values (Sloan *et al.*, 2013). Motivations and practices relating to these largely three-dimensional concerns differ depending on the hotel size as well as its brand or chain affiliation. Yet, the existing sustainability literature either focuses on the business case for large corporations that engage in sustainable practices or labels other efforts as merely socially responsible practices. Small to medium enterprises (SMEs) and family-owned and managed hotels have been given little attention throughout the service sector and especially in the hospitality industry.

The primary reason for this is that, in comparison with large corporations, SMEs have different motivations, challenges and practices (Morsing and Perrini, 2009). Furthermore, while large corporations engage with sustainability more often through formalized plans, policies and strategies, SMEs, which are in general managed by their owners, engage in sustainability initiatives through lifestyle choices and habits informed by values rather than conscious actions (Matten and Moon, 2008). Decision-making in family businesses often reflects the owner-manager's personality and characteristics and shapes its culture, values and habits whereas larger business concerns are, more often than not, shaped by economic concerns such as profit maximization or market share (Fassin *et al.*, 2011). While small tourism enterprises have the advantage of being flexible enough to react quickly to address sustainability issues, they also have the disadvantage of lacking information on market demands and business opportunities (Condon, 2004). They often grapple with insufficient resources such as finances, time, and limitations in the space and type of building (Font *et al.*, 2014).

A review of the literature suggests that nearly all hotels first engage with sustainability for cost reduction and resource efficiency reasons to accrue a direct operational and internal benefit and gain a competitive advantage. This rather economic focus on sustainability is further encouraged by government policies and legislation that emphasize the business case of sustainability, aimed at increasing the sustainability engagement of the private sector. Yet, some hotels go further than economic concerns and take sustainability actions visible or expected by others. In such cases, societal legitimization or stakeholder relations can be considered another motivation to understand sustainability-related practices of hotels, characterized by various stakeholder interests that are integrated into the sustainability decision-making. However, it is often the case that owners of small to medium-sized hotels also manage these hotels, and so owners' values and lifestyle play a significant role in their sustainability-related motivations and initiatives. Thus, lifestyle and moral values, rather than competitive elements that have traditionally dominated the literature, may largely account for their business sustainability level in the first place.

A review of the literature also suggests that although small to medium sized hotels are prevalent in the hospitality industry, there is scarcely any evidence in the few best practice case studies in which sustainable hotels' motivations, challenges and practices are demonstrated. Indeed, the business implications of sustainability in small businesses merit greater scrutiny, as consumers and the public generally associate smaller companies with "green" consciousness (Hoffman, 2000).

It has long been argued that SMEs' owners/managers have a good grasp of sustainability concepts without knowing the theory (Fassin *et al.*, 2011). There are few studies that analyse SMEs' CSR/sustainability practices from a qualitative perspective, and the assessment of a best practice's business sustainability positioning with regard to motivational concerns, organizational perspective and value creation, as well as certain aspects of its sustainability culture, is still to be explored.

In the sustainability literature, organizational culture serves as an invaluable tool to explain a company's sustainability orientation and progressive sustainability strategies. However, there is very little theoretical underpinning of the relationship between sustainability-related organizational culture dynamics and the business sustainability levels of small family-owned and managed hotels. Owners/managers are considered to be the major decision-making forces of businesses, and their view of what constitutes sustainability influences their willingness to implement the concept (Spence *et al.*, 2003). Thus, understanding the values represented by owners/managers of small to medium-sized businesses is crucial in understanding how their sustainability journey evolves. Extant literature reveals that small businesses tend to be independent, managed by owners and characterized by multitasking, a limited flow of money and a personal relationship management style. Thus, small businesses differ from their larger counterparts not only in size but also in nature (Holliday, 1995). Given the general characteristics of small to medium-sized hotels, we think that it is crucial to consider factors related to the owners'/managers' values, habits and sustainability orientation.

More importantly, due to their size and their scope of operation, small hotels are embedded in the networks or communities and these present many opportunities to develop sustained relationships and socialization (Nahapiet and Ghoshal, 1998). Thus, sustainability actions to influence stakeholder perceptions become imperative for small hotels, especially those in protected environments, to gain social capital that shapes their relationships with their environments (Werner and Spence, 2009). Social capital is defined as "the nature of power and meaning that exists as structures and mechanisms guiding every day social practice" (Fuller and Tian, 2006). This includes intangible assets such as trust, legitimacy and reputation, which are often influenced through behaving responsibly towards customers, suppliers and society in general (Russo and Tencati, 2009). Adler and Kwon (2003) also argue that since small enterprises are normally embedded in their local communities, as in the case of Beechenhill, developing social capital becomes essential for their sustainability. This social capital, which resides in the value of the individual or organization's network, is achieved through engagement and contribution to those communities. Thus, the concept of social capital is suitable for understanding the business sustainability level of small and independent hotels.

In the Beechenhill Farm Hotel case study, we therefore seek to discover certain aspects of Beechenhill's sustainability culture, which is a major contributor to its social capital, and assess its contribution to the hotel's overall business sustainability positioning based on the Dyllick/Muff Business Sustainability Typology (Dyllick and Muff, 2013). Considering Beechenhill's organizational culture could well explain the hotel's distinct profile and its successful implementation of sustainability—even in a protected environment such as the Peak District National Park where the hotel is located.

Thus, the main research goals of this case study are to:

1. Assess the business sustainability position of the Beechenhill Farm Hotel as a best practice, family-owned and managed hotel in the hospitality industry

2. Understand how Beechenhill got to its current business sustainability position through transformational shifts in its sustainability journey and in its organizational culture

3. Identify the organizational perspective (approach) through which Beechenhill addresses and resolves sustainability issues (inside-out vs. outside-in)

4. Contribute to a multiple-case analysis of a wider pool of sustainable companies from various industries and to facilitate an exchange of know-how among practitioners, academia and the business world

The Dyllick/Muff Business Sustainability Typology (Appendix) was chosen as the optimal overarching framework to guide the case, as its typology is particularly helpful in understanding the business sustainability motivations and practices of companies in regard to today's and tomorrow's sustainability challenges. The typology uses the three elements of a business process model, which are: concerns, processes (approach) and value creation, all of which have so far remained an under-explored issue in the sustainability literature.

The structure of this case study is as follows: first, a review of the literature on the phases of change towards sustainability in the hospitality industry is conducted, to understand the motivations of hotels to move beyond compliance, to more complex and demanding strategies. Second, the case study methodology is explained. Third, our findings are presented in a way to reinforce an understanding of the different sustainability phases in Beechenhill's timeline. Fourth, Beechenhill's sustainability journey is developed. Fifth, Beechenhill's business sustainability positioning is discussed in the light of the Dyllick/Muff Business Sustainability Typology.

Sixth, Beechenhill's values-based sustainability culture is described. These findings are then contextualized in a discussion, which relates to the broader field of research on sustainability and organizational culture. Seventh, to ensure the success of the hotel's progressive sustainability strategies, the conclusion is made that the Prince family's values, mind-set, lifestyle, habits and routines largely contribute to the hotel's success as a leading sustainability role model.

While the findings do not allow us to make any definitive claims about how the family business values and owners' lifestyles and habits affect the financial performance of Beechenhill, the survey and interview data are used to reinforce recent research about the crucial role of embedding some aspects of sustainability into the personal values and lifestyle choices of a family business in a protected area. Our first main finding suggests that Beechenhill's extensive network of stakeholder relationships constitutes the heart of its social capital, and is driven by sustainability-related knowledge sharing, and communicating the success and failure of sustainability efforts transparently. Our second main finding suggests that Beechenhill's overarching mission statement is a very good example of a business that creates triple bottom line (TBL) value. Although communicating sustainability messages and sharing sustainability know-how make positive contributions to social value creation, Beechenhill largely leverages its social capital to please its direct stakeholder group and "please the planet" simultaneously—ensuring their guests return. Our third main finding relates to why this is the case. We find that the owner-manager's strong sustainability values and sustainable lifestyle choices are important contributors to the hotel's social capital, and play a key role in the hotel's TBL value creation.

Our analyses suggests that in terms of its sustainability timeline, Beechenhill's sustainability strategy has, over the years, evolved from a fairly compliant and economically sustainable business strategy into a more balanced, three-dimensional strategy that aligns its social, environmental and economic concerns in an integrated approach. Complying with laws and regulations as well as with voluntary third party accreditation criteria, Beechenhill has successfully gained recognition as an exemplar organic farm hotel that reduces the environmental impact of an integrated farming and tourism business on a protected landscape. Furthermore, over the past couple of years, the farm hotel appears to have gone further, focusing on not only caring passionately about the environment, but also on engaging with a multitude of stakeholders in sharing their sustainability experience and know-how to educate others. This can be considered as a shift of focus from the "business case of sustainability" toward the "business case for sustainability". It is a novel approach to have deliberately defined goals that create social and environmental values that transcend economic parameters.

> **shift of focus from the "business case of sustainability" toward the "business case for sustainability"**

As far as Beechenhill's current business sustainability level is concerned, Beechenhill possesses all the criteria associated with a business that manages for the triple bottom line (people, planet, profit). The hotel aligns its social, environmental and economic concerns with the TBL values of sustainability in an integrated approach with a broadened stakeholder perspective. Its mission statement emerges from the multi-dimensional concerns of TBL values, largely from the traditional focus on guests. The value proposition clearly reflects the three dimensions of the TBL. Beechenhill's primary stakeholders are visitors and guests, yet its concern is not only with pleasing guests, but rather sharing with them, engaging them, and educating them about sustainable practices such as sustainable living and sustainable transportation. This way, Beechenhill not only contributes to environmental value creation but also to social value creation, both of which further contribute to its economic sustainability.

a value-driven sustainability orientation justifies the hotel's strong culture of sustainability

In terms of organizational culture, Beechenhill's success in sustainability appears to have come from the owner-manager's values, which all family members truly believe in. Such a value-driven sustainability orientation justifies the hotel's strong culture of sustainability, which is built on integrity (treating guests with helpfulness, fairness and compassion), honesty (listening hard and telling the facts of sustainability), respect (acknowledging and sharing the sources of inspiration and knowledge), quality (using the best materials and products), service with heart (community at work and having fun), and environmental awareness through action (decreasing environmental impact and having the desire to continuously innovate and improve to differentiate itself from others). Furthermore, the owner-manager's personal leadership style reflects a combination of both feminine and masculine values, which is ideal in a multi-faceted field like sustainability. Finally, Beechenhill's social capital resides in the value of the owner-manager's and the family's network, which is continuously reconstructed through the communication of sustainability achievements and awards and the sharing of their success (and failure) with others.

Thus, this case study provides a nuanced analysis of how Beechenhill, as a small family business, engages sustainability as a best practice in the hospitality industry. This case draws attention to how the owner-manager's strong sustainability values and sustainable lifestyle choice contribute to a successful sustainability performance in small family-run hotels. The case study is one of several produced by the Business School Lausanne that aims to provide best practice examples for implementing business sustainability in different industries and settings. This case aims to serve the Beechenhill Farm Hotel but also other sustainability-oriented hotels in their journey toward becoming truly sustainable businesses by translating sustainability challenges into business opportunities. A limitation should be pointed out also. It is highly likely that our findings are only applicable to small and medium-sized businesses located in protected areas.

Literature review

Phases of change towards sustainability

In the face of troubling scientific facts and figures about the diminishing planetary resources and increasing societal challenges such as social equity, gender equality or poverty, an accelerating number of hotels have started to engage in some sort of sustainability-related hotel practices over the past few years. A sustainable hotel operation, according to the American Association, Green Hotels, is the following: "Green Hotels are environmentally sustainable properties whose managers are eager to institute programs that save energy, save water and reduce solid waste while saving money to help protect our one and only earth."

Sloan *et al.* (2013), on the other hand, define a sustainable hospitality operation as: "A hospitality operation that manages its resources in such a way that economic, social and environmental benefits are maximized to meet the need of the present generation while protecting and enhancing opportunities for future generations."

While the Green Hotel's definition highlights the business case for hotels based on environmental friendliness, Sloan *et al.* (2013) refer to a broader meaning of sustainable business that sees sustainability as managing for the triple bottom line values of sustainability—a process by which firms manage their financial, social and environmental risks and opportunities (Network for Business Sustainability, 2012).

Indeed, corporate leaders are feeling pressure to address environmental and social concerns along with financial performance (Holliday, 2001; Livesey and Kearins, 2002). Goodno (1994) argues that hotels are situated in a context squeezed between the push of legislation, the pull of consumer pressure groups and economic concerns related to cost savings. Hotels have focused primarily on cost savings as the initial step in their multi-faceted sustainability journey (Chong and Verma, 2013). As cost savings are largely associated with "green" practices, several authors have long criticized the tourism industry, particularly the hotel industry, for their intense focus on the environmental dimension to become "sustainable" (Font and Harris, 2004; Roberts and Tribe, 2008). Yet, environmental initiatives can be the stepping-stone towards sustainability and hotels could evolve to include social and ethical aspects as well as become more integrated in the community (Kernel, 2005).

A review of literature, in fact, suggests that companies often go through phases starting with simple, easy-to-implement strategies and progressing towards more complex and potentially rewarding approaches (Mirvins and Googins, 2009; Hoffman and Bansal, 2012). As companies evolve through the phases, they assume more complex responsibilities, increase their interactions with stakeholders, and strive to align their business model or corporate culture with sustainability goals (Miller and Serafeim, 2014). Nidumolu *et al.* (2009) posit that the first steps most companies take in the long sustainability journey usually arise from the law. Similarly, a 2009 BCG Report, *The Business of Sustainability*, found that the biggest drivers of corporate sustainability investments were government legislation, consumer concerns and employee interest in sustainability, of which, government legislation was the principal driver of sustainability efforts by nearly all the industries analysed. While the nature and number of phases differ, nearly all hotels first engage with sustainability by focusing on legal compliance, for the purpose of managing economic risks and opportunities, saving costs and increasing shareholder value.

However, a more recent study found that only 9% of survey respondents who said they adopted sustainability strategies as a result of legislation reported that their sustainability practices added to their profitability (MIT and BCG Report, 2012). Thus, smart companies comply with the most stringent rules and do so before they are enforced, simply to harness substantial first-mover advantages in terms of fostering innovation (Nidumolu *et al.*, 2009). As Bronn and Vidaver-Cohen (2009) assert, it is actually more desirable for businesses to have less regulation in order to have more freedom in decision-making to be able to meet market and social factors. Yet, a 2012 Gram Green Paper[2] into the UK hospitality industry's attitudes towards sustainability, for instance, shows that although 83% of hoteliers want their business to be greener than it is now, the majority of hoteliers (53%) actually believe that they do not have the financial resources to realize this ambition, largely citing budget restrictions as the main barrier (William Reed Business Media, 2014).

In addition to legal standards, hotels also feel compelled to abide by voluntary codes—general ones, such as the Greenhouse Gas Protocol, or sector-specific ones, such as the Green Tourism Business Scheme (GTBS)—to exhibit socially responsible behaviour. Once hotels have learnt to manage risks and efficiencies through compliance, many of them further evolve to engage in some sort of corporate social responsibility (CSR) activity such as charity projects and community involvement that reflect deeply held values. Some even go further and become proactive about environmental issues to make their value chains sustainable. Although the initial aim making value chains sustainable is usually to create a socially responsible corporate image, most companies capitalize on reduced costs or creating new businesses as well

---

2 Gram is the UK's leading refrigeration supplier with over 35 energy efficient products listed and takes its commitment very seriously with its strong presence on the Energy Technology List (ETL). In 2012, Gram teamed up with the leading channel associations within the industry including: Considerate Hoteliers Association, LACA (Local Authority Caterers Association), NACC (National Association of Care Catering), Sustainable Restaurant Association and TUCO (The University Caterers Organization), to produce a third Green Paper to add to its legacy.

(Nidumolu *et al.*, 2009). Deale (2013) asserts that hotels aim to increase efficiencies throughout the value chain with separate CSR activities in the form of donations of goods, services and more recently volunteer hours. In the hotel industry, CSR projects are believed to lead to guilt-free hotel operations, enhanced corporate reputation in the eyes of eco-minded hotel guests and even attraction of new guests (Euromonitor International, 2012).

Hitchcock and Willard (2009) assert that CSR leads to positive public relations, legitimacy and improved corporate image with shareholders and community, and thus can be a differentiating factor and a source of competitive advantage for businesses. Legitimization can be a valid driver of sustainability by both large and small hotels although methods and motivations for societal legitimization would differ between small and medium hotels (Font *et al.*, 2014). A previous study shows that large hotels, hotels with a classification between three and five stars and chain hotels were more likely to experience positive CSR benefits than small, two star classified and independent hotels (Kirk, 1998). Interestingly, this search for competitiveness is based on the assumption that CSR and corporate financial performance (CFP) are positively related (Carroll and Shabana, 2010). Yet, extant research finds positive, neutral and negative relationships between CSR and CFP, making this relationship debatable (Griffin and Mahon, 1997; Margolis and Walsh, 2001). Furthermore, there are two pitfalls associated with traditional CSR strategies: first, business is pitted against society rather than recognizing their interdependence; and, second, CSR is relatively a defensive concept rather than a strategic lens (Porter and Kramer, 2011).

Once hotels have enjoyed the benefits of managing legal compliance coupled with voluntary CSR practices, they see themselves integral to society. It may well be this relatively recent concept of CSR that provides an understanding of evolution in the meaning of sustainability from *green* to *sustainable*. They tend to easily recognize the relevance and the need to respond to social and environmental concerns along with economic concerns. This is often the outcome of a radical shift in mind-set from doing things better to doing new things. They simply move from operational optimization and *defensive* CSR activities towards a strategically focused organizational transformation phase (Antonis *et al.*, 2011; Visser, 2010). This shift is argued to be the result of recognition that current models of CSR have largely been ineffective at solving societal challenges (Visser, 2010; Moore and Westley, 2011; Porter and Kramer, 2011). While traditional CSR programmes comprise activities such as employee volunteer programmes or charitable giving and philanthropy, *strategic* CSR reframes sustainability and social benefits as a driver of business innovation, value creation and competitive advantage (Hoivik and Shankar, 2011; Porter and Kramer 2007, p. 2).

Thus, in this phase, three-dimensional concerns of people, planet and profit take precedence with a broadened focus on stakeholders. Businesses in this phase of sustainability relate economic, environmental and social concerns to the triple bottom line (TBL) values of sustainability (Dyllick and Muff, 2013). The concept of TBL measures the multi-dimensional business contributions to sustainability (Elkington, 1997). It is a synergistic search for creating economic, environmental and social value through the adoption of sustainability efforts (Hart and Milstein, 2003). Hotel sustainability strategies entail new programmes and initiatives that are developed and implemented with the aim of addressing specific sustainability issues or stakeholders.

Developing sustainable offerings or redesigning existing ones to become eco-friendly leads to "becoming sustainable" (Nidumolu *et al.*, 2009). This is in line with Orsato's (2006) eco-branding strategy which asserts that environmental product differentiation would create greater environmental benefits or impose smaller environmental costs, compared to similar products. Although this may lead to increased operating costs, such differentiation would simply satisfy the green market niche willing to pay a premium for environmentally friendly products (Blanco *et al.* 2009), which would, in turn, enable the hotel to command a price premium or increase market share (Reinhardt, 1998). A main pitfall of managing for the TBL is the confusion created with regard to measuring and comparing the trade-offs between economic, social and environmental values. While environmental initiatives are easily measurable in the short-term with objective data, social initiatives require a longer time span and subjective data that is harder to measure (Sasidharan *et al.* 2002). Different social dimensions such as health and education cannot be summed or aggregated since their outcomes are not additive.

A more recent development of TBL is the concept of Creating Shared Value (CSV), which argues for economic value creation in a way that simultaneously creates societal value. In this sense, it represents one particular model of implementing strategic CSR in larger organizations. CSV can be defined as creation of meaningful economic and social value whereby new benefits exceed the costs for the business and society simultaneously (Porter and Kramer, 2011). In other terms, it is a business strategy for companies to create measurable shareholder value by identifying and addressing social problems that intersect with their business. This creates new opportunities for companies, civil society organizations, and governments to leverage the power of market-based competition in addressing social problems (Shared Value Initiative website).

InterContinental Hotels Group (IHG), the largest hotel company in the world, for example, identified water and waste as environmental and social issues with significant shared value potential and launched its group-wide online environmental management system Green Engage in 2009 by testing various options for reducing water, waste and energy to lower its environmental footprint while also driving down hotel operating costs. In 2011, Green Engage further became aligned to LEED, making IHG the first hotel company to have an existing hotel programme aligned. This way, IHG transparently communicates to its customers the true value of how they are "saving the planet" by quantitatively measuring environmental performance. Furthermore, the hotel group recognized the need for increased capacity building in the industry and thus set up the IHG Academy to ally with community and educational institutions to give people real-world hospitality knowledge. The IHG Academy raises job skills and creates economic opportunity around the IHG hotels while creating a pipeline of prepared and engaged potential recruits.

A major limitation of CSV is that it overlaps with CSR, thus it is not always clear what builds a "core" business approach to Shared Value (SV). Furthermore, there is still the need for practical drivers for companies that seek SV, which makes it difficult to make a business case. The *how* of measuring SV is still not completely clear considering the overlapping areas of *defensive* CSR and CSV. For example, while IHG's Green Engage programme aggregates the total cost savings generated by resource use reductions (e.g. water, energy and waste), it cannot compare resource reductions with the workforce development outcomes of its IHG Academy programme, although the company could compare the two programmes' financial returns. This may be due to the infancy of the concept in the sense that operational tools and measurement of SV have only recently started to be developed (Bockstette and Stamp, 2011). Finally, time lags between improving the competitive context and profit maximization are not deeply explored, partly due to the fact that investments in societal value creation are likely to bring about up-front costs.

Although the concept of shared value creation is a state-of-the-art contribution towards linking corporations to society at large, and thus a progressive leap from the opposing views of shareholder value management (Rappaport, 1988; Friedman, 1970) and stakeholder value management (Freeman, 1984), it is limited to those issues and concerns that emphasize the *business case* for sustainability and thus economic value for business (Dyllick and Muff, 2013).

In these times of escalating societal challenges, however, there is great need for businesses to move forward and become eco-effective or socio-effective by solving sustainability issues of societies (Dyllick and Hockerts, 2002). Social businesses promise a higher effectiveness in addressing sustainability challenges than commercial businesses as the social mission supersedes financial benefits as their primary objective. Felber's (2010) Economy for the Common Goods movement (ECG) and Sukhdev's (2012) Corporation 2020 are examples of new business models that support social businesses and social entrepreneurs. Sabeti *et al.* (2009) highlight a *fourth sector* of organizations oriented towards social benefits, like government agencies and NGOs, yet unlike them, who are able to earn their income themselves. Similarly, B-Corporation in the US and community interest companies in the UK are some examples of privately owned organizations that prioritize their social mission over economic value creation. Although changing the mind-set from the traditional *business case* to the societal good may be too idealist for commercial businesses including hotels, there is clearly a market for new organizational forms with a clear social purpose (Dyllick and Muff, 2013).

In light of this extant theory and literature, Dyllick and Muff (2013), in their Business Sustainability Typology, posit that a truly sustainable business translates sustainability challenges into business opportunities making "business sense" of societal and environmental issues. By starting out with societal challenges such as public health, poverty, climate change, biodiversity or social justice, a truly sustainable business makes a positive contribution to society and the planet rather than reduce its environmental impacts only. The authors draw attention to the prevalent *inside-out* organizational perspective most business approaches derive from, and further highlight the need to frame business sustainability through a different approach—an *outside-in* organizational perspective—which they believe will lead companies to true sustainability.

Significance of a culture of sustainability for implementing sustainability strategies

Yet, such an *outside-in* organizational perspective requires a radical shift in mind-set from commercial self-interest to societal good. Caring for the well-being of other stakeholders directly creates value for shareholders (Freeman *et al.*, 2010; Porter and Kramer, 2011), as well as drawing attention to the performance implications of a corporate culture of sustainability (Godfrey, 2005; Margolis *et al.*, 2007; Porter and Kramer, 2011). An organization's culture guides the decisions of its members by establishing and reinforcing expectations about what is valued and how things should be done. Thus, culture is often described as "the way we do things around here" (NBS, 2010). Over time, a company builds up its own culture and this culture is continuously reinforced and reshaped through the daily practices of its members. Although there is a lack of consensus regarding a common definition of the term "organizational culture" (Ashkanasy *et al.*, 2000), there is a range of definitions from shared values, ideologies and beliefs (e.g. Schwartz and Davis, 1981), to notions of accepted behavioural rules, norms and rituals (e.g. Trice and Beyer, 1984), and most commonly, shared patterns of meaning or understanding (Louis, 1985; Smircich, 1983).

Corporate culture describes and governs the ways a company's owners, management and employees think, feel and act. A company's organizational culture can be founded on beliefs included in its vision or mission statement. Organizational culture can be a useful tool for organizational change programmes as the values and ideological underpinnings of a company's culture affect how sustainability is implemented (Cameron and Quinn, 2006; Jarnagin and Slocum, 2007). Thus, it plays a vital role in the success or failure of sustainability strategies in becoming a truly sustainable business (Miller-Perkins, 2011).

In this case study, a culture of sustainability, thus, is one in which organizational members hold shared assumptions, values and beliefs about the importance of balancing economic efficiency, social equity and environmental accountability (NBS, 2010). It is assumed that a stronger culture of sustainability is attained if values and beliefs underlie the mission or vision of the organization. Furthermore, a culture of sustainability has been found to increase the effectiveness of leadership commitment and external stakeholder engagement, which, in turn, fosters trust, innovation and mechanisms for execution (Eccles *et al.*, 2012).

To date, however, the role of leaders' values has been largely overlooked in the discourse on execution of CSR activities and sustainability performance (Orlitzky *et al.*, 2011). Emerging research demonstrates that corporate success depends on leaders' perceptions of and actions on the challenges and demands of CSR and corporate social performance (CSP) (Waldman, 2011). Indeed, degree of accountability towards others and breadth of stakeholder group focus have been found to determine various responsibility orientations of leaders (Pless *et al.*, 2012).

Pless *et al.* (2012) identified four orientations that leaders may use to exhibit responsibility and implement CSR: traditional economist, opportunity seeker, integrator and idealist. While the traditional economist has an orientation of short-term economic value creation aimed at shareholders, the opportunity seeker takes on social responsibility as part of the strategy of longer-term value creation with the aim of realizing competitive advantages such as a better reputation or new market opportunities. These two orientations imply a low degree of accountability towards others and are limited to legal and economic concerns. Orientations of idealistic and integrative leaders, however, derive from a broader degree of accountability to go beyond these two concerns and include business responsibilities that are relevant to society as a whole (e.g. sustainability challenges). While the integrator considers profits to be an outcome that is likely to result from running a purposeful and responsible business for multiple stakeholder groups, the idealist sees leadership as a servant-based responsibility and aims to serve the needs of a specific stakeholder group (Van Dierendonck, 2011).

Understanding cultural elements of organizations fosters successful execution of sustainability strategies. Attitudes towards specific aspects of sustainability such as leaders' values concerning environmental and social issues are certainly relevant as the above-mentioned most recent research highlights. Yet, specific characteristics of culture such as flexibility, external orientation, stability, control and tolerance for ambiguity could be equally significant, to manage challenges in execution even when the organization's sustainability strategy is well set and clear (Miller-Perkins, 2011).

Thus, the Beechenhill case study has been crafted in light of the Dyllick/ Muff Business Sustainability Typology as well as Beechenhill's organizational culture, to better understand the framing of its business sustainability in the sustainability journey.

Methodology

In this case study, two interrelated methodologies were used to gather data on the Beechenhill Farm Hotel. A Sustainability Culture and Leadership Assessment (SCALA) survey was conducted in order to understand certain aspects of Beechenhill's sustainability culture, as well as primary elements of the Dyllick/Muff Business Sustainability Typology in terms of concerns considered (inputs), the organizational perspectives applied (processes and approach) and the type of value created (outputs). The typology was also used as the overarching framework to craft semi-structured interview questions that would provide a more detailed and clearer picture of the Beechenhill Farm Hotel's business sustainability level in the sustainability journey. The study provides insights into the Beechenhill Farm Hotel's business sustainability level and organizational culture and emphasizes the important role an owner-manager's personal values and family culture play in the successful implementation of sustainability strategies in small to medium-sized hospitality businesses.

SCALA survey

The Sustainability Culture and Leadership Assessment (SCALA) survey was used as a support tool to assess and describe organizational culture and climate. The SCALA survey was developed by Miller Consultants in 2012. Set up in 2010, Miller Consultants is a US-based consulting company, which specializes in sustainability research that focuses on the sustainability culture and sustainability leadership in corporations. The SCALA instrument is composed of items pertaining to culture and leadership. The items derive from a review of the public literature and interviews with thought leaders. To construct SCALA, data from across many surveys was gathered (Miller-Perkins, 2011). Thus, each item in the assessment is tied to a specific survey item or derived from a characteristic uncovered in previous research reviews. The assessment contains both sustainability-specific content as well as more general organizational climate content that has been found to impact the execution of sustainability strategies.

The SCALA survey serves to contribute to research objective 2 in the "Introduction", which aims to explore the transformational shifts in Beechenhill's timeline as well as in its organizational context. The SCALA data helps one to understand the impact of and changes in organizational culture and also contributes to the understanding of an overall business sustainability level and how it was achieved in research objectives one to three. Collecting data through the SCALA survey also helps us to understand how certain aspects of the Beechenhill's family-oriented organizational culture supported or hindered the development of sustainability initiatives, as well as how these initiatives influenced its culture. In addition, it aids in the identification of the hotel's capacity for executing progressive sustainability strategies.

The SCALA survey consisted of four sections and a total of 43 questions, of which the first four in section I were general questions on location, gender, age group and company position of the interviewees. The next 26 questions in section II were related to cultural characteristics on sustainability and correspond to research objective 2, while the following 11 questions in section III were related to business sustainability positioning of the hotel based on the Dyllick and Muff (2013) typology and correspond to research objectives 1, 2 and 3. Finally, the two questions in section IV explored an understanding of the hotel's health and well-being focus and awareness of the importance of personal values and beliefs that could lead to future health and well-being initiatives. These do not correspond to any specific research objective, yet aim to understand a potential area of concern for the hotel, on which the researcher and the hotel could work together for a mutual learning opportunity in a possible "next step". The questions in section II were further sub-categorized under organizational leadership (eight questions), organizational systems (four questions), organizational climate (five questions), change readiness (three questions), and internal (three questions) as well as external stakeholders (three questions), respectively. As such, Section II questions serve to assess levels of change readiness to support sustainability initiatives, measure similar or varying perceptions across stakeholder groups, identify company strengths that can be leveraged to meet sustainability goals, and improve on areas of possible concern regarding sustainability goals. The survey used a mixture of semi-open, open and mainly Likert scale questions.

The sample consisted of four family members, who were the only permanent staff at Beechenhill. The survey was administered as hard copies for ease of following up the survey turnarounds by the researcher who was accommodated at the hotel and also conducted the interviews. It was conducted in April 2014 and yielded quantitative data that complemented the qualitative data from semi-structured interviews and the literature review.

Interviews

The interviews aimed to explore research goals 1 to 3 and to shed light on the business sustainability position of the Beechenhill Farm Hotel in detail. The sample for the interviews was chosen from the hotel's internal and external stakeholders who appeared to have extensive knowledge of and engagement in Beechenhill's sustainability journey. The interviews were preceded by an initial phone interview with the owner-manager of the hotel as the key informant. The researcher further worked in collaboration with the owner-manager in choosing interviewees, based on their level of experience and engagement in the sustainability initiatives. The total number of interviewees listed was 12. Ten participated in the study. Some of the potential interviewees were not available during the interview period. The interviews were ultimately conducted with four Beechenhill family staff members and six external stakeholders. Table 1 provides a detailed list of the interviewees.

Table 1 Interviewee list and their engagement with Beechenhill

Name	Title	Years of engagement with Beechenhill's sustainability initiatives
Sue Prince	Owner-Manager	30 years
Terry Prince	Farm Operations Manager	30 years
Alexandra Gray	Accommodation and Events Manager	5 years
Rob Gray	Hotel Operations Manager	4.5 years
Dr Andy Tickle (external stakeholder)	Director of the Friends of the Peak District Charity	10 years
Dr Xavier Font (external stakeholder)	Professor in Sustainable Tourism at the Leeds Metropolitan University; manager of a consultancy service for small firms to audit their sustainability marketing and communications	More than 5 years
Ruth Nutter (external stakeholder)	Freelance Project Manager for an arts programme, a repeat Beechenhill guest	6 years
Faith Johnson (external stakeholder)	Director at the Environmental Quality Mark Community Interest Company	10 years
Diane Roberts (external stakeholder)	Acting Staffordshire Business & Environment Network (SBEN) Manager at the Staffordshire County Council	More than 5 years
Cathy Bower (external stakeholder)	Wedding Photographer at Indigo Photography	More than 5 years

As can be seen in Table 1, nine of the ten interviewees have more than five years of engagement with the hotel's sustainability initiatives and thus were able to easily provide invaluable insights into the hotel's sustainability orientation that has been evolving over the past few years. The interviews were conducted in the social room at the hotel. They were administered in person from 23 April to 2 May 2014. Prior to the interviews, interviewees were contacted by the researcher and were provided with an outline of the interview question topics. Each interview lasted approximately 50 minutes.

The interview questions in the interview guide were based on the Dyllick/Muff Business Sustainability Typology and were divided into four general themes, as identified from the literature review and expert faculty review.
The first part of the interview covered the general attitudes towards sustainability such as the understanding of sustainability and sustainable business practices. The second part attempted to identify the type of business sustainability in terms of concerns and the type of value created. The third part of the interview explored the current sustainability practices and future plans in resolving sustainability issues. Finally, the fourth part expanded on the hotel's approach (inside out vs. outside in) to address and resolve sustainability challenges, with regard to strategic focus and implementation.
For a smooth read, the interview and the SCALA survey findings are presented in a dispersed rather than concentrated manner throughout the case study.

Thriving on sustainable thinking in a protected landscape

Beechenhill Farm Hotel is a relatively small, 37-hectare organic[3] dairy farm in the Staffordshire Peak District National Park[4] in the centre of rural England, which offers eco-tourism accommodation (including facilities for wheelchair users), eco-weddings and conferences. The farm hotel lies between Ilam and Stanshope in the limestone plateau pastures of the White Peak. Perched on

---

3 Organic farms are farms where organic farming is carried out, and food of optimum quality and quantity are produced, using methods that seek to co-exist with, and not dominate, natural systems. Organic farming maximizes the wildlife and landscape value of productive farmed land as well as non-farmed areas. Organic farming relies on sound rotations, natural nitrogen fixation, biologically active soil life, recycled farm manures and crop residues, appropriate cultivation, biological pest control and ethical livestock systems.

4 "National Parks are the most beautiful and dramatically different expanses of the country in England and Wales where people can enjoy a wide range of open-air recreation", as the Countryside Agency states. Ten National Parks were established during the 1950s. More areas are currently being proposed. National Parks are run by National Park Authorities, which is a public body made up of two groups of people—members and officers.

a south-facing hill above the picturesque village of Ilam on the Staffordshire-Derbyshire border, Beechenhill cares passionately about the environment and tries to be as sustainable as possible, priding itself on being one of the UK's leading sustainable small hotels.

The National Park landscape, which has developed as a result of thousands of years of farming, is recognized by the nation as an exceptionally valuable one, and is key to Beechenhill's success as a tourism business. For Beechenhill, the landscape is indeed an important part of their lives and business. The landscape is well worth caring for, not only because they appreciate it and proudly look after it but also because it supplements a proportion of their family income. The owner-manager and her family, for instance, designed a farm trail at Beechenhill to enhance some landscape features. They share information and understanding about the environment with their guests who enjoy being able to explore and learn about their farm and its environs. The family considers farming in the Peak District National Park to be a positive and beneficial experience, and this is reflected in Beechenhill's diversified business model where tourism and farming are firmly integrated in this protected landscape. In the Peak District, one cannot thrive without the other, and diversification plays a key role in the sustainability of the 2,500 farms located in the Peak District National Park.

The family-run farm hotel strives to be sustainable through reducing its environmental impact, enabling others to experience and appreciate a sustainable lifestyle, supporting its local community and contributing to the global community. Addressing rural resource efficiency, economic pressures and reducing the carbon footprint of the farm and tourism business in ways that protect the National Park, are the overarching drivers for the owners of Beechenhill, as stated by owner-manager Sue Prince:

> The pristine protected landscapes of England are under ever increasing pressure. As we face the challenges of climate change, a steadily increasing population and economic difficulties, people everywhere try to find economic solutions. Some of these solutions could increase the risk to our protected landscapes, and once we have lost them, they can never come back.

Thus, in order to fully *walk the walk and talk the talk*, Beechenhill has long considered sustainability in all its daily decisions and operations: The farm hotel gradually replaces equipment and exchanges inefficient, eco-unfriendly systems with more sustainable versions. Local organic produce is Beechenhill's first choice in food purchasing, followed by British Organic and British Fair Trade produce, respectively. Furthermore, as Beechenhill is an organic farm, no synthetic chemicals are used on the 37 hectares. The farm is carefully managed to encourage flora and fauna, using only clover and composted manure to support fertility and encourage insect life, which in turn attracts birds. In addition to eco cleaning products and recycled paper, there are recycling and composting facilities for guests and all farm waste. Finally, while the farm's main income is from organic milk, the bed & breakfast (B&B) generates its main income from eco-weddings organized in the Hay Barn.

The accommodation section consists of two rooms in the main building (one double and one family room); a romantic cottage for two; and a converted barn for six (including wheelchair users). Thus, groups of up to 14 can be accommodated in comfort during reunions, get-togethers and celebrations. The farm also boasts a Swedish-style hot tub, heated cave and barrel sauna with outdoor shower and fireplace. The warm Hay Barn is at hotel guests' disposal, and there is also an eco-venue for hire (for conferences, courses, weddings and ceremonies of up to 60 people). The farmhouse breakfasts are prepared with a wide range of local and organic produce such as cereals, fruit, homemade organic yoghurt, porridge and bread as well as homemade jam and honey from the farm.

The majority (70%) of Beechenhill's guests are repeat customers who are always keen to see the new developments on the farm, from the dry stone wall along the drive to the trees planted in the Millennium Avenue where trees are planted by Beechenhill on behalf of guests. This is reflected in the following quote from Sue Prince in 2014: "The secret of our success in sustainability is making the 'eco-experience' at Beechenhill celebratory and fun for visitors, as well as sharing our eco-experiences".

The family can learn from many repeat customers, businesses and organizations demonstrating good practice. Learning from good practice and sharing success indeed lie at the heart of Beechenhill's success. For Beechenhill, creating environmental awareness, to a large extent, starts with guests' eco- experience at the hotel. Beechenhill values its guests' feedback and continuously builds on it. The 2014 Beechenhill eco-survey (shared by the family with its various stakeholders) "How is Beechenhill doing eco-wise?" (https://www.surveymonkey.com/results/SM-65CXFCH) highlights Beechenhill from a guest perspective.

The Beechenhill eco-survey had 49 respondents (both repeat and first time Beechenhill guests), and was administered through an online survey tool (SurveyMonkey), the link for which was included on the Beechenhill website during the months of April and May 2014. The survey consisted of eight questions that the Beechenhill family members thought were important in order to be able to progress in their sustainability journey. The questions included: the frequency of guest stays at the hotel; what guests think of Beechenhill as an eco-holiday place; the eco-friendly additions that respondents noticed at Beechenhill (those which they thought were important and which they already do at home or they might start to do at home); what respondents thought about Beechenhill's eco-friendly performance; and how likely it was that respondents would recommend the hotel to family or friends as an eco-holiday place.

When asked about how well guests thought the hotel was doing in providing them with an eco-friendly place to stay, 24 out of 49 respondents (57.14%) mentioned that they enjoyed themselves more because Beechenhill is so eco, while 17 respondents (40.48%) mentioned that the hotel's outstanding eco-friendly performance was the reason why they keep coming over and over again to Beechenhill. Furthermore, when asked about what respondents have seen in other places that they think Beechenhill should be doing to make their stay even better for them and the planet, the majority of the 21 respondents (28 respondents skipped this question) mentioned the fact that nothing springs to mind, with the rest having mentioned a few suggestions such as geothermal energy, more promotion of Beechenhill's eco-cleaning products through advertising, and the possibility of filling stations for milk where guests can buy milk directly on the farm in their own containers. The question that sought to determine what guests saw, heard about, felt important, already do at home and intend to do at home, led the Beechenhill team to order a new electrical vehicle charging unit that will be much more visible, as indicated in the majority of guest comments on that topic. The eco-survey is clearly a good example of Beechenhill's commitment to advancing its sustainability journey, to add to the recognition it has achieved through various awards and accolades.

Beechenhill is a holder of a Peak District Environmental Quality Mark (PD-EQM)[5] and has a Gold Green Tourism Business Scheme (GTBS)[6] award. In November 2012, the farm hotel was one of the few English finalists in the carbon reduction category of the Virgin Responsible Tourism Awards[7] and in

---

5 Environmental Quality Mark (EQM) is a Peak District Environmental Quality Mark award presented to businesses that put pride in the Peak District at the heart of their operations; actively safeguard and improve the Peak District environment and heritage; safeguard natural resources; promote their values to their customers; add to the well-being of their communities and work together with businesses in other sectors, use and promote their produce and services.

6 The Green Tourism Business Scheme (GTBS) is an outgrowth of the understanding of the UK Government that sustainability is not a trend that is going away. The scheme has led to the development of a number of very popular green tourism initiatives including Green Tourism for London. The Green Tourism Business Scheme award recognizes places to stay and visit that are taking action to support the local area and the wider environment. It is the largest sustainable (green) scheme to operate globally and assesses hundreds of fantastic places to stay and visit in Britain. Businesses that meet the standard for a GTBS award receive a Bronze, Silver, or Gold award based on their level of achievement. Areas that a business is assessed on include: management and marketing, social involvement and communication, energy, water, purchasing, waste, travel, natural and cultural heritage and innovation. The Gold Award is the highest standard a business can achieve within the GTBS scheme and is only awarded to businesses that have demonstrated excellence in sustainable tourism.

7 Virgin Responsible Tourism Awards recognize industry leaders in sustainability and recognize individuals, companies and organizations in the travel industry that are making a significant commitment to the culture and economies of local communities and are providing a positive contribution to biodiversity conservation. The central

the same year they won the Environmental Business Award in the Sentinel Business Awards.[8] As a winner of the UK Green Hotelier[9] 2013 competition, Beechenhill is also very proud to have won the Gold Award in the sustainable tourism category of the Visit England Awards for Excellence[10] 2013.

Beechenhill's sustainability journey

Beechenhill's sustainability journey indeed reflects the sustainable thinking mind-set elaborated on in the previous section. The journey starts with the purchase of the Beechenhill Farm with the intention of diversifying into the hotel business to ensure the sustainability of their business. In the first years,

tenet of the Awards is that all types of tourism—from niche to mainstream—can and should be operated in a way that respects and benefits destinations and local people. The Responsible Tourism Awards are different from other awards in that winners are nominated by tourists. One of the founding principles of the Awards is to always seek out new responsible tourism ventures that deserve to be celebrated and tourists' nominations are fundamental to this process.

8 Sentinel Business Awards is a celebration of business in Staffordshire and South Cheshire and enjoys a reputation for being the premier event in those areas. It grows in popularity with the business community every year who view it as an ideal platform to promote their products and services. It rewards the achievements of businesses that have proven to be the most successful during the year, showing innovation, commitment and tenacity. There are a series of 12 individual awards which are: Entrepreneur of the Year, Apprentice of the Year, Business Innovation Award, Business of the Year, Growth Award, International Trade Award, Science and Technology in Business Award, Small Business of the Year, Training Excellence Award, Young Business Person of the Year, Lifetime Achievement, and Community Engagement Award.

9 Green Hotelier competition is an initiative of the online *Green Hotelier* magazine which is published by the International Hotels Environment Initiative, an industry initiative that produces an environmental action guide for hotels, produces reports on environmental best practices and conducts workshops and conferences worldwide. The Green Hotelier competition seeks to find the UK's most innovative green hotel, B&B or hostel. The sustainable initiatives implemented at participating hotels are categorized under the following topics: Energy & Carbon, Water, Education & Training, Community and Events. Entries are judged on innovation, environmental impact/savings and green plans for the future.

10 Visit England Awards for Excellence celebrate the best of English tourism. They promote healthy industry competition and high standards, helping to ensure England's place as a world-class destination. The 16 categories for the 2013 awards included: Access for all Tourism Award, Bed & Breakfast/Guest Accommodation of the Year, Best Tourism Experience, Business Tourism Award, Caravan Holiday Park, Large Hotel (over 35 bedrooms), Large Visitor Attraction (over 100,000 visitors), Self-catering Holiday of the Year, Small Hotel of the Year (under 35 bedrooms), Small Visitor Attraction (under 50,000), Sustainable Tourism Award, Taste of England Award, Tourist Information Service, Tourism Pub of the Year, Tourism SuperStar, and Travel Article of the Year.

Sue and her husband Terry decide to invest in the farmhouse harnessing every regulatory incentive that presents an opportunity for diversifying into the tourism business. They simultaneously invest in the farming business and in the construction of the farm's accommodation units, driven by a strong desire to achieve resource efficiencies and cost savings. The couple's strong sustainability values and orientation lead them to that very decision—to go organic in the farming business. The successful conversion of Beechenhill into a fully organic farm gives a real sense of achievement to the couple, which they further extend into their hotel business. Their environmental awareness and love of the Peak District further leads them to invest in *green technology*, which not only helps the hotel save costs and become more efficient but also makes a positive contribution to eco-hotel industry standards, showcasing how a small hotel can increase its social capital through collaborating with various stakeholders such as policy-makers and educational institutions. While establishing these networks proactively, Beechenhill simultaneously contributes to the local and global community through donations to various charities.

The couple's strong values-orientation, their desire to communicate with and educate others throughout their sustainability journey, their realization of the links between voluntary environmental and social activities and economic well-being, has helped them to continuously decrease the farm hotel's environmental impact, innovate and increase their social capital, which are key factors inherent to this case study. The rest of this section will elaborate on how Beechenhill has gradually been evolving on their sustainability journey:

Capitalizing on regulatory incentives and going organic

In 1984, the Prince family bought Beechenhill Farm and started a bed and breakfast business with two bedrooms. They thought that linking farming with tourism was crucial for the sustainability of their farm business, and Beechenhill seemed like the ideal farmhouse in which to realize their life-long desire to run a farm hotel. In 1985, Beechenhill Cottage (with accommodation for two guests) was converted from an old stallion pen, and farm visits were started in cooperation with the Peak District National Park Authority (PDNPA). Again, in the same year, the family planted 250 indigenous trees, in what is now called Millennium Avenue. In 1987, a milking parlour was built and a small shelterbelt for wildlife was planted. In 1990, the Cottage by the Pond—a wheelchair-accessible cottage—was completed. The family won a Nat West National Farmers Union (NFU) National Venture Cash Competition for the concept of the Cottage by the Pond, and the way it was marketed. In 1991, Beechenhill won the Holiday Care Service Award for accessible accommodation and 0.75 hectares of indigenous woodland was also planted. The family further restored a tiny lake with an established population of great crested newts.[11] In 1993, the family planted a further 1,000 trees in Millennium Avenue.

The year 1997 marked a break-through in Beechenhill's business strategy. While listening to Peter Day on BBC Radio 4's *In Business* talking about globalization, she suddenly realized that what he was referring to could actually apply to her own business. The famous business correspondent and broadcaster was talking about how ultimately white goods (fridges and washing machines) would be made wherever in the world it is cheapest to produce—and that same fate could be said to await milk production as well! In the same year she met an organic farming lecturer at a friend's and discussed the possibility of converting Beechenhill and decided to investigate it further. Consequently, she contacted the Ministry of Agriculture, Fisheries and Food (MAFF)[12] about organic milk production. The result of the first organic adviser visit to Beechenhill was to set the stage in going organic, one consequence of which was the cessation of the routine giving of antibiotics to dairy cows. In the same year, a new 2,500-litre milk tank was also purchased. In 1998, Beechenhill had the second free advice visit, this time from an organic adviser with financial expertise, who showed the family how to prepare conversion plans and registration information for the Soil Association, and how to apply for the MAFF Organic Aid Scheme. A search for organic feed companies was also started. Subsequently, registration forms were sent off to the Soil Association for conversion from 1 June 1998 which culminated in the first Soil Association inspection being administered, and 25% of the farm entered organic conversion.

In 2000, Beechenhill became a fully organic farm and gathered its first crop of organic big bale silage. The cows started their organic diet (until then the cows ate ordinary GMO-free[13] concentrated food) and their diet became 90% organic. Beechenhill joined the organic feed buying group.

---

11 The northern crested newt, also known as the great crested newt or warty newt (*Triturus cristatus*) is a newt in the family Salamandridae, found across Europe and parts of Asia. Great crested newts are a European protected species whose eggs, breeding sites and resting places are protected by law. A licence may be obtained from Natural England if an activity is planned and disturbing them or damaging their habitats (ponds and the land around ponds) cannot be avoided.

12 The Ministry of Agriculture, Fisheries and Food (MAFF) was a United Kingdom Government department created by the Board of Agriculture Act 1889, and at that time was called the Board of Agriculture. The Ministry was formally dissolved in 2002, at which point its responsibilities were merged into the Department for Environment, Food and Rural Affairs (Defra), which is currently the ministry responsible for agriculture in the UK.

13 GMO means genetically modified organism, which is a novel organism created by scientists when they genetically modify or engineer food plants. Scientists have cited many health and environmental risks with genetically modified (GM) foods. As a result of these risks, many people in the United States, Canada, Europe, Japan, and other nations are demanding non-genetically modified (non-GMO) foods.

In September 2000, milk became organic after three months of organic feeding. Beechenhill started selling organic milk and won a Heart of England Sustainable Tourism Award. The family also planted 20 more trees in Millennium Avenue, each dedicated to guests who had visited regularly over the previous ten years. However, becoming organic was just the onset of the new challenges in Beechenhill's sustainability journey. Having gone fully organic in 2000, Beechenhill further continued its sustainability journey along with "green" investments, which were thought to be essential in coping with rural resource efficiency, economic pressures and the carbon footprint of the farm and hotel business.

Investing in green technology

Competition regarding environmental performance is strong within the hotel industry, driven in part by concerns about resource efficiency. Possessing this *green* consciousness, Beechenhill has invested in the following green initiatives, which helped Beechenhill not only to realize direct savings in operational costs, but also to set industry standards in order to gain competitive advantage from these initiatives. Thus, the family business further raised the bar for excellence, to a level to which others have to aspire.

Heating

Beechenhill tries to operate without oil. The hotel has a new wood boiler, which provides hot water and heating to the entire accommodation and hay barn. The only oil used is in the Rayburn and that has a new burner that uses 40% less oil. The Rayburn cooker conversion has led to a saving of 2.5 tonnes of carbon. An induction cooker also helps save energy and costs. Finally, Beechenhill found under floor heating to be a really effective way of warming interiors, as a lower water temperature is required than the use of radiators. At Beechenhill, insulation is done using sheep's wool from a neighbouring farm and lime plaster. Lime plaster with Pearlite insulates efficiently while retaining the character of the building making it the best for rural and old buildings. Finally, all accommodation is double-glazed and has wooden window shutters.

Lighting

There is low-energy lighting installed everywhere—from the farm's floodlights to the fairy lights used in barn weddings. While movement sensors on all public lighting reduce energy usage and light pollution, sun tunnels in windowless rooms also remove the need for artificial lighting during daylight hours. Where possible, there are low rated appliances to reduce energy consumption, and the energy monitors in the cottages help guests see how much energy they use. In 2013, low energy lighting helped Beechenhill achieve a carbon saving of approximately 0.75 tonnes. The two 4-kW solar photovoltaic arrays on the cowshed roof provide about half of the farm's electricity and generate 14% more electricity per kWh than conventional panels. These innovative, lightweight solar PV arrays are very suitable for fragile roofs, which are typically found on farm barns and warehouses—and helped Beechenhill achieve a carbon saving of 4.3 tonnes.

Water

The farm has rainwater flush toilets in two cottages and the Hay Barn wedding barn. The cisterns use an existing 8,000-gallon rainwater tank situated behind the farmhouse, where water is collected from the north-facing roofs. Water from the south-facing roofs, on the other hand, is collected and feeds a restored pond, which is home to a colony of rare great crested newts. There are dual flushes on some WCs. Solar panels are also used in various places around the property.

Waste

There are recycling and composting facilities for guests and all farm waste. On-site recycling and composting led to a reduction in the quantity of un-recyclable waste. While three bins of rubbish were being produced weekly, now one and a half are being produced every two weeks. Furthermore, eco cleaning products and recycled paper products are used throughout the farm.

Beechenhill further invested in two electric bikes, which are offered for hire, allowing guests to explore the nearby countryside rather than driving all day. Having invested in the above-mentioned "green technology", the Prince family felt the need to test themselves in competitions and make sure they were moving in the right direction. So, in 2003, Terry Prince applied for the Peak District Environmental Quality Mark (PDEQM) for his farming business and Sue Prince applied for the award for her tourism business. After a rigorous inspection process, both applications were successful.

Beechenhill's further plans in sustainability include the creation and installation of an innovative, low-tech, small-scale bio digester dome to make methane from cow manure. The low energy lighting is gradually being replaced with LEDs, and better-rated white goods are purchased when replacements are needed. As decorating happens in rooms and cottages, rainwater flushes will be installed in more toilets and induction hobs will replace conventional. Finally, the hotel plans to invest in more electric bikes.

The simultaneous pursuit of contributing to the local and global community

Although regulation, reputation and social licence have clearly been a driver for big business, smaller businesses have been less exposed to these factors and driven more by a sense of social responsibility. Similarly, although smaller businesses can sometimes be less capable of sustainability investment and less cognizant of how sustainability relates to their business, i.e. not just recycling initiatives, Beechenhill has been well aware of the opportunities for continuous improvement and driven largely by a sense of social responsibility for the much appreciated protected landscape of the Peak District. Sue and the family's sense of social responsibility are largely embedded in the values-based management style they pursue, as will be detailed in the following paragraphs.

Locally, Beechenhill supports the local community in lots of different ways. The owner-manager, an artist renowned for Swedish folk art, contributed to the creation of a community website for Ilam village and its businesses. The farm hotel further contributes to the funding of various charities: 1) Practical Action, which finds practical solutions for ordinary people living in difficult conditions; 2) Wetton and Alstonefield First Responders who are trained by the ambulance service to respond immediately in emergencies; and 3) Friends of the Peak District, which is an independent charity dedicated to a vision of a living, working Peak District that changes with the times but remains beautiful forever. Social responsibility largely derives from the owner-manager's personal values, which understandably derive from her personal involvement with various stakeholders, mainly with public bodies and third parties. From 2009 to 2013, she also held various responsibilities as a commissioner on a high level expert panel of Defra's growth review in tackling rural disadvantage in England. Finally, between 2010 and 2011, she contributed to the review and renewal of the Peak District Environmental Quality Mark (PD-EQM); customized it for Staffordshire County Council and got the scheme validated by Visit England. EQM is now a white label scheme[14] for any organization or destination.

Globally, from 2006 to 2009, Sue Prince carried out missions at the Foundation ADEPT, to deliver website design, strategic advice, training and practical tourism workshops for a rural development project that gave economic value to the traditional way of life that protects one of the most valuable European landscapes, the Transylvanian landscape in Romania. In 2007, the owner-manager also worked at the Prince's Charities Foundation where she facilitated the initial development of Transylvania Authentica, a Romanian version of the Peak District Environmental Quality Mark (EQM), and the presentation of the economic benefits of a protected landscape to the Romanian Prime Minister's Office. Feeling socially responsible at the global level, she has been delivering marketing, research, design and rural development concepts to substantial eco-tourism investments in Europe since 2007.

---

14 A white-label scheme is a scheme produced by one organization (the producer) that other organizations (the marketers) rebrand to make it appear as if they had made it.

As can be seen, by donating to charitable causes, Beechenhill provides resources to help strengthen communities and lend a hand in times of need. And, given the myriad of issues that could benefit from more resources, Beechenhill's choice of which causes to support with corporate philanthropy appears to be driven by Sue and the family's personal values as well as the moral convictions of stakeholders. These shared values may indeed explain Beechenhill's ability to understand how their strategy and operating context intersect with key societal needs, as well as their business case for sustainability, which will be elaborated in the following section.

Creating a business case for sustainability

Creating a business case for sustainability requires identifying, creating and strengthening the links between economic success on one hand and non-monetary social and environmental activities on the other. Having realized the links between voluntary environmental and social activities and corporate economic success, Sue and the family have managed and innovated these links and improve economic success through voluntary social and environmental activities. They have simply redesigned Beechenhill's business model—farming with tourism—with cost and efficiency-oriented measures like the Pilot Light Project, and elements for improvement such as environmentally and socially outstanding products and services like the Wedding Weekend Package. The following paragraphs will elaborate on these changes in Beechenhill's sustainability journey.

2007 saw changes in environmental legislation in the UK. In 2007, all subsidies changed due to the European review of the Common Agricultural Policy 2005–2011. From schemes based on the number of animals kept (headage), they changed to schemes based on the amount of land held—the new scheme was named Single Farm Payment (SFP). Farmers received financial remuneration for the land they farmed regardless of cropping or stock reared. The government hoped that this would encourage farmers to get closer to the market, produce goods that would give them a profit and improve the environment. Thus, the government has split England into three zones—Lowland, Severely Disadvantaged Area (SDA) and Moorland. As many National Parks and special landscapes are Severely Disadvantaged, this was considered bad news for the upland regions of England where the farmers received £100 less per hectare (ha) than their lowland competitors, making them even more severely disadvantaged. The government further introduced an Uplands Entry Level Scheme (UELS) to alleviate this disadvantageous situation. The government started to give additional payments for environmental works such as the Entry Level Scheme (ELS) and organic farm incentives that were £30/ha extra. UELS for Higher Level Scheme (HLS) also became available for farms with special environments and was up to £60/ha.

Having realized these positive incentives to encourage environmentally friendly farming in the Peak District, the Prince family decided to act on these voluntary incentives and was entitled to Single Farm Payment (SFP) worth £6,000 per year and Organic Entry Level Scheme (OELS) worth £2,000 per year. Organic farming as an environmental activity had simply created a positive economic contribution to their corporate success.

Furthermore, having understood how the drivers of a business case can be positively influenced by societal and environmental activities, Sue Prince decided to diversify further into a new field of opportunity for the family business. In 2008, she developed the eco-wedding business, where families could book the whole farm for the weekend, decorate the Hay Barn, eat local food, have local live bands and have their guests put up at some of the many tiny B&Bs and cottages in the surrounding three-mile radius. Crucially, Beechenhill works with its local coach company to arrange delivery and collection of guests to and from the celebration. Diversification into the eco-wedding business helped to increase Beechenhill's sales and profit margins, reputation and brand value, as well as innovative capabilities. Wedding weekend packages currently provide a new main income for the forward-thinking farm hotel while providing a sense of getting married in the country home of friends who care about visitors and the planet.

In 2009, as a way of reducing their environmental impact, continuing to diversify, innovate and offer a distinctive experience to visitors, Sue Prince developed the Pilot Light Project—the greening of farming and tourism in a protected landscape. The purpose of the project was, first, to address rural resource efficiency, economic pressures, and reduce the carbon footprint of a tourism business in the Peak District National Park. And, second, to demonstrate the range of technologies to various stakeholders concerned with sustainability. The project served as an engagement tool with various stakeholders such as Keele University, Marches Energy Agency, The Peak District National Park Authority and Staffordshire Business Environment Network. Furthermore, Aberystwyth University has been involved in monitoring the ecological effects of certain initiatives and guests were also encouraged to get involved in recording changes to wildlife. Since the introduction of the Pilot Light Project, the carbon footprint of the farm has been reduced from 41 tonnes to 14.4 tonnes—despite the addition of the wedding venue and an additional dwelling. A 120 kW biomass (pellet) boiler and mini district main, which boasts 90% fuel efficiency, has helped reduce the carbon footprint by replacing two oil CH boilers and four immersion heaters, leading to a carbon saving of approximately 19 tonnes. The farm has also experienced a 90% reduction in the amount of oil used. In the same year, the family planted 500 indigenous trees in the Millennium Avenue.

As can be seen from Beechenhill's sustainability journey since 2007, Beechenhill's economic success is created through voluntary social and environmental activities that are deliberately pursued. The "journey" that sincerely originates from the imperative-for-the-sustainability-of-business, is enriched with increased stakeholder relationships, local and international charity activities and finally enhanced innovative capabilities—including the invention and integration of the eco-wedding business into Beechenhill's business model and eco-friendly product innovations such as the Wedding Weekend Package. Beechenhill indeed has evolved from the sustainability of business towards the business of sustainability throughout its journey.

A meaningful core strategy: harnessing sustainable practices to communicate with and educate others

It is very important to us that we share our place with you—after all, what is the point of standing alone in a lovely place saying "wow isn't it lovely!" We are proud of our place, proud of our eco-ventures and we delight in sharing it with you (Sue Prince, 2013).

As can be seen from the above quote, Beechenhill possesses a broader view of social and environmental responsibility and takes sustainability beyond the company walls. Sue Prince and the family have built their business on a strong belief in values-based management. For Sue, *meaning* comes from engagement in positive work that challenges a person's capacity, making a larger contribution to the overall well-being of humanity and the planet. The way things are done—sharing with others—sets the direction, the ambition and the values they would like to see exhibited in the family business and with their stakeholders. At its core is the triple bottom line principle, the foundation of their ability to create long-term value for the business itself and contribute to a more sustainable society. Delivering a memorable guest experience, which respects the environment and builds a respectful and thriving business, is seen as a great contribution Beechenhill makes to society and sustainable development, yet Beechenhill believes that there is a higher purpose than this, "to tell other people that sustainability is working".

> **Sue Prince and the family have built their business on a strong belief in values-based management**

Sue and the family truly act on their beliefs when they see systems or markets fail that hinder people from living sustainable lifestyles. They use sustainable practices to educate others and spread the word around in the wider community. For instance, they set targets to decrease their environmental footprint so successfully that they now guide others by sharing their success and challenges along their sustainability journey. They simply reach out to holiday guests, individuals, government bodies, academicians, fellow hoteliers and third parties to seek best ideas and share their learning in sustainability, co-create solutions and answers. This is reflected in Sue Prince's comments when she referred to the biggest benefit of the Pilot Light Project that she developed in 2009:

A key part of the project is the other organizations and individuals that have got involved in measuring the impact of our sustainability initiatives and giving their advice. What we end up taking home is much greater than what we contribute.

> **Beechenhill is well aware that consumers are becoming more and more environmentally conscious**

Beechenhill is well aware that consumers are becoming more and more environmentally conscious and are looking to businesses to take the lead. For Beechenhill, using "green" technologies makes sense both for increased guest comfort and a business's bottom line, yet what is essential is to demonstrate to planners, influencers, small businesses and individuals that "if Beechenhill can do it, then you can too". For Beechenhill, being sustainable also involves staying in the minds of others having demonstrated a sustainable way of living. The biggest benefit of the Pilot Light Project to the farm hotel, for instance, has been sharing the lessons they have learnt with other small businesses and encouraging and enabling others to make sustainable decisions in the future. In the three years from 2010 to 2013, 4,000 people have become aware of and experienced the environmentally friendly changes at Beechenhill Farm Hotel (annually 700 staying guests, 700 wedding guests and 300 day visitors, school groups, and Pilot Light Demo day participants for three years).

"While the Pilot Light Project has provided huge savings on carbon, the real benefits have come from having demonstrated that being environmental does not mean being 'worthy or preachy'", as the owner-manager puts it. With all the "green" technology built in the Pilot Light Project to be climate sensitive, Beechenhill guests have an improved experience through a sustainable way of living. Sue and the family further think that it is crucial to talk about ideas and concerns by visiting other businesses that have already made changes, and they firmly believe that there is nothing better than "talking to someone in the same boat".

> **Beechenhill's core strategy centres on using sustainable practices and initiatives to communicate with and educate others**

Beechenhill's core strategy centres on using sustainable practices and initiatives to communicate with and educate others. A deliberate pursuit of these voluntary social activities to share with others will in return, create positive social value through which a positive economic effect will be created.

Managing for the triple bottom line

Having assessed the important phases of evolution in Beechenhill's sustainability timeline, and its core strategy, this section will assess Beechenhill's sustainability positioning based on the relevant criteria of the Dyllick/Muff Business Sustainability Typology. The three criteria of the typology reflect elements of a typical business process model: 1) the relevant concerns (drivers, motivations); 2) the organizational perspectives applied (starting with societal challenges (outside-in) vs. starting with existing business, strategy or product-lines (inside-out)); and 3) type of value created.

Focus on three-dimensional concerns

Sustainability requires a multi-faceted perspective indeed; while the traditional business perspective is one-dimensional with economic concerns, the sustainability perspective typically includes the three concerns of social, environmental and economic issues. Corporate sustainability strategies are therefore challenged to recognize both market sustainability as well as social and environmental sustainability, equally (Parnell, 2008).

Beechenhill's mission statement "to please you so that you return, in a way that pleases the planet and pleases us, too", entails a broadened stakeholder perspective. As the mission statement explicitly shows, while Beechenhill's primary concern about "pleasing guests so that they return", implies its economic concern, "the manner in which they return to please the planet and people" implies its social and environmental concerns.

The interview findings are aligned with Beechenhill's mission statement in the sense that when interviewees were asked about Beechenhill's strategic focus regarding sustainability, 90% of the interviewees (nine out of ten) mentioned that the hotel exhibits stakeholder concerns with environmental and social concerns, while only one interviewee mentioned a shift of focus from customer to societal concerns. Furthermore, when interviewees were asked about the impact of the economic downturn on the hotel's commitment to sustainability, more than half of the respondents (seven out of ten) cited that the downturn affected Beechenhill positively in the sense that many from the luxury hotel segment that cut down on their international holiday experiences downgraded to environmentally and socially responsible eco-hotels such as Beechenhill. The same interviewees further mentioned that the economic downturn highlighted the demand of stakeholders that the hotel industry needed to communicate effectively on their environmental and social commitment. While only one interviewee mentioned a stronger concern with the bottom line, two interviewees mentioned more concern with society and the planet.

The interview findings further confirmed that altruism and the owner-manager's values and lifestyle significantly influenced Beechenhill's concern on stakeholders and customers. All ten interviewees thought that Sue Prince's personal values (altruism, feeling socially responsible) and lifestyle largely accounted for Beechenhill's engagement with various stakeholders and communities. This finding suggests the importance of a company leader's personal values and lifestyle—especially for small businesses.

SCALA findings also align with the interview findings. In the SCALA survey, "Awareness of our responsibility to the environment" (100%) and "Desire for innovation and growth" (100%) were the two most widely cited motives that led the hotel to start addressing sustainability issues; the "Desire to create long-term value for stakeholders" (50%) and the "Recognition of how our company could address societal needs" (50%), were also cited. As can be seen, these motives support the aforementioned personal values that are perceived to have led to Beechenhill's noteworthy sustainability performance, and reflect the owner-manager's awareness of the three-dimensional concerns of sustainability.

Indeed, the Beechenhill team is well aware of the environmental and social issues it addresses, as well as the future concerns they feel they should address. In the SCALA survey, treating guests well and fairly, and engaging with the community through school visits, social inclusion of ethnic minority groups, and social and fitness classes, were the most widely mentioned social issues that respondents believed the hotel addresses especially well. Another social issue that was mentioned was education. Furthermore, extending use of the Hay Barn to more village events, more frequent group visits and more disabled visitors were mentioned, as social issues that the hotel is not currently addressing but that they wished it would address. All these issues mentioned truly relate to Beechenhill's social concerns.

Regarding the environmental issues that the hotel addresses especially well, climate change, biodiversity, pollution control, resource efficiency, recycling, reducing use of chemicals for cleaning, self-sufficiency, using nature friendly chemicals, and reducing water and energy use, were the most widely cited issues in the survey. Furthermore, being organic and using rainwater, were cited among the environmental issues the hotel also addresses well. When asked about the environmental issues that Beechenhill is not currently addressing that the respondents wished the hotel would address, the following issues were mentioned: public transport, training people to switch off lights, making sure all car journeys are necessary, turning down farmhouse temperatures to avoid wasting heat, more water management, using drinking water bottles, and making electric car charger and electric bikes more visible. All these issues mentioned truly relate to Beechenhill's environmental concerns.

When assessed with regard to the *concerns* criteria, Beechenhill appears to have three-dimensional concerns, typically seen in businesses that manage for the triple bottom line. Beechenhill's mission is a proactive one that entails all the three dimensions of the TBL, in a way that not only seeks to minimize negative impacts, but also seeks to please various stakeholders and provide a positive social value.

Social, environmental and economic value creation

Triple bottom line value creation is a broad concept and requires aligning the three-dimensional concerns with the values it seeks to create—relating economic, environmental and social concerns to the TBL values of sustainability. Beechenhill's triple bottom line value creation is reflected in the SCALA results where three of the four respondents think that the company is creating economic, social and environmental value by addressing sustainability issues, with only one respondent having mentioned positive contribution to solving critical societal challenges. Similarly, in the interviews the majority of the interviewees (nine out of ten) think that Beechenhill's strategic focus is on triple bottom line value creation. The same interviewees further mentioned the development and implementation of new strategies and programmes aimed at sustainability issues in a proactive way.

When further asked about "in what aspects Beechenhill contributes to societal well-being" (positive common good), the most widely cited aspect was educating relevant stakeholders, especially customers (cited nine times); and creating awareness of sustainability through increased communication and demonstration of a sustainable lifestyle. This was followed by quality of life, which entailed feeling good, empowered and valued (cited three times). Educating guests, suppliers, employees and the local community clearly seem to be Beechenhill's primary contribution to society at large.

Finally, the most widely cited societal challenge the interviewees thought that "Beechenhill can solve capitalizing on its current resources and relationships", was "more education of guests, consumers and suppliers" (cited eight times), followed by "engagement of disadvantaged people" (cited two times) and "biodiversity" (cited two times). Other invaluable interviewee insights included: "accommodating single mothers", "organizing more school trips to show children where organic food comes from", "showing people that luxury and sustainability can actually go hand in hand" and "overcoming lack of awareness in sustainability".

As can be seen, Beechenhill balances economic, social and environmental dimensions of sustainability to a certain extent; and invents, produces and reports measurable results in well-defined sustainable development areas (energy saved, carbon emissions avoided in waste management, trees planted, number of people reached out for awareness of issues) while doing this in an economically sound and profitable way. Figure 1 is a synopsis of Beechenhill's business sustainability positioning based on Dyllick and Muff's Business Sustainability Typology, as detailed in terms of concerns, organizational perspective and type of value created.

> **Beechenhill balances economic, social and environmental dimensions of sustainability**

Figure 1 Beechenhill's business sustainability positioning in the Dyllick/Muff Business Sustainability Typology

Source: Developed for this case study

Business Sustainability 2.0 – Beechenhill Farm Hotel

Concerns	Organizational perspective	Values created
Three-dimensional concerns	Inside-out	Triple bottom line

From managing risks toward managing for the triple bottom line

Social concerns
- Community engagement
- Learning from others and sharing the relevant learning and experience in sustainability
- Offering a distinctive eco experience to visitors of the Peak District
- Using sustainable practices to educate others and spread the word around the wider community

Environmental concerns
- Climate change/CO_2 footprint
- Reducing, reusing and recycling initiatives
- Rural resource efficiency

Economical concerns
- Investment for sustainable actions (Economic pressures)
- Product innovation
- Business model innovation (Diversification into tourism)

To please visitors, so that they return, in a way that pleases the planet and pleases Beechenhill

Social Value
- Sharing information and facts about organic food production.
- Enabling consumers to value products and to make sustainable decisions (responsible consumerism)
- Creating awareness of a sustainable lifestyle
- Raising the bar for excellence in sustainability and showcasing how a family-run small business can pioneer in sustainability

Environmental Value
Maintaining or enhancing the Peak District environment that supports the integration of tourism and farming (diversification).

Economical Value
Strengthening the links between non-monetary social and environmental activities on the one hand and economic success on the other hand

An "inside-out" organizational perspective

Dyllick and Muff (2013), in their typology, posit that companies usually start off with their existing business, strategy or product-lines and work on making them more sustainable (inside-out perspective), with the aim of creating social, environmental and economic values (triple bottom line). This "inside-out" perspective leads to initiatives and actions that are by nature limited in their contributions to solving sustainability challenges.

Beechenhill indeed displays this *inside-out* perspective to business by establishing its concerns within well-defined sustainability areas: social, environmental and economic. Having started out with a proactive and multi-dimensional mission statement, the hotel strives to create triple bottom line values. It first looks at the internal environment within which it operates and asks itself what it can do to address societal and environmental issues. It engages in developing and implementing new strategies and programmes, addressed at specific sustainability issues or stakeholders, such as climate change, decreasing natural resources, and education of people through sustainable lifestyles. The hotel exhibits a continuous pattern of active exchange with a broad group of stakeholders such as the Staffordshire Business and Environment Network (SBEN),[15] the National Park Authority,

---

15 The Staffordshire Business & Environment Network (SBEN) was launched in 1992, providing a membership scheme entitling members to subsidized and free initiatives

Green Tourism Business Scheme and charities such as the Friends of the Peak District. It further explores new market opportunities such as the eco-wedding business or green conference business. Although Beechenhill does not question the societal value of its products and services, it adapts existing products/services and develops new ones with improved triple bottom line value creation. In this respect, the Pilot Light Project has been harnessed to decrease the hotel's environmental impacts leading to green investments, from the biomass boiler to the double-glazed windows in the guestrooms.

> The hotel exhibits a continuous pattern of active exchange with a broad group of stakeholders

Importantly, in the interviews, all ten interviewees see Beechenhill as a true integrator, that is, the hotel's sustainability goals are seen as fully integrated into daily operations. This is also demonstrated in the SCALA where all Beechenhill team members strongly agree that the hotel's sustainability is integrated into the operating procedures and policies.

Triple bottom line management is a proactive approach to sustainability as companies create value not just as a side-effect of their business activities, but also as the result of deliberately defined goals and programmes addressed at specific sustainability issues or stakeholders. This approach is also reflected in the survey findings whereby three of the four respondents mentioned that Beechenhill's current approach to sustainability is proactive, with the one respondent having described it as an active approach. Moreover, all four respondents further thought that the hotel is very engaged with sustainability. Finally, this proactive approach to sustainability implementation was supported in the interviews, where the majority of the interviewees (seven out of ten) thought sustainability implementation is purely a business responsibility rather than the responsibility of the public sector or third parties. While two interviewees saw business responsibility as the responsibility of all parties (government, business, third parties), one interviewee believed that the responsibility belonged to government bodies.

It is this proactive approach that distinguishes Beechenhill from other hotels whose main purpose is to reduce costs and business risks, to increase reputation, thereby increasing profits and competitiveness. As far as the interviewees' justification for seeing sustainability implementation as a business responsibility was concerned, while nine interviewees mentioned the business opportunities inherent in environmental and social issues, one interviewee highlighted the advantages inherent in new business models,

---

from within the SBEN portfolio. Its mission is to support organizations to achieve long-term sustainability and maximize their business opportunities through innovative environmental activity. The Network helps raise business awareness through seminars and enhance skills and knowledge through environmental training and counselling. It also provides practical advice on developing and implementing environmental policies as well as promoting examples of good environmental practice. With Staffordshire County Council providing its support and also acting as secretariat, SBEN has a proven track record and an enviable reputation for quality and customer service.

facilitated through sector-wide or cross-sectoral collaborations with others. The results clearly suggest that the Beechenhill team does not only feel responsible for the environment, but also has a nose for business, which senses business opportunities inherent in environmental awareness.

True sustainability, however, works the other way around by starting with sustainability challenges, and questions how company resources and competences can be used and adapted to make *business sense* of these challenges. This requires the organizational perspective to shift from *inside-out* to *outside-in*. Overall, when judged with regard to the *organizational perspective* criteria of the Dyllick and Muff's Business Sustainability Typology, Beechenhill appears to possess an *inside-out* organizational perspective, typical in businesses that manage for the TBL.

After having positioned Beechenhill as a business that manages for the TBL, we now look at the organizational and cultural underpinnings of this TBL strategy. While organizational culture plays an important role in organizational strategies, it matters even more with sustainability strategies due to the unique and challenging context they require. Most sustainability-related research over the past few years showed that culture is important in the success of sustainability strategies (Miller-Perkins, 2011).

Thus, the following section will focus on understanding various aspects of Beechenhill's sustainability culture, which largely accounts for the hotel's success as a best practice hotel in the field of sustainability, and may also serve as the building block for the hotel's future sustainability strategies.

A values-based sustainability leadership and culture

Creating a new or reviving a mission statement for a business is one thing and rallying team members around this new mission and bringing about a true mind-set shift in sustainability is another. Sustainability lies deep in Beechenhill's culture. It means that environmental and social concerns are not a one-man duty, but rather a whole organizational commitment. In Beechenhill's case, business operations are underpinned by a strong values system, and decisions and actions are always considered in relation to the owner-manager's values. Thus, this purpose shift and the recognition of social and environmental concerns in addition to economic concerns, appear to have happened more easily as the owner-manager Sue and her family typically set out to meet an environmental or social concern based on consistent values across the family business. A strong sustainability values system, which is espoused both widely and deeply in a company, can help ensure that sustainability performance is not jeopardized by questionable practices elsewhere in the company. Finally, shared values are essential to developing and implementing triple bottom line value creation, establishing cross-sector partnerships and educating others through using sustainable practices.

Organizational culture includes norms and personal values regarding appropriate and desirable actions with others outside and within the walls of the organization (Miller Perkins, 2011). A strong corporate values system is the building block for a positive and constructive organizational culture that is associated with more positive staff morale, improved service quality, and greater sustainability of existing and future sustainability initiatives (Glisson, 2007). Thus, understanding how sustainability culture and values relate to sustainability implementation is of utmost importance to practitioners in facilitating sustainability transformation. For instance, lifestyle and value-driven companies communicate the greater number of environmental, social and economic activities, compared with competitiveness-driven companies that practice fewer eco-savings activities, and legitimization-driven companies that report a broad spectrum of activities that are harder to quantify (Font et al., 2014).

To describe in more detail how Beechenhill's sustainability culture and shared values support the implementation of its sustainability strategy, we rely on the SCALA results, which are presented below.

Organizational leadership

Organizational leadership refers to those who are in formal positions of authority from the executives at the top of the organization down through the ranks of the organization (Miller-Perkins, 2011). Companies whose leaders have a clear vision for sustainability would be in a better position to achieve sustainability-related goals. It appears that Sue is highly driven by values that are both feminine such as cooperation, intuitive and holistic thinking, and masculine such as competition and rational thinking. A balanced combination of these values is indeed ideal for sustainability leadership. According to the SCALA results, all four respondents agreed that their leader has a clear vision for sustainability. All respondents further agreed that their leader takes a long-term view when making decisions.

Previous research shows that companies that have a sound business case for their sustainability strategies in the first place are likely to find it easier to integrate sustainability into their decision making (Miller-Perkins, 2011). This is also the case with Beechenhill, as three out of the four respondents agreed that their leader has a clear business case for pursuing the goals of sustainability, with one respondent having expressed neutrality. Yet, when asked about whether their leader integrates sustainability into their decision-making, all four respondents agreed.

Another important aspect of effective governance is smooth implementation of strategies and goals. This applies to sustainability as well. It is noteworthy that in the interviews held with the Beechenhill team and its external stakeholders, it was neither the disengagement of employees nor internal resistance to change that presented a challenge facing Beechenhill. Rather, insufficient resources (financial, time, type of building) were the most widely cited challenge (eight out of ten) in the hotel's implementation of sustainability. While one interviewee saw communication and marketing of sustainability as a challenge, another interviewee commented on the disadvantage of being a first mover as a small hotel engaged with sustainability.

Two other indicators regarding Beechenhill's governance and leadership success are how the team perceives the hotel's as well as their leader's performance relative to those of other companies in the industry. In the SCALA survey, all four respondents rated Beechenhill better than other companies in the industry with regard to sustainability leadership. Similarly, all respondents reported that their leader compared better than the leaders of other companies in their region with regard to commitment to sustainability.

Companies with leaders who can inspire others with their visions would be more apt to create momentum for their sustainability initiatives. This appears to hold true for Beechenhill, as all respondents agreed that the leader of their company is able to inspire others about sustainability-focused issues and initiatives.

Finally, success with sustainability requires corporate leaders to possess a clear understanding of the issues and the personal commitment to address them. The literature indicates that leadership commitment is critical to successful implementation of sustainability strategies (Eccles *et al.*, 2012). Furthermore, courage to take risks plays a crucial role in leading companies to incremental or radical improvements in the journey. The Beechenhill SCALA data show that all four respondents agreed that the leader of the company is willing to take measured risks in pursuit of sustainability. All four respondents further agreed that the leader of the hotel is knowledgeable of the issues pertaining to sustainability. Finally, all four respondents agreed that their leader is personally committed to issues pertaining to sustainability.

Organizational systems

Organizational systems are the mechanisms through which work is regulated and results are measured and communicated (Miller-Perkins, 2011). The author further asserts that in order to meet sustainability goals, organizations need systems for regulating work and measuring and communicating results. The Beechenhill SCALA data show that all four respondents agree that the hotel has embedded sustainability into the operating procedures and policies. Yet, when asked about whether the hotel utilized an enterprise wide management system, consensus was lower (two respondents only). Similarly, two respondents agreed that the company has integrated sustainability-related goals into the performance management system. Finally, when asked about whether rewards and compensation are clearly linked to the organization's goals, two respondents strongly agreed whereas the other 50% expressed neutrality.

These findings were also supported in the interviews where the majority of the interviewees (nine out of ten) mentioned that sustainability was fully integrated into line functions, with one interviewee having mentioned a new business model centred on societal challenges with new alliances and partners.

Organizational climate

Miller-Perkins (2011) defines organizational climate as the characteristics of the internal environment as experienced by its members. The long-termism of sustainability entails uncertainty, which can be challenging for organizations. Thus, understanding of the organizational climate can contribute to more predictable corporate behaviour and sustainability implementation. Levels of trust are an important indicator of organizational climate in an environment of uncertainty. In the SCALA survey, all respondents agreed that the level of trust within their organization is high. Also, all respondents agreed that most people in the hotel believe that a commitment to sustainability is essential to the company's success in the long term.

The degree to which an organization supports learning is another aspect of organizational climate as leaders may consider enhancing the organizational climate to succeed in uncertainty. Three of the four Beechenhill team members agreed that continual learning is a core focus of their organization, with one respondent having expressed disagreement. One way of facilitating organizational learning is to encourage people to learn from external sources. In the SCALA survey, all four respondents agreed that their company encourages people to learn about sustainability from external sources.

Finally, organizational cultures that are willing to take risks and are committed to innovation are highly likely to thrive when faced with ambiguity (Miller-Perkins, 2011). The Beechenhill data show that three of the four respondents agreed that their company rewards innovation, whereas one respondent reported neutrality.

Change readiness

Sustainability goals and strategies require organizational change; thus, organizational cultures that excel in the capability of handling change are more likely to thrive with their sustainability initiatives (Miller-Perkins, 2011). Handling change entails both the ability to sense and act on change signals as well as the ability to experiment rapidly and economically to learn new and better ways of coping with change (Reeves *et al.*, 2012). This is reflected in the degree to which people actively challenge the status quo. In the SCALA survey, all four respondents think that the hotel actively challenges the status quo.

Previous research suggests that the best predictor of future behaviour is often past behaviour; thus, past change efforts are an important indicator in assessing change readiness. Three of the Beechenhill team members reported that the hotel has a strong track record of implementing large-scale change successfully while one respondent reported neutrality. When small, incremental change was considered, all team members agreed that their company has a strong track record for implementing incremental change successfully.

Internal stakeholders

Internal stakeholders are groups or individuals within the bounds of the organization who can affect or are affected by the achievement of the sustainability objectives (Miller-Perkins, 2011). Sustainability efforts are successfully implemented in organizations where employees feel valued by the company, and care about the company and its values. Such organizations further believe that sustainability means more than an added cost to the hotel. Beechenhill's internal stakeholders are the family members, who make up its corporate culture. In the SCALA survey, all four respondents believe that the hotel has a clear strategy for engaging all internal stakeholders in its sustainability efforts. Regarding perceptions of congruence between sustainability goals and strategies, again all of the Beechenhill team believes that they are engaged in work that is connected to sustainability goals. Furthermore, all team members believe that the hotel values them and their contribution.

External stakeholders

External stakeholders are groups or individuals outside of the organization who can affect or are affected by the achievement of the sustainability objectives (Miller-Perkins, 2011). External stakeholders play a crucial role in giving organizations a systems advantage as they enable organizations to extend their adaptive capacity beyond their own organizational boundaries to include a network of partners and collaborators in the broader ecosystem (Reeves *et al.*, 2012). The adaptive capacity increases as organizations continuously go through the social interactions that external stakeholders provide as learning platforms. Thornton *et al.* (2012) assert that social exchanges serve as the tool to organizational change and that social interactions provide the key motor that transforms organizational practices.

Beechenhill indeed has an extensive range of external stakeholders, which include visitors, previous guests, suppliers, consultants, the National Park Authority members, Staffordshire Business and Environment Network (SBEN) members and various charities such as Friends of the Peak District. This is demonstrated in the SCALA survey whereby all four respondents believe that the hotel has mechanisms in place to actively engage with external stakeholders about its sustainability efforts. Beechenhill further appears to possess a consistent and integrated engagement strategy that deliberately targets key external stakeholders. In the SCALA survey, all team members agreed that their company sends a clear and consistent message about the hotel's commitment to sustainability.

Finally, Beechenhill's focus appears to have shifted from *the firm* to *the ecosystem*. This is strikingly evident in the hotel's sustainable sourcing strategy that builds on the capabilities of its suppliers. Beechenhill is aware of the fact that the hotel does not operate in isolation from its surroundings and that, to compete and thrive, it needs reliable local suppliers that believe in the benefits of sustainable practices. In the SCALA, all four respondents believe that the hotel encourages sustainability in its supply.

The "distinctive" role of sustainability values in creating social capital

Values as building blocks of corporate culture

As the SCALA findings highlight, Beechenhill's culture is well aligned with its sustainability strategy and goals. The hotel has a clear business case for sustainability and excels in integrating its mission and sustainability goals into the sustainability decisions, and into its operating policies, procedures and performance management systems. Rewards and compensation, to a certain extent, are linked to Beechenhill's sustainability goals. The owner-manager appears to be knowledgeable, inspiring, risk loving and personally committed to sustainability. Furthermore, all team members believe that a commitment to sustainability is essential to the company's success in the long term. The level of trust, continual learning and focus on innovation are also prevalent. The small family business has a strong track record for implementing both large-scale and incremental change successfully, which explains its continuous progress in the sustainability journey, and can signal progressive sustainability strategies toward becoming a truly sustainable company. Finally, the hotel is quite capable of actively challenging the status quo and engaging both internal and external stakeholders in its sustainability initiatives. Thus, Beechenhill appears to possess a balanced mix of externally focused, adaptable and flexible organizational culture as well as an internally focused, stable and durable culture. As the timeline suggests, the hotel appears to be evolving more towards the externally focused end of the continuum with increasing stakeholder relationships, which largely constitute Beechenhill's social capital.

Understandably, values, ideologies and beliefs play a crucial role in understanding a company's culture, and have been viewed as a reliable representation (Howard, 1998). The organizational learning literature has largely focused on organizational values to assess and measure organizational culture. A number of studies suggest that the successful implementation of culture change for business sustainability might be largely dependent on the values and ideological underpinnings of a company's culture, and that these in turn affect how business sustainability is implemented (Cameron et al., 1993; Jarnagin and Slocum, 2007). Indeed, a manager's/owner's view of what constitutes sustainability does influence the interpretation and implementation of their sustainability practices.

The SCALA findings for Beechenhill do support this fact, as all Beechenhill team members agree that the hotel's sustainability initiatives are mainly influenced by their personal values, beliefs, perception of environmental imperatives and awareness of the type of action required. Interviews with Beechenhill family members and external stakeholders further shed light on Sue's personal values, which have largely permeated Beechenhill's culture. The most cited values were: authentic hospitality with passion and service with heart; environmental awareness through action; treating visitors and guests with helpfulness and compassion as members of a family; community at work and having fun; and finally, desire to continuously innovate and improve. As the interview findings suggest, Beechenhill's strong lifestyle and values orientation largely stem from living in the valued landscapes of the Peak District, which often means that the sustainability component is critical in a protected environment where natural resources have to be cared for. This is understandable as Sue and the family naturally behave in a sustainable manner through their lifestyle choices.

Finally, the owner-manager Sue's personal leadership style for business sustainability largely relies on feminine principles: caring, making intuitive decisions, having a sense of work as being part of their life and not separate from it, putting the family's labour where their love is, being responsible to the world in how they use their profits, and recognizing that the bottom line should stay at the bottom. One explanation for this may be that the degree of environmental commitment and sustainability varies across cultures as culture values differ (Randall et al., 1993). For instance, in masculine cultures, the dominant values in society are success, money and possessions, whereas in feminine cultures the dominant values in society are caring for others and the quality of life and well-being (Hofstede, 1981, 2001). Similarly, more feminine cultures will exhibit higher levels of environmental sustainability (Park *et al.*, 2007). Although various studies have found cultural aspects to affect environmental sustainability, elaborating on this cultural aspect of sustainability such as masculinity versus femininity falls outside the scope of this case study.

Values as a major contributor to social capital

Strikingly, research suggests that lifestyle and value-driven tourism businesses report the greater number of environmental, social and economic activities, which in turn help increase their social capital (Font *et al.*, 2014). Social capital resides in the value of the owner-manager's and the family's network. Defined as "the nature of power and meaning that exists as structures and mechanisms guiding everyday social practice" (Fuller and Tian, 2006), social capital includes intangible assets that compose the guiding principles of the long-term performance of SMEs: reputation, trust, legitimacy and consensus (Russo and Tencati, 2009). Furthermore, this is often influenced through caring for business stakeholders, environment and society at large. In this context, sustainability is associated with responsibility and is defined by the owner-manager's values, which are articulated as integrity, honesty, respect, quality, service and sustainability (www.beechenhill.co.uk/sueprinceartist) in Beechenhill's case. As such, Sue Prince explains her reasons for sustainability engagement as a moral and ethical argument together with pride and the sense of *doing the right thing*. This can be linked to the development of social capital, with most benefits being unquantifiable and most businesses not preferring to look at sustainability in economic terms, even when such benefits were also realized (Tzschentke *et al.* 2004, 2008).

Although small firms are generally found to be shy to communicate their sustainability messages and make limited use of their sustainability actions to attract customers, we clearly see that Beechenhill has successfully managed to capitalize on transparency, communication and sharing the eco-experience with others in its sustainability journey. The communication of sustainability achievements and awards gained helps create social capital that can create competitive advantage through protecting reputation (Font *et al.*, 2014). Although Sue Prince mentions feeling uncomfortable *boasting*, she states that she is simply using communication rather than marketing to promote Beechenhill's sustainability achievements, rather than gaining some commercial advantage from its sustainability endeavours. The interviews strikingly highlight that this has largely to do with the owner-manager's personal leadership style and values. The interviews also demonstrate that decision-making at the hotel is often carried out as an extension of the owner-manager's personal values and lifestyle, which appears to have largely shaped this small farm hotel's culture and enacting values in ways other than shaped by profit.

Discussion and outlook

This section discusses the findings of the interviews and the SCALA survey in light of the prevalent literature. First, the distinct phases of Beechenhill's sustainability journey with reference to the phases of change in the relevant sustainability literature will be scrutinized, highlighting the motivations and drivers behind Beechenhill's sustainability initiatives in the journey. Then, implications of its key strategy of engaging and educating others through sustainable practices will be discussed from the perspective of consumers and the scale of business. Next, based on the Dyllick/Muff Business Sustainability Typology, the hotel's business sustainability positioning as a triple bottom line approach, and how this pinpoints the way forward to its becoming a truly sustainable hotel will be evaluated and justified. Then, Beechenhill's values-led organizational culture and the role of its social capital will be further discussed in order to explain the business's successful implementation of sustainability as a small hotel. Finally, the section will round off with the implications and limitations of the case study for practitioners, policy-makers and academia, respectively.

As Beechenhill's sustainability journey shows, the hotel initially started off with a voluntary compliance-oriented strategy to simultaneously go organic and differentiate. In complying with laws and non-mandatory policies as well as with voluntary third party accreditation criteria, Beechenhill started making investments in "green technology" both driven by cost savings (e.g. through resource efficiency) as well as through the responsibility to decrease environmental impact on the valued Peak District landscape. Indeed, the sustainability literature shows that core drivers of sustainability are found to be costs and cost reduction (Christmann, 2000; Epstein, 1996); sales and profit margin (Porter and van der Linde, 1995); risk and risk reduction (Schaltegger and Wagner, 2006); reputation and brand value (Marrewijk, 2003); innovative capabilities (Cohen and Winn, 2007; Schaltegger and Wagner, 2011); and attractiveness as an employer (Revell *et al.* 2010). Revell *et al.* (2010) go further to identify that cost reductions are seen as the most promising driver, followed by aspects such as dealing with regulatory risks, attracting and retaining staff, attracting new customers and increasing market share, as well as attaining good reputation. As for the tourism industry, Brown (1996) posits that one of the most influential benefits of incorporating environmental commitment in tourism accommodations is cost saving.

Although cost savings may seem like a reactive and defensive strategic behaviour that is directed towards both the protection of the existing business and revenue generating rationale (Prahalad and Bettis, 1995) and a pure compliance strategy (Roome, 1992), it is a justifiable proactive strategy since the core business and all its operational processes and products/

services are directed towards sustainability—as is the revenue logic. This refers to what Roome (1992) calls "commercial and environmental excellence". It is noteworthy that Beechenhill has been pursuing voluntary social and environmental activities not just as a by-product of business activities, but also as the result of deliberately defined goals and programmes. The initial diversification strategy as realized by Beechenhill—linking organic farming with tourism—was a proactive one as it developed its sustainability initiatives with the intention to contribute to the solution of societal and environmental issues. It launched initiatives that created a positive business effect and had a clear and convincing business case for sustainability characterized by creating economic success through (and not just along with) a certain social or environmental activity (Dyllick and Muff, 2013).

Beechenhill's sustainability journey further reflects the simultaneous pursuit of contributing to the local and global community, with the awareness of responsibility for the environment and a desire for resource efficiencies and cost savings. The hotel's pursuit of charitable activities is clearly reflected in the SCALA survey. The survey shows "recognition of how Beechenhill could address societal needs" and "desire to create long-term value for stakeholders" as the two equally perceived secondary motives behind the hotel's sustainability-related activities, after "awareness of responsibility for the environment" and "desire for innovation and growth", which are the equally perceived primary drivers that led the hotel to start addressing sustainability issues. Beechenhill's investments in CSR projects and donations, such as the funding for Practical Action, the Wetton and Alstonefield First Responders and the Friends of the Peak District, are highly likely to contribute, directly or indirectly, to the hotel's bottom line. This is certainly in line with Waldman and Siegel's (2008) assertion that CSR derives from instrumental thinking to maximize the wealth of the firm. However, Beechenhill's understanding of responsibility goes beyond charitable donations, and further entails sharing the *eco-experience* with others and educating them on quality of life issues such as a sustainable lifestyle.

As one could see from the hotel's journey from 2008 onwards, the farm hotel has progressively improved the quality, quantity, cost and reliability of its inputs and operational processes while simultaneously acting as a steward for essential natural resources of the Peak District and driving economic and social development. This has consequently led to reconceiving differentiated products and services such as the eco-wedding business, and a new conference offer which utilizes the converted Hay Barn for conferences, workshops and meetings of up to 50 delegates. Currently, plans for organizing an annual prize for the greenest wedding on site is under consideration. Indeed, improving value in one area —such as resource efficiency—gives rise to opportunities in other areas, such as accessing new markets or lowering costs through innovation (Porter and Kramer, 2011, p. 7).

Overall, Beechenhill appears to have a convincing business case for sustainability. Its proactive strategy integrates environmental and social objectives as part of the core business logic. As our findings explicitly show, both Beechenhill's farm and tourism business processes and products are directed towards sustainability, as is its revenue logic. The farm hotel clearly addresses efficiency and cost-related aspects, develops sustainability-oriented innovation capabilities and addresses customer issues as well as societal *non-market* issues such as enabling others to make sustainable choices and practices. In other words, Beechenhill strives for business leadership through outstanding sustainability performance and creates a justifiably persistent *halo effect* by consistently sharing its outstanding performance and sustainability experience with others, as awareness about sustainability and local community contribution tend to affect consumers' purchase intentions (Lee and Shin, 2010). Similarly, sharing information and providing awareness for guests on environmental issues, promoting sustainability-oriented local businesses and encouraging organic product consumption and/or sustainable lifestyles would benefit hotels to engage more guests in their sustainability initiatives (Scorcher and Brant, 2002; Rosenzweig, 2007).

Unsurprisingly, Beechenhill successfully engages guests in the hotel's sustainability practices. For instance, upon request, couples are directed toward sustainable caterers and suppliers to turn their wedding celebration into a green one. As some studies about guests' preferences among hotels' sustainability activities reveal, guests mostly value guest experience-related activities rather than those focusing on minimizing ecological impacts (McGehee and Andereck, 2009). Furthermore, the literature suggests that engaging consumers is akin to *building a reservoir of goodwill*, and that consumers feel a sense of attachment or connection with companies engaging in sustainability initiatives they care about, which is called *consumer–company identification* (Bhattacharya and Sen, 2004). It may be this identification that prompts Beechenhill's visitors and guests to engage in the hotel's sustainability initiatives and a variety of behaviours favourable to the hotel (e.g. word of mouth, loyalty)—and in this respect, it may be a pivotal driver of the positive effects of Beechenhill's sustainability initiatives on company stakeholders' patronage behaviour.

Yet, while some literature informs us that small businesses lack sufficient influence or resources to sufficiently attend to stakeholder concerns and societal social issues (Spencer and Heinze, 1973), more recent literature suggests that small businesses may indeed be more generous in the support of society compared to larger corporations. Indeed, in many cases, it is the smaller businesses that are prominent examples of companies gaining competitive advantage by employing environmental strategies (Hoffman, 2000). In this sense, Beechenhill is a very good example of how a small business makes "business sense" of environmental and social issues, and implements TBL value creation.

Through a triple bottom line approach, Beechenhill contributes to environmental and social value creation, in addition to the economic imperatives businesses are driven by. As such, the hotel not only decreases its negative impact on the environment but also contributes positively to the creation of social value by sharing the eco-experience with others and enabling others to learn from their experience and lead sustainable lifestyles. Importantly, Beechenhill's economic success is not increased while performing environmental and social issues, but rather a positive economic effect is created based on these intended social and environmental activities and initiatives. Beechenhill indeed harnesses a good understanding of how the drivers of a business case can be positively influenced by environmental and societal activities. Beechenhill's approach to sustainability is in line with literature, which posits that a sustainable hotel at its best refers to a hotel that voluntarily implements sustainable practices to reconcile social, environmental and economic concerns, to create a triple bottom line (people, planet, profit) value (Sloan *et al.* 2013). Yet, Dyllick and Hockerts (2002) argue that businesses need to go beyond multi-dimensional business contributions to sustainability and become eco-effective or socio-effective by solving the sustainability issues of societies. Similarly, Dyllick and Muff (2013) posit, in their Business Sustainability Typology, that truly sustainable businesses have a holistic approach and thus question their businesses' societal value rather than economic, social and environmental value creation. This would require that, in addition to adapting existing and developing new products with improved triple bottom line value creation, they also need to question the societal value and actively respond to societal challenges which may occur as a result of collaboration with new partners (Dyllick and Muff, 2013).

Beechenhill excels in TBL value creation, largely due to its most precious asset—its organizational culture—which comprises their values, beliefs and sustainable lifestyles. As Tzschentke (2008) argues, sustainability largely relies on the capacities and abilities of managers to implement them. Indeed, a values-based sustainability leadership constitutes the heart of Beechenhill's success as a small and leading sustainable hotel. Beechenhill's motivations and practices relating to three-dimensional concerns of the TBL are largely based on values rather than the resource-based view of the firm (Prahalad and Hamel, 1990; Barney, 1991), typically seen in large corporations. Understandably, small to medium-sized businesses (SMEs) are not *little big companies* adopting scaled-down versions of the products and processes of bigger companies to engage in sustainability through standard CSR activities (Morsing and Perrini, 2009; Jenkins, 2006).

> **Beechenhill excels in TBL value creation, largely due to its most precious asset—its organizational culture**

As the interview and SCALA findings demonstrate, at Beechenhill, decision-making is often carried out as an extension of the owner-manager's personal values and lifestyle, which appears to have shaped this small farm hotel's culture by enacting values and habits in ways other than shaped by profit

(Fassin *et al.*, 2011). This is in accordance with Matten and Moon's (2008) research, which shows that in SMEs, sustainability-orientation is embedded through good habits and dictated by the very nature of the environment, product or service, rather than formalized plans or procedures. It may also be that assuming a profit maximization view of the world is unhelpful in understanding small firms' sustainability behaviour, considering the particular nature of SME ownership and management (Font *et al.*, 2014). Indeed, sustainability research demonstrates that the main reason for small and medium accommodation enterprises acting responsibly is altruistic, arising from the managers' and owners' values and lifestyles (Garay and Font, 2012). Sustainability perfectly fits in with lifestyle, habits and routines for most small to medium-sized hotels and this is positively correlated with improving performance (Font *et al.*, 2014).

Finally, and most importantly, knowing that the relationship between small hotels and their environment is shaped by social capital rather than rules and policies (Werner and Spence, 2009), it becomes crucial for Beechenhill to develop its social capital—its engagement and contribution to the communities and the value of Sue and the family's networks—which will highly likely constitute the building block of its future sustainability endeavours, as a small hotel in a protected landscape.

This case study has several implications for hoteliers, policy-makers as well as academia. While it showcases to hoteliers, especially the owner-managers in protected landscapes, how small hotels in conserved environments can transform their sustainability strategies from a focus on "sustainability of business" towards "business of sustainability", it also demonstrates to policy-makers that the "business case of sustainability", which emphasizes eco-saving commercial reasons to the disengaged profit-driven businesses, might not really work as a true motivator for altruistic and value-driven small businesses. Rather, this case study emphasizes "the business case for sustainability" which entails voluntary social and environmental activities that are based on intended management activities to improve sustainability through which a positive economic effect is created. As for academia, previous studies have focused on using large companies' language with emphasis on systems and policies, and also focusing on eco-savings (Lopez-Gamero *et al.*, 2009; Pereira-Moliner *et al.*, 2012) in the search to identify how sustainability improves business performance. Thus, this case study contributes to the scarce evidence base about best practice case studies, where sustainable hotels' motivation, challenges, practices and business sustainability positioning are demonstrated with a broader focus that also includes various organizational factors such as organizational culture, concerns, type of value created, and organizational perspective used.

Finally, regarding the limitations of this study, our findings are highly likely to be applicable only to small businesses, and thus the findings cannot really be generalized either to large or chain-affiliated hotels or to hotels in non-protected areas. Furthermore, complementary research in adult and organizational learning would be invaluable to understand the sustainability journey of other small to medium-sized hotels like Beechenhill.

Peering over the horizon

As Sue finished reading the comprehensive case study, she felt blessed be to living in a protected area, which she believed had led her family and herself to seek lifestyles based on eco-friendly "alternative values", as opposed to ones centred on profit maximization alone. She was also grateful for the fact that the Peak District was designated as a protected area which meant that these values included sustainability. Ultimately, however, it was their family habits and routine—rather than a conscious managerial structure—that had made their sustainable lifestyle choices part of Beechenhill's DNA. Indeed, she was convinced that their personal ethics and altruism were a determinant and key in their lifestyle behaviour, and were crucial factors in providing a quality service in their sustainability journey.

It was true that Sue and her family had indeed been creating their social capital over the years, but more importantly, based on the case findings, Sue felt more confident that her daughter and son-in-law would build on these well-established, intangible assets that were the guiding principles of Beechenhill's long-term, sustainability performance. She believed that practising what she preached, and enabling others to learn from each other, had proved to be the most effective tool in her sustainability leadership.

Feeling thankful for the Lausanne Business School's nomination and for its objective case study, with its vindication that her beliefs and ideals were instrumental to the success of Beechenhill, she got up to find Terry and share the findings, with great hopefulness that the future of this meaningful legacy that they had passionately constructed together was on track. Remembering the famous sustainability guru, Peter Senge's saying, "Building a responsible company takes forever", she had a "eureka" moment—the idea of a potential mutual learning project in collaboration with this leading Swiss innovator in sustainability education. Such a learning opportunity could well be Beechenhill's next step on the inexorable path to perfection in the sustainable business world, where a company such as theirs not only helps to resolve societal challenges, but also succeeds in capturing people's minds and hearts as it journeys towards environmental and social stewardship.

Bibliography

Adler, P.S. & Kwon, S.W. (2002). Social capital: prospects for a new concept. *Academy of Management Review*, Vol. 27, 17-40.

Barney, J. B. (1991). Firm resources and sustained competitive advantage. *Journal of Management*, Vol. 17, 99–120.

Bhattacharya, C.B. & Sen, S. (2004). Doing better at doing good: When, why, and how consumers respond to corporate social initiatives. *California Management Review*, Vol. 47, No. 1, Fall, 9-24.

Brown, M. (1996). Environmental policy in the hotel sector: Green strategy or stratagem. *International Journal of Contemporary Hospitality Management*, Vol. 8, No. 3, 18-23.

Cameron, K. S., Freeman, S. J. & Mishra, A.K. (1993). Downsizing and Redesigning Organizations. G.P. Huber and W.H. Glick (Eds.). *Organizational Change and Redesign*, 19-63. New York: Oxford University Press.

Christmann, P. (2000). Effects of best practices of environmental management on cost advantage: The role of complementary assets. *Academy of Management Journal*, Vol. 43, 663-680.

Cohen, B. & Winn, M.I. (2007). Market imperfections, opportunity and sustainable entrepreneurship. *Journal of Business Venturing*, 22(1), 29-49.

Condon, L. (2004). Sustainability and small to medium sized enterprises: How to engage them. *Australian Journal of Environmental Education*, 20(1), 57-67.

Dyllick, T. & Hockerts, K. (2002). Beyond the business case for corporate sustainability. *Business Strategy and the Environment*, 11, 130-141.

Dyllick, T., & Muff, K. (2013). *Clarifying the meaning of sustainable business: Introducing a typology from business-as-usual to true business sustainability*. Retrieved from http://ssrn.com/abstract=2368735.

Eccles, R.G., Ioannou, I. & Serafeim, G. (2012). The impact of a corporate culture of sustainability on corporate behavior and performance. *Working Paper 12-035*, May 9, 2012. Boston: Harvard Business School.

Epstein, M.J. & Roy, M. (1996). *Measuring Corporate Environmental Performance: Best Practices for Costing and Managing an Effective Environmental Strategy*. Chicago: Irwin Professional Publ.

Fassin, Y., Van Rossem, A. & Buelens, M. (2011). Small business owner-managers' perceptions of business ethics and CSR-related concepts. *Journal of Business Ethics*, Vol. 98, 425-453.

Font, X., Garay, L. & Jones, S. (2014). Sustainability motivations and practices in small tourism enterprises. Retrieved from http://repositoryintralibrary.leedsmet.ac.uk/open_virtual_file_path/i4004n769149t/Font%20Garay%20Jones%20JCP%20pre%20publication%20version.pdf.

Fuller, T. & Tian, Y. (2006). Social and symbolic capital and responsible entrepreneurship: An empirical investigation of SME narratives. *Journal of Business Ethics*, 67, 287-304.

Garay, L. & Font, X. (2012). Doing good to do well? Corporate Social Responsibility reasons, practices and impacts in small and medium accommodation enterprises. *International Journal of Hospitality Management*, 31(2), 328-336.

Glisson, C. (2007). Assessing and changing organizational culture and climate for effective services. *Research on Social Work Practice*, 17, 736-747.

Hoffman, A. (2000). *Competitive Environmental Strategy*. Washington, D.C.: Island Press.

Hofstede, G. (1981). Culture and organizations: International studies of management and organizations, 10(4), 15-41.

Hofstede, G. (2001). *Culture's Consequences: Comparing Values, Behaviors, Institutions, and Organizations across Nations*. Thousand Oaks, CA: Sage.

Holliday, R. (1995). *Investing Small Firms: Nice Work?* London: Routledge.

Howard, L.W. (1998). Validating the competing values model as a representation of organizational cultures. *The International Journal of Organizational Analysis*, 6(3), 231-250.

Jarnagin, C. & Slocum, J.W. Jr. (2007). Creating corporate cultures through mythopoeic leadership. *Organizational Dynamic*, 36, 288-302.

Jenkins, H. (2006). Small business champions for corporate social responsibility. *Journal of Business Ethics*, 67(3), 241-256.

Lee, K.H. & Shin, D. (2010). Consumers' responses to CSR activities: the linkage between increased awareness and purchase intention. *Public Relations Review*, 36(2), 193-195.

Lopez-Gamero, M.D., Molina-Azorin, J.F., & Claver-Cortes, E. (2009). The whole relationship between environmental variables and firm performance: Competitive advantage and firm resources as mediator variables. *Journal of Environmental Management*, 90(10), 3110-3121.

Marrewijk, M. van (2003). Concepts and definitions of CSR and corporate sustainability, between agency and communion. *Journal of Business Ethics*, 44(2/3), 95-105.

Matten, D. & Crane, A. (2005). Corporate citizenship: toward an extended theoretical conceptualization. *The Academy of Management Review*, 30(1), 166-179.

Matten, D. and Moon, J. (2008). Implicit and explicit CSR: a conceptual framework for comparative understanding of corporate social responsibility. *The Academy of Management Review*, 33(2), 404-424.

McGehee, N. G., & Andereck, K. (2009). Volunteer tourism and the volunteered: The case of Tijuana, Mexico. *Journal of Sustainable Tourism*, 17(1), 39–51.

Miller-Perkins, K. (2011). Sustainability culture: Culture and leadership assessment. *Miller Consultants Inc.* Retrieved from www.millerconsultants.com/sustainability.php.

Morsing, M. & Perrini, F. (2009). CSR in SMEs: Do SMEs matter for the CSR agenda? *Business Ethics. A European Review*, 18(1), 1-6.

Nahapiet, J. & Ghoshal, S. (1998). Social capital, intellectual capital, and the organizational advantage. *Academy of Management Review*, 23, 242-266.

Park, H., Russell, C. & Lee, J. (2007). National culture and environmental sustainability: A cross-national analysis. *Journal of Economics and Finance*, 31, 104-121.

Parnell, J. (2008). Sustainable strategic management: Construct, parameters and research directions. *International Journal of Sustainable Strategic Management*, 1(1), 35-45.

Pereira-Moliner, J., Claver-Cortes, E., Molina-Azorin, J.F., & Jose Tari, J. (2012). Quality management, environmental management and firm performance: Direct and mediating effects in the hotel industry. *Journal of Cleaner Production*, 37, 82-92.

Porter, M. & Kramer, M. (2011). Creating shared value: How to reinvent capitalism and unleash a wave of innovation and growth. *Harvard Business Review*, Jan-Feb, 62-77.

Porter, M.E. & Linde, C. van der (1995). Toward a new conception of the environment/ competitiveness relationship. *Journal of Economic Perspectives*, 9(4), 97-118.

Prahalad, C. K. & Bettis, R.A. (1995). The dominant logic: Retrospective and extension. *Strategic Management Journal*, 16(1), 5-14.

Prahalad, C. K., & Hamel, G. (1990). The core competence of the corporation. *Harvard Business Review*, 68(3), 79-91.

Randall, D.M., Huo, Y.P., & Pawelk, P. (1993). Social desirability bias in cross-cultural ethics research. *International Journal of Organizational Analysis*, 2, 185-202.

Reeves, M., Haanaes, K., Love, C. & Levin, S. (2012). Sustainability as adaptability. *Journal of Applied Corporate Finance*, 24(2), 14-22.

Revell, A., Stokes, D. & Chen, H. (2010). Small businesses and the environment: Turning over a new leaf? *Business Strategy and the Environment*, 19(5), 273-288.

Roome, N. (1992) Developing environmental management strategies. *Business Strategy and the Environment*, 1(1), 11-24.

Rosenzweig, P. (2007). Misunderstanding the nature of company performance: The halo effect and other business delusions. *California Management Review* 49(4), 6–20.

Russo, A. & Tencati, A. (2009). Formal vs informal CSR strategies: Evidence from Italian micro, small, medium-sized and large firms. *Journal of Business Ethics*, 85, 339-353.

Schaltegger, S. & Wagner, M. (eds.) (2006). *Managing the Business Case for Sustainability.* Sheffield: Greenleaf.

Schaltegger, S. & Wagner, M. (2011). Sustainable entrepreneurship and sustainability innovation: categories and interactions. *Business Strategy and the Environment*, 20(4), 222-237.

Scorcher, M. & Brant, J., Are you picking the right leaders? *Harvard Business Review*, February 2002.

Shrivastava, P. (1995). *Greening Business: Profiting the Corporation and the Environment*; Cincinnati: Thompson Executive Press.

Sloan, P., Legrand, W. & Chen, J.S. (2013) *Sustainability in the Hospitality Industry: Principles of Sustainable Operations.* 2nd edition. New York, NY: Routledge.

Spence, L., Schmidpeter, R., & Habisch, A. (2003). Assessing social capital: Small and medium sized enterprises in Germany and the U.K. *Journal of Business Ethics*, 47, 17-29.

Spencer, H. & Heinze, D. (1973). Decision making for social involvement: Some criteria and model theoretic. In Green, T. & Ray, D. (1973), *Academy of Management Proceedings, 33rd Annual Meeting, Boston, Mass, August 19-22*, 601-607.

Stawiski, S., Deal, J.J. & Gentry, W. (2010). Employee perceptions of corporate social responsibility: The implications for your organization. *Quick View Leadership Series*, Center for Creative Leadership: USA.

Thornton, P.H., Ocasio, W. & Lounsbury, M. (2012). *The Institutional Logics Perspective: A New Approach to Culture, Structure and Process*. Cambridge: Oxford University Press.

Tzschentke, N., Kirk, D., & Lynch, P.A. (2004). Reasons for going green in serviced accommodation establishments. *International Journal of Contemporary Hospitality Management*, 16(2), 116-124.

Tzschentke, N., Kirk, D., & Lynch, P.A. (2008). Going green: Decisional factors in small hospitality operations. *International Journal of Hospitality Management*, 27(1), 126-133.

Waldman, D.A. & Siegel, D.S. (2008). Theoretical and practitioner letters: Defining the socially responsible leader. *Leadership Quarterly*, 19, 117-131.

Werner, A. & Spence, L.J. (2009). Literature review: Social capital and SMEs. In L. J. Spence, A. Habish, and R. Schmidpeter (Eds.) *Responsibility and Social Capital: The World of Small and Medium Sized Enterprises*. (pp. 7-24). New York, NY: Palgrave Macmillan.

Appendix: The Dyllick/Muff Business Sustainability Typology

The Dyllick/Muff Business Sustainability Typology uses three elements of a typical business process model: the relevant concerns considered (inputs), the type of value created (outputs), and the organizational perspectives applied (processes) (Dyllick and Muff, 2013). Dyllick and Muff draw attention to the fact that the broader sustainability perspective typically entails social, environmental and economic concerns, in contrast to the traditional business perspective that entails economic concerns only. Regarding the type of value created, Dyllick and Muff highlight the need for businesses to contribute to the positive common good by going beyond triple bottom line value creation. They envisage true business sustainability as one that contributes to resolving environmental, social or economic issues on a regional or global scale. Finally, regarding the organizational perspectives applied, the authors turn around the traditional *inside-out* perspective that aims to invent, produce and measure within the three-dimensional sustainability aspects, to an *outside-in* perspective that starts with sustainability challenges that lie beyond the company boundaries (see Fig. A1). The typology aims to serve scholars and practitioners by clarifying the drivers and aims of business sustainability (Hashmi and Muff, 2014). As Business Sustainability (BS) evolves from 1.0 to 2.0 and 3.0, respectively, the relevance and contribution to resolve societal issues increase, with Business Sustainability 3.0 exhibiting "true business sustainability".

Figure A1 Typology of business sustainability and their key characteristics
Source: Dyllick & Muff 2013

BUSINESS SUSTAINABILITY TYPOLOGY (BST)	Concerns (What?)	Values created (What for?)	Organizational perspective (How?)
Business-as-usual	Economic concerns	Shareholder value	Inside-out
Business Sustainability 1.0	Three-dimensional concerns	Refined shareholder value	Inside-out
Business Sustainability 2.0	Three-dimensional concerns	Triple bottom line	Inside-out
Business Sustainability 3.0	Starting with sustainability challenges	Creating value for the common good	Outside-in
The key shifts involved:	1st shift: broadening the business concern	2nd shift: expanding the value created	3rd shift: changing the perspective

At the level BS.1, a business responds to extra-market business challenges that result from environmental or social concerns that are typically voiced by external stakeholders. Thus, managing economic risks and opportunities takes precedence as a strategy. While the focus is primarily on managing risks, embracing opportunities typically follows later. Existing strategies, outlooks, products and services remain unchanged. There are often no changes in the corporate structure in terms of governance and leadership focuses on seeking opportunities. There is often a central function or unit in charge of or coordinating response to sustainability challenges, and the reporting is mostly on good news and economic benefits. Primary corporate attitude is basically reacting to societal pressures for the purpose of refined shareholder value.

At the more advanced BS.2 level, the stakeholder perspective is broadened with the aim of creating social and environmental values in addition to economic value; in other words, the business manages for the triple bottom line through particular programmes that are consequently measured and reported. The primary focus is on developing and implementing new strategies and programmes that are addressed at specific sustainability issues or stakeholders. The business further reconceives new products and markets. While existing products and services are adapted, new products and services are also developed to improve triple bottom line value creation, yet without questioning their societal value. Sustainability goals are integrated into planning and reporting cycles as well as into management and governance structures, mainly through cross-functional committees, policies and guidelines. Furthermore, sustainability goals and activities are embedded in line functions as part of sustainability implementation. While internal reporting includes differentiated triple bottom line activities and results, external reporting includes reporting on sustainability goals and achievements, which is often externally verified. Primary corporate attitude entails a pattern of active exchange with a broad group of stakeholders for the purpose of social, environmental and economic values (triple bottom line), yet still with an "inside-out" organizational perspective.

Finally, at the BS.3 "true business sustainability" level, there is a shift in mind-set from minimizing negative impacts to creating positive impacts in significant issues relevant to the society and the planet. This derives from an "outside-in" organizational perspective, unlike those prevalent in the lower levels of business sustainability. Capabilities and resources are redefined to resolve societal issues that form the baseline for new strategies, business models, products and services. At this advanced level, companies engage in changing the collective rules of the game through sector-wide or cross-sectoral strategies. The primary focus is on societal concerns that supersede focus on customers. Furthermore, markets and strategies derive from societal challenges. New products and services are created as a voluntary and proactive response to societal challenges, likely in collaboration with new partners. The company governance structure includes relevant societal representatives who contribute to the relevant decision-making processes throughout the organization. The company re-organizes around the societal issues it addresses and includes new players in these open and dynamic structures. Reporting entails societal value creation with different societal stakeholders. Primary corporate attitude entails a pattern of voluntary, proactive as well as interactive collaboration with new players for the purpose of creating value for the common good.

✉ Armand Calinescu Street no.19, Sector 2, Bucharest, Romania

☎ +90 532 2618027

💻 gulen.hashmi@bsl-lausanne.ch

Interloop Limited

A journey from ethics to business sustainability

Shamaila Gull

Business School Lausanne, Switzerland

Introduction

This case study is aimed to highlight the distinguishing attributes of sustainable organizations in comparison with their traditional counterparts in the context of a developing country. The insights gained from this case study will be beneficial for the managers of other local textile organizations which are at the early stages of adopting sustainability as an emerging paradigm. The case study is written in the form of an organized journey comprising history, current status and future perspectives of the organization. Additionally, the case study examines the sustainability culture of the chosen organization for a deeper understanding of cultural characteristics of sustainable organizations. The interpretation of the organization with the Business Sustainability Typology Matrix will help us to understand the multiple concerns, the values created and perspectives adopted by sustainable organizations. Moreover, the case study will help practitioners and academics to learn about the business sustainability practices from the perspective of a developing country by serving the following objectives:

▶ Assess the sustainability position of Interloop based on the ongoing business practices

▶ Understand the cultural dimensions of Interloop from sustainability perspective

▶ Analyse the positioning of Interloop on the Business Sustainability Typology Matrix presented by Dyllick and Muff (2015)

▶ Contribute to a wider pool of case studies of sustainable organizations from various industries of different regions, to facilitate an exchange of know-how among practitioners as well as between academia and the business world

The case study is part of a doctoral dissertation at the Business School of Lausanne (BSL), Switzerland and it is part of a cohort of similar case studies in different industries and in different regions of the world. The task includes identifying two sustainability leaders in a specific region of the world and analysing their cases from a sustainability perspective. The organizations chosen are also recognized for their achievements and contributions to adopt and implement sustainability in their local geographical region.

The sample chosen for this research work is from the textile sector of Pakistan and the objective is to identify the core characteristics of sustainable organizations in the Pakistani textile sector and share them with the purpose of facilitating other such organizations aspiring to adopt sustainability. The research work is based on both secondary and primary sources of data used to highlight the sustainability perspective of the organization. Additionally, the organization was chosen based on the following points:

> It had to be geographically located in Pakistan

> It had to be a recognized sustainability leader in this region with some awards or third party certifications in this regard

> It had to have significant contributions from social and environmental perspectives

> It had to be ranked on the business sustainability typology from level Sustainability 1.0 to Sustainability 3.0

> It had to be from the textile sector in order to provide a comparison base with other organizations of the same sector

Once the organization was selected based on the above criteria, secondary data collection was done to gain an insight about the organization. Organizational news letters were also considered to gather the secondary data. The primary sources of data were SCALA survey results (which will be explained in later sections) and interviews. For qualitative data, interviews were conducted for which six internal stakeholders and one external stakeholder were taken as the sample. An interview protocol was approved by the instructors of BSL keeping in view the specific research requirements. The details of interviewees are shown in Table 1.

Table 1 Interviewees

Sr No.	Name	Designation
1.	Mr Musaddaq Zulqarnain	Chief Executive Officer (CEO)
2.	Mr Ghulam Qasim	Deputy General Manager EHS
3.	Mr Muhammad Maqsood	Director Finance
4.	Ms Fareha Zafar	Deputy General Manager OD
5.	Ms Rahat	Deputy Manager Internal Audits
6.	Mr Ghulam Mohauddin	Deputy General Manager Taxation
7.	Mr Roudy Damen	CEO Euro Sox

Overview of textile sector of Pakistan

The textile sector is considered to be the backbone of Pakistan's economy. Pakistan is the eighth largest exporter of textile products in Asia. This sector contributes 9.5% to the GDP and provides employment to about 30% of the manufacturing workforce of the country (Tribune, 2013). According to this report, Pakistan is the fourth largest producer of cotton with the third largest spinning capacity in Asia after China and India, and contributes 5% to the global spinning capacity. For Pakistan as one of the leading producers of cotton in the world, the development of a textile industry, thereby making full use of its abundant resources of cotton, has been a priority area towards industrialization. There are 1,221 ginning units, 442 spinning units, 124 large spinning units and 425 small units which produce textile products. The significance of the textile industry in Pakistan's economy can be gauged from the fact that it contributes more than 67% to the total export earnings of the country, makes up 27% of added industrial value, and constitutes 31% of total manufacturing investment.

Among the crucial challenges that the Pakistani textile industry is facing today, the most important are how to improve labour exploitation and reduce its environmental footprint to international standards. At present, the textile sector is not only depleting natural resources but also seriously affecting the quality of life. For instance, there is random disposal of industrial waste water along with substantial atmospheric pollution by the textile sector. Such activities require proper legislation by the regulatory authorities, for instance, the Pakistan Environmental Protection Act (PEPA), in order to control the environmental issues. However, the compliance requirements for textile exporters are the main driving force in this industry. Compliance with internationally defined standards for air emissions, waste water disposal and use of hazardous chemicals is a global demand by end users thus encouraging the organizations to reduce their environmental footprint (Interview Qasim).

Similarly, another major challenge faced by the industrial sector of Pakistan is the social and ethical impacts of the business activities. The textile sector not being an exception faces the pressures of social and ethical compliance like other business sectors in the country. Lack of awareness, low literacy rate, workforce exploitation, inappropriate safety measures and discrimination are major causes of social and ethical challenges faced by the industry. The current global business environment is motivating organizations to consider the full social and ethical impacts of their corporate activities and policies. Global warming, depletion of the ozone layer and child labour are examples which have forced the corporate world to reconsider and redesign their business so as to reduce the negative social and environmental footprints. Those companies which are able to demonstrate a responsible approach towards broader social and ethical issues gain a competitive edge and inspire the confidence of stakeholders such as clients, investors, local communities and consumers. Moreover, in order to address these issues and to satisfy their stakeholders, local textile organizations are increasingly gearing towards social certifications such as OHSAS 18001[1] (occupational health & safety assessment series) and SA8000.[2]

The textile sector like other sectors of the country is striving for sustainable development by addressing the environmental and social issues along with economic interests. However, social, cultural and economic barriers are hindering any effort to solve these environmental and social issues. Textile organizations are adopting different measures to comply with international standards by addressing the burning environmental and social issues. The textile organizations well understand the fact that international clients can only be attracted by addressing these issues which will ultimately improve the economic situations as well. This is mainly because international clients demand socially and environmentally sustainable supply chains (interview Zulqarnain). The demands of big international clients such as Nike, Puma, Adidas and many more have changed the nature of competition in the textile sectors of Asian countries and as a result these countries are making changes in their textile manufacturing according to the needs and demands of modern customers at the global level which has helped them to stay in the competition (Tahir & Mughal, 2012). China can be taken as one of the best examples in this regard.

The enhanced focus on social and environmental issues in the developed world has influenced the developing world as well. One reason for this influence is the international trade between the organizations operating in developed and developing regions of the world. For instance,

while human rights clauses have been included in all new general cooperation and trade agreements negotiated by the EU since 1995, in 2008 they began also to include sustainable development chapters. These contain obligations to

---

1 OHSAS 18001 is an Occupation Health and Safety Assessment Series for health and safety management systems. It is intended to help an organization to control occupational health and safety risks. It was developed in response to widespread demand for a recognized standard against which to be certified and assessed. Essentially, OHSAS helps in a variety of respects. It helps to: minimize risk to employees/etc.; improve an existing OH&S management system; demonstrate diligence; gain assurance; etc. The benefits can be substantial (OHSAS 18001, 2015). 2 "The SA8000 Standard is the central document of our work at SAI. It is one of the world's first auditable social certification standards for decent workplaces, across all industrial sectors. It is based on the UN Declaration of Human Rights, conventions of the ILO, UN and national law, and spans industry and corporate codes to create a common language to measure social performance. It takes a management systems approach by setting out the structures and procedures that companies must adopt in order to ensure that compliance with the standard is continuously reviewed. Those seeking to comply with SA8000 have adopted policies and procedures that protect the basic human rights of workers" (SA 8000 Standard, 2015).

respect labour and environmental standards, with a clear reference to core labour standards as defined by ILO conventions (Ambrogio, 2014).

This report was focused on textile sectors of Asian countries, Pakistan being one of them. International organizations operating in economically developed regions of the world and having advanced knowledge about social and environmental issues want their suppliers to be as responsible towards these issues as they are. As the textile sector of Pakistan serves many international clients so it becomes more vulnerable to losing its clientele if it fails to meet the social and environmental standards defined by its sustainable customers. However, it is important to mention that with the increased awareness among developed societies about the challenges faced by the planet, the concerns of the industrial sector in Pakistan have also started moving beyond compliance towards addressing environmental, social and economic concerns altogether.

About Interloop

With increased awareness concerning societal challenges, organizations around the globe have started realizing their responsibility towards the social and environmental concerns in addition to their economic challenges. Among these companies is Interloop Limited, located in the subcontinent region of South Asia, Pakistan. Interloop is an unlisted public company with majority shares owned by one family. The company is one of the world's largest sock manufacturers and exporters with hosiery being its core business. It has an annual turnover exceeding $250 million (Company Business, 2014). Besides hosiery, Interloop is a reputed manufacturer of quality yarn. It is a vertically integrated organization with in-house spinning, yarn dyeing, knitting and finishing facilities. Interloop Limited was established in 1992 with only 10 knitting machines on the floor but currently, Interloop houses over 3,500 knitting machines, 46,704 ring-spinning spindles and has more than 13,000 employees (Company Business, 2014). The company offers a wide range of socks with various quality levels and price points in line with all types of customers including brands, retailers and speciality stores, in addition to its quality yarns for denim, hosiery and the weaving industry.

In-house designing, product development facilities and a recently established Research & Innovation Center, with a team of technical experts, have paved the way to serve Interloop customers' needs well and in time. Being a full service supplier, Interloop offers a unique set of services besides offering a quality product. This includes, but is not limited to market intelligence, trend projections, product design and development support, VMI[3] (vendor

---

3 "Vendor-managed inventory (VMI) is a family of business models in which the buyer of a product (business) provides certain information to a vendor (supply chain) supplier of that product and the supplier takes full responsibility for maintaining an agreed

managed inventory) services and distribution centres offering pick and pack services across the globe (Company Business, 2014). This unique combination of product and service differentiates Interloop from the rest of the textile companies in the world and hence Interloop has the privilege of providing services to such leading retailers as JCPenny, H&M, SportMaster, Tesco, C&A, Penney, Primark, ASDA, Payless, Family Dollar and Lidl. For brands, it is serving Nike, CK, Puma, Tommy Hilfiger, Reebok, Medipeds, Wilson and CAT.

Ethical foundation of the company

This family owned business is considered to be a progressive organization in the local textile industry with annual turnover exceeding $250 million and impressive international clientele. This perception about the company is primarily based on the ethical values of its owners which they brought in from their family background and embedded in their business operations for community welfare. The ethical mind-set of Interloop's owners became a primary motive for them to accept the social, environmental and economic challenges faced by the company. Furthermore, this ethical perspective of Interloop makes compliance pressures from customers a secondary motive to address these challenges. While starting the discussion about his organization, the CEO of Interloop said,

> This business evolved in a slightly different way as we based all our functions on ethical grounds. The purpose was never to make money but the emphasis was on developing our human resources and achieving financial sustainability from a community point of view (interview Zulqarnain).

The CEO explained that the company has always wanted to gain financial sustainability as a result of its ethical practices and not by doing its business in a traditional way with a core focus on profit maximization. The above mentioned words show the commitment that since its foundation in 1992, Interloop Limited has adopted the ethical business practices for the larger good of the community. However, these practices were initially not included in the company's formal terminology such as corporate social responsibility or sustainability. Additionally, adopting ethical practices was itself a challenge while operating in Pakistan as there was no role model or guiding institution in this part of the world during the decade of the 1990s, especially in the textile sector (interview Zulqarnain). Interloop's preliminary business perspective was conventional and focused on meeting the economic expectations of its owners and investors. However, this

---

inventory of the material, usually at the buyer's consumption location (usually a store). A third-party logistics provider can also be involved to make sure that the buyer has the required level of inventory by adjusting the demand and supply gaps... This is one of the successful business models used by Walmart" (Wikipedia).

conventional focus never set aside the ethical principles of the founders which they brought in from their family values. The CEO explained that the economic responsibilities were never met at the cost of community and employees' health and safety. This ethical mind-set of the top management not only trickled down inside the organization but it was also very much appreciated by the employees. One of the employees shared her views about being affiliated with Interloop as follows: "People feel proud and safe at Interloop. They have mental satisfaction for being associated with a company that ethically owns its responsibilities without any legal requirement" (interview Rahat).

The journey of sustainability

The journey of sustainability covered by Interloop took many different turns while progressing towards sustainability. The reflections of this journey of sustainability at Interloop start with its commitment to go beyond compliance for the welfare of society at large. This first phase, i.e. *going beyond compliance*, initiates with the organization's engagement in CSR activities for internal stakeholders and steadily moves along the challenges of CSR for the external stakeholders of the company. The second phase, *triple bottom line approach (TBL)*, focuses on addressing the broader social and environmental issues faced by the company along with its economic concerns. These phases will be described through the historical milestones achieved by the organization over a period of time. The case study will then continue with the current status of Interloop explained through the interpretation of the SCALA survey results and positioning of Interloop in the Dyllick and Muff Business Sustainability Typology Matrix (Dyllick & Muff, 2015). Lastly, future perspectives of the organization will be discussed along with a crucial enabler that was adopted by Interloop to implement sustainability.

Historical milestones

This section will cover the historical milestones of Interloop Limited which were achieved during the journey of sustainability. These achievements will be described in two phases: going beyond the compliance and TBL approach to adopt business sustainability. The discussion will provide an insight as to how Interloop became the only choice, in the local region, for its international clients such as Nike, Puma, Adidas and many more which wanted to do their business with a company free of social and environmental charges.

The competitive challenges have forced the textile sector of Pakistan to comply with their customers' codes of conduct on social and environmental practices. These compliance pressures act as the main driving force for the local textile organizations to move beyond their economic interests.

The complexities of the external environment are increased by the need for compliance with global standards on issues such as health and safety, quality management, labour practices, ethical and environmental concerns. Meeting such standards is considered increasingly necessary to enter into global value chains in textiles, garments and horticulture (Nadvi, 2009).

However, Interloop's ethical perspective has made these compliance pressures a secondary motive behind their responsible business operations. The organization started its journey towards sustainability by voluntarily owning the responsibility to think and go beyond the economic interests and compliance pressures. Interloop had initiated the community welfare projects since the early years of its foundation by engaging in CSR endeavours. This initial focus was mainly triggered by the ethical mind-set of Interloop's management which embarked the organization on this remarkable journey of sustainability. The CSR contributions of Interloop which were made beyond the compliance pressures from its international customers are described below.

voluntarily owning the responsibility to think and go beyond the economic interests and compliance pressures

Internal CSR engagements

The concept of CSR is widely understood by the corporate world in its true meaning. There are many definitions of the concept with a common base line of doing well for society beyond the economic and legal obligations. One such definition is: "Actions of firms that contribute to social welfare, beyond what is required for profit maximization, are classified as Corporate Social Responsibility (CSR)" (McWilliams, 2000).

Some of the CSR initiatives of Interloop which they took in the early years by acknowledging their ethical responsibility are described below. These initiatives set an example for other local textile organizations to see beyond their strategic interests for the betterment of their internal stakeholders.

Employee safety

Things began with an increased focus on improving the working conditions and safety measures for the employees. The safety of the employees was assured at every level to keep the employees committed and motivated. Workplace safety requirements were met by following successful HR practices and creating awareness among employees through related training programmes. Regular training programmes were conducted in this regard which not only created awareness for workplace safety among employees but also made them cautious about how to avoid workplace hazards. This enhanced focus of Interloop's management on humanizing their work environment also resulted in creating an inspiration for other local textile organizations to achieve their corporate goals without compromising on the basic social issue of employees' safety (interview Mohauddin).

Changing the culture of blue collar supervisors

Labour exploitation in the form of child labour, unhealthy working conditions and discrimination are common issues in developing countries such as Pakistan, India and Bangladesh. These issues are mainly faced by the blue collar workers of the industry and the key reason behind these issues is the uneducated and untrained supervisors working in different industrial sectors including the textile sector. In the mid-1990s, Interloop started focusing on changing the culture of blue collar supervisors by emphasizing the need for considerate behaviour towards the skilled labour by understanding the fact that skills are a "hard kept secret" for any organization (interview Zulqarnain). The purpose was fulfilled by bringing in more educated and skilled people who could understand the need for social reforms within the organization. These social reforms emerged out of the ethical values of Interloop's management and were a step forward towards reducing the labour exploitation of blue collar workers from the textile sector of Pakistan.

Adopting NEQs and PEPA

Doing business in an environment lacking proper legislation and accountability is a big challenge for almost every organization. Law enforcement in this region of the world has always been weak and left the companies in a void with regard to their social and environmental responsibilities. Given these circumstances, this makes those organizations exceptional that fulfil their legal obligations on a voluntary basis. Along with social transformation, Interloop was also concerned about the environmental situation and implemented all the National Environmental Quality Standards (NEQs) (The Gazette of Pakistan, 1993) as required by the law. Interloop was among the pioneer organizations in the textile sector of Pakistan which started paying attention towards environmental protection at a time when no significant organization in this region was highlighting the potential threat of environmental hazards by following the parameters mentioned in NEQs. Moreover, the adoption of the Pakistan Environmental Protection Act (PEPA, 1997) further strengthened the image of Interloop as an environmentally responsible organization. PEPA was established for the protection, conservation, rehabilitation and improvement of the environment, for the prevention and control of pollution, and promotion of sustainable development. Adopting PEPA when no other organization in the textile sector was even aware of such laws identified Interloop as one of the pioneer organizations. Moreover, addressing the potential environmental threats of land, air and water pollution and implementing the NEQs and PEPA were important steps for Interloop to gain the status of a very progressive organization in the region.

For Interloop, their ethical and legal engagements not only created their good will as an ethically responsible organization but also led the organization to accept the challenges of social responsibility beyond the compliance pressures.

External CSR engagements

Ethical foundations were at the basis of Interloop's thinking which centred on the larger good of the community. The decision to engage in CSR activities for the company's external stakeholders was made easy due to the positive outcomes of the internal engagements, such as increased employee commitment, decreased employee turnover and improved clientele. The ethical values of the top management, inherited from their family and which they brought into their family business, acted as a main driving force for Interloop to serve the larger community even outside the organization. Moreover, Interloop's management was fully aware of the responsibility of giving back something to the society which had allowed them to run their business successfully over the years. The top management wanted to extend the social transformation, which initiated within the organization, to the wider community around them.

Investing in community welfare projects was a big step taken by Interloop in the local textile sector. These investments to community welfare projects created good will for Interloop not only among internal but also among its external stakeholders. Moreover, this step was taken in a context where limited resources, lack of basic necessities such as electricity, lack of proper infrastructure, lack of technological facilities and above all lack of ethically responsible attitudes among employees had always been hindrances for local textile organizations to invest in such projects. Due to these hindrances, many other organizations still consider these CSR commitments an extra burden on their profitability which is already limited in a developing country like Pakistan.

In the following discussion a few prominent CSR contributions of Interloop for the external community will be described. These contributions changed the organization's image in the minds of its stakeholders and served as a base to embrace the idea of business sustainability.

SOS Villages

In line with its ethical and social commitments, Interloop got involved with SOS Children's Villages Foundation in Faisalabad, Pakistan chapter, in 1998.

An independent housing block for 10 SOS Villages were built in collaboration with a client Dobotex International,[4] one of the ethically and socially responsible organizations which donate generously for such noble causes (In the Loop, 2013). This contribution came out of the socially responsible mind-set of Interloop's top management. It strengthened the image of the company among the external community members as it was a step towards raising the quality of life for less privileged children.

Rehabilitation of earthquake victims

Another evidence of the CSR engagement of Interloop was witnessed when there was a disastrous earthquake in the northern areas of Pakistan in 2005 causing massive destruction in the affected areas and displacing more than 200,000 families (The News, 2012). The catastrophe witnessed devotion and humanity from people of all walks of life including the corporate sector. Interloop quickly made a plan to set up a tent village in the most affected area, Muzzaffarabad, to accommodate victims that had been displaced from their homes. Many international organizations such as Caritas (an international NGO), Oxfam, UNICEF, WHO and WPF also came forward to help Interloop in this noble cause of rehabilitating victims. The efforts made by Interloop for the rehabilitation of homeless people of the affected area after this earthquake were admired not only by the public but also by the corporate sector of Pakistan.

MOU with The Citizens Foundation

For CSR purposes, Interloop cooperates with non-profit organizations (NPOs) which are doing something worthy for the development of the nation and which are sustainable themselves (interview Zulqarnain). An important achievement in this regard is the establishment of 14 schools, for less privileged children, in collaboration with a NPO, The Citizens Foundation (TCF).

In 2009, Interloop signed a Memorandum of Understanding with TCF which is Pakistan's leading non-profit organization in the field of formal education. This was another social welfare contribution which marked Interloop as an ethically and socially responsible organization in the minds of both the internal and external stakeholders. Initially, four schools were built again in collaboration with Dobotex International and later the number of schools increased over a period of time. Interloop proudly owns this contribution and gladly expresses its efforts for providing quality education

---

4 Dobotex International is the exclusive licensing partner of various worldwide A brands in fashion, sport and sport-lifestyle segments. Founded in 1979 and located in Netherlands. It mainly deals with Puma and Tommy Hilfiger (www.dobotex.nl/).

to the less privileged in its newsletters as well. "Interloop is committed to increase the literacy rate and provide quality education to the less privileged children without delaying it any further" (In the Loop, 2013).

Investing in the educational field was highly admired by the stakeholders of the organization as the purpose was purely to educate under-privileged children. The employees took pride in their affiliation with an organization that was committed to the societal welfare beyond its own economic interests. By 2014, the number of schools had reached 14 and it will be 30 according to the vision 2020 of Interloop (interview Zulqarnain). A life-time endowment fund was established by Interloop to make these schools financially sustainable for a longer time period.

Flood relief activities

Pakistan has been affected by floods periodically. There was a disastrous flood in 2010 which severely damaged many parts of the country affecting around 20 million people. Interloop mobilized quickly to play its role and set up the Flood Relief Fund to collect donations. To support the displaced people, 90 houses were built at a cost of Rs.28 million. Moreover, 100 tonnes of food essentials were distributed among sufferers with the help of Pakistan Armed Forces (CSR, 2014). This level of spirit for social service is rarely revealed by the corporate sector in Pakistan because of lack of interest, awareness and resources to be spent on social causes.

National outreach programme

In 2013, Interloop signed an MOU with a leading national university of the country to support students from under-privileged backgrounds. To start with, an endowment fund was set to support one student per year. This programme is the continuation of efforts taken by Interloop to support and spread quality education, from primary to higher levels, in order to raise the social standards for the less privileged class in Pakistan. The CEO of Interloop shares his views about the programme as: "Our purpose to invest in the field of education is to enable the children to get a quality education without any class barrier" (interview Zulqarnain).

All the above mentioned CSR endeavours were accomplished beyond what was required to be a compliant organization. The ethical mind-set which was trickled down from the founders to the lower levels of the organization created an acceptance and encouragement for the CSR engagements. The organizational journey started with being an ethically responsible organization, gradually accomplishing different milestones by extending its concerns from within the organization to the outer community. As a result, the positive responses from different stakeholders encouraged Interloop to further look for the wider societal issues.

> **positive responses from different stakeholders encouraged Interloop to further look for the wider societal issues**

In the early 21st century transformations of the corporate world gained speed. Researchers further developed the concepts of "business ethics" and "corporate social responsibility". "The story of CSR in the 21st century is a story of progressive business sensitization to systems and dynamics of governance beyond government, regulation beyond law, and responsiveness beyond responsibility" (Horrigan, 2007).

In doing so, the traditional notion of CSR was replaced, in many contexts, by the term **sustainability** which started to strike the corporate world in a unique way. Sustainability is based on three pillars identified as the **triple bottom line** approach (Elkington, 1994) as compared to the more confined term of CSR (Horrigan, 2007). The three pillars or principles of the triple bottom line approach are defined to be environmental sustainability, social sustainability and economic sustainability.

Since the emergence of sustainability, the organizations were trying to balance out their economic concerns with social and environmental aspects thus serving the purpose of the triple bottom line approach of sustainability. This was in stark contrast to the traditional business approach where corporate responsibility was more or less confined to profit maximization. However, the introduction of the triple bottom line approach changed the business perspectives of the corporate world altogether. There was an increased focus on social and environmental concerns by organizations in all parts of the world which very often also enhanced their financial strength. Financial strength serves the economic dimension of sustainability, which is one of the three pillars of sustainability. Subsequently, sustainability has become the emerging paradigm for those organizations who want to contribute to making this planet a safe place to live.

From its engagement in CSR activities for the internal stakeholders to the engagements for external stakeholders, Interloop kept on darkening its shade of "green". Moving further, investing in environmental initiatives such as waste water treatment, biogas plants and waste management gave Interloop a first mover advantage as no other textile organization launched any significant environmental protection initiative at that time. The environmental initiatives along with the company's engagement in CSR activities created a paradigm shift at Interloop from addressing two dimensional concerns, i.e. economic and social, to three dimensional concerns, i.e. economic, social and environmental. These three concerns represent the triple bottom line approach of *sustainability* contributing to the sustainable development of the organization in a longer-term perspective. In order to serve these sustainability concerns, Interloop changed its business model to create value without compromising on any of these concerns. This change in business model mainly involved a position of making

change in business model mainly involved a position of making profit without damaging the environment and social values

profit without damaging the environment and social values. For instance, the installation of water treatment plants not only protected the environment but also attracted various sustainable international clients for Interloop who were sensitized to sustainability challenges. Moreover, the change in business models and practices enabled the organization to get various third party certifications in recognition of their efforts in support of environmental and social concerns.

The environmental and social certifications, which will be explained later, along with its strong ethical foundation enabled Interloop to formally adopt *sustainability* as a new outlook. This was a turning point for Interloop as it resulted in adding to its clientele a number of highly renowned international brands such as Nike, Puma, Adidas and more. Such business giants had a clear focus on sustainability and were looking for sustainable suppliers as expressed by one of the representatives of Interloop. "Top brands of the world consider sustainability as an important factor in selecting their suppliers. These brands believe in sustainability and encourage their suppliers to adopt sustainability measures (interview Maqsood).

These attractive customers proved to be a profit generating source for Interloop, thus, strengthening the growth of the organization. Economic growth of Interloop in turn enabled the organization to invest more in environmental protection and social uplifting of its employees, thus serving the true spirit of sustainability.

Environmental and social certifications

Organizations in Pakistan have also started responding to the sustainability challenges, like other organizations in different parts of the world. Keeping their ethical paradigms intact, the management of Interloop also started focusing on addressing the social and environmental issues in a formal way. For this purpose, a more formal *Environmental Policy* was designed in 2002 that emphasized protecting the environment by reducing all types of air, land and water pollution. The new policy involved more stringent measures of environmental protection including a tight control on air emissions, installation of water treatment effluent plants, solid waste management techniques and use of hazardous chemicals. This environmental policy changed the nature of Interloop's business perspective to a more responsible one as compared to the competitors. These persistent efforts for environmental protection, driven by both ethics and compliance pressures from the customers, gave grounds for Interloop to get tangible proof of its environmentally responsible business operations. For this very purpose, in 2004, Interloop was certified with ISO 14001 by SGS (Certifications, 2014) for adopting and practising environmental protection measures in its business operations. SGS is the world's leading inspection, verification, testing and certification company which helps other companies to operate in a more sustainable manner. This certification helped Interloop to implement, maintain and improve on its environmental management system through its stated environmental policy. In the same year the Worldwide Responsible Accredited Production[5] (WRAP) certificate was also awarded to Interloop for socially and environmentally conscious business practices. "The WRAP Principles are based on generally accepted international workplace standards, local laws and workplace regulations which encompass human resources management, health and safety, environmental practices, and legal compliance including import/export and customs compliance and security standards" (WRAP, 2015).

Along with the environmental issues, social compliance was also dealt with responsibility at Interloop in order to make sure that the organization follows all the international standards and laws of social compliance, i.e. child labour laws, health and safety laws and discrimination. This social compliance with international standards and laws led to another achievement of certifying the organization with SA8000 and OHSAS 18001 (Certifications, 2014) for fulfilling social responsibilities, awarded in 2005 and 2008, respectively. These certifications ensure the safe working environment of the employees through continuous social audits on the following issues:

- Child labour
- Forced or compulsory labour
- Health & safety
- Freedom of association
- Discrimination
- Disciplinary practices
- Working hours
- Remuneration
- Counselling and psychology

For this purpose, a huge investment was made on employee health & safety measures taken by Interloop in terms of health screening of the employees working on plants, fire safety measures, handling dangerous chemicals and better and secured infrastructure. This enhanced focus by Interloop on safeguarding the social concerns helped the organization to secure third party recognitions thus ensuring its clients a safe and sound working system intact with its business operations. These third party certifications gave a competitive advantage to Interloop as there was no other significant

---

5 WRAP is the world's largest independent certification programme primarily focused on the apparel, footwear and sewn product sectors. It is mainly social compliance certification given to the companies after ensuring their compliance with WRAP's 12 principles (www.wrapcompliance.org).

organization in the textile sector of Pakistan which was certified for social practices at that time.

The compliance pressures from the foreign customers of Interloop were the main drivers for these environmental and social certifications. The certifications resulted in retaining the lucrative foreign customers for Interloop who preferred to have suppliers with environmental friendly business operations. These customers contributed in improving the economic dimension of Interloop thus further strengthening the triple bottom line approach of the organization. People at Interloop understand this fact and express it by saying: "Along with other factors such as your values, goals and culture, financial health of a company is also a must for long-term sustainability" (interview Maqsood).

Establishment of an EHS department

An important milestone in the journey towards sustainability was to establish an independent Environment, Health & Safety (EHS) department in 2007. This department was established in response to the emerging societal and environmental priorities and expectations (EHS, 2014). The EHS department was part of the paradigm shift that showed the importance of environmental and social concerns in the business operations. This department, since its establishment, has made historic contributions in reducing the environment and social risks for the organization as well as community. The department operates in four sections:

► **Compliance with Customer Code of Conduct (COC) and certification.** This section is primarily responsible for ensuring conformance to applicable laws, regulations, policies and standards. It monitors the system and procedures to comply with legal, environmental and social requirements and reports on them.

► **Safety.** The occupational health and safety practitioners at Interloop strive to foster the development of safety consciousness among employees in order to minimize the risk of injury to persons and damage to facilities on a proactive basis. Education and training leads to safer practices among workers and are an integral part of the occupational health and safety programme at Interloop.

► **Medical Health Unit.** Interloop has established a round-the-clock medical health unit which provides not only the first aid treatment but also medical personnel and facilities to manage any possible workplace injury and infirmity. This initiative is to ensure the health and well-being of the company employees. Additionally, the unit is equipped with necessary medications, medical supplies and ambulances.

► **Environment.** This section is responsible for taking measures to ensure that business activities do not harm the environment and are not instrumental in global climate change. Reducing the environmental footprint through energy substitutes, waste management, waste water treatment and other innovative ideas are the responsibilities of this section of the EHS department.

The EHS department ensures the occupational health and safety of the employees by developing safety consciousness among them through various measures including specialized training programmes. These training programmes, since their induction, have helped in reducing the workplace hazards at the organization's premises by equipping employees with proper knowledge to deal with health and safety issues. Such efforts are highly exceptional in the Pakistani textile sector where labour exploitation is considered to be a norm. Deplorable working conditions, occupational health and safety hazards and long working hours are compounded by denial of basic human rights for a large number of workers in the labour market of Pakistan (Ghayur, 1996). However, serious efforts of EHS have played a vital role in making Interloop one of the safest organizations to work in the local community through its safety measures such as fire safety, noise testing, safe use of chemicals and health awareness among employees. For instance, Interloop has maintained the accident rate at around 0.1 for the last four years. The required limit of this rate is 0.5 according to the international standards defined by OSHA[6] for the textile sector. Moreover, extremely bad working conditions for employees in many other textile organizations due to a purely money-making mind-set has resulted in the lowest employee turnover rate, less than 5% at Interloop for the last four years (interview Din).

The EHS department is committed to operating in a manner that reduces environmental, health and safety risks to its stakeholders (EHS, 2014), especially its employees and people living in the surroundings of the factory premises. The department is responsible for monitoring the proper adoption and implementation of environmental standards. Persistent environmental monitoring makes sure that air, land and water discharges are within the permissible limits identified through various standards such as NEQs. This department is also responsible for taking innovative measures for developing and adopting substitutes for natural energy sources. An important step in this regard is to produce energy through food waste materials collected from within the organizational premises.

The management of Interloop is very keen to enhance the department's capabilities by investing in new and innovative measures for protecting the environment. This department is not only contributing to Interloop's success in becoming a sustainable organization but it is also setting a benchmark for other local organizations, as said by the CEO of Interloop.

---

6 OSHA is part of the United States Department of Labor. Its mission is "to assure safe and healthful working conditions for working men and women by setting and enforcing standards and by providing training, outreach, education and assistance" (https://www.osha.gov/about.html).

We needed to have a specialized department which has the professional expertise and reports directly to the top management. This department has its own key performance indicators (KPIs) entirely focused on providing healthy environment not only to our employees but also to the community as a whole. This department sets benchmark in the textile sector of Pakistan (interview Zulqarnain).

These KPIs mainly include: health and safety, waste management, energy conservation, water purification and emissions control. Various steps and measures taken by the EHS department to address the sustainability concerns are explained below. All these efforts by Interloop have contributed to safeguarding the environment through multiple means in a context where the majority of organizations lack resources as well as the will to invest in such measures.

Air and noise testing

In continuation of the efforts exerted to address the social and environmental concerns of sustainability, Interloop started conducting air and noise testing for its employees in 2009. These tests are conducted by professionals from renowned laboratories such as "At Waste" and "Global Environmental Lab" (GEL) on a periodic basis. The quarterly monitoring of air emission sources is carried out to ensure that the emissions are under permissible limits. If there is any deviation from the permissible limits, the operation of that equipment is shut down immediately for subsequent remedial measures. Similarly the noise level within the premises is checked periodically to avoid any potential danger caused due to a high level of noise generated by machines. These tests ensure not only the health and safety of people working within the organization, but also safeguard the environment for the community members living in the surroundings of the factory.

LEAN Resource Group

Since the adoption of sustainability formally in 2008, there was an aggressive development in social and environmental protection measures taken by Interloop. Another stepping stone in this regard was establishing the LEAN Resource Group in 2010 as part of the Company's vision 2015. The purpose of this resource group is to adhere with lean manufacturing practices, thus emphasizing eliminating the non-value added activities such as waste from business operations. Interloop started its war on waste in 2009 and invested massively in training its teams to gain knowledge about lean practices. One of the Interloop customers, Nike, trained all the plant managers in its lean manufacturing training facilities in Vietnam and Sri Lanka (Lean, 2014) for minimizing waste. Interloop has a dedicated Lean Resource Group headed by an Executive Director to lead the transformation towards practising lean in its processes. An example in this regard is to produce socks from regenerated yarn which is made after recycling the wasted socks which would have been added otherwise to the organization's waste. Interloop is fully capable with this technique to eliminate the wasted products by recycling them. This activity of recycling wasted socks and regenerating yarn is certified by the Global Recycle Standard. "The Global Recycled Standard is intended for companies that are making and/or selling products with recycled content. The standard applies to the full supply chain and addresses traceability, environmental principles, social requirements, and labeling" (Global Recycle Standard, 2015). According to the CEO of Interloop, such practices have resolved the waste management problems at the factory's premises and a culture is developed for waste management pursuing the company's zero waste targets.

Implementation of 3R in waste management

A variety of waste streams and waste products are generated throughout Interloop's facility for which Interloop has an extensive waste management programme focused on the 3R principle, reduce, reuse and recycle. All the wastewater produced from textile processing undergoes treatment before it is discharged to the environment. The hazardous wastes are safely handled and stored, and are sent either for recycling or for incineration. The non-hazardous waste, which includes left over socks, polythene bags, cardboard, paper cones and cartons are collected from each department and are stored in a waste store before these are disposed of to recyclers. The aim is to minimize waste from all of the business activities and apply sustainable waste management and disposal methods through the waste management hierarchy of "avoid, reduce, recycle, recover, treat and dispose". Such activities help to safeguard the purity of the environment for all living beings.

> **aim is to minimize waste from all of the business activities and apply sustainable waste management**

Biogas plant

Innovating and developing substitutes for natural resources to avoid their depletion is one of the most important requirements of sustainability. Keeping in view of this fact, Interloop is determined to conserve energy by all means. One of the several measures that Interloop has taken in this regard is the installation of a food waste treatment plant (or biogas plant) in 2012 to utilize solid food/kitchen waste. It is part of their comprehensive waste management system that emphasizes source reduction, reuse and recycling, and is based on the dictum that "nothing should go to waste". The biogas plant is a modern portable organic waste treatment plant. It consists of kitchen waste shredding facilities, an anaerobic digester, biogas collection and compression systems, and piping for compressed biogas to take it to the canteen for use as part of a fuel substitute for liquefied petroleum gas (LPG). The plant has a capacity to treat 200 kg/day of food waste and if operated at full capacity, will be able to produce biogas equivalent to 200 kg of LPG/month (EHS, 2014). Although the gas produced through this plant does not meet the total energy requirements of the system, however, it fully consumes the kitchen waste of the company which would have otherwise been added into the environment. Therefore, this investment contributes to environmental protection through waste management, generating renewable energy source and LPG cost reduction.

Water treatment effluent plant

In 2001, Interloop established its first wastewater treatment effluent plant for reducing the water pollution created by discharge of hazardous materials into water drainage. This water pollution is dangerous not only for human lives but also for other living beings. However, lack of awareness in this developing region has multiplied this problem many times, for instance, reduced marine life in the main river streams of the country due to contaminated water discharged by the industries. Interloop again acted as a pioneer in establishing such a water treatment plant to avoid the discharge of contaminated water into watercourses.

As the business activities of Interloop grew with the passage of time, this effluent plant became insufficient to treat the wastewater produced. Therefore, in continuation of its strong concern for environmental protection as part of sustainability measures, Interloop installed another state-of-the-art effluent treatment plant in 2012. As the effluent from the textile dye house is the potential environmental issue, Interloop now has state-of-the-art effluent treatment plants at every manufacturing unit to effectively undertake treatment requirements. The organization considers these effluent treatment plants as an investment for future generations (EHS, 2014) because the world's clean water resources are depleting with every passing day. Water pollution is the biggest threat to clean water resources and the problem is becoming worse with industrial expansion especially in developing countries where the level of awareness is not high. Interloop understands the responsibility towards its environment and always takes measures to reduce such impacts on the environment. The operation of these activated sludge-based effluent treatment plants is round the clock, meeting not only the standards defined by NEQs, but also some more stringent parameters of environmental protection from the world's leading brands. The largest effluent treatment plant at Interloop has the capacity of treating 180 m³ of waste water per hour which is far more than the capacity held by many national/international organizations of the same size. The current capacity of Interloop for treating the waste water again gives it a competitive advantage over its competitors because the average capacity of effluent plants in the local textile sector ranges between 50 and 70 m³/hour. Moreover, Interloop also has a centralized laboratory to closely monitor the defined parameters

> **Water pollution is the biggest threat to clean water resources**

and ensure that the effluent discharged into the environment is within safe limits.

Measuring carbon footprint

Carbon discharge in our environment is exceeding the ecological thresholds resulting in diverse environmental issues such as global warming and climate change (Rockstrom *et al.*, 2009). This activity has created a global impact and organizations around the globe are trying to reduce their carbon footprint by adopting different stringent measures. Interloop, being an environmentally responsible organization, has been measuring its carbon footprint since 2012 on a voluntary basis. An integrated and organization wide effort is being done not only to reduce carbon emissions, but also to measure the carbon footprint of the organization. Currently, Interloop is the only organization in the local textile sector which is measuring its carbon footprint. Serious efforts in this regard have resulted in fulfilling the purpose and soon carbon footprint measures will be part of the reports published by the organization to show its sustainability contributions (interview Zulqarnain).

Redefined company values

Change in operational paradigms at Interloop for adopting and implementing sustainability also involved redefining the company values for its stakeholders. Three-dimensional organizational perspectives broadened the focus from shareholders to stakeholders involving the larger community for the larger common good. The cultural values redefined by Interloop are depicted as **i-Care**. The organization emphasizes these values to show its commitment towards having a safer place to work and live in. Interloop defines **i-Care** as:

> **Three-dimensional organizational perspectives broadened the focus from shareholders to stakeholders**

▸ i, integrity

▸ c, care

▸ a, accountability

▸ r, respect

▸ e, excellence

These words encompass the three-dimensional responsibilities, environmental, social and economic, owned by the organization for making this planet a safe and healthy place to live. Environmental protection, social uplifting and economic strength serve the three-dimensional purpose of sustainability showing care for all the direct and indirect stakeholders of the organization. This slogan of cultural values at Interloop is very popular among the employees and makes them committed to sustainability goals and practices. A diagrammatic presentation of company values is given in Figure 1.

Figure 1 Diagrammatic presentation of organizational values

The description given above about the journey of sustainability at Interloop shows an incremental progress of the organization since its foundation. An organization which was started with an ethical perspective soon indulged itself in CSR endeavours and persistently entered the realm of sustainability by adopting the TBL approach. This journey shifted the organization's two-dimensional perspectives, economic and social, into three-dimensional business perspectives, environmental, social and economic. Interloop's journey can be exemplified to various traditional organizations in this or other developing regions of the world for identifying the possible ways by which they can start moving towards sustainability.

Current status

The historical milestones achieved by Interloop established it with the status of a sustainable organization following the triple bottom line approach as its core business perspective. This approach has secured a special position for Interloop in the textile sector of Pakistan as no other organization in the local textile sector has done much significant work to address sustainability issues.

The efforts done by Interloop towards a safe and healthy planet for future generations to live in have altogether changed the image of organizations which are based in developing countries. The organizations which are at the initial stages of adopting sustainability can learn a great deal from the past and current status of sustainability leaders such as Interloop.

Interloop today is considered to be a non-traditional organization with a long-term focus on strengthening the business finances without compromising the environmental and social factors. In this section of the case study, the current status of Interloop will be explained with the help of the SCALA survey results and interviews. These results will explain how Interloop today is known as one of the sustainability leaders in the textile sector of South Asia, Pakistan.

The SCALA survey was used as a quantitative measure of data to be used in the case study. It was conducted organization-wide as an online survey through self-administered questionnaires sent to employees via their email addresses. The survey comprised 30 questions developed by Miller Consultants, ten questions added by Business School Lausanne (BSL) and two questions added by the researcher to gain an insight into specific research needs. The sample size was N= 84 after having a response rate of almost 70%. The sample was chosen in consultation with Interloop's management through a random sampling technique and it represented almost 20% of the population: executives/managers of all management levels. Demographically, the respondents were 93% male and 7% female. The organization-wide survey involved one C-level executive, 19 senior managers, 49 mid-level managers, 14 first-line managers and two from other positions. According to age groups, three respondents belonged to the age group of 51–60 years, 24 respondents were of 41–50 years of age, 53 respondents belonged to the 31–40 years age group and 4 respondents were between 20 and 30 years of age. The Deputy Manager Protocol and Travel, Ms Faryal Sohail, was the coordinator in the sample selection for the survey as well as the interviews.

It is important to mention that the SCALA survey shows highly positive results for Interloop on various dimensions. This is possibly because no other significant Pakistani textile organization has yet taken environmental and social initiatives to this extent. These highly positive results were also endorsed by the stakeholders who were interviewed for the purpose of developing this case study.

SCALA survey

The purpose of the Sustainability Culture and Leadership Assessment (SCALATM) is to provide organizations with information about their organization's current capacity for executing sustainability strategies. The

SCALA survey at Interloop was done in collaboration with Miller Consultants and Business School Lausanne, Switzerland, to understand the extent to which sustainability is embedded into the culture of Interloop. The survey provides an insight into the organization's sustainability culture regarding six categories:

- ▷ Organizational leadership
- ▷ Organizational systems
- ▷ Organizational climate
- ▷ Change readiness
- ▷ Internal stakeholders
- ▷ External stakeholders

The results of the six categories mentioned above will now be explained to understand the culture of Interloop regarding sustainability. All the results are available in the report provided by Miller Consultants for Interloop Ltd.

Organizational Leadership

Responsible organizational leadership is required to implement sustainability within an organization. The commitment of responsible leadership gives a firm standing to the sustainability goals pursued by an organization (Bertels, Papania, & Papania, 2010).This responsible organizational leadership has a vision to assess the successful implementation of sustainability strategies and their consequences. According to the SCALA survey 97.6% (N=84) of the respondents agree or strongly agree that the leadership of Interloop has a clear vision for sustainability while 92.9% of respondents agreed that the leadership has a long-term view when making sustainability decisions. Interloop's historical commitments with environmental and social factors of sustainability clearly show that the leadership of Interloop has been personally committed to issues related to sustainability claiming their ethical base. SCALA results prove this personal level of commitment of Interloop's leadership with sustainability issues as 97.6% of respondents agreed that Interloop has a clear business case for pursuing the goals of sustainability.

Sustainable organizations tend to integrate sustainability strategies into their decision making. This organizational tendency proves to be true for Interloop too as 96.5% of respondents agreed that Interloop's leadership integrates sustainability into decision making. At Interloop this integration is done through engaging the heads of all the departments in designing the organizational goals and strategies including sustainability. This engagement ensures the diffusion of sustainability perspective to all the other employees of the organization working in various functional units. The EHS department plays a crucial role in this regard as it goes on to measure the sustainability related performance of these functional units. The performance is measured based on meeting the environmental and social standards set by third party audit teams such as WRAP, ISO and OHSAS.

The commitment of top management to organizational goals cannot be trickled down unless the employees get inspired by the examples and practices set by the management itself. Interloop's sustainable practices including an enhanced focus on environment protection, employees' health and safety and waste management techniques have inspired not only the employees but also many other stakeholders. SCALA results verify this quality of Interloop's leadership as 94.1% of respondents (N=84) agreed with the statement that their leadership inspire others about sustainability-focused issues and initiatives. This inspiration successfully attracted big international brands such as Puma, Nike, Adidas and many more to look for a sustainable supplier in this developing part of the world. Such clientele strengthened the economic base of the organization and also encouraged it to adopt more sustainability measures for environmental safety. Along with the international clients, other stakeholders also became inspired and showed their trust in doing business with Interloop due to its sustainable and ethical reputation in the market. Director Finance at Interloop was of the view that stakeholders get inspired by the sustainable practices and ultimately show their commitment to work with a sustainable organization. He further said:

> All financial institutions of the country want to do business with us due to our ethical practices. Investing in sustainability is not an expense rather it is an investment for our future generations which pays back to the organization on long-term basis (interview Maqsood).

SCALA results also show that 96.6% of respondents (N= 84) perceive Interloop's leadership to be knowledgeable about the issues pertaining to sustainability. This is evident from various measures that Interloop has taken in order to address environmental and social concerns such as renewable energy sources, water conservation and workplace health and safety. These measures taken by Interloop are unique in the local region as competitive organizations lack knowledge as well as the will to address sustainability issues. This lack of knowledge and will restricts the organizations from taking measured risks in pursuit of their strategies including sustainability. However, the opposite happens at Interloop where 96.5% of respondents agreed that the leadership is perceived to be willing to take measured risks related to sustainability.

lack of knowledge and will restricts the organizations from taking measured risks in pursuit of their strategies including sustainability

It can be inferred from the above discussion that organizational leadership (i.e. top management) at Interloop is fully committed with sustainability initiatives and is trying to diffuse the phenomenon to a larger community through its sustainable governing practices. These practices have become part of the organization's culture due to continuous engagement and commitment of the leadership.

The head of EHS department at Interloop claimed that sustainability is embedded into their daily operations and systems due to continuous reinforcement of its importance and benefits for the society as a whole (interview Qasim). This claim is endorsed by the SCALA results where 83.9% of the respondents (N=84) agree with the statement that the company has embedded sustainability into the operating procedures and policies. For this Interloop has adopted an organization wide approach by involving people working at all levels of management into sustainability concerns through frequent training and other awareness programmes. This is further confirmed by SCALA respondents as 79.1% agree that the organization has an enterprise-wide management system for sustainability. Sustainability goals assigned to various departments are continuously monitored and measured by the EHS department. The organization's leadership also rewards the innovative ideas addressing sustainability issues and such rewards are linked with sustainability based performance. The case is endorsed by SCALA results where 74.7% of respondents agreed that the company has integrated sustainability-related goals into the performance management system and 64.6% of respondents agreed with the statement that rewards and compensation are clearly linked to the organization's sustainability goals. However, 23% of the respondents neither agreed nor disagreed with the statement which is possibly because these employees are not sure of the fact that the company has taken sustainability as one of the criteria for giving rewards and compensation to employees as endorsed by the majority of the respondents.

When sustainability is embedded into the daily operations/systems of the organization, a *sustainable culture* is developed within that organization. This sustainable culture in turn supports the development of new business models focused on the betterment of the environment, society and economic well-being of that organization. Interloop over a period of time, has developed such capabilities which are required to instil a sustainable culture within the organization.

The organizational climate is one of the most commonly used variables to describe the organization's internal context (Zhang & Liu, 2010). SCALA measured the perception of employees about the internal context/environment of Interloop by taking trust, learning and innovation into consideration to understand the organizational climate. According to SCALA results 86.2% of respondents (N=84) of Interloop agree or strongly agree to have a high level of trust within the organization and 89.6% of respondents believe that a commitment to sustainability is essential to the company's success in the long term. Interloop's commitment to implement sustainability strategies have made their organizational climate more conducive for learning as depicted by SCALA results where 100% of the respondents agree or strongly agree that learning is the core focus at Interloop Ltd. However, in the SCALA survey 78.1% of respondents agree that their organization encouraged them to learn about sustainability from external sources. It can be inferred from these results that sustainable organizations tend to have their core focus on learning and development of their employees. Similarly, a very high percentage of respondents, 93.1%, believe that the rewards are directly linked with innovation at Interloop. Endorsing the SCALA results about organizational climate, an interviewee responded by saying: "We have suggestion boxes throughout our premises and employees are encouraged to give ideas on how to improve the environmental and social conditions. Innovative and good ideas are rewarded which makes employees feel proud" (interview Rahat).

Overall responses of SCALA results show that Interloop's climate is encouraging towards bringing positive changes such as sustainability practices into the organization's internal environment.

Change readiness

Change readiness describes how committed employees of an organization are to implement the organizational change (Weiner, 2009). Interloop has always been keen to bring incremental changes within the organization which could ultimately impact the environment and the society as a whole in a positive manner. This has also been endorsed by SCALA results in which 97.7% (N=84) respondents believe that Interloop has a strong track record for implementing incremental change successfully while 88.5% support the view of having a strong track record for implementing large-scale change successfully at Interloop. However, interviewees stated some change resistance among employees while adopting non-traditional business practices, focused on environmental protection and social uplifting, which was dealt with amicably through training and other awareness programmes.

An organization basically challenges the status quo when it decides to bring in some positive change in its practices. SCALA survey shows that 69.1% of respondents agreed that Interloop actively challenges the status quo. As the implementation of sustainability strategies was considered to be a change in traditional ways of doing business and required a high level of change readiness among employees, as a result, the current status of Interloop makes it a strong case for a sustainable organization considering the past behaviour of the organization.

Internal stakeholders

Sustainable organizations understand that internal stakeholders (i.e. employees) play an important role in sustainable development of an organization. Such organizations are more concerned about the career development, skill enhancement and safe working conditions of their employees (Eccles, Ioannou, & Serafeim, 2011). This enhanced concern for employees' interests and needs not only creates employee motivation and engagement but also develops an atmosphere of trust within that organization resulting in transformation of behaviours to support sustainability (Eccles, Perkins, & Serafeim, 2012). Interloop being an ethical organization has always valued its employees and therefore won the trust of its employees resulting in increased employee engagement.

The engagement of internal stakeholders/employees is ensured at all levels of the organization and personal sustainability goals are assigned to employees for which their evaluation is also done (interview Rahat). SCALA results support the same argument of engaging internal stakeholders in sustainability efforts with 82.7% of respondents (N=84) agreeing or strongly agreeing. Similarly, 90.8% of respondents perceive that by and large, people are engaged in work that is connected to sustainability goals. Furthermore, 87.4% of respondents of the survey also believe that Interloop values them and their contribution. These results clearly show that the importance of employees is well understood by Interloop and is of utmost significance for creating long-term values. The CEO of the organization stated his view about sustainability and internal stakeholders as: "Our company gets the attention of talented workforce due to our sustainability practices" (interview Zulqarnain).

External stakeholders

An organization cannot implement its business strategies without engaging its external stakeholders. The external stakeholders may include customers, suppliers, business partners, competitors, related non-profit organizations, government and other pressure groups (Robbins & Coulter, 2010). Sustainability as an emerging business strategy needed to have an active stakeholders' engagement which was well understood by Interloop right from the initial stages. The details are as follows:

Interloop is engaged with such business partners that have a clear vision for sustainability. SCALA survey results show that Interloop has mechanisms to actively engage with external stakeholders about its sustainability efforts. This view was supported by 77% of respondents (N=84) of the survey. "Business sustainability is an added value and it has a return but for that organization must return some of its profit back to the society" (interview Damen).

The CEO of Euro Sox (one of the international clients and strategic partner of Interloop), Roudy Damen, admired the progressive pace of Interloop towards sustainability and mentioned sustainability as one of the main reasons for their partnership. He was of the view that they could not find any better business partner, in this region, as the value cannot be created without being ethical and sustainable. He also emphasized on advertising and publicizing the sustainability practices in outer circles for its larger impact. He further said: "Interloop is realizing and owning the responsibility based on personal ethics and values. Interloop is not doing it as a legal demand like its counter parts rather it owns the responsibility to make the environment and society more sustainable" (interview Damen).

Interloop has always engaged its suppliers while taking decisions regarding sustainability. It is because of the sustainable efforts of the company that big supplier companies are eager to work with Interloop (interview Zulqarnain, 2014). In the SCALA results 85% of respondents of the survey (N=84) agree on the opinion that Interloop encourages sustainability in its supply chain. Similarly, ethical practices which were transformed into sustainability strategies have raised the trust level of financial institutions for Interloop. This is basically because the company has never defaulted on any payment and more importantly, investment in environmental safety has attracted the financial institutions towards Interloop (interview Din).

The adoption of sustainability practices has also attracted premium customers to become engaged with Interloop. This engagement has resulted in the continuous increase in the profitability of Interloop over the past few years (Investor Information, 2014). The CEO of Interloop said: "Most of the premium customers who want to do business in this region have long-term business plans with us as they don't want to work with non-sustainable companies" (interview Zulqarnain).

It can be inferred from the above discussion that engagement of external stakeholders may be considered as a key to success for sustainable organizations. This is affirmed through SCALA survey in which 89.6% of respondents agreed that the company sends a clear and consistent message to external stakeholders about its commitment to sustainability. However, the organization needs to develop such mechanisms which involve the external stakeholders into the sustainability goals more actively and deeply.

So far the case study has studied what Interloop has done in the adoption and incorporation of business sustainability, but we also need to see how far the company has travelled on the path of embracing true business sustainability. For this purpose, we shall position Interloop in the Dyllick/Muff Business Sustainability Typology Matrix.

Business Sustainability Typology and Interloop

The discussion presented in the case study so far enables the reader to understand the historical achievements and contributions of Interloop from ethics to sustainability along with the cultural assessment of the organization regarding sustainability. The primary motive behind all these endeavours had been the ethical mind-set of the top management of Interloop which trickled down to lower levels through continuous reinforcement and personal commitment of top management with such issues. The leadership/top management owned this responsibility of social welfare and environmental protection beyond the legal obligations as also said earlier by a business partner, Roudy Damen.

The discussion will now proceed by examining Interloop's positioning according to the Business Sustainability Typology Matrix presented by Dyllick and Muff (Fig. 2).

Figure 2 Business sustainability: from business as usual to true sustainability

BUSINESS SUSTAINABILITY TYPOLOGY (BST)	Concerns (What?)	Values created (What for?)	Organizational perspective (How?)
Business-as-usual	Economic concerns	Shareholder value	Inside-out
Business Sustainability 1.0	Three-dimensional concerns	Refined shareholder value	Inside-out
Business Sustainability 2.0	Three-dimensional concerns	Triple bottom line	Inside-out
Business Sustainability 3.0	Starting with sustainability challenges	Creating value for the common good	Outside-in
The key shifts involved:	1st shift: broadening the business concern	2nd shift: expanding the value created	3rd shift: changing the perspective

This sustainability typology assesses organizations based on three different business perspectives: concerns, value creation and organizational perspective. The assessment then places an organization on the sustainability matrix which describes three stages of business sustainability: Sustainability 1.0, Sustainability 2.0 and Sustainability 3.0. Interloop's positioning will now be assessed based on the three business sustainability stages mentioned above. The discussion will be justified with the help of SCALA results and interviews where required.

> **typology assesses organizations based on three different business perspectives: concerns, value creation and organizational perspective**

Concerns

According to Dyllick and Muff, the traditional business perspective (business-as-usual) is to focus on economic concerns mainly. The sustainability perspective (Sustainability 1.0, Sustainability 2.0 and Sustainability 3.0), however, involves a long-term focus on sustainability issues with a purpose to have an impact on society at large. These sustainability issues are catered to preserve the natural and social capital along with financial management for a balanced approach to business sustainability practices (Dyllick & Muff, 2014). This practice will ultimately result in contributing to the macro level sustainability of society.

Interloop, with its founding ethical values, has been trying to address all three concerns of sustainability as described through the historical journey of the company and the SCALA survey.

▶ **Environmental concerns.** The environmental concerns were mainly dealt with through a keen focus on waste management techniques, biogas plants, periodic air and noise testing, efforts to measure carbon footprint and water treatment effluent plants.

▶ **Social concerns.** The social concerns were primarily addressed by ensuring health and safety of employees through workplace safety measures including noise testing, fire protection and other safety related training programmes. The educational projects for providing quality education to the less privileged children of society are also a landmark contribution in addressing social concerns. Moreover, the external community members were also indirectly taken care of through the company employees by knowledge sharing.

These long-term concerns of Interloop to safeguard the natural and social resources of the organization have helped the organization to contribute to the macro level sustainability in a developing society through environment protection and social uplifting.

▶ **Economic concerns.** The economic concerns have also been a focus for Interloop's management. This is evident from the above discussion in the form of retaining profitable customers, reduced employee turnover rate, trustworthy relations with stakeholders and modified and resilient business operations.

The assumption of having these multiple concerns is further confirmed by the SCALA results as 97.6% of respondents agreed that Interloop has a clear business case for pursuing the goals of sustainability. The Head of EHS department stated the business concerns of Interloop by saying: "We don't take them as an expense rather these are the investments for our future generations which will not only make people safe but our society, equipment and environment will also be safe" (interview Qasim).

According to Sustainability 1.0 "the relevant concerns considered by business mostly shift from purely economic concerns to include social and environmental concerns related to sustainability issues faced by society". Therefore, based on the above discussion, we can safely categorize Interloop as a Business Sustainability 1.0 organization for addressing the three-dimensional concerns of sustainability. The following discussion will further elaborate the position of Interloop on this typology.

Values created

Dyllick and Muff explained value created by sustainability perspectives as follows:

> Sustainability perspectives are broader and include different kinds of values, typically balancing economic value, environmental value and social value, the triple bottom-line of people, planet and profits. They serve a broader set of stakeholders and also include stakeholders who are only indirectly affected by business activities, or include in an even more abstract sense the "common good" (e.g. society as a whole, future generations, health of the planet) (Dyllick & Muff, 2015).

According to Dyllick and Muff, the sustainable organizations create values as a result of their deliberately defined sustainability goals and not as a side effect of their business practices. The purpose of such goals is to generate multiple values to make this planet a safe and healthy place to live in.

It is evident that Interloop is creating value through its TBL approach as described in earlier sections. This approach depicts a broader way of creating values by aligning the three-dimensional environmental, social and economic concerns with TBL values of sustainability. The assumption is further endorsed by SCALA survey where 69.8% of respondents (N=84) endorse this view that the organization is creating economic, social and environmental values.

Finally, Interloop balances the environmental and social dimensions of sustainability (renewable energy sources, waste management, waste water treatment, health and safety, emissions control and education projects) while doing its business in an economically sound and profitable way. Hence, the aforementioned discussion further advances the position of Interloop on the business sustainability typology and makes it a strong case to be considered as a Sustainability 2.0 organization for following the TBL approach and addressing the three-dimensional concerns of sustainability.

Organizational perspective

The business sustainability typology by Dyllick and Muff described two types of organizational perspectives, inside-out approach and outside-in approach. The "organizations usually initiate the process from the existing business, strategy or product-line and work on making them more sustainable" (inside-out). This approach is mostly adopted by Sustainability 2.0 organizations and advances on the continuum of sustainability by following the outside-in approach in which "sustainability challenges are used as the starting point to define possible contributions by a business that also makes business sense" (Dyllick & Muff, 2015). According to Dyllick and Muff's business sustainability typology only Sustainability 3.0 organizations follow the outside-in approach.

All efforts that have been made by Interloop in following the TBL approach show its commitment to manage its economic concerns along with the environmental and social concerns faced by the organization. It is a proactive approach to address the sustainability issues while managing the business risks. This argument is justified through SCALA results where 96.5% of respondents believe that leaders of this company are willing to take measured risks in pursuit of sustainability. Furthermore, this has enabled the organization to manage its business operations in a way that is supportive to create TBL values. This is evident through various measures taken by the organization such as waste water treatment, energy conservation, 3R waste management and the Lean Resource Group to make its business processes environmentally safe and sustainable. These technologies are adopted by utilizing the organization's existing resources or procedures thus, following the inside-out approach. Similarly, social sustainability initiatives also involve the current business practices to benefit the community in a direct or indirect way. According to Dyllick and Muff, the perspective of deliberately defining the sustainability goals within the organization, for well-defined sustainability issues of society, by utilizing existing business resources is an "inside-out" perspective of sustainability. An inside-out sustainability perspective encourages the organizations to monitor, identify and solve sustainability issues but this approach limits the scope of sustainability related decisions and actions due to the entire dependence on the existing business model (Dyllick & Muff, 2015). However, keeping in view the geographical context of Interloop, adopting an inside-out perspective of sustainability is considered to be a significant step towards addressing environmental and social concerns. This context and consistent efforts of Interloop towards sustainability have differentiated Interloop from its counterparts in a significant manner and it was made possible by identifying the sustainability challenges and resolving them proactively. The SCALA survey results confirm this assumption for Interloop where 58.1% of respondents believe that Interloop's current approach to sustainability is proactive. It can therefore be inferred from the above discussion that Interloop possesses an inside-out organizational perspective which is usually followed by the organizations that create values by managing the TBL approach.

arguments clearly justify Interloop to be placed among Sustainability 2.0 organizations

The above arguments clearly justify Interloop to be placed among Sustainability 2.0 organizations on Dyllick and Muff's Business Sustainability Typology. However, an initiative of Interloop for providing quality education to the less privileged children of society can be considered as an outside-in approach, thus identifying Interloop as Sustainability 3.0 organization for this particular aspect. Sustainability 3.0 is "true business sustainability as the most advanced form of business sustainability. The focus shifts from reducing the negative impact of business to making a positive impact in critical and relevant areas for society and the planet". This educational initiative addresses a broader societal challenge of illiteracy faced by the Pakistani society and which will ultimately create a highly positive impact in raising the quality of life for people living in an under-privileged society. The argument is also justified through SCALA survey where 17.4% of respondents (N=84) supported the view that Interloop is making a positive contribution towards solving critical societal challenges.

Future business perspective

Interloop has not completed this journey of sustainability to its ultimate end. The organization understands the need to continuously address the challenges faced by this planet. The TBL approach has given a direction to Interloop for moving forward on the sustainability perspective. The slogan of "i-Care" has changed the mind-set of people associated with Interloop by introducing a shift in business paradigms to address sustainability issues. Among the future business concerns of Interloop are the following:

> **TBL approach has given a direction to Interloop for moving forward on the sustainability perspective**

▷ Innovating and using more substitutes for natural energy sources to deal with the challenge of natural resource depletion

▷ Introducing organic cotton in manufacturing socks which will reduce the consumption of cotton grown with the use of pesticides and other toxic chemicals thus reducing the environmental footprint

▷ Formal reporting of sustainability efforts and challenges by publishing a Sustainability Report encompassing global sustainability challenges

▷ Providing participative training to the employees for better application of sustainability plans

Keeping in mind such future business perspectives will engage the organization in sustainability efforts on a continuous basis. The CEO of Interloop expressed his views as follows:

It doesn't end here. We have two things in mind now: 1. continuous training and development programmes for the employees to take forward the sustainability objectives of the company. 2. Sustained financial models to support the sustainability issues. We want communities to be sustainable and not only the organization... At least we are putting our share (interview Zulqarnain).

A crucial enabler

> 'Training' as a crucial enabler that facilitated Interloop in advancing on the journey of sustainability

Lastly, it is important to highlight "Training" as a crucial enabler that facilitated Interloop in advancing on the journey of sustainability. This enabler was adopted as a strategic tool to implement sustainability practices in an effective and efficient manner.

While Interloop was running its business on ethical principles, the top management at Interloop was also concerned to transfer these ethical values to the lower levels as well. According to the CEO of Interloop, it was not very difficult to convince people as the top management set a very strong example of ethical practices themselves (interview Zulqarnain). The concerns of the management towards employees' health and safety, employee empowerment, workplace hazards, environment safety and waste management were the main inspirations for the employees to be ethically sustainable. However, in order to practically change the mind-set of people working at Interloop, periodic training programmes played a vital role as a crucial enabler to implement sustainability. Management of Interloop well understood the fact that without changing the mind-set of people working in the organization, it would not be able to bring paradigm shifts in the business. This was more of a reason that sustainable organizations well understand the importance of employees for their sustainable development and has their enhanced focus on transforming the behaviours of their employees to support sustainability (Eccles, Perkins, & Serafeim, 2012).

Changing the traditional ways of doing work is a challenge for most of the organizations during transitional phases. Similar conditions were faced by the management of Interloop as stated by the head of the EHS department (interview Qasim). In order to address this challenge and facilitating the shift in operational paradigms, management decided to adopt training programmes as an effective tool. For this purpose, intense and frequent training programmes were conducted for all levels of hierarchy in the organization. Both in-house and out-sourced facilities were used for conducting these training programmes. Experts with relevant knowledge of environmental protection and social concerns were involved for the said purpose. These intense and frequent training programmes not only created awareness among employees regarding sustainability issues but also imparted technical know-how to achieve sustainability goals. Employees of Interloop benefited from such training programmes and took them as a means of professional learning and development. Head of the Organizational Development (OD) department at Interloop said:

> Adopting and implementing sustainability was not possible without training programmes. We have training calendars to regularly arrange training programmes at all levels of the organization. These training programmes not only create awareness about social and environmental issues among employees but also educate them on doing self-audit (interview Fareha).

Apart from these periodic training programmes, employees are continuously engaged in reinforcing their perceptions of sustainability. This is done by celebrating various occasions and events, related to both environmental and social issues, at the company premises involving everybody working for the organization. These occasions and events are mostly celebrated annually and mainly include:

▶ **Celebrating Sustainable Energy week**. To reinforce the need for energy conservation for sustainable living. Employees are encouraged and rewarded to bring in innovative ideas for energy conservation and suggestion boxes are also placed throughout the premises for such ideas

▶ **Celebrating World Water day**. To reinforce the need for conserving clean water and avoiding its shortage

▶ **Celebrating Respiratory Protection week**. To reinforce the need for respiratory protection and raise awareness among employees to protect themselves against environments with insufficient oxygen and hazardous air contaminants

▶ **Celebrating Hepatitis Prevention day**. To reinforce the importance of healthy living by providing the employees with awareness on preventive measures for hepatitis

▶ **Celebrating Dengue (epidemic) Prevention day**. To reinforce the need for an epidemic-free workplace to address the social concerns.

▶ **Celebrating International Women's day**. To reinforce the non-discriminatory and equal employment opportunity practices of the organization.

Employees of Interloop fully engage themselves in such celebrations and learn the best practices of not only their personal health but also environmental safety. Moreover, such celebrations along with training programmes not only engaged the employees but also helped in changing the mind-set that was required to implement sustainability practices at Interloop. It is imperative to mention that these celebrations have wider impacts crossing the organizational boundaries when the employees of Interloop bring all these learnings with them out to their families. This is helping in spreading the knowledge of sustainable practices outside the organization to a larger community for the common good of society and the environment.

Conclusion

It is concluded from the discussion in the case study that the corporate sector needs to recognize its responsibilities to safeguard social and environmental issues without compromising the financial health of the organization. Addressing the sustainability issue can provide a solid base to the organizations to differentiate themselves from traditional organizations especially in the context of the developing world. This transformation of an organization from traditional business perspectives to sustainability perspectives needs ethical values as the founding stone as witnessed in this case study. Ethical practices of Interloop's leadership led the organization on this remarkable journey of three-dimensional sustainability perspectives. Development of sustainable culture and the responsible role of the organization's leadership had been the key points for implementing sustainability at Interloop. Moreover, training programmes, as a crucial enabler, used by Interloop proved to be effective in adopting and implementing sustainability at Interloop.

Organizations with traditional business perspectives can learn the possible ways of adopting sustainability practices from the historical milestones of Interloop to achieve the status of a sustainable organization. Adopting these practices has given long-term benefits to Interloop in the form of a healthy workforce, profitable customer relationships, less employee turnover, reduced environmental footprint, cost reduction and above all, status of a sustainable organization. Moreover, complying with laws, third party recognitions and addressing a triple bottom line approach of sustainability has portrayed Interloop as a sustainability landmark in the textile sector of Pakistan. Similarly, active involvement of internal and external stakeholders has also played a vital role in categorizing Interloop as a sustainability leader in the local textile sector. Interloop has successfully engaged the premium international customers as its clientele mainly due to its responsible approach to address sustainability issues. However, improved mechanisms are required to deeply engage the external stakeholders, such as investors and suppliers, in sustainability issues addressed by the organization.

sustainable organizations can leverage the long-term relationships with their stakeholders on sustainability issues

It may then be inferred that sustainable organizations can leverage the long-term relationships with their stakeholders on sustainability issues resulting in financial sustainability for such organizations. Additionally, sustainability issues need persistent and devoted efforts by the corporate sector to bring a meaningful change in business paradigms focused on sustainability.

Bibliography

Ambrogio, E. D. (2014). *Workers' conditions in the textile and clothing sector: just an Asian affair? Issues at stake after the Rana Plaza tragedy.* European Parliamentary Research Service.

Bertels, S., Papania, L., & Papania, D. (2010). Embedding sustainability in organizational culture. Retrieved from www.nbs.net.

Dyllick, T., & Muff, K. (2014). The Business sustainability typology, A briefing for organizational leaders and academic scholars. Retrieved from http://www.bsl-lausanne.ch/research-and-publications/the-business-sustainability-typology.

Dyllick, T., & Muff, K. (2015). Clarifying the meaning of sustainable business: introducing a typology from business-as-usual to true business sustainability. *Organization & Environment.* Retrieved from: http://www.truebusinesssustainability.org/?page_id=7.

Eccles, R. G., Ioannou, I., & Serafeim, G. (2011). *The Impact of a Corporate Culture of Sustainability on Corporate Behavior and Performance.* Harvard: Harvard Business School.

Eccles, G. R., Perkins, M. K., & Serafeim, G. (2012, June). How to become a sustainable company. *MIT Sloan Management Review, 53*(4), 43-50.

Elkington, J. (1994). Towards the sustainable corporation: Win-win-win business strategies for sustainable development. *California Management Review, 36*(2), 90-100.

Ghayur, S. (1996). Labour market issues in Pakistan: Unemployment, working conditions, and child labour. *The Pakistan Development Review, 35*(4), 789-803.

Global Recycle Standard. (2015). Global recycle standard. Retrieved from: http://textileexchange.org/sites/default/files/te_pdfs/integrity/GRS%20Presentation.pdf.

Government of Pakistan. (1993, August 29). The gazette of Pakistan. Retrieved from http://cmsdata.iucn.org/downloads/national_environmental_quality_standards_1993.pdf

Horrigan, B. (2007). 21st century corporate social responsibility trends – an emerging comparative body of law and regulation on corporate responsibility, governance, and sustainability. *Macquarie Journal of Business Law, 4,* 85-122.

Interloop, L. (2013). *In the Loop.* Faisalabad: Interloop Limited.

Interloop, L. (2014a). Certifications. Retrieved from: http://interloop-pk.com/certifications.php.

Interloop, L. (2014b). Company business. Retrieved from Interloop: http://interloop-pk.com/companybusiness.php.

Interloop, L. (2014c). CSR. Retrieved from: http://interloop-pk.com/corporatesocialresponsibility.php.

Interloop, L. (2014d). EHS. Retrieved from: http://interloop-pk.com/ehs.php.

Interloop, L. (2014e). Investor information. Retrieved from: http://interloop-pk.com/investor_info.php.

Interloop, L. (2014f). Lean. Retrieved from: http://interloop-pk.com/lean_our_practices.php.

McWilliams, A. (2000). *Wiley Encyclopedia of Management*. New York, NY: John Wiley & Sons Inc.

Nadvi, K. (2009). Globalisation and poverty: How can global value chain research inform the policy debate? *ResearchGate*.

OHSAS 18001. (2015, April). What is OHSAS 18001? Retrieved from: http://www.ohsas-18001-occupational-health-and-safety.com/what.htm.

PEPA. (1997, September 3). Pakistan Environmental Protection Act. Retrieved from https://www.elaw.org/system/files/Law-PEPA-1997.pdf.

Robbins, S. P., & Coulter, M. (2010). *Management*. New Delhi: Pearson Education.

Rockstrom, J., Stephen, W., Noone, K., Persson, A., Chapin, F. S., Lambin, E. F., . . . Scheffer, M. (2009). A safe operating space for humanity. *Nature*, 461, 472-475.

SA 8000 Standard. (2015, April). SA8000® standard and documents. Retrieved from http://sa-intl.org/index.cfm?fuseaction=Page.ViewPage&PageID=937.

SCALA. (2014). *Sustainability Culture and Leadership Assessment Survey*. Louisville, KY: Miller Consultants Inc.

Tahir, M., & Mughal, D. K. (2012). Pakistan textile industry and the neighbouring countries (a globalization effect). *Far East Journal of Psychology and Business*, 8(2), 66-70.

The News. (2012, October 8). Bitter memories of October 5, 2008 earthquake still fresh. *The News*. Lahore, Punjab: Pakistan.

Tribune. (2013, March 18). Statistics on textile industry of Pakistan. *The Express Tribune*.

Weiner, B. J. (2009, October 19). A theory of organizational readiness of change. Retrieved from http://www.implementationscience.com/content/4/1/67.

WRAP. (2015). WRAP's 12 principles. Retrieved from http://www.wrapcompliance.org/12-principles.

Zhang, J., & Liu, Y. (2010). Organizational climate and its effects on organizational variables: an empirical study. *International Journal of Psychological Studies*, 2(2), 189-201.

✉ Institute of Business and Information Technology, Quaid-e-Azam Campus, University of the Punjab, Lahore, Pakistan

💻 shamaila.gull@gmail.com

☎ +92-42-99230826

Dynamic Sportswear Ltd: compliance or muddling through sustainability?

A perspective from the Pakistani textile industry

Shamaila Gull

Business School Lausanne, Switzerland

Introduction

As the eighth largest exporter of textile products in Asia, the fourth largest producer of cotton in the world with the third largest spinning capacity in Asia after China and India, the Pakistani textile sector has become a significant textile contributor in the region. The economic output from this sector comprises 9.5% of the GDP, hence, making this sector the economic backbone of the country. Moreover, this sector employs more than 38% of the manufacturing workforce, contributes more than 63–68% of the total export earnings of the country and is a major source of foreign exchange earnings (Cleanclothes, 2015), thereby enhancing the significance of this sector.

Increased competition among clothes retailers has triggered a high demand for low cost strategies. As a result, the location of the suppliers has shifted from relatively high wage countries to low wage countries in developing regions such as South Asia including Bangladesh and Pakistan (Graafland, 2002). This shift has increased the competition among the textile organizations of these countries. In order to remain competitive in the international market, Pakistani textile organizations need to organize their efforts for addressing social and environmental issues, for example, unsafe working conditions. These issues have primarily resulted from the increased awareness of the social and environmental challenges faced by the global corporate sector. As a result, there have been increasing demands from the international customers of the local textile sector to address these issues. These demands have set standards resulting in compliance pressures on the local textile organizations doing business with the international customers. For this purpose, the local textile organizations regularly conduct compliance audits to ensure their customers that they meet the

International buyers
want their suppliers
to be socially and
environmentally
responsible

internationally expected business standards. These audits can help the organizations to identify risks, non-compliance with laws and company policies, and areas that need improvement (cengage, 2015). However, these audits can only be effective when supplier organizations are empowered to manage their social and environmental responsibility themselves and buyer organizations ensure a greater security for their suppliers by engaging in long-term business relationships with them (BSR, 2007). The cited BSR[1] report also states that a conflict exists between buyers' desire to ensure socially and environmentally responsible business and their commercial purchase objectives. International buyers want their suppliers to be socially and environmentally responsible without increasing the purchasing prices. As long as buyer organization do not align the strategic goals of their sustainability or CSR departments with the economic goals of the purchasing department, the local textile industry will be confronted with an unsolvable conflict: acting responsibly while still being economically viable for its international clients. The economic constraints faced by the Pakistani textile organizations further complicate this situation of dealing with the compliance pressures and doing business in a profitable way.

Keeping in view the importance of this sector in the Pakistani industry, the textile sector of Pakistan was selected to be part of case studies written by research cohorts at Business School Lausanne, Switzerland, as part of doctoral dissertations. The primary purpose of writing these case studies was to add a knowledge base to the business sustainability perspective and related cultural dimensions of sustainable organizations in different regions of the world. The organizations selected from Pakistan not only belonged to the textile sector but they also had a comparative base of being exporters of hosiery products to some famous international brands such as Nike, Puma, Levi's, Dockers, Adidas and many more. The focus of this case study is to highlight the existing business sustainability practices and the challenges related to their implementation faced by the textile organizations operating in Pakistan. One of the most popular definitions of business sustainability is given by John Elkington which considers sustainability as "accounting and reporting framework that measures an organization's progress along three lines: economic prosperity, environmental quality and social justice" and he even said it more simply in defining the triple bottom line (TBL) approach of "People, Planet and Profit" (Elkington, 1994).

In this developing region of South Asia, Pakistan is classified as a low-income economy by many rating agencies (Malik, 2002), thus restricting the financial growth of the local textile industry. Despite limited economic resources,

---

1 Business for Social Responsibility (BSR) is an organization that works with businesses to create a just and sustainable world. Their role is catalysing change within business by integrating sustainability into strategy and operations, and to promote collaboration among companies and their stakeholders for systemic progress toward a just and sustainable world (www.bsr.org/en/about/).

local organizations are still trying to do their share in safeguarding the social and environmental resources for a better living. However, the organizations addressing sustainability issues are far fewer in number in this developing region. Due to economic constraints, most organizations are operating on the concept of separating the firm's interests from the stakeholders' interests thus hiding the actual practices of the organization from what stakeholders actually demand (Crilly, Zollo, & Hansen, 2012). This happens when stakeholders do not have the same level of information because the information is retained by the management about the organization's affairs (Iqbal, Ahmed, Basheer, & Nadeem, 2012). For instance, despite the compliance pressures from multiple stakeholders such as NGOs, worker unions, community groups and customers, nothing much has been done to deal with the issue of fire safety at factory premises. Most of the local textile organizations still lack proper fire safety measures even after the horrible incident of a factory fire in 2012 killing more than 300 workers (Zia-ur-Rehman, 2012). Many indicators of environmental hazards such as air pollution further show a dismal situation. Similarly, although Pakistan is a signatory to many social conventions such as International Labor Organization (ILO), most of the textile organizations are not responding appropriately to address the issues related to social compliance (Sheikh, 2004). On the contrary, compared with what is practised by most of the Pakistani textile organizations, there are few organizations that have shown the responsibility to address the social and environmental issues beyond what is legally and ethically required. Such sustainable organizations are taking effective measures to meet internationally expected social standards along with a focus on preserving the natural environment. Dynamic Sportswear is one of such organizations which are trying to be conscious in owning their corporate responsibility towards social and environmental uplifting by adopting and implementing sustainability practices. The organization has started addressing the sustainability challenges by accepting the internationally expected business standards. Although the organization's efforts to address sustainability issues are obvious, the organization's position in the sustainability typology used in this case study analysis is still at an initial level, Business Sustainability 1.0, as will be described in later sections.

Keeping in view the above mentioned discussion points, this case study will shed light on the business practices of Dynamic Sportswear (Private) Limited from a sustainability perspective. The main objectives of the case study will be to:

1. Assess the sustainability position of Dynamic Sportswear based on the ongoing business practices

2. Understand the cultural dimensions of Dynamic Sportswear from a sustainability perspective

3. Analyse the positioning of Dynamic Sportswear on the Business Sustainability Typology Matrix presented by Dyllick and Muff (2015)

4. Contribute to a wider pool of case studies of sustainable organizations from various industries of different regions to facilitate an exchange of know-how among practitioners as well as between academia and the business world

In preparing this case study, we started with a comprehensive understanding of the sustainability concept and the relevant textile industry context from the literature. The literature review of both topics enabled the researcher to gather the relevant information that was required to serve the purpose of accomplishing the objectives of the case study. The information gathered from the literature review is used in the case study where required to support the arguments. The case study proceeds to describe the different phases of organizational change towards sustainability at Dynamic Sportswear with the help of theoretical literature, company documents and interviews conducted with various stakeholders. The discussion of these phases serves objective 1 of the case, emphasizing the past and current business practices of the organization for moving towards sustainability. Interviews with the company's stakeholders also provided important insights about the sustainability practices at Dynamic Sportswear Ltd. The details of interviewees are shown in Table 1.

Table 1 Interviewees

Sr No.	Name	Designation
1.	Mr Mobeen	Chief Executive Officer (CEO)
2.	Mr Rao Muhammad Shahbaz	Manager Finance and Corporate Affairs
3.	Ms Zill-e-Huma	Chief Merchandiser
4.	Ms Rabia Arif	Supply Chain Manager
5.	Ms Neelma Kazmi	Human Resource Officer
6.	Mr Muhammad Shahzad	Compliance Specialist
7.	Mr Muhammad Naveed	Production, Planning and Control Manager
8.	Mr Shad Mustafa	Chief Executive Officer, Textile Marketing Company (Supplier)

In order to understand the sustainability culture of Dynamic Sportswear which serves objective 2 of the case study, the Sustainability Culture and Leadership Assessment (SCALA™) survey was done in collaboration with Miller Consultants and Business School Lausanne, Switzerland. This survey examined the cultural dimensions of Dynamic Sportswear from a sustainability perspective through six variables: organizational leadership, organizational systems, organizational climate, change readiness, internal stakeholders and external stakeholders. The analysis of these six cultural dimensions can be helpful in understanding the cultural characteristics of sustainable organizations. Moreover, the SCALA survey highlights different cultural aspects of Dynamic Sportswear which have supported the organization to reach its current position on the Business Sustainability Typology Matrix (Dyllick & Muff, 2015). This typology helps us to understand the current and future sustainability challenges by focusing on concerns, values created and organizational perspective of sustainable organizations, thus, fulfilling objective 3 of the case study.

The case will now proceed with a brief company background followed by various business phases of organizational change for Dynamic Sportswear over time. The sustainability culture at Dynamic Sportswear will then be assessed by using the findings of the SCALA survey by discussing its six dimensions. The discussion of the business phases and the cultural assessment will be used as the foundation for positioning Dynamic Sportswear on the Business Sustainability Typology matrix presented by Dyllick and Muff (2015). The case study closes with a discussion of key challenges faced by the local textile organizations with respect to sustainability.

Company overview

Dynamic Sportswear (Pvt) Ltd is a family owned business that has been manufacturing and exporting socks from Pakistan since 1992. The company produces all types of socks (sports/athletics/casual) for men, ladies and children. The company is considered to be one of the largest manufacturers and exporters of sport socks from Pakistan, with more than 600 employees, 333 knitting machines, covering an area of 220,000 square feet, a turnover of US$18.0 million annually, and with a capacity of 70 million pairs per annum exporting to USA, Canada and Europe on a regular basis (Dynamic Sportswear (Pvt) Ltd, 2015).

Dynamic Sportswear is a fully integrated vertical unit. The company has unlimited design capability and can manufacture all types of heel formats (i.e. Y-heel, reciprocated/real, pouch, tube) using the latest computerized Italian machines, equipped with the latest in-house toe linking and over-locking, dyeing and finishing machines. The company is able to meet the most stringent and discerning requirements ranging from the upscale to the bulk economy market of socks. Moreover, the company is equipped to provide quality socks at the most competitive prices. Its customer portfolio includes prestigious organizations such as Levi's, Dockers, Nine West, Fruit of the Loom, Wrangler, Converse, Dunlop, Umbro and department store chains C&A and Tesco. Moreover, their socks can also be found at chain stores such as Target, Walmart, Kohl's and Mervyn's (Dynamic Sportswear (Pvt) Ltd, 2015).

Dynamic Sportswear believes in and practices total quality management and all of their product range is certified by the OekoTex Standard 100[2] Certification (TESTEX Swiss Textile Testing Institute). The company is also Worldwide Responsible Accredited Production[3] (WRAP) and ISO 9001:2008[4] certified. Various compliance audit companies such as SGS (the world's leading inspection, verification, testing and certification company), Intertek,[5] Cal Safety Compliance Corporation (CSCC) and Bureau VERITAS[6] (BV) annually monitor the company's commitment with the customers' as well as certification organizations' codes of conduct. These certification companies do audits for multiple social (workplace safety, child labour, safety-related trainings) and environmental issues (waste management, emissions control, waste water treatment). The factory is also equipped with its own waste water treatment unit to meet international environmental standards (Dynamic Sportswear (Pvt) Ltd, 2015).

The above description shows that Dynamic Sportswear is engaged in third party certifications for various standards. The main reasons behind this are the social and environmental challenges faced by the textile sector of the country. As mentioned above, these challenges are mostly compliance-driven in the industry of a developing country like Pakistan. This view is also endorsed by the interviewees of this case study. However, a consistent commitment of organizational leadership at Dynamic Sportswear with

---

2 The OEKO-TEX® Standard 100 is an independent testing and certification system for textile raw materials, intermediate and end products at all stages of production. It mainly deals with the impact of textiles and their chemical ingredients on the health and well-being of humans (https://www.oeko-tex.com/en/manufacturers/concept/oeko_tex_standard_100/oeko_tex_standard_100.xhtml). The Oeko-Tex Standard is one of the most successful consumer health and safety standards in the textile industry (https://center.sustainability.duke.edu/sites/default/files/documents/ecolabelsreport.pdf).

3 WRAP was formed out of the desire to create an independent and objective body to help apparel and footwear factories around the world verify that they are operating in compliance with local laws and internationally accepted standards of ethical workplace practices (www.wrapcompliance.org/).

4 ISO 9001:2008 sets out the criteria for a quality management system and is the only standard in the family that can be certified (although this is not a requirement). It can be used by any organization, large or small, regardless of its field of activity. This standard is based on a number of quality management principles including a strong customer focus, the motivation and implication of top management, the process approach and continual improvement (www.iso.org/iso/home/standards/management-standards/iso_9000.htm).

5 Intertek Pakistan provides expert services to clients requiring independent and world-class, testing, inspection, certification and consulting services. As part of the global Intertek network, Pakistan supports clients operating inside the country and internationally (www.intertek.com/pakistan/).

6 Created in 1828, Bureau Veritas is a global leader in testing, inspection and certification (TIC), delivering high quality services to help clients meet the growing challenges of quality, safety, environmental protection and social responsibility (www.bureauveritas.com/wps/wcm/connect/bv_com/group/home/about-us/our-business/certification).

product quality, without any compromise on social and environmental aspects, has enabled them to meet the compliance requirements.

Phases of organizational change for sustainability

Dynamic Sportswear went through different business phases while progressing on its journey towards sustainability. This journey was a challenge for an organization operating in a developing country with corresponding contextual constraints. According to research by Kazmi and Takala (2014), the current constraints faced by the textile sector of Pakistan involve:

> ▶ Obsolete technological solutions and infrastructure

> ▶ Unskilled or poorly trained human resources

> ▶ Lack of capacity to meet the certified standard levels

> ▶ Lack of automated industrial operations

> ▶ Lack of proper and effective marketing of textile products

> ▶ Environmental challenges

Additionally, deprivation of labour rights, dangerous working conditions in the factories and discrimination against female workers are among the big issues in Pakistan's textile industry (Cleanclothes, 2015). In the presence of these constraints, it becomes very difficult for an organization to think beyond its economic interests and meet the internationally expected business standards. However, the commitment of Dynamic Sportswear's leadership to gain economic benefits without compromising on the social and environmental issues has facilitated the company to start travelling on the path of sustainability. The organization started its business with an initial phase: **Phase 1** of capitalizing on business economy with an ethical perspective. This phase describes the founding perspective of the organization with ethics as a base for having a long-term competitive edge.

Moving forward, **Phase 2** shows the progress of the business practices of Dynamic Sportswear on the sustainability continuum with mostly social concerns. In this regard, compliance with internationally defined social standards has helped the organization to win the trust of its foreign clients, thus, enabling the organization to compete with other compliant organizations on an international level.

Later on, **Phase 3** shows a consistent and progressive engagement of Dynamic Sportswear towards sustainability by involving a broader perspective of economic and social concerns along with environmental protection.

This tri-faceted business perspective facilitated the organization to address the sustainability issues. The journey of Dynamic Sportswear from a one-dimensional economic perspective to a three-dimensional sustainability perspective is explained below by showing the organization's progress towards sustainability over a period of time.

Phase 1: capitalizing on business economy

Dynamic Sportswear started its business operations as a family owned business in 1992 with only 10 knitting machines on its floor. The business was started in a traditional way with profit maximization as the main organizational goal. However, Dynamic Sportswear faced industrial constraints (mentioned above) thus limiting the organization's growth opportunities. The only possible way to progress and take the limited opportunities available in the market was to maximize the shareholders' wealth. This sole economic business concern of Dynamic Sportswear was addressed by a strong commitment of the top management to the quality of its products. While pursuing this commitment, the organization got the ISO 9001 certification for its product quality in 2004. Moreover, this commitment for product quality also secured profitable customers for Dynamic Sportswear initially at the national and later on at the international level. An enhanced focus on product quality served the economic base of the organization through customer satisfaction, finally resulting in profit maximization. However, this economic perspective never compromised on ethical norms of the business (interview Mobeen) as will be described later.

According to the interviewees at Dynamic Sportswear, "Quality and Commitment" had been keys for the organization to achieve its economic goals. For this, organizational leadership never compromised on the quality of their products at any point in time. This "Quality and Commitment" business perspective is strongly related to the ethical perspective of the leaders of Dynamic Sportswear. At this phase of the company's development the family values of the organization's owners were the foundation of the company's ethical climate. Business practices, led by these corporate ethical values, directly influenced the employees' performance at Dynamic Sportswear in a positive manner (Sabir, Iqbal, Rehman, Shah, & Yameen, 2012). The leadership of the organization used these ethical practices as a tool to achieve an improved performance of the employees at Dynamic Sportswear that resulted in economic gains. However, these ethical practices at Dynamic Sportswear were in contrast to the prevailing industrial norms during the 1990s.

The working conditions for the workers were below average and labour exploitation was a norm in the subcontinent in this era, with the Pakistani textile industry being no exception. This was mainly due to weak law enforcement, lack of awareness and a high rate of illiteracy in the region.

There was no significant textile organization that paid attention to raising the product quality without compromising on the basic business ethics. However, Dynamic Sportswear differentiated itself from other textile organizations based on its concern for raising product quality through ethical considerations for the employees which finally resulted in employees' commitment and loyalty for the organization. Additionally, these ethical considerations not only resulted in better product quality but also attracted a skilled workforce from the market and reduced employee turnover rate (interview Naveed). Some examples of ethical practices adopted by Dynamic Sportswear are mentioned below.

Always paying the employees the minimum wage rate had been a practice at Dynamic Sportswear since its foundation in 1992 (interview Mobeen). This is one example of Dynamic Sportswear's ethical practices that they adopted to reduce the impact of labour exploitation common in the industry. The organization had always paid the employees according to the wage rate set by the local government. This practice distinguished the organization from the rest of the local textile companies that did not pay the legal minimum wage, because the relevant authorities did not effectively enforce the law. This distinguishing practice of Dynamic Sportswear resulted in employees' commitment and better performance for the organization. It is important to mention that the current minimum wage rate paid by the organization is Rs.13,000 (approximately $130) per month as required by the local government in 2015. However, the minimum industrial wage is still Rs.7,000 (approximately $70) per month (Cleanclothes, 2015) which shows the dire state of workers' rights. It is important to mention that these low wages of the employees of supplier organizations are a result of low prices demanded by the international buyers due to increased global competition (Graafland, 2002).

Providing employees with a safe and hygienically sound working environment shows ethical commitment of the organization's leadership. The organization improved the working conditions of its employees through an increased focus on cleanliness by considering the need for hygiene for its employees. Since its beginnings, the organization has been engaged in proper waste disposal in order to provide a clean and healthy working environment for its employees. Being rare in the local textile industry, such practices also won the trust of the employees leading to better performance.

The core business process of knitting is known for its heavy production of liquid waste. This waste water was one of the main components of pollutants being discharged into main watercourses by textile organizations. Despite legislation from relevant authorities in the mid-1990s, no proper mechanism was adopted by the textile organizations to deal with this waste water generated as a result of bleaching and dyeing. In 1998, Dynamic Sportswear took the initiative of installing a waste water/effluent treatment plant (ETP) to treat this waste water, before dumping it into the main watercourses. It was purely an ethical responsibility assumed by the management of Dynamic

Sportswear without any pressure from law enforcing agencies or customers at that time. This practice won the trust of Dynamic's customers resulting in retaining and attracting a lucrative customer base for the organization and ultimately enhancing the organization's economic value.

A canteen was also opened within the factory premises in 1999 for providing the employees with clean and hygienic food at a very nominal price. The food was provided to the employees at subsidized rates by the organization with no quality difference for any hierarchical level. Employees from all the managerial and non-managerial levels enjoy the same kind of food with the same services for all. In a developing country like Pakistan, where social class discrimination is common and the majority of the corporate sector has a money-making mind-set, such ethical initiatives create an exception in the industry especially for the workers.

Finally, Dynamic Sportswear has always taken its prime responsibility to run this family-owned business in an ethical way. The ethical considerations guided the organization's dealings with its multiple stakeholders including customers, employees and suppliers, resulting in profitable and trustworthy relations with these stakeholders. For instance, a supplier mentioned ethics as the main reason for their business partnership with Dynamic Sportswear. He said; "They always had a clear ethical footprint which is the main reason of doing business with them for over 20 years. Good moral and ethical background of the owners had been keys for the success of their business" (interview Mustafa).

Ethical motivation could be considered as the only possible reason for avoiding labour exploitation and dealing responsibly with the stakeholders when there was weak law enforcement and monitoring by relevant authorities in the local textile industry. The implementation of the ethical practices helped the organization to capitalize on its economic success (through employees' commitment, profitable customers, trustworthy suppliers), thus, creating a competitive edge for the long-term survival of the organization. Moreover, the ethical values held by the founders helped the organization to pave its way for moving forward towards a broader perspective of responsible business with social responsibilities as a top priority.

> The implementation of the ethical practices helped the organization to capitalize on its economic success

Phase 2: managing social issues

With the growth in business Dynamic Sportswear also broadened its frame of responsibilities. The ethical mind-set of the organization's leadership led it to include corporate responsibilities towards social issues. In an operative context where labour exploitation, child labour, poor health and safety conditions and violation of laws are considered to be the norm, it becomes difficult for the organizations to go against the odds. However,

Dynamic Sportswear became an exemplary organization by addressing the social concerns faced by the local textile industry at the time when no other significant organization acted responsibly. For instance, contrary to the common practice in the industry, the management of the organization strictly followed the laws of child labour. According to the Pakistani Employment of Children Act 1991, the minimum age limit for a child to work is 14 years. However, "the 18th amendment in the constitution has actually raised the minimum age up to 16 years without amending the labour laws, so contradiction continues" (paycheck, 2015). It is very important for textile organizations to abide by the laws of child labour due to the dangerous nature of work and the handling of chemicals at a textile organization. Because of this, Dynamic Sportswear had always employed persons who were above 18 years of age, going even beyond child labour laws and common sustainability standards. This perspective has enabled the organization to capitalize on human resources of the organization by dealing with a social issue that may restrict the entry of local textile organizations to the international markets, if not addressed.

When Dynamic Sportswear entered the American market to export its products to brands such as Levi's, it further enhanced its focus on resolving the social dilemmas present in the industry (interview Shahbaz). In pursuing this, Dynamic Sportswear again set an example by conducting its first social compliance audit in 1998 when such audits were still unheard of in the local textile industry. This compliance audit was done to assure the foreign clients about safe practices adopted by the organization for its employees. However, it was not an easier task for the organization to fulfil the formal requirements of the audit as there were no examples present at that time in the local textile industry. But the responsible leadership of the organization did not let these hurdles stop it from meeting its obligations towards a better working environment. Instead of doing this audit as mere window-dressing to satisfy its customers, Dynamic Sportswear sought help from one of its customers, Levi's, to guide their staff in the audit requirements and procedures (interview Shahbaz). It is important to mention that fake compliance audits are highly common in practice in the local industry due to corruption. Many textile exporters bribe the auditors to get fake compliance certificates to authenticate their malpractices (interview Mustafa). Due to the strong ethical culture at Dynamic Sportswear corrupting auditors was not an option here. The organization only had to organize its procedures according to the compliance requirements along with a few additional measures.

Dynamic Sportswear considers workplace health and safety measures an integral part of its business operations (interview Huma). Consequently, the organization conducts safety-related trainings, measures to reduce accident rates and noise testing. The organization started training its employees for fire safety and other workplace hazards as an initial step in collaboration with Civil

> **Dynamic Sportswear considers workplace health and safety measures an integral part of its business operations**

Defence Services.[7] These training programmes equipped the employees with basic knowledge to deal with workplace mishaps. Additionally, supervisors are trained to further facilitate safety measures to lower level staff (interview Rabia).

Similarly, reducing the accident rate has also been a priority of Dynamic Sportswear. The top management has been committed to provide a safe and sound work place to its employees but illiteracy poses a big challenge to educate the employees in adopting safe work practices. The labour-intensive nature of the textile industry, with lack of education and awareness, further complicates the problem in a developing country's context. However, despite these challenges, Dynamic Sportswear is determined to reduce the operational hazards to a minimum. In this regard, guiding posters were pasted everywhere in the factory premises with precautionary signs for the employees to remember and follow. These posters helped the employees to follow the safety measures on a routine basis thus reducing the workplace casualties. The guiding signs in these posters include wearing masks, metal gloves and earplugs while working in the assembly area. All such measures have reduced the accident rate at Dynamic Sportswear to a significant extent. Figure 1 shows the record of accidents and injuries at Dynamic Sportswear for the year 2014. The record shows that only minor injuries, i.e. small cuts and bruises, occurred while no major injury such as physical disability or death happened in 2014 because of the safety measures adopted by the organization.

Figure 1 Summary record of accidents and injuries

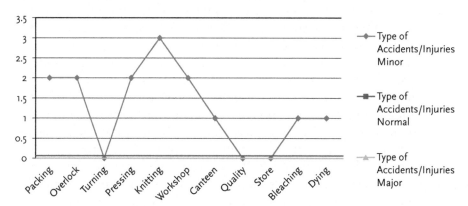

Textile manufacturing organizations cause a serious threat to the health and safety of their employees through air and noise pollution, if not handled

---

7 "Civil Defence in modern times is essential for a civilized society. As the Civil Defence is always ready for the protection of any person, property, place or thing during any hostile attack, whether from air, land or sea. During the peace times humanity also faces other most dangerous calamities whether these are man-made or natural" (www. civildefence.gov.pk/page.php?id=1).

properly. The employees working in assembly areas are specifically under threat of air and noise pollution generated by machines. Dynamic Sportswear realized this fact and adopted proper measures to secure its employees from these threats. The organization is engaged with renowned laboratories, which conduct air and noise testing for the employees on a regular basis (interview Naveed). This regular monitoring of air and noise in the factory premises is also a non-practised norm of the local textile industry and significantly differentiates Dynamic Sportswear from its competitors in a positive way. Moreover, this measure has addressed not only the social aspect of this issue but also helped in reducing the environmental impact of air and noise pollution.

In short, Dynamic Sportswear owns its responsibility to cater to the social issues faced by the local textile industry. The compliance audits, prevailing wage rates, healthy and safe working environment, educating and training the workers are significant contributions that have given long-term benefits to the company in the form of social and economic values (interview Naveed). Due to this engagement with social issues Dynamic Sportswear has become a preferred employer in the industry. However, the pressure from international customers to fulfil social standards on the competitive textile manufacturers is growing (interview Arshad). Dynamic Sportswear's willingness to accept the compliance challenges enabled it to get the third party social certifications. These certifications mainly include WRAP and OEKO-TEX Standard 100 certifications. Additionally, the organization is participating in the Business Social Compliance Initiative[8] (BSCI) code of conduct.

> the pressure from international customers to fulfil social standards on the competitive textile manufacturers is growing

In addition to workplace safety, local labour laws and the third party certifications require the organizations to meet the workplace standards related to working hours, rest times, freedom of association, discrimination, harassment and unions. Dynamic Sportswear strictly follows these standards by allowing a maximum of 54 work hours (including overtime) per week for the workers. These work hours include 1 hour rest time after every 5 hours work shift. Moreover, the company also facilitates the freedom of employees to have their religious, professional or political associations. In this regard,

---

8 The BSCI Code draws on important international labour standards protecting workers' rights such as International Labor Organization (ILO) conventions and declarations, the United Nations (UN) Guiding Principles on Business and Human Rights as well as guidelines for multinational enterprises of the Organization for Economic Co-operation and Development (OECD). It sets out 11 core labour rights, which participants and their business partners commit to implementing within their supply chains in a step-by-step development approach (www.bsci-intl.org/content/bsci-code-conduct). It is important to mention that a few standards such as BSCI also face criticism from researchers and related activists due to the unacceptable methods of implementation of such standards. For instance, there is a marginal role of stakeholders in the design and governance level of the organizational systems supported by BSCI standards.

a workers' welfare council (workers' union) has also been established which has elected members from all the sections of the organization. Female workers are also part of this council without any discrimination. This council ensures the workers' rights by raising its voice against any workplace harassment or abuse.

Finally, strict law enforcement is required to deal with the societal issues, such as corruption, often faced by developing societies. In the Pakistani textile industry, this issue has resulted in getting fake certifications to meet compliance standards. Such societal issues run against the true spirit of the compliance pressures and the results are mere window-dressing. However, in the case of Dynamic Sportswear, the organization's ethical foundation opened a way to accept the compliance pressures and act appropriately accordingly without fraud. Dynamic Sportswear's deliberate efforts to address the social issues faced by the local textile industry created social values (safe working environment, employee training, no to child labour) for its stakeholders along with a positive economic impact. These deliberate efforts embarked the organization on the journey of sustainability with an additional focus on environmental concerns.

Phase 3: moving to business sustainability

Creating a business case for sustainability requires identifying economic opportunities and further harnessing these opportunities with social and environmental initiatives. Along with its economic and social concerns, Dynamic Sportswear managed to invest in such initiatives that were helpful in reducing the organization's environmental footprint. These investments for environmental protection, along with the initial two business concerns, economic and social, facilitated the organization to embrace the idea of sustainability. It is important to mention that addressing the social and environmental issues was primarily triggered by the ethical mind-set of the organization's top management that was brought in from the family values of the owners. However, compliance pressures from foreign customers also played a vital role in this regard. The following paragraphs will shed light on Dynamic Sportswear's sustainability journey with more focus on environmental initiatives.

In order to reduce the environmental footprint, Dynamic Sportswear laid down a 3 km long drainage pipe in 2004. This drainage pipe was laid down with the approval of relevant authorities to dispose of the wastewater generated by the production site into the main drain of the city. Dynamic Sportswear paid the entire cost of the drainage pipe. In contrast to this responsible behaviour, the other organizations operating in the vicinity used to put their wastewater into the nearby clean water irrigation canal. This criminal negligence was happening due to weak monitoring by regulatory authorities. Dynamic Sportswear, however, recognized its responsibility to reduce the environmental footprint of polluting the clean canal water used for irrigation purposes by investing in this drainage pipe. This drainage pipe has also reduced the environmental hazard for the community living near the factory.

As discussed earlier, an effluent treatment plant (ETP) was installed by the organization to treat the wastewater produced by the company caused by the bleaching of the yarn. The growth in business, in later years, also involved the dyeing of yarn and socks that generated a more harmful kind of wastewater. This wastewater required an advanced ETP with a capacity to treat the pollutants in a more effective way. For this purpose, a state-of-the-art ETP was installed in 2012 that operates round the clock. This ETP has a capacity to treat around 50–60 m³ of wastewater per hour which is slightly above the average capacity of many local textile organizations of the same size (i.e. 40–50 m³/hour). It is important to mention that in contrast to the around-the-clock operation of the ETP at Dynamic Sportswear, most of the other textile organizations run the ETP plants on a need basis merely for getting the audit approvals (interview Mobeen). Investing in ETP and treating waste water before discharging it into the drains is an important environmental contribution by Dynamic Sportswear towards community safety at large.

> an effluent treatment plant (ETP) was installed by the organization to treat the wastewater

An independent Health & Safety committee was established in 2012. This committee is responsible for ensuring social and environmental safety and for reducing the negative impacts of business operations. The members of this committee have expert knowledge of social and environmental issues faced by the textile industry. These members meet on a regular basis to deliberate on issues such as the energy crisis, operational risk assessment and related training programmes (interview Neelma). The committee is also responsible for formulating social and environmental goals. These goals are incorporated in the performance evaluations of the employees for proper assessment and implementation. Major contributions of this committee, so far, have been to take measures for energy conservation and placing the safety posters in the native language of workers for a better understanding. These posters also helped to reduce the number of accidents while working in the assembly area (interview Shahzad). In short, establishing this committee facilitated the implementation of sustainability practices with a combined focus on social, environmental and economic concerns.

Energy conservation and innovating renewable energy sources are also part of the company's sustainability initiatives. "The ecological footprint of humans on earth increases with energy use and we have to address the compromises of our relationships with non-renewable energy" (Weinstein, Turner, & Ibanez, 2013). Dynamic Sportswear realizes the importance of renewable energy sources and is trying to adopt energy substitutes to reduce its environmental footprint. These energy substitutes include: solar panels, steam from boilers and light-emitting diodes (LED). In 2013, solar panels were installed as a measure to reduce the energy consumption from non-renewable sources such as fossil fuels. These solar panels have started contributing to the energy system of the organization in an effective way. Although the current contribution of these solar panels is less than 10% of the total energy requirement of the organization the management of Dynamic Sportswear is determined to install more solar panels.

> solar panels were installed as a measure to reduce the energy consumption from non-renewable sources

Another important step to save energy was taken in 2013 in the form of using steam from boilers. This steam is used as an energy substitute to run the chillers which otherwise operate on power from fuel. This particular initiative has also contributed to reducing the carbon footprint of the organization to a significant extent.

Similarly, in 2014 LED lights were installed in most of the factory premises. These LED lights operate by consuming very little power and thus help the organizations to save energy as well as cost. Electric meters were also installed at various sections of the organization to monitor the energy usage. These electric meters also help the employees to do self-audits of their energy consumption. Moreover, the LED lights and electric meters helped in reducing the energy cost of the organization by almost 20% (interview Shahbaz).

Finally, energy conservation measures taken by Dynamic Sportswear have reduced the consumption of energy from sources such as oil, thus reducing the carbon footprint by 15,935 kg in 2014. This carbon reduction is equivalent to planting 797 trees for safeguarding the natural environment.

It is evident from much global research that clean drinking water sources are quickly depleting. This has posed a serious challenge for all the responsible entities of society to adopt strict measures for preserving clean water sources. In this regard, Dynamic Sportswear has installed a clean drinking water plant for its employees. The main reason behind this plant was the limited access to drinking water in the remote area where the factory is located. The organization invested in this initiative in order to provide the employees with clean and safe drinking water. The purpose, however, does not end here. Keeping in view the importance of clean water, the organization put water meters at different consumption sites in the factory premises to monitor the water consumption on regular basis. These water meters not only allow the regular monitoring of water consumption for various purposes but also make the employees conscious about the worth of clean water.

> A proper system for waste management has been adopted to deal with the solid waste

A proper system for waste management has been adopted to deal with the solid waste generated by the business operations. The organization has collaborated with waste management vendors such as A.T. Waste Management,[9] which is approved

---

9 http://atwm.com.pk/

by the relevant authorities for their specialized services in this regard (interview Shahbaz). These vendors are responsible for disposal of the hazardous waste materials such as ETP sludge and chemical packaging. The management of Dynamic Sportswear fully coordinates with the waste vendors to ensure the safe disposal of waste materials.

Apart from these major environmental protection and work safety initiatives, the organization is also concerned about other relatively minor issues that can affect the environment: paper wastage control, lead free packaging, use of dangerous chemicals and BHT[10] free poly bags. These minor but important concerns also help in reducing the environmental footprint caused by the production site.

All the above mentioned phases of organizational change highlight the economic, social and environmental concerns of the business. These economic (employee commitment, profitable customers, reduced employee turnover), social (wage rates, safe working conditions, noise testing) and environmental (waste management, energy conservation, clean water conservation) concerns addressed by Dynamic Sportswear serve the sustainability perspective of the organization. Additionally, these concerns facilitated the organization to travel upon the path of sustainability by giving it a long-term competitive advantage in the local textile sector.

Sustainability Culture and Leadership Assessment (SCALA) survey

It is very important for an organization to understand the role of leadership and culture in adopting sustainability. The pathway for the adoption of business sustainability leads through the implementation of a sustainability-oriented organizational culture (Linnenluecke & Griffiths, 2010). Sustainability values cannot be created without making them part of the accepted values and norms of the organization, i.e. organizational culture. These accepted values and norms then embed sustainability into the daily operation of the business. Therefore, it is important for practitioners to understand the dynamics of sustainability culture for the overall implementation of sustainability by an organization. In order to understand

---

10 Plastic packaging material, like poly bags, can contain BHT (butylated hydroxytoluene). This is an antioxidant that prevents ageing of the plastic and can be transferred to the fabric. There are many studies which demonstrate that BHT accumulates over time in the body, having a toxic impact on the lungs, liver and kidneys among other negative effects (http://thegoodhuman.com/2009/09/24/what-is-bht-butylated-hydroxytoluene-and-why-you-should-avoid-it/).

the depth of the sustainability culture at Dynamic Sportswear, the SCALA survey was conducted. The SCALA™ survey…

> is an assessment instrument composed of items pertaining to culture and leadership. The assessment contains both sustainability-specific content as well as more general organizational climate content that has been demonstrated or asserted in other research to impact the execution of sustainability strategies (SCALA, 2014).

This survey will help the readers to assess the perception of Dynamic Sportswear's employees regarding sustainability culture and the performance of the leadership to create sustainability values.

The SCALA survey was used as a quantitative measure in this case study. It was conducted organization-wide as an online survey by sending the questionnaires to employees via their email addresses. The survey comprised 30 questions developed by Miller Consultants, 10 questions added by Business School Lausanne (BSL) and 2 questions added by the researcher to gain an insight about the employees' perspective of organizational sustainability. The questionnaire was in English, and the questions were a mix of open and close-ended questions. Close-ended questions were answered on a five-point Likert scale with responses ranging from "strongly agree" to "strongly disagree".

The sample was chosen from the population of 40 executive level employees. The survey was conducted online by sending the questionnaire to 24 employees based on the email addresses provided by the company. The sample size was N= 13 after having a response rate of almost 50%. The sample was chosen in consultation with Dynamic Sportswear's management through a random sampling technique and it represented senior, middle and first-line management of the organization. Demographically, the respondents were 77% male and 23% female. The organization-wide survey involved two corporate-level executives, two senior managers, six mid-level managers, two first-line managers and one from other positions. According to age groups, one respondent belonged to the age group 51–60 years, two respondents were of 41–50 years of age, four respondents belonged to the 31–40 years age group and six respondents were between 20 and 30 years of age. The survey consisted of questions related to the following six variables:

> ▸ Organizational leadership

> ▸ Organizational systems

> ▸ Organizational climate

> ▸ Change readiness

> ▸ Internal stakeholders

> ▸ External stakeholders

The survey results for the above mentioned variables will now be explained to get a better understanding of Dynamic Sportswear's culture regarding sustainability.

Organizational leadership

Organizational leadership refers to those who possess formal authority from the top of the organization and at various organizational ranks (Miller-Consultants, 2015). The long-term success of the organization depends on the strength of its leadership. Organizations whose leaders have a clear vision for sustainability will be in a better position to achieve the goals of sustainability. The SCALA results for Dynamic Sportswear show that 54% of the respondents (N=13) either agree or strongly agree that their leaders have a clear vision for sustainability. Similarly, 85% of the respondents agreed that leaders of this company take a long-term view when making decisions.

Furthermore, while expressing their views about Dynamic Sportswear's leadership in the SCALA survey, 69% of the respondents (N=13) either agree or strongly agree that leaders of this company integrate sustainability into their decision-making; 62% of the respondents also believe that leaders of this company are able to inspire others about sustainability focused issues. When asked about the willingness of the leaders to take measured risks in the pursuit of sustainability, 54% agreed and 15% of the respondents strongly agreed with the statement.

Two important aspects of effective leadership are commitment and knowledge possessed by the organization's leaders. In the SCALA survey, 69% of the respondents (N=13) agreed or strongly agreed that leaders of this company are personally committed to issues pertaining to sustainability. A very high percentage of respondents, 92%, also believe that leaders of this company are knowledgeable about the issues pertaining to sustainability. Finally, 85% of the respondents agree or strongly agree with the statement that the leaders of this company have a clear business case for pursuing the goals of sustainability.

leadership of Dynamic Sportswear is striving to diffuse the sustainability phenomenon into the company culture

It can be inferred from these results that the leadership of Dynamic Sportswear is striving to diffuse the sustainability phenomenon into the company culture. However, continuous engagement and commitment of leadership is required to develop a sustainable culture.

Organizational systems

The SCALA survey also assessed the employees' perception about embedding sustainability in the organization's systems. "These systems consist of a structured framework of practices and procedures that enable the organization to execute in a consistent and lasting manner" (Eccles, Perkins, & Serafeim, 2012). The SCALA data for Dynamic Sportswear shows that 54% of the respondents (N=13) agree or strongly agree that the company has embedded sustainability into the operating procedures and policies; 75% of the interviewees also endorsed the SCALA results for embedding sustainability into the organization's daily operations.

Additionally, 69% of the respondents also believe that the company has integrated sustainability-related goals into the performance management system. However, only 31% of the respondents agree that rewards and compensations are clearly linked to the organization's sustainability goals. These contradictory results lead to an assumption that the performance management system of Dynamic Sportswear not yet fully includes sustainability as an integral part. This could be done by assigning sustainability goals to the employees with measurable outcomes and linking these outcomes with rewards and compensation.

According to a previous research "sustainable companies are far more likely to have enterprise-wide management systems for executing sustainable strategies" (Eccles, Perkins, & Serafeim, 2012). The SCALA survey results for Dynamic Sportswear show that 62% of respondents agree to the statement that the organization has an enterprise-wide management system for sustainability.

Lastly, the SCALA survey results show that although the organization has systems in place there is a need for continuous sustainability-related efforts to fully integrate sustainability into these organizational systems.

Organizational climate

Organizational climate refers to the characteristics of the internal environment of an organization. These characteristics may include trust, innovation and learning. According to Eccles *et al.*, "companies with an established organizational culture that includes strong capabilities for change, a commitment to innovation and high levels of trust have a significant advantage" (Eccles, Perkins, & Serafeim, 2012). Forty-six per cent of the respondents (N=13) of the SCALA survey agreed with the statement that the level of trust within this organization is high. While 38% of the respondents agree or strongly agree that the organization rewards innovation. These results again show that the organization needs to incorporate the sustainability perspective more into its culture by promoting trust, innovation and learning among its employees. An organization cannot become sustainable without these sustainability-related cultural aspects.

The extent to which an organization supports learning of its employees is another aspect by which to gauge its organizational climate. In SCALA 85%

of the respondents (N=13) agree or strongly agree with the statement that continual learning is a core focus of this organization. Furthermore, 38% of respondents are of the view that people in this organization are encouraged to learn more about sustainability from external sources. This result may lead to an assumption that the organization does not put much focus on employees' formal training regarding sustainability. There are very few training programmes that are focused on sustainability issues as also stated by the interviewees.

Finally, 77% of respondents either agree or strongly agree that a commitment to sustainability is essential to the company's success in the long term. It can be inferred from these results that Dynamic Sportswear needs more persistent efforts to make its organizational climate supportive to implement sustainability practices.

Change readiness

Change readiness is an important cultural element that enables the process of sustainability (Eccles, Perkins, & Serafeim, 2012). With regard to this, the SCALA survey shows that 62% of the respondents (N=13) believe that the company has a strong track record of implementing large-scale change successfully while 69% of respondents believe the same for implementing incremental (small, continuous) change. Five out of eight interviewees also endorsed the SCALA results for change readiness through their personal experiences with Dynamic Sportswear.

Moreover, challenging the status quo is also an indicator to bring positive changes in organizational practices. In this regard, 77% of the respondents agree or strongly agree that people in this company actively challenge the status quo. These results support the view that Dynamic Sportswear has started travelling towards sustainability by promoting sustainable business practices that are unfortunately not yet commonplace in Pakistan.

Internal stakeholders

The execution of any sustainability strategy needs the personal engagement of employees (Eccles, Perkins, & Serafeim, 2012). The SCALA survey shows that the company has a clear strategy for engaging all internal stakeholders in its sustainability efforts: 54% of the respondents agree with the statement while 69% agree and 15% strongly agree that by and large, people in this company are engaged in work that is connected to sustainability goals. Thirty-eight per cent of the respondents agreed with the statement that employees feel valued in Dynamic Sportswear while 38% of the respondents also believe that the desire to engage employees also led the company to start addressing sustainability issues. These low percentage results are an alarm call for

> **sustainable culture requires a higher level of employee engagement for achieving the sustainability goals**

the organization to consider what needs to be done to improve the employees' perception of feeling valued. This is mainly because sustainable culture requires a higher level of employee engagement for achieving the sustainability goals.

External stakeholders

According to Eccles *et al.* (2012), "companies that thrive with a sustainability strategy realize the importance of reaching beyond their own internal boundaries to a variety of external stakeholders". In this respect, the SCALA survey shows that 46% of the respondents agree or strongly agree with the statement that the company has mechanisms in place to engage actively with external stakeholders about its sustainability efforts. The result implies that there is a need for more effective mechanisms to engage external stakeholders in adopting and implementing sustainability.

Additionally, 62% of the respondents believe that the company encourages sustainability in its supply chain while 62% of the respondents also agreed that the company sends a clear and consistent message to external stakeholders about its commitment to sustainability. For instance, the organization's corporate policy statement is:

> It is Dynamic Sportswear's policy to operate in a safe and responsible manner that respects the environment and the health of our employees, our customers and the communities where we operate. We will not compromise environmental, health or safety values for profit or production.

In short, an enhanced focus is required to engage the external stakeholders of the organization in sustainability-related goals and efforts for a significant impact.

The sustainability culture assessment of Dynamic Sportswear shows that although the organization has started implementing sustainability practices in its operations, there is still a lot more to do in this regard. For example, the performance management system needs to be more effective in terms of measuring the impact of sustainability practices. Similarly, measures should be taken to properly train the employees about sustainability issues in a more comprehensive way so that they can understand the impact of social and environmental values created by the organization. More effective mechanisms to engage the internal and external stakeholders in achieving sustainability goals are also required to develop a value-driven sustainability culture. Finally, the percentage results show that the development of sustainability culture at Dynamic Sportswear is at its initial stages. Dedicated and persistent efforts in organizational leadership are required to implement credible and effective sustainability practices.

> **persistent efforts in organizational leadership are required to implement credible and effective sustainability practices**

The case study so far has enabled the readers to know about different organizational phases of Dynamic Sportswear while progressing on the journey towards sustainability. The SCALA survey assessment further explored the journey by understanding the strength of the sustainability culture of the organization. These two sections of the case study, the phases of the organizational development overview and the SCALA survey, will now lead to positioning Dynamic Sportswear on the Business Sustainability Typology Matrix (Dyllick & Muff, 2015). This positioning will gauge how far the organization has travelled to embrace the idea of true sustainability.

Positioning Dynamic Sportswear on Business Sustainability Typology Matrix

This business sustainability typology presented by Dyllick and Muff (2015) examines the sustainability progress of an organization based upon three elements: 1) concerns; 2) values created; and 3) organizational perspective (see Fig. 2). The assessment of these three elements then places an organization on one of the three stages of business sustainability:

▶ Business Sustainability 1.0 (redefined shareholder value management)

   ▶ Business Sustainability 2.0 (managing for the triple bottom line)

      ▶ Business Sustainability 3.0 (true sustainability)

Dynamic Sportswear's position on this typology will be determined based on the information gathered in previous sections of the case study.

Figure 2 Framework presenting different stages of business sustainability

BUSINESS SUSTAINABILITY TYPOLOGY (BST)	Concerns (What?)	Values created (What for?)	Organizational perspective (How?)
Business-as-usual	Economic concerns	Shareholder value	Inside-out
Business Sustainability 1.0	Three-dimensional concerns	Refined shareholder value	Inside-out
Business Sustainability 2.0	Three-dimensional concerns	Triple bottom line	Inside-out
Business Sustainability 3.0	Starting with sustainability challenges	Creating value for the common good	Outside-in
The key shifts involved:	1st shift: broadening the business concern	2nd shift: expanding the value created	3rd shift: changing the perspective

According to Dyllick and Muff, traditional business organizations focus entirely on their economic concerns by maximizing the profit for shareholders. In contrast to this, the sustainability perspective is broader with a combined focus on economic, environmental and social concerns (Dyllick & Muff, 2015). This multi-faceted focus of sustainable organizations gives them a long-term competitive advantage in terms of sustainability. As shown in the previous discussion, Dynamic Sportswear addresses the sustainability challenges by adopting its three-dimensional concerns: environmental, social and economic.

The environmental concerns at Dynamic Sportswear are mainly addressed in the form of solid waste management, effluent treatment plants, energy conservation by installing solar panels and LED lights, water usage monitoring, carbon footprint reduction, paper wastage control, biodegradable (BHT free) packaging and installing a drainage pipe to save the clean water irrigation canal.

The social challenges have always been a focus of the organization. These challenges emerged out of the ethical approach of the business owners. Safe working environment, reduced operational risks, saying no to child labour, training and education, paying according to the prevailing wage rates, air and noise testing, a hygienic workplace and providing the employees with clean drinking water are the examples of social sustainability contributions by Dynamic Sportswear.

The economic concern is depicted through the phase 1 of organizational change in the earlier section of this paper. An initial business focus resulted in addressing economic concerns by raising the product quality, reducing employee turnover rate, creating a profitable customer base and long-term relationships with stakeholders.

multi-dimensional sustainability concerns identifies Dynamic Sportswear as a Business Sustainable 1.0 organization

Addressing these multi-dimensional sustainability concerns identifies Dynamic Sportswear as a Business Sustainable 1.0 organization. However, according to Dyllick and Muff's Business Sustainability Typology (2015), Dynamic Sportswear might already be a Sustainability 2.0 organization because it does address social, environmental and economic concerns. To verify if Dynamic Sportswear has already made this jump from 1.0 to 2.0 we need to explore how Dynamic Sportswear fulfils the other two elements of the BST: values created and organizational perspective.

Values created

For Sustainability 1.0 organizations, "business success still is evaluated from a purely economic view and remains focused on serving the business itself and its economic goals. The values served may be somewhat refined, but still oriented toward the shareholder value" (Dyllick & Muff, 2015). However,

"Business Sustainability 2.0 means broadening the stakeholder perspective and pursuing a triple bottom line approach. Value creation goes beyond shareholder value and includes social and environmental values" (Dyllick & Muff, 2015).

The earlier discussion about Dynamic Sportswear's sustainability journey clearly shows that the organization is striving to address the sustainability challenges by managing its economic gains. The economic gains are achieved by addressing the social issues through employees' training and education, improved working conditions, health and safety measures and reduced accident rates. These social considerations leverage the economic interests of the organization; maximizing the shareholders' value by increasing the employees' commitment and winning the trust of international customers. The results of the SCALA survey also endorse this assumption as 54% of the respondents believe that the organization is addressing sustainability issues in order to manage its risks and compliance standards. Additionally, 46% of respondents believe that the "desire to improve efficiency and impact the company's bottom line" led the organization to start addressing the sustainability issues. Both of these characterize redefined shareholder value management as adopted by Sustainability 1.0 organizations.

In addition to the social challenges, the organization is also trying to maximize the shareholders' value by addressing environmental issues. These environmental issues include: carbon reduction, waste management, energy saving, reduced usage of dangerous chemicals and wastewater treatment. The environmental initiatives help in preserving the natural environment of the planet. However, from a sustainability perspective, these issues are being addressed without compromising on the economic values of the business.

Managing this redefined shareholder value has also given a competitive edge to Dynamic Sportswear in the local textile sector of Pakistan. The SCALA survey supports this view and 69% of respondents think that Dynamic Sportswear is a better or much better company in the local textile industry with regard to sustainability. This is mainly due to the developing context of the country where the majority of organizations focus only on traditional ways of doing business. In this case, the values created because of the redefined shareholder value management identify Dynamic Sportswear as a Business Sustainability 1.0 organization, which adopts approaches with "attempts that are oriented primarily toward increasing shareholder value by reducing the business footprint rather than creating sustainable value in its broader meaning" (Dyllick & Muff, 2015).

Organizational perspective

Business Sustainability 1.0 organizations usually follow the inside-out organizational perspective: "organizations usually initiate the process from the existing business, strategy or product-line and work on making them more sustainable" (Dyllick & Muff, 2015). This perspective encourages the organizations to actively monitor, identify and solve the sustainability challenges. Dynamic Sportswear displays this inside-out business perspective by aligning its social and environmental concerns with economic values. For this purpose, the organization used its existing business model to address the sustainability challenges faced by the local textile industry. The argument is also supported by the above mentioned SCALA results: Dynamic Sportswear has been addressing sustainability issues by embedding it into its existing operations and systems. Furthermore, when asked, all the interview responses showed that sustainability goals are integrated into the daily operations of the organization. This integration has enabled the organization to deal with sustainability challenges (energy conservation, water conservation, waste management, safe and healthy working environment, training and education, safe packaging) in an effective way.

The implementation of sustainability by using the existing business model and resources supports the inside-out perspective for Dynamic Sportswear. The SCALA results confirm this argument for Dynamic Sportswear as 85% of respondents agree that the company has a clear business case for pursuing the goals of sustainability. The organization is also trying to embed the sustainability goals into its organizational systems as discussed earlier. Finally, an inside-out perspective limits the scope of sustainability-related decisions and actions due to the entire dependence on the existing business models (Dyllick & Muff, 2015). However, it may be considered as a significant step towards addressing the sustainability issues in a developing country's context.

The above discussion clearly positions Dynamic Sportswear as a Business Sustainability 1.0 organization in Dyllick and Muff's sustainability typology. Although the above mentioned organizational phases show a glimpse of the triple bottom line (TBL) approach, the current practices have not yet successfully embraced this concept which goes beyond the compliance requirements. In order to move towards Business Sustainability 2.0 which applies a TBL approach, Dynamic Sportswear needs to have a visible and measureable impact of sustainability practices. Moreover, persistent and dedicated efforts are needed to travel along this path towards true sustainability. Sustainability 3.0 means that "sustainability challenges are used as the starting point to define possible contributions by a business that also makes business sense" (Dyllick & Muff, 2015).

> persistent and dedicated efforts are needed to travel along this path towards true sustainability

The challenge

Dynamic Sportswear is operating in a developing country context which has low per capita income, poor social conditions, energy and water shortage, weak governance, political instability, uncertainty and security threats (Abid,

2013). These issues have resulted in an adverse situation for businesses to operate in. Limited economic opportunities in a developing country such as Pakistan often lead to dismal business conditions, thus, limiting the business concerns to the extent of maximizing shareholders' wealth. In this adverse scenario, the organizations lack resources and will to move beyond the economic concerns towards a better society. However, some external pressures bound the business organizations to operate in a responsible way. These external pressures may come from government, non-profit organizations (NPOs), labour unions and customers. Complying with the demands of these pressure groups is the only way for the businesses to survive and remain competitive in a developing economy.

The textile sector of Pakistan, which contributes 63–68% of total country exports, also faces compliance pressures from the above mentioned pressure groups, especially international customers. International trade, which has increased many times in the last 15–20 years, has imposed serious challenges for the Pakistani textile sector to compete with global textile competitors such as China and Bangladesh. These challenges include "meeting strict quality and compliance requirements, not only from a product-specific and technical perspective, but also from regulatory, social, environmental, performance, and customer-specific standpoints" (Ehsan & Khanum, 2014). The sustainable customers from developed economies specify compliance standards. The Pakistani textile organizations strive to meet these compliance standards even in the presence of existing contextual constraints. Furthermore, these compliance standards have shifted the organizational concerns from one-dimensional (i.e. economic) to three-dimensional (i.e. economic, social and environmental). In order to address these multi-dimensional concerns local textile organizations are taking measures to reduce their negative social and environmental impacts. The importance of third party certifications has also increased in the prevailing scenario of meeting the compliance standards. These third party certifications for the textile sector may include WRAP, ISO 9000, Oeko-Tex 100 and many more (Ehsan & Khanum, 2014).The compliance pressures have divided the local textile industry into compliant and non-compliant organizations (interview Mobeen).

> local textile organizations are taking measures to reduce their negative social and environmental impacts

Dynamic Sportswear is no exception, facing similar compliance pressures from its customers. According to a business supplier of Dynamic Sportswear, 90% of the textile organizations are trying to be sustainable due to compliance pressures (interview Mustafa). This view is also supported by the SCALA survey where 38% of respondents consider the company's current approach to sustainability as "reactive". Moreover, 54% of respondents consider the need to manage risk and compliance as a basic motive, which led the company to start addressing the sustainability issues. However, Dynamic Sportswear's investments in social and environmental initiatives have to be seen in the context of the current adverse business conditions of the country. These investments have not only generated economic benefits for the company but also won the trust of the stakeholders by creating social and environmental values. However, in the presence of the challenges faced by a developing country like Pakistan, these investments have raised a serious question for all the compliant organizations of the country. These organizations need to understand whether these investments are mere compliance initiatives or are they committed to becoming truly sustainable? Answering this question is a big challenge for practitioners who claim to be sustainable in this developing region. In this regard, research states:

> Today companies must choose whether to start the journey to become sustainable or to adhere to the more traditional model. Although each company must make that choice for itself, we believe that changing social and investor expectations will only increase the pressure on companies to adopt the sustainable model. Doing so requires unswerving leadership commitment, without which the journey cannot begin. In reframing its identity, the company must learn to engage openly with external stakeholders. Maintaining transparency without recourse to defensive strategies is integral to a sustainable strategy. As this strategy is implemented through broader-based employee engagement and disciplined mechanisms for execution, a new identity can emerge: that of a sustainable company (Eccles *et al.*, 2012).

Although Dynamic Sportswear has started travelling along the sustainability path it is not the journey which is travelled by only one organization. In order to see a visible impact of sustainability efforts on the local society there must be a combined struggle from the whole textile sector of Pakistan. These combined efforts would enable the local textile organizations to remain part of sustainable supply chains operating globally. A few significant textile associations such as APTMA[11] need to come forward to add social and environmental values to society beyond just being compliant organizations. These associations could play a vital role in facilitating industrial progress on the sustainability path with combined efforts from all the member organizations.

the industry should focus on improving the capacity building for sustainability-based performance

Additionally, the industry should focus on improving the capacity building for sustainability-based performance. This capacity building would facilitate the organizations to align their social, environmental and economic concerns. For instance, training could be adopted as an enabler to enhance the understanding and communication of sustainability issues among textile workers. In summary: industrial collaboration could be the key to achieving a level of sustainability that goes beyond compliance for the local textile organizations and their international clients.

---

11 All Pakistan Textile Mills Association (APTMA) is the premier national trade association of the textile spinning, weaving, and composite mills representing the organized sector in Pakistan. APTMA emerges as the largest association of the country as it represents 396 textile mills out of which 315 are spinning, 44 weaving and 37 composite units (www.aptma.org.pk/).

Bibliography

Abid, R. (2013). *Economy of Pakistan Challenges and Prospects*. Islamabad: Weeklypulse.

Bertels, S., Papania, L., & Papania, D. (2010). Embedding sustainability in organizational culture. Retrieved from www.nbs.net.

BSR. (2007). *Beyond Monitoring: A New Vision for Sustainable Supply Chains* . New York, NY: Business for Social Responsibility.

Cengage. (2015, August 13). The social audit. Retrieved from http://www.cengage.com/resource_uploads/downloads/1439042314_215907.pdf.

Cleanclothes. (2015, August 11). Facts on Pakistan's garment industry. Retrieved from http://www.cleanclothes.org/resources/publications/factsheets/pakistan-factsheet-2-2015.pdf.

Crilly, D., Zollo, M., & Hansen, M. T. (2012). Faking it or muddling through? Understanding decoupling in response to stakeholder pressures. *Academy of Management Journal*, 55(6), 1429-1448.

Dyllick, T., & Muff, K. (2015). Clarifying the meaning of sustainable business: introducing a typology from business-as-usual to true business sustainability. *Organization & Environment*. Retrieved from: http://www.truebusinesssustainability.org/?page_id=7.

Dynamic Sportswear (Pvt) Ltd. (2015, May). Dynamic Sportswear. Retrieved from http://www.dynamicsportswear.com.

Eccles, G. R., Perkins, M. K., & Serafeim, G. (2012, June). How to become a sustainable company. *MIT Sloan Management Review*, 53(4), 43-50.

Ehsan, S., & Khanum, A. (2014). Compliance with global quality requirements in Pakistan's export sector. *The Lahore Journal of Economics*, 19, 244-266.

Elkington, J. (1994). Towards the sustainable corporation: Win-win-win business strategies for sustainable development. *California Management Review*, 36(2), 90-100.

Graafland, J. J. (2002). Sourcing ethics in the textile sector: The case of C&A. *Business Ethics: A European Review*, 11(3), 282-294.

Iqbal, N., Ahmed, N., Basheer, N. A., & Nadeem, M. (2012). Impact of Corporate Social Responsibility on financial performance of corporations: Evidence from Pakistan. *International Journal of Learning & Development*, 2(6), 107-118.

Kazmi, S. A., & Takala, J. (2014). An overview of Pakistan's textile sector from operational competitive perspective: A suggestive analysis. *World Journal of Engineering and Technology*, 2, 124-130.

Linnenluecke, M. K., & Griffiths, A. (2010). Corporate sustainability and organizational culture. *Journal of World Business*, 45, 357-366.

Malik, A. S. (2002). *Impact of Environmental Regulations on the Textile Sector of Pakistan*. Geneva.

Miller-Consultants. (2015, August). Developing leaders. Retrieved from http://millerconsultants.com/developing-leaders.

Nadvi, K. (2009). Globalisation and poverty: How can global value chain research inform the policy debate? *ResearchGate*.

Paycheck. (2015, August 11). Child labor and Pakistan. Retrieved from http://www.paycheck.pk/main/labour-laws/fair-treatment/minors-and-youth/child-labour.

Sabir, M. S., Iqbal, J. J., Rehman, K. U., Shah, K. A., & Yameen, M. (2012). Impact of corporate ethical values on ethical leadership and employee performance. *International Journal of Business and Social Science*, 3(11), 163-171.

SCALA. (2014). *Sustainability Culture and Leadership Assessment Survey*. Louisville, KY: Miller Consultants Inc.

Sheikh, D. H. (2004). Social compliance in Pakistan's textile industry. *Pakistan Textile Journal*.

Weinstein, M. P., Turner, R. E., & Ibanez, C. (2013). The global sustainability transition: it is more than changing light bulbs. *Sustainability: Science, Practice & Policy*, 9(1), 4-15.

Zia-ur-Rehman. (2012, September 12). More than 300 killed in Pakistani factory fires. *The New York Times*.

✉ Institute of Business and Information Technology, Quaid-e-Azam Campus, University of the Punjab, Lahore, Pakistan

💻 shamaila.gull@gmail.com

☎ +92-42-99230826

ICI Pakistan Ltd

Sustainability through adversity

Syeda Nazish Zahra Bukhari

Business School Lausanne, Switzerland

Introduction

Pakistan is a developing country as categorized by the World Bank in its 2015 list of developing nations. The countries are categorized based on their gross national income (GNI) per capita per annum. Countries with a GNI of US$11,905 and less are defined as developing nations (Developing Countries, 2015). Pakistan falls into this category with a GNI of $1,360 as reported by the World Bank (2013). However, this categorization does not display the whole picture. According to the *CIA World Fact Book* (2014):

> Decades of internal political disputes and low levels of foreign investment have led to slow growth and underdevelopment in Pakistan. Agriculture accounts for more than one-fifth of output and two-fifths of employment. Textiles account for most of Pakistan's export earnings, and Pakistan's failure to expand a viable export base for other manufacturers has left the country vulnerable to shifts in world demand. Official unemployment was 6.6% in 2013, but this fails to capture the true picture, because much of the economy is informal and underemployment remains high. Over the past few years, low growth and high inflation have led to a spurt in food prices. As a result of political and economic instability; the Pakistani rupee has depreciated more than 40% since 2007. Pakistan remains stuck in a low-income, low-growth trap, with growth averaging about 3.5% per annum from 2008 to 2013.

In order to put the country on the path of sustainable growth, the Government of Pakistan adopted 16 targets and 41 indicators, to achieve the Millennium Development Goals (MDGs), against which the sustainable growth of the country would be measured. The MDGs are eight international development goals, to be achieved by 2015 by all 189 United Nations member states and at least 23 international organizations (UNDP, 2015). These are:

1. To eradicate extreme poverty and hunger

2. To achieve universal primary education

3. To promote gender equality and empower women

4. To reduce child mortality

5. To improve maternal health

6. To combat HIV/AIDS, malaria, and other diseases

7. To ensure environmental sustainability

8. To develop a global partnership for development

> **Pakistan as a nation is not sustainable or even heading down the path of sustainable development**

Each goal has specific targets and deadlines to achieve those targets. Out of the total 41 indicators adopted by the Government of Pakistan, time-series data is available for only 33 of these indicators. It reveals that out of a total of 33 indicators, Pakistan is on track to achieve the targets on nine indicators, whereas its progress on 24 indicators is off track. The reasons for missing most of the indicators include internal and external economic and non-economic challenges as stated by the country's Planning and Development Minister.

The data paint a very bleak picture of the country. Pakistan as a nation is not sustainable or even heading down the path of sustainable development. Pakistan must address serious issues related to government revenues and energy production in order to increase the amount of economic growth that is vital for its survival in the long term. Other long-term challenges include escalating investment in the fields of education and healthcare, building the competences to adapt to the effects of climate change and natural disasters, and reducing dependence on foreign donors. The country also faces serious concerns about rising demand for energy inputs and the volume of greenhouse gas (GHG) emissions (Pakistan Economy, 2014).

> **The adversities faced by businesses in Pakistan include: almost no support from the government, a prevailing mind-set in the country's culture that does not give any importance to the concept of well-being, an extremely challenging economic environment, and virtually no precedent of any organization that has adopted the concept of business sustainability in its true spirit**

In such circumstances, it is very hard for businesses to grow and develop sustainably. The adversities faced by businesses in Pakistan include: almost no support from the government, a prevailing mind-set in the country's culture that does not give any importance to the concept of well-being, an extremely challenging economic environment, and virtually no precedent of any organization that has adopted the concept of business sustainability in its true spirit. However, an organization's and the country's sustainable development are dependent on each other. In the words of the former United Nations Secretary-General, Kofi Annan:

In today's world, the private sector is the dominant engine of growth the principal creator of value and managerial resources. If the private sector does not deliver economic growth and economic opportunity equitably and sustainably—around the world, then peace will remain fragile and social justice a distant dream (Annan, 1997).

ICI Pakistan: from corporate philanthropy to corporate sustainability

ICI Pakistan Limited is a manufacturer and trader of a diversified range of products. It has been operating in this geographic area for nearly 70 years. It is a leading chemical company supplying products to almost every industry in Pakistan. It employs approximately 1,100 people; the company is headquartered in Karachi whereas operations are spread all across Pakistan. The company is currently owned by the Yunus Brothers Group (YBG). YBG is a conglomerate with diversified interests in textile, cement and power generation. YBG is the first Pakistani national company to own ICI Pakistan; before them, the ownership of the company was passed on between international organizations (ICI, 2014).

The four main businesses of ICI Pakistan are:

- Polyester
- Soda ash
- Chemicals
- Life sciences

The four businesses produce the following products:

- Polyester staple fibres
- POY chips
- Light and dense soda ash
- Sodium bicarbonate
- Speciality chemicals
- Polyurethanes
- Adhesives
- Pharmaceutical
- Animal health products manufactured
- Agricultural products including field crop seeds and vegetable seeds

Total company turnover in 2014 was 42.7 billion rupees (approximately €0.37 billion), with each business contributing the following share to the total turnover (ICI, 2014):

- ▶ Polyester, 46%
- ▶ Soda ash, 26%
- ▶ Life sciences, 17%
- ▶ Chemicals, 11%

The history of ICI Pakistan can be traced back to the Imperial Chemical Industry (ICI), which was a British chemical company and was among the largest manufacturers of chemicals in Britain for many years. ICI was formed in Britain in 1926 by the merger of four British corporations (Brunner Mond, Nobel Explosives, the United Alkali Company, and British Dyestuffs Corporation). Its headquarters was in Millbank, London (ICI, 2015).

In the late 1920s, Lord McGowan, who was the founding Chairman of ICI in Britain, sent Richard Banks (an employee of ICI) to the subcontinent (the part of South-East Asia containing India, Pakistan, and Bangladesh jointly under British rule at that time) to explore new business opportunities. ICI decided to set up a soda ash factory in Khewra (Pakistan) since it was at the heart of a large salt range that could supply limestone and rock, the two major raw materials for the upcoming industries of glass, soap, textiles, leather and general chemicals in the subcontinent. The plant started commercial production around the mid-1940s as part of the Alkali Chemical Corporation of India (ACCI), which was controlled by the British headquarters of ICI.

The history of ICI Pakistan's sustainability journey can be divided into three parts based on the three phases the company went through. ICI Pakistan's journey of corporate sustainability is one that has much resemblance to the development of the concept of sustainable development in the business world. ICI Pakistan started off with the practice of "corporate philanthropy" and steadily moved towards embracing the idea of "corporate social responsibility", and ultimately to the concept of "corporate sustainability". "Mix sustainable development, corporate social responsibility, stakeholder theory and accountability, and you have the four pillars of corporate sustainability. It's an evolving concept that managers are adopting as an alternative to the traditional growth and profit-maximization model" (Wilson, 2003).

1939–1990s: corporate philanthropy

In 1947 when the subcontinent was given independence from British rule and divided into two separate independent countries, Pakistan and India, the control of the soda ash factory was vested to the head office of the new ICI

Pakistan. Throughout the 1950s and early half of the 1960s, ICI Pakistan functioned as a small soda ash business and a large trading business importing ICI manufactured chemicals, dyes and other allied chemicals from over 100 overseas suppliers to Pakistan. In 1965, a major development in the history of ICI Pakistan occurred when Yusuf M. Khan was made the Chairman of ICI Pakistan by the international headquarters. He was the first Pakistani to be entrusted with the leadership of the company.

In the second half of the 1960s the company went on a large-scale expansion with the addition of a textile auxiliary plant, a pharmaceutical factory, the acquisition of the Fuller Paints Factory (an already established paint business in Pakistan) and the expansion of the soda ash factory in Khewra. At this time, ICI Pakistan established two additional companies under the parent brand of ICI Pakistan (ICI P), ICI Pakistan Manufacturers Ltd (ICI PML), which consisted of the soda ash business and the new textile auxiliaries' business, and Paintex Ltd, which was the newly acquired paint business. In the late 1980s the company expanded further with the start of ICI's polyester business, which was set up to cater to the growing textile industry of Pakistan at that time. In addition to this, ICI Pakistan also diversified into the areas of pharmaceuticals, agrochemicals and some general chemical like polyurethanes, trioxide, and water treatment chemicals (Hamid, 2012).

Along with the growth in business activities, the philanthropic activities of the company can be traced back to the start of its operations when the company first broke ground in Khewra for the construction of the soda ash plant in 1939 (ICI, 2014). Most of the activities fell under the umbrella of corporate philanthropy, which is defined in the business dictionary as:

> the charitable donations of profits and resources given by corporations to nonprofit organizations. Corporate philanthropy generally consists of cash donations, but can also be in the form of use of their facilities or volunteer time offered by the company's employees. The donations are generally handled directly by the corporation or by a foundation created by the firm.

Some examples of the company's philanthropic work at that time are listed below:

▶ ICI's Winnington Hospital, which was founded in 1943 and is located on-site at the soda ash plant in Khewra, Pakistan. The hospital is equipped with a well-established operating theatre and serves as a hub of medical activity for the benefit of the Khewra community. The hospital is used to conduct regular immunization for all community children against infectious diseases. The hospital team also conducts weekly medical camps in the nearby vicinity (ICI, 2009).

▶ In c. 1944 the company installed water taps for facilitating 24-hour community access to clean and running water for domestic use. Before that the community had no access to domestically usable running water (ICI, 2008).

▷ The ICI Pakistan Foundation was created under a trust in 1991 to channel the company's support of various social development initiatives in the healthcare and education sectors. The foundation allocates a percentage of the company's profit every year for philanthropic activities (ICI, 2008). Various members of the company's top management are part of the ICI Foundation's board of directors. Any employee in the organization can highlight a particular cause and suggest it for support. This is then investigated, analysed and judged for genuineness and worth by the foundation's board of directors (Z. Farid, personal communication, 28 October 2014).

▷ ICI Pakistan continued helping the Khewra community, where its soda ash plant was situated, with their various basic needs, including healthcare. In 1991, the company started its 2-day monthly eye clinic programme. This programme was offered free of cost to the Khewra community in the ICI Winnington hospital with the assistance of Layton Rahmatulla Benevolent Trust doctors. The services include outpatient department consultation and surgeries. An intraocular lens (IOL) bank has also been established, carrying 50 IOLs at any given point for cataract patients (ICI, 2008).

▷ ICI initiated a project in Khewra called Project Green in 1992. This was basically an initiative to bring greenery to the dried-up lime beds of Khewra (ICI, 2008). As the Vice President of ICI's Soda Ash division, said:

> **if you have the will to do something good you will ultimately succeed**

In Khewra, the land is very barren because of a huge quantity of salt in the water. Back in 1992 we decided to plant trees in the dry trenches present over there. Everyone thought it to be an impossible task; however, we had hope. We filled the dry trenches with river soil and planted trees in them. Then we used the recycled water, obtained after treating the waste water from the manufacturing of soda ash, to water the trees. Now we have a nice green patch of land that is welcoming for both humans and animals. It stands there as a proof that if you have the will to do something good you will ultimately succeed (S.A. Khan, personal communication, 6 November 2014).

The land spread over 152 acres with a total of 300,000 trees planted and a survival rate of 85%. The major water sources are the rain and recycled water from the company's soda ash plant (ICI, 2008).

> **corporate philanthropy practices usually are not sustainable. Anything a business does out of goodwill alone will not last, because there is no true link between an organization's strategy and its philanthropic activities**

However, corporate philanthropy practices usually are not sustainable. Anything a business does out of goodwill alone will not last, because there is no true link between an organization's strategy and its philanthropic activities. The practice is often observed in Pakistan; it was found in research conducted by the Pakistan Center for Philanthropy that almost 50% of the country's publicly listed companies donate 1% of their profits to charitable causes. But, what the companies do not realize is that corporate philanthropy often becomes a means to ease the corporate conscience instead of an established part of business strategy (Balkhi, 2015). According to research, the concept of corporate philanthropy is popular in Islamic countries like Pakistan, because philanthropy is derived from religious beliefs, according to which philanthropy should not be conducted to reap the reputation rewards from the society, but to serve God. So the donor does not close the loop by reporting the good that he did, he just leaves it to God to judge (Siddiqui, 2009). This analysis is reinforced by a survey done by Pakistan's Center for Philanthropy (PCP) which shows that, despite challenging economic conditions in Pakistan, the country's businesses contributed Rs3.8 billion (approx. $0.037 billion) towards philanthropic activities in 2011 (The News, 2011). This is a large amount for an economically challenged developing nation since for the same year a survey conducted by the Committee Encouraging Corporate Philanthropy (CECP) showed that 214 leading companies, including 62 of the top 100 companies in the Fortune 500 donated $20 billion to various charities (CECP, 2012).

By the early 1990s, ICI Pakistan became a large, broad-based and profitable organization. At this time, the international holding company, ICI PLC, merged the previously formed three groups, ICI P, ICI PML and Paintex, into a single entity called ICI Pakistan. Because of its tremendous growth and future potential, ICI PLC, decided to make its largest investment yet in Pakistan. In 1995, a plant was set up with an investment of Rs.450 million to produce pure terephthalic acid (PTA) in Pakistan. It was planned that this business would derive commercial and technological support from a very strong global ICI PLC business in PTA. Along with the rapid expansion in the company's business portfolio the management also focused on developing the company's in-house capabilities in the areas of utility service, corporate services and communication, technology acquisition and development, project construction and management, and safety, health and environment management (Hamid, 2012).

Health, safety, environment and security (HSE&S)

According to the Technical General Manager of ICI Pakistan:

I joined ICI back in 1980. At that time, there was no concept of "Safety" far less of "Sustainability". We took our first sustainable steps in the smaller playing field of workplace safety. Actually, the impact of "safety" is felt immediately; the impact of "health" is felt over a person's lifetime, but the impact of "sustainability" is felt over generations (I. Haider, personal communication, 28 October 2014).

the impact of "safety" is felt immediately; the impact of "health" is felt over a person's lifetime, but the impact of "sustainability" is felt over generations

According to research done by the Sustainable Development Policy Institute in 2012, 20% of the registered industries in Pakistan are considered highly polluting with 23 industrial sectors falling under the category of "most hazardous" on the basis of industrial effluents and 11 industrial sectors reported as "most hazardous" on the basis of their gaseous discharge (Khwaja, 2012). In 1988, ICI Pakistan attained a compliance certification from the European Chemical Industry Council (CEFIC), which is one of the main trade associations within the chemical industry in Europe (About CEFIC, 2015). The CEFIC compliance project in ICI Pakistan was a 36-month effort that the company's Health, Safety, and Environment Department undertook. The company also helped two of its partners develop the technical expertise and systems required to meet the rigorous CEFIC road safety guidelines for chemical transportation and handling (ICI, 2008). ICI Pakistan took up the initiative of health, safety, environment, and security (HSE&S) management at the time when it was not a legal obligation, nor considered a moral or social obligation by the majority of the organizations operating in Pakistan. In Pakistan, there was no Environmental Protection Act before 1997 and the government of Pakistan developed National Environmental Quality Standards (NEQs) through the self-monitoring and reporting/SMART programme in 2001 for all industrial sectors across the country. Under such external conditions, the company also created a Health, Safety, Environment and Security (HSE&S) Department and a yellow book of rules was formed containing rules, regulations and policies for all operational levels and areas as part of their internal development programme.

Even today the concept of workplace safety or safe handling of precarious materials is not commonly being implemented very seriously by the government nor is it being practised in its true spirit by the businesses. The chemical industry generates huge quantities of hazardous waste, and no proper chemical waste disposal facilities exist in the larger setups as well. As a result, chemical wastes spread all over the country with adverse implications for all the stakeholders. Furthermore, no central database has been created by the government concerning the chemical waste sites. Most often hazardous waste is handed over to contractors by the manufacturers, who then release the waste in broken ground close to roads and residential areas, cultivable lands or water bodies, generating irreparable damage. In the cities of Pakistan, flammable and toxic chemicals are sold just like everyday grocery items. The tanneries discharge huge amounts of untreated chemical waste into the environment. For example, the toxic industrial waste discharged by tanneries in the city of Sialkot is causing serious diseases such as cancer and diverse lung diseases (Jaspal and Haider, 2014). In a study done on the drinking water of the Sheikhupura industrial estate (Pakistan), where ICI's polyester factory is located and which houses more than 190 industrial units of various business groups, it was found that the drinking water had bacterial contamination, a high level of total dissolved solids, elevated chromium level (0.6 mg/L), and increased levels of arsenic and manganese, all of which are greatly hazardous to human health (Gilani et al., 2013).

According to its HSE&S policy (ICI, 2014), ICI Pakistan's core values are:

▷ Protecting the health and safety of employees, contractors, customers and neighbours

▷ Maintaining the security of people and assets

▷ Protecting the environment and working in close cooperation with customers, suppliers and distributors to do the same

▷ Complying with all relevant laws and regulatory requirements

▷ Ensuring that all activities are conducted in a manner consistent with ICI Pakistan health, safety, environmental and security standards and guidelines

▷ Ensuring that business activities are conducted to prevent harm to customers, employees, contractors and the public, other stakeholders and the environment

▷ Developing, manufacturing and marketing products with full regard of HSE&S aspects as well as ensuring compliance with the ICI Pakistan product stewardship management system and sell only those products that can be transported, stored, used and disposed of safely

▷ Protecting peoples, assets, intellectual property and critical information from accidental or deliberate harm, damage or loss

▷ Openly communicating on the nature of activities, encourage dialogue and report progress on health, safety and environmental performance

▷ Regularly monitoring the application of this policy

HSE&S management system

The HSE&S policy is implemented on an organization-wide level through ICI's health, safety, environment and security management system. The key elements are the policy, standards, guidelines, localized management system (procedures), and training management, self-assessment and audit, performance reporting and policy review. The line management was made responsible for HSE&S performance, the implementation of local regulatory requirements and ICI Pakistan's HSE&S policy, standards and guidelines.

The implementation is based on (ICI, 2014):

▷ **Equipment**. Designed and maintained "fit for purpose"

▷ **Procedures/system**. Locally developed and documented "robust"

▷ **People**. Trained and involved, contributing to HSE&S improvement

In 2000, Pakistan had just 59 industrial units that had any type of ISO certification, only 37 IEE/EIA reports were submitted to the Environmental Protection Agency (EPA) and the investment in environmental sustainability measures by the industrial sector in 1996 was Rs.7,570 million (Khwaja, 2012) which was extremely small compared to the revenue being generated by the industrial sector of the country at that time with a GDP of $75 billion (Economy of Pakistan, 2014). In a survey done by the *Financial Daily* newspaper of Pakistan it was observed that:

> About 40 per cent of the corporate companies in Pakistan think CSR means merely paying taxes. 30 per cent believe CSR is contributing to community welfare or donating to organizations for social development purposes and community development, while 15 per cent think that CSR equates employee welfare, and 10 per cent think CSR means working in areas where the company's interests lie. Only five per cent clearly understand CSR means directly implementing social development activities and projects (Arifeen, 2013).

Research from the Global Reporting Initiative (GRI), a leading organization in the sustainability reporting field, shows that in Pakistan, where 73% of the country's population lives on or below US$1 a day (UNDP), the sustainability performance of the companies operating in their country is not the primary concern of the majority of the country's population (Hils, 2011). The same perspective was shared by an ex-CEO of ICI when he said that "the sustainability-related expectations in Pakistan's emerging market environment can be generous and forgiving" (ICI, 2008). In such an external environment ICI Pakistan, in addition to internal audits, conducted external audits of its HSE&S programmes and entered into a Self-Monitoring and Reporting Program (SMART). It was a voluntary programme, in which the organizations worked along with the National Environmental Protection Agency (I. Haider, personal communication, 28 October 2014) and reported their environmental footprints, audited by a third party (Z. Farid, personal communication, 28 October 2014). This was done purely on a voluntary basis as there was no legal or regulatory requirement for SMART reporting by the Government of Pakistan until 2001.

"the sustainability-related expectations in Pakistan's emerging market environment can be generous and forgiving"

Continuing with its focus on environmental responsibility ICI Pakistan started working with World Wide Fund for Nature (WWF) in 1999 on the Save the Marine Turtle programme in Karachi, where the company's life sciences business was located. This was part of ICI's collaboration with WWF, to educate the local community about the importance of the marine turtles in the local ecology and factors causing their extinction. Many of the company employees took place in the activity on a voluntary basis and participated in cleaning the nesting place of the turtles. The corporate communication and public affairs department started publishing an internal magazine by the name of *Engage* in which various corporate social responsibility initiatives taken by the company were published for the internal stakeholders of the company (Z. Farid, personal communication, 28 October 2014). Various societal and environmental projects pursued by the company through active and voluntary employee participation during this time period are listed below (ICI, 2008):

▷ ICI financially supported the ABSA School, which caters to hearing impaired students.

▷ The company's polyester business supported a local primary school in an underdeveloped area of the country through both financial and qualified personnel assistance.

▷ The company's paints business supported the SOS village in Lahore through monetary donations as well as voluntary work done by the company's employees.

▷ The company continued to serve society through its monthly eye-camps, donations to a charitable cancer hospital, free kidney dialysis centre and through the provision of clean water in an underdeveloped area of the country

During this time period ICI Pakistan's parent company ICI PLC was struggling to manage its international portfolio. ICI PLC categorized its businesses into two groups, the "heavy end" business, comprising its traditional basic chemicals and other high capital structures where profitability was heavily dependent on the cost of manufacturing, and the "light end" business, consisting of low capital but high research and development cost businesses that produced high value-added products, which could earn high margins in the market. In addition to the parent company's categorization, ICI Pakistan was itself struggling with its own categories of businesses, including the "regional business" that catered to national markets and were bounded by local heavy tariff barriers and the "international business" that was capable of achieving a major global market share. ICI Pakistan felt that the heavy end regional businesses were slowing down the more profitable light end businesses. The parent company also preferred the light end businesses based on shareholder value maximization. So it demerged its most promising light end businesses, i.e. pharmaceuticals, agrochemicals and seeds, into Zeneca PLC, a separate entity, and it also acquired a group of light end businesses from Unilever to reposition the company internationally. ICI PLC also divested the pure terephthalic acid (PTA) business to DuPont and a large part of its heavy end portfolio to Huntsman Corporation of USA. Thus internationally the company was only left with paints as its strong heavy end business.

Unfortunately, the newly acquired light end business did not prove to be as successful as expected. All this greatly impacted ICI Pakistan since investment from the international parent company became scarce. Also, the regional soda ash and the polyester business had no attraction to the parent company which had already divested its international soda ash and fibre business. In addition to this, it was becoming increasingly difficult to sustain the now regional PTA business since it had lost the support of ICI PLC, which had divested the international PTA business to DuPont. ICI Pakistan, nevertheless, continued to acquire whatever investment it could get from ICI PLC and also managed to get some external non-ICI funding for expansion, restructuring and improvement of the company both technically and organizationally (Hamid, 2012).

Among this strategic turmoil, the company did not derail from its journey towards the adoption of corporate sustainability. Rather, it progressed from the "social responsibility" mind-set towards thinking sustainably. Evidence of this is the initiatives taken by the company during the following years.

2005–2015: corporate sustainability

> **I immediately fell in love with the concept and regretted all the time we had lost not knowing and following corporate sustainability in its true spirit**

I have been working in ICI Pakistan for the last 14 years and I myself learned about sustainability when we as an organization moved from the various paths of health, safety, environment, caring for our people and community to the enchanting path of sustainability. I immediately fell in love with the concept and regretted all the time we had lost not knowing and following corporate sustainability in its true spirit (S.A. Khan, personal communication, 6 November 2014).

ICI Pakistan adopted the concept of corporate sustainability under the leadership of its international holding company ICI PLC. A company database was developed for the collection, analysis, sharing and reporting of various critical data in the early 2000s. A Sustainability Council was formed, which was part of the International Sustainability Council of the parent company. The formal start of corporate sustainability was marked by the development of a sustainability framework for the company.

Sustainability framework

The company's sustainability framework is based on the triple bottom-line concept of economic, social and environmental parameters against which they measure their sustainability performance (ICI, 2014). The parameters to measure the company's performance in the three dimensions were laid down as shown in Table 1.

Table 1 ICI Pakistan's sustainability framework

Economic performance	Social performance	Environmental performance
Integrity management	Health, safety & security	Emissions control
Sourcing	Employment practices	Water usage
	Community investment	Waste management
		Product stewardship
		Energy efficiency

These were the major areas identified by the company's top management as critical to the sustainable development of the organization. After the framework was in place the management started to align all the other operational and administrative procedures. In 2005, the company started its Chairman and CEO's Leadership Award for Sustainability. This was an internal company award that was granted based on the best sustainability initiative and output produced by a business. Five-year sustained improvement-based target programmes were rolled out in 2000 and again in 2005 by the name of Challenge 2005 and Challenge 2010, respectively. In 2007, a global audit was conducted in the area of corporate sustainability under the supervision of Richard Moss, the then global representative of ICI Pakistan's international holding company in ICI Pakistan's Sustainability Council (Z. Farid, personal communication, 28 October 2014).

At this point in time, the company was in the first stages of business sustainability in which sustainability concerns are being considered in decision making and actions, but the business objectives remain focused on creating shareholder value (Dyllick & Muff, 2015). In the international arena ICI PLC's post-Zeneca demerger strategy was not going as planned and the company was weakening both financially and strategically in the global market. Because of this, AkzoNobel, a world-leading coating company, acquired ICI PLC globally in 2008 primarily to gain a stronger position in its core business of paints (Hamid, 2012). The current chief executive of ICI Pakistan, Asif Jooma states, "the attraction of AkzoNobel to acquire ICI PLC was its coatings and paint business, which were highly synergistic to Akzo's strategic portfolio" (Baig, 2013).

ICI Pakistan as part of AkzoNobel Group

AkzoNobel is a Fortune 500 company dealing with paints, coatings and speciality chemicals. It is listed on the Euronext Amsterdam Stock Exchange. It is among the chemical industry leaders in the Dow Jones Sustainability Indexes, and it is included in the FTSE4Good Index (ICI, 2008). AkzoNobel is a company that takes its commitment towards sustainable development very seriously. In AkzoNobel 50% of the CEO's annual incentive is directly linked with the company's performance in the Dow Jones Sustainability Index. The Dow Jones Sustainability Indexes (DJSI) are a family of indexes evaluating the sustainability performance of the largest 2,500 companies listed in the Dow Jones Global Total Stock Market Index. They are the longest-running global sustainability benchmarks worldwide (Dow Jones Sustainability Index, 2014). AkzoNobel was ranked number one, out of more than 350 companies in the materials industry group, in the DJSI for the third consecutive year in 2014 (ICI, 2014). One of the biggest steps that ICI Pakistan took on the path of sustainable development was the start of sustainability reporting in 2008. In 2008, ICI Pakistan released its first Annual Sustainability Report as part of its annual report.

This was a big step in the country's business environment at that time as a report on Asian sustainability in 2009 stated:

> Disclosure in Pakistan (with regard to sustainability) is generally poor with only three companies making it into the top of the overall ASR (Asian Sustainability Report). What little disclosure there is in Pakistan seems to revolve around the provision of information about general policies, codes and governance issues. Less than one in five companies provides any information on the environment, supply chains and community and development, all issues that are particularly important in the context of Pakistan. There is a great opportunity for companies to take a lead in engaging with sustainable development in a country like Pakistan. Our Research tends to demonstrate that in most cases that is not the case, however (Siddiqui, 2009).

ICI is, however, an exception to this as is evident from the comprehensive sustainability key performance indicators reported by the company and externally audited by third parties. In 2010, the company formulated the first sustainability report, which was separate from the company's annual report. The company used the G3 Reporting Framework issued by the Global Reporting Initiative (GRI). An independent sustainability audit was conducted by Ernst &Young, the results of which were incorporated into the improvement plans (ICI, 2010). For this report, ICI won the Best Sustainability Report Award and the runners-up award for its 2011 Sustainability Report. This award was introduced by the Institute of Chartered Accountants of Pakistan (ICAP) based on the internationally recognized framework: G3 Guidelines of Global Reporting Initiative (ICI, 2011). In 2010, ICI developed its key performance indicators (KPIs) for sustainability reporting for each segment in alignment with the basic parameters defined by AkzoNobel (ICI, 2010).

The various initiatives taken by the company, as part of the AkzoNobel group, demonstrate the sustainability concerns of the company. We will explore the sustainability-related developments through the triple bottom line approach.

Economic performance

Under the leadership of AkzoNobel, the company continued to prosper economically. In 2008, the company's profit after tax crossed the Rs.2 billion mark for the first time in the company's history showing an increase of 16% from the previous year (ICI, 2008). The positive economic performance of the company continued in the coming years with a 10% increase in the company's profit after taxes in 2009; furthermore the company paid the shareholders the highest ever dividend per share in the company's history (ICI, 2009). In 2011, however, the impact of a severe gas shortage in the country adversely impacted ICI Pakistan's bottom line through an increase in the operating costs by Rs.825 million. This lowered the company's profitability compared to the previous year (ICI, 2011). In April 2011, ICI Pakistan's Board of Directors received a proposal from its international holding company AkzoNobel to demerge the paint business into a separate listed entity. This was approved in May 2011 by the Board of Directors of ICI Pakistan, and two distinct companies were formed: AkzoNobel Pakistan and ICI Pakistan, though at the time, both were owned by AkzoNobel (Tirmizi, 2012).

Social performance

In the area of employee productivity, the company invested in the training of its 901 employees in 2008 (ICI, 2008), with four executives attending leadership programmes in INSEAD and Oxford University. A new Code of Conduct was approved by the ICI Board in October 2008, which stressed the values of sustainable development at every single level of management and front-line workers. The Speak Up programme was initiated, a whistle blowing system to report corrupt, unethical or illegal behaviour—if employees do not feel able to use the normal management routes. In 2008, it was accessed eight times by employees. Each instance was investigated by the senior executives of the group with actions taken to resolve the situation (ICI, 2008). ICI Pakistan launched an employee engagement programme in early 2009. It was a voluntary programme in which many employees enthusiastically contributed their time and efforts for a variety of community welfare initiatives (ICI, 2009).

Since the start of its operations, ICI Pakistan has been engaged in supporting the development of its value chain partners and the community. Shakoor and Company, a local transportation company state:

> We started off with four 10-ton Bradford vehicles with a carrying capacity of 280 tons. Now it has increased up to 7,800 tons and 485 employees. We have grown with and through ICI Pakistan. In 1998, ICI worked with us to help us become CEFIC (European Chemical Industry Council) compliant. It was a 36-month long effort that ICI's HSE&S department helped define. ICI helped us develop the technical expertise and systems required for the safe transportation and handling of chemicals. We now have professional management, which is still far from the norm in our industry. Even our Human-Resource system is modeled after ICI.

My father always says "Whatever we are now; almost all of it is because of ICI"
(A. Shakoor, personal communication, 6 November 2014).

Environmental performance

In Pakistan, the chemical industry has been one of the major contributors to the country's economy since the start. However, the issue of environmental pollution has always been associated with this industry. Even after having anti-pollution laws, the environmental protection authorities are taking little action to handle the adverse environmental situation developed as a result of the hazardous emissions from these units (Rehman, 2010). A report released by the World Bank states that the air quality in Pakistan will further worsen over time and proper government intervention is required to tackle the problem. According to a World Bank study:

> Ambient concentrations of health-damaging particulate matters in Pakistan are, on average, more than four times above levels recommended in World Health Organization (WHO) guidelines. The harm caused by air pollution in Pakistan's urban areas is the highest in the South Asian region and exceeds most other high profile causes of mortality and morbidity in the country (Ahmed, 2014).

The report further highlights significant implementation gaps in the environmental protection policies of the country. In Pakistan, only 1% of waste being generated by the various industries is being treated before discharging it into the rivers and drains. In Pakistan, a meagre 0.003% (Rs.763 million) was allocated towards environmental protection in the Federal Budget of 2012–2013 (Dawn, 2012). Even in such conditions ICI Pakistan always remained committed to its vision of environmental sustainability. By 2008, the finishing machines at the soda ash plant had become old, and the sealing arrangement of these machines contained hazardous asbestos. These machines were replaced with steam cleaners, thus significantly lowering the generation of hazardous, non-product output (NPO). Project Salvage was initiated during 2008 at the polyester plant for the reduction of non-hazardous NPOs generated during the production of polyester. The waste generated was recycled, significantly reducing NPOs. In the past the treated water used at the paints plant was disposed of as waste. In 2008, the company started storing the water and processing it through an effluent treatment plant on-site. This water is then used for washing purposes. With 100% recycled water being used for washing purposes, the site's total water usage was reduced by 45% compared to the baseline year, 2005 (ICI, 2008). Energy has been a major problem in Pakistan for many years (Kazmi, 2014), and it had proven a challenge for ICI Pakistan also (I. Haider, personal communication, 28 October 2014). However, in 2008 the company acted in a sustainable manner and in order to produce more electricity, gas turbines operating on natural gas were substituted for dual fuel engines operating on furnace oil and natural gas. This reduced energy-related emissions of CO_2 in the polyester business by 23% compared to 2005.

ICI's steps to conserve natural resources were vital in a country where water availability is decreasing at an alarming rate. The 1951 per capita availability of water in Pakistan was 5,300 cubic metres, and it has now decreased to 1,200 cubic metres, which is just touching the water scarcity level of 1,000 cubic metres. Less than 50% of the population have access to safe drinking water and adequate sanitation (Environment and Sustainable Development, 2014) and no national plan for disaster risk management to cater to environmental hazards, climate change and ozone-depleting substances impacts exists. The soda ash business commissioned its reverse osmosis (RO) water purification plant in 2010. This new plant accomplished 100% water reduction, which meant that every single drop of water processed through the plant was being utilized in one process stream or another and not a single drop of water was being wasted during the soda ash production cycle (ICI, 2010). For the sustainable development of society as whole initiatives were taken in all of ICI's businesses, which included an internal company awareness campaign to save water wastage by the soda ash team which resulted in saving 240 million litres of water. The paint business experimented by utilizing rainwater directly in water-based paint manufacturing and as a result saving 5,000 litres of water. The polyester plant invented a system of recycling waste to greatly reduce its harmful effect on the environment and additionally save the company millions on treatment and raw material costs. In 2011, a total of 135 drums of waste were recycled completely and converted into valuable and consumable 39 tonnes of chips, ensuring zero inventories (ICI, 2011).

One innovative initiative taken by the company was the use of oxo-biodegradable technology, which is a "green" material that degrades like natural minerals and helps reduce chemical impact on the environment. ICI decided to test this technology and as a start replaced the paper envelopes used in everyday mailing with oxo-biodegradable bags. Little did they know that what was an experimental technology for them at that point in time, would make a breakthrough in the market. The vendor with whom they had developed the bags started receiving successive orders from other corporations that followed ICI's lead and decided to adopt the technology in their operations. ICI used 75,000 biodegradable bags with paper savings worth an estimated 31 trees. The company is now introducing this technology for packaging their products as well.

From a strategic point of view, AkzoNobel's main interest in ICI Pakistan was the paint business. The ownership had plans to set up a state-of-the-art paint manufacturing facility in Pakistan, which would serve the needs of not only the local markets, but also the Middle East and possibly the European market in the future. So after the demerger of the paint business into a separate entity in May 2011, the process to find a buyer for ICI Pakistan (soda ash, polyester and life sciences) began on 13 June 2012. Initially, three parties bid for ICI Pakistan: the Yunus Brothers Group, the Nishat Group (the largest private sector conglomerate in Pakistan), and a consortium of ICI Pakistan's employees backed by a Dubai-based private-equity firm Fajr

Capital. In the end, the Yunus Brothers Group (YBG) bought a 75.8% stake in ICI Pakistan from AkzoNobel for Rs14.4 billion in July 2012 ($152.5 million) (Tirmizi, 2012).

ICI Pakistan as part of Yunus Brothers Group (YBG)

This was the first time in the history of the company that ICI Pakistan was owned by a Pakistani company. As discussed in the previous sections the attitude of most of the local businesses towards corporate sustainability was not very proactive in Pakistan, making the employees at ICI a little doubtful about the importance the new leaders will place on business sustainability. A report on Pakistani organizations' behaviour regarding business sustainability stated:

> It is somewhat surprising that Standard Chartered, Royal Bank of Scotland and GlaxoSmithKline; all find themselves in the bottom quartile of the Asian Sustainability Report. This reflects an often cited accusation that multinational corporations sometimes have sophisticated policies and systems relating to sustainability in their home countries, but that does not adequately translate into the same types of activities in developing countries where stakeholder pressure is not as significant (Siddiqui, 2009).

However, the company's performance after acquisition by YBG demonstrated a continued commitment towards business sustainability. It was communicated to the employees that the performance appraisal criterion of the Chief Executive Officer (CEO) would be the achievement of a number of quantitative and qualitative value driven objectives. The quantitative objectives were related to the growth and financial performance of the business, and the qualitative objectives were related to the company's performance on sustainability parameters. This gave a strong message to the employees about the new ownership's attitude towards adopting business sustainability (ICI, 2013). We will study the journey of ICI Pakistan under the YBG ownership through the performance of the company on the triple bottom line parameters.

Economic performance

The new management changed the accounting period from January–December to July–June in order to align ICI Pakistan with the YBG's other businesses. ICI Pakistan posted net sales of PKR18.3 billion for the first half of 2013, which were 9% higher compared to the same period in the previous year, and profit after tax was also reported to be 37% higher. In the first half of 2014 the company achieved a 5% growth in net sales. The company also signed an agreement with Unibrands Pvt Ltd, an international concern, for the import, marketing and distribution of nutrition products of Morinaga Milk Industry Co. Limited in Pakistan. The current CEO of ICI Pakistan stated: "Sustainability is integral to us, and we believe in actively participating with our internal and external stakeholders to build a cleaner environment and efficient and safe operating procedures" (ICI, 2013).

Social performance

ICI Pakistan continued serving the communities in which they were operating through various social development programmes. The life sciences business, along with some external stakeholders, ran a breast cancer awareness campaign for the females living in under-privileged conditions and having little or no knowledge of the disease. According to the Pink Ribbon foundation in Pakistan, almost 40,000 females die because of breast cancer every year and one of the major reasons for this high death rate is low female literacy rates and lack of preventive health awareness among the public (A. Malik, personal communication, 6 November 2014). The new ownership adopted a participative approach for the development of social sustainability in communities. In 2013, ICI Pakistan discussed with the residents of Kakapir village (Pakistan) what developmental programmes would be most beneficial for their sustainable growth. The participants of the discussion highlighted the high level of illiteracy as a critical area, and a large number of females expressed the desire to be educated so that they can teach their children and support their families. As a response to this feedback, ICI Pakistan launched an adult literacy programme in collaboration with a non-profit organization. The programme was run for women of all ages living in under-privileged conditions. In May 2014, 28 women from Kakapir village graduated from this programme, and a parallel programme was started in Lyari (Karachi, Pakistan) in which 22 students were enrolled. The employees of the polyester business started a basic household electric wiring course of 6-months duration for under-privileged youth near the polyester plant. The purpose of this free training course was to impart technical skills to the uneducated youth through which they can earn a livelihood.

The employees of ICI Pakistan continued demonstrating the spirit of social sustainability under the new ownership. A group of employees visited the far-flung rain-affected area of Nagarparkar (Pakistan). The area is usually associated with long droughts so when heavy rain fell in this area, in 2013, it resulted in complete destruction of the homes and livelihoods of the residents. ICI employees voluntarily took time off from their work and started a rehabilitation programme for the people of Nagarparkar. This included monetary donations and building permanent houses for the community, which would protect them from future rains. They used some of the company's old banners and flex (outdoor promotional material) to rainproof the newly built houses. The company also built a computer facility for the residents of the undeveloped Bhit islands (a small fishing community on the coast of Karachi, Pakistan). Over 800 students benefit from this facility every day. In 2013, the company donated paint worth Rs.0.74 million (approximately $7,265) to a government hospital in Karachi. A hygienic drinking water programme was started in the province of Sind (Pakistan) in 2013, which provides access to safe and clean drinking water to over 20,000 people every day. The project is being developed further with the installation of water purification plants in the underdeveloped areas of the province (ICI, 2013).

In 2013, the company conducted HSE&S awareness sessions for a number of its customers along with arranging a customer conference in Istanbul (Turkey) for the better understanding of customer needs through an interactive session. The YBG group understood that the employees of the company had gone through a strategic transition, with the new ownership taking over, and to help them cope with this change, a series of CEO sessions were arranged throughout the company in March 2013. In these sessions, the CEO met with all the company's staff (managerial and non-managerial) and shared the top management's vision for the company's future and also listened to issues being faced by various employees after the takeover.

Environmental performance

2013 continued with the company getting external recognition for its sustainability initiatives in the form of the Best Sustainability Report award at the ACCA-WWF Pakistan Environmental Reporting Awards. The company's internal 2012 Chief Executive HSE&S Trophy was awarded to the chemical business based on the health, safety, and environmental performance and the award of Best HSE initiative was given to the soda ash, polyester and chemical businesses. This best award is based on a yearly competition held between the company's business units. In this competition, each business identifies significant hazards and actions taken to remove those hazards.

The development of a database was started, for measuring the company's performance in the areas of health, safety, energy, and environment. Earlier, this data was monitored globally by AkzoNobel. The new database will help ICI Pakistan monitor and track the company's impact on the environment. ICI participated in the Earth Hour global initiative and managed to save 2.063 MW of electricity at five of the company's work sites by switching off unnecessary lights, and Earth Day was celebrated on 22 April 2013 when employees voluntarily planted trees in various areas. The polyester business converted 250,000 wrappers of its packaging (bale wrappers) to biodegradable packaging, and the life sciences business also started the use of biodegradable bags for the packaging of one of its products, sunflower seeds. These biodegradable bags were especially designed for a customer of ICI Pakistan, the Food and Agriculture Organization (FAO) of the United Nations (UN) (ICI, 2013).

In 2014, two of the company's head offices were converted to LED (light-emitting diodes) tubes in place of the usual light tubes. LEDs are very energy-efficient and consume up to 90% less power than the regular incandescent bulbs. The new LED tubes are being run through solar panels thereby further reducing energy usage and cost. Because of the severe shortage of natural gas in the country, ICI Pakistan installed HTM heaters and power and steam generation plants, which is specialized equipment for efficient running of the polyester manufacturing plant. These machines are using coal-fired boilers instead of the formerly used natural gas. Before commencing the project the HSE department of the polyester business arranged a public hearing of the Environmental Impact Assessment (EIA) department. The EIA procedure is a legal requirement in Pakistan, according to which the potential impacts of proposed projects on the physical, chemical, biological, cultural and socioeconomic components of the total environment must be assessed. The project was passed by the respective authority, but ICI Pakistan without any legal requirement, ensured that the desulfurization technology was incorporated in the project's scope. This technology would adequately mitigate the adverse impacts of any hazardous gaseous emissions from the coal-fired boilers. This greatly increased the cost of the project; making it a 2 billion rupees (approximately $19.63 million) project. The technology removes sulphur dioxide from the boiler and furnace exhaust gases and is thus termed as a "clean-coal technology" (ICI, 2014).

Sustainable Culture and Leadership Development (SCALA) survey

The next step in the case study was observing and analysing the employee's perceptions about the role of leadership and different dimensions of culture in the company's approach towards sustainability. For this, a survey developed by Miller Consultants Inc. was administered at the various work sites of the company. The SCALA™ survey "is an assessment instrument composed of items pertaining to culture and leadership. The assessment contains both sustainability-specific content and general organizational climate content that has been demonstrated or asserted in other research to impact the execution of sustainability strategies" (SCALA, 2014).

In ICI Pakistan, SCALA was administered in August 2014 under the new leadership on a total sample of 40 respondents across the company. The respondents were selected through the process of cluster sampling in which managerial level employees were selected randomly out of three clusters, the three major company work sites. The mode of administration was paper based. The survey was administered at the three major work sites of the company by the researcher:

> ▸ ICI's polyester plant (Sheikhupura City)

> ▸ ICI's head office (Lahore City)

> ▸ ICI's soda ash plant (Khewra City)

A total sample of 40 employees was taken, and the survey had a 100% response rate. The respondents belonged to senior level, middle level and first-line level managers from the different business units. Out of the total 100% respondents, 20% were senior managers, 63% were middle managers, and 17% were first-line managers; 95% of the respondents were male, and the remaining 5% were females. In terms of age, 30% of the respondents belonged to the age group 20–30 years, 30% were about 31–40 years of age, 33% were within the 41–50 year age bracket, and 7% were between the ages of 51 and 60, thereby having representation from all the age groups. The survey instrument consisted of 30 questions pertaining to the following sections:

▷ Organizational leadership

▷ Organizational systems

▷ Organizational climate

▷ Change readiness

▷ Internal stakeholders

▷ External stakeholders

Ten questions were added to the survey by Business School Lausanne, tailored towards answering the case study's research questions and two questions were included by the researcher in order to gain greater understanding of the employees' perspective of the organization's sustainability. The questionnaire was in English, and the questions were a blend of open and close-ended questions. Close-ended questions were answered on a five-point Likert scale with responses ranging from "strongly agree" to "strongly disagree".

We will analyse the employee's responses with respect to the six sections of the SCALA survey in order to assess ICI employees' perceptions about the sustainability performance of the new leadership.

Organizational leadership

Organizational leadership plays a key role in the adoption and development of business sustainability. Successful leaders optimize employee well-being, social responsibility, job commitment, and financial performance all at the same time (Fry and Slocum, Jr, 2008). In the words of Hargreaves and Fink (2003):

Sustainable leadership matters, spreads and lasts. It is a shared responsibility, that does not unduly deplete human or financial resources, and that cares for and avoids exerting negative damage on the surrounding educational and community environment. Sustainable leadership has an activist engagement with the forces that affect it, and builds an educational environment of organizational diversity that promotes cross-fertilization of good ideas and successful practices in communities of shared learning and development.

The employees in ICI Pakistan had a very positive perception about the role of their leadership in the adoption and development of business sustainability within their organization. A greater percentage of the employees "strongly agreed" or "agreed" with the viewpoint that the new leadership is fulfilling its role in the area of sustainability leadership. This is evident through the following observed response rates.

Of the employees surveyed, 63% strongly agreed and 35% agreed that the current leaders of the company had a clear vision for business sustainability. Further elaborating their viewpoint, 45% of the employees strongly agreed and 53% agreed with the statement that the leaders integrate sustainability into their decision making as well. Thirty per cent strongly agreed and 58% agreed that the leaders of the company are able to inspire others about sustainability focused issues. When asked whether the leadership is willing to take measured risks in pursuit of sustainability 20% strongly agreed and 68% agreed with this statement. Forty-three per cent of the employees were in strong agreement along with 55% and 48% agreeing with the statements that the leadership is knowledgeable about sustainability issues and were personally committed to sustainability issues, respectively. Sixty per cent of the respondents thought that the leaders of the company are "much better" compared to the leaders of other companies with respect to their commitment towards sustainability, and 35% of the respondents termed the leadership as "better" than the others.

Organizational systems

The employees were surveyed about how much the company has embedded sustainability in their organizational systems. The responses showed a high degree of awareness among the organization's managerial staff regarding the organizational incorporation of business sustainability: 53% of the employees surveyed strongly agreed and 45% agreed that ICI Pakistan has embedded sustainability into the operational procedures and policies. Ninety-five per cent of the respondents were aware of the company's enterprise wide management system for sustainability; the high rate depicts their direct or indirect involvement in the system during their job performance. Twenty-eight per cent strongly agreed and 55% of the respondents agreed that the company had integrated sustainability-related goals into its performance management system. Fifteen per cent of the employees surveyed strongly agreed and 53% agreed that the rewards and compensations are clearly linked with the company's sustainability goals.

The positive feedback about the integration of sustainability objectives into the organization's systems was further strengthened by the responses generated through the open-ended question, in which the respondents were asked to briefly speak about any sustainability initiative in which they had been involved. All the 40 respondents narrated a number of sustainability projects that they were a part of during their time in ICI Pakistan. One of the respondents said:

I was actively involved in the introduction of biodegradable packaging for our finished goods along with the introduction of paper-free invoice, packing list and order delivery report for our customers. It is a great feeling playing a positive role in reducing the burden on our environment.

Another respondent shared:

I am an active part of the free eye camp project at our soda ash work site This programme is so famous in the community that people recognize ICI Pakistan because of this programme. I am proud of this initiative of my company.

> **I am an active part of the free eye camp project at our soda ash work site This programme is so famous in the community that people recognize ICI Pakistan because of this programme. I am proud of this initiative of my company**

Organizational climate

A positive organizational climate was portrayed by the respondents with 43% of the employees strongly agreeing and 45% agreeing that the level of trust within ICI Pakistan is high. Thirty-eight per cent strongly agreed and 50% of the employees agreed that continual learning is a core focus of the organization under the new leadership, and 38% strongly agreed and 53% agreed that the new leadership rewards innovation. Thirteen per cent of the employees showed strong agreement and 49% agreed that the company encourages its employees to learn about business sustainability from external sources. The high percentage of positive responses showed that the employees perceived that the new leadership had developed a supportive climate for the adoption and facilitation of sustainability within the organization.

Change readiness

Change has been an integral part of the company's history, with the company going through several changes in its product portfolio along with changes in the corporate ownership. Many of the employees have witnessed these changes throughout their careers in the company. An employee working in the soda ash business says:

One look around ICI, and you will find people who have been working here for 10, 20, or 30 years. That is something extraordinary and rarely found anywhere else. If you delve deeper, you will know that ICI Pakistan has been a second home for many.

> **One look around ICI, and you will find people who have been working here for 10, 20, or 30 years. That is something extraordinary and rarely found anywhere else. If you delve deeper, you will know that ICI Pakistan has been a second home for many**

The company's ability to manage change positively is shown in the responses of the employees surveyed: 38% strongly agreed and

52% agreed that ICI Pakistan has a strong track record for implementing both large-scale and incremental (small, continuous) change successfully and 15% strongly agreed whereas 63% of the respondents agreed that the company actively challenges the status quo.

Internal stakeholders

With respect to the company's internal stakeholders 38% of the respondents strongly agreed and 64% agreed that the company has a clear strategy for engaging all internal stakeholders in its sustainability efforts. While 35% strongly agreed and 58% agreed that, by and large, people are engaged in work that is in some way connected to sustainability goals of the company. Thirty-five per cent of the employees strongly agreed that the employees feel valued in ICI Pakistan and 48% agreed with this statement. When the respondents were asked what they thought the company was trying to achieve by addressing sustainability issues, 83% of the respondents opted for "creating economic, social and environmental value". Seventy per cent of the respondents rated ICI Pakistan as "much better" than the other companies in the same industry while 53% thought the company's approach towards sustainability was "proactive" and 45% thought it was "active".

External stakeholders

Twenty per cent of the respondents strongly agreed and 60% agreed that the company has a mechanism in place to actively engage with external stakeholders about sustainability efforts and that the company encourages sustainability in its supply chain. The survey results reveal a very positive assessment of the employees with respect to the company's sustainability leadership and culture. The respondents gave a favourable assessment of the new ownership with regard to its role in integrating sustainability within the organization's culture and actively involving all the stakeholders in their sustainability vision. The survey results are supported by the evidence of the new leadership's sustainability initiatives, discussed in the previous section. The employees were told about the company's sustainability vision by the new CEO himself. They were informed that the performance appraisal of the CEO would also be based on the company's performance on the sustainability KPIs. This highlighted the importance of business sustainability for the leadership.

Up until this point in the case study, we have investigated what the company has done in the adoption and incorporation of business sustainability, but we also need to gauge how far the company has travelled along the path of embracing true business sustainability. For this purpose, we place another filter on ICI Pakistan in the shape of the Dyllick/Muff Business Sustainability Typology.

Redefined shareholder value management

According to Dyllick and Muff (2015) a huge disconnect exists between the intentions of organizations with respect to business sustainability (BST) and the actual significant improvements being made on a global level. This disconnect has been linked to the lack of understanding regarding the true meaning of business sustainability in both the academic and the corporate world. Thus a new typology of business sustainability has been developed that defines three levels of business sustainability:

> ▶ Business Sustainability 1.0 (redefined shareholder value management)

> ▶ Business Sustainability 2.0 (managing for the triple bottom line)

> ▶ Business Sustainability 3.0 (true sustainability)

In order to place an organization in this typology the organization's approach for integrating sustainability in the business is analysed through the "input-process-output" model. This can be clearly understood through the framework presented in Figure 1 (Dyllick & Muff, 2015).

Figure 1 A framework for considering different approaches of business sustainability

BUSINESS SUSTAINABILITY TYPOLOGY (BST)	Concerns (What?)	Values created (What for?)	Organizational perspective (How?)
Business-as-usual	Economic concerns	Shareholder value	Inside-out
Business Sustainability 1.0	Three-dimensional concerns	Refined shareholder value	Inside-out
Business Sustainability 2.0	Three-dimensional concerns	Triple bottom line	Inside-out
Business Sustainability 3.0	Starting with sustainability challenges	Creating value for the common good	Outside-in
The key shifts involved:	1st shift: broadening the business concern	2nd shift: expanding the value created	3rd shift: changing the perspective

ICI Pakistan's business sustainability position is defined on the basis of the information gathered in the previous sections of the case study. BST 1.0 has been defined as "an approach to business that creates shareholder value by embracing opportunities and managing risks deriving from economic, environmental and social developments". This is considered as the first step towards the adoption of true BST by Dyllick and Muff (2015) in which organizations recognize that new business challenges exist outside their markets and raise social and environmental concerns. ICI Pakistan is currently positioned on the BST 1.0 level.

Concerns

The BST 1.0 companies are addressing economic, ecological, and social concerns. As discussed ICI Pakistan's sustainability approach is focused on these three dimensions. The sustainability KPIs, which they reported on in the last six years, are shown in Figure 2.

Figure 2 ICI Pakistan's Sustainability Key Performance Indicators

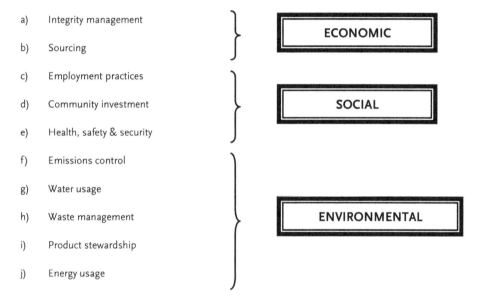

a)   Integrity management

b)   Sourcing

c)   Employment practices

d)   Community investment

e)   Health, safety & security

f)   Emissions control

g)   Water usage

h)   Waste management

i)   Product stewardship

j)   Energy usage

ECONOMIC

SOCIAL

ENVIRONMENTAL

Environmental

The various initiatives being pursued by ICI Pakistan include water usage reduction, production waste reduction and recycling, working on the use of alternative and sustainable energy sources in the form of solar panels and clean coal technologies, use of biodegradable materials in internal communication and packaging of some products, and continuous hazardous emission reduction from all the work sites.

Social

Some examples of social sustainability are: working for the betterment and advancement of the communities in which the company operates, continuous focus on employee safety, training and career advancement, and working with supply chain partners to improve sustainability of the processes. The new leadership has launched a number of projects to address the social concerns of diverse communities in which the company is operating. They include an adult literacy programme, establishment of water purification plants in places where people had no access to clean drinking water, awareness campaigns about breast cancer among illiterate women, funding of various schools being run for the under-privileged youth of the nation, and vocational training being given voluntarily by ICI employees. ICI Pakistan has an employee engagement survey conducted each year by an outside research organization "Gallup Pakistan". In 2012, the engagement survey score was 4.35 on a 5-point scale (with 5 being the highest positive indicator on the scale), placing ICI at the 74th percentile within the Gallup global database. The company also ranked third in the Best Place to Work 2012 survey conducted by Engage Consulting (an international research organization).

Economic

Economic concerns have also been the focus of the management, which is evident from the ownership shifts the company went through in the recent past. As explained in the company's historical timeline the underlying reason behind the acquisition by Yunus Brothers Group and the sale of the company by AkzoNobel was economic.

ICI Pakistan can be characterized as BST 1.0 in accordance with Dyllick and Muff (2015). In BST 1.0 companies "the underlying objective of all the company's activities remains economic. While introducing sustainability in the business will generate positive side effects in the environmental and social fields, business success still is evaluated from a purely economic view".

Values created

According to Dyllick and Muff (2015) the company on the BST 1.0 level addresses the three dimensional concerns in order to create redefined shareholder value. In this section ICI Pakistan is analysed on the basis of the particular values it is creating or preserving, through the input-process-output model. In the input-process-output model *values created* is the output being delivered by the company.

When the employees were asked what the company is primarily trying to achieve by addressing sustainability initiatives, 53% chose "the desire to improve efficiency and impact the company's bottom line", 48% selected "the desire for innovation and growth" and 33% opted for "awareness of our responsibility to the environment". This reinforces the BST 1.0 positioning of the company, as the sustainability initiatives are perceived to be creating and enhancing shareholder value. The BST 1.0 value creation approach is seen in the company's definition of its value creation areas as well. The company defines the following areas as its refined shareholder value creation:

▷ Customer care

▷ Supply chain partner management

▷ Innovation in business operations and products

▷ Employee well-being

▷ Value creation for shareholders

ICI Pakistan has termed its customers, supply chain partners, employees, and shareholders as the entities for which it is generating value through its business processes. This demonstrates a refined vision towards a shareholder definition in contrast to the business-as-usual definition of the typical capital investing shareholder. Along with the primary business of the company, ICI Pakistan is also creating value for its supply-chain partners, employees, community and the natural habitat in which it operates. However, all these activities are being done as support functions of their economic sustainability, therefore, positioning the company on the BST 1.0 level. This can be further understood by looking at the "process" part of the input-process-output model; the part that clarifies *how* the company addresses the identified concerns for creating the "refined shareholder value".

Organizational perspectives

Two types of organizational perspective have been defined in the Dyllick/Muff Business Sustainability Typology (2015), the "inside-out approach" and the "outside-in approach". "Usually, companies start from their existing business, strategy or product-lines and work on making them more sustainable (inside-out). This may lead them to incremental or radical improvements, depending on their cultural readiness and how far-sighted and courageous they are".
This is opposite to the "outside-in" approach in which "sustainability challenges are used as the starting point to define possible contributions by a business that also makes business sense". According to the typology only BST 3.0 companies are following the "outside-in" approach.

If we study the product portfolio of ICI Pakistan, we can see that the business units of the company have been pretty much the same with various additions and demergers through time. The company has not yet designed any product that addresses or offers a solution to any of the triple bottom line concerns; rather it has tried to redesign or improve its production processes, supply chain and operational procedures in order to make them more sustainable. The company is also investing in the acquisition of sustainable alternatives for energy production.

This is evident through the different initiatives taken in the area of energy conservation through the use of solar panels and LEDs in the work sites along with sustainable resource utilization (reduced water usage for the existing production processes, water recycling, switching production to recycled raw materials for the production of existing products, using biodegradable packaging for existing products, etc.). Furthermore, the company is incurring an additional cost to eliminate the hazardous gas emissions from its new coal-fired boiler plant. This technology is being used to make a business process environmentally safe and is thus an "inside-out" approach in which the company takes the existing products or procedures and tries to make them more sustainable. The social sustainability initiatives of the company also focus on the areas in which the company is currently operating thereby facilitating the community that is directly or indirectly associated with the company's existing operations.

The challenge

> ongoing turbulent political condition and continued energy shortages in Pakistan" as one of the biggest challenges for the company

ICI Pakistan has started its journey on the path of business sustainability by taking the initial steps under an international ownership. Now the company is owned and managed by a local group, and the data show that the new leadership is following in the footsteps of the previous owners. However, the company has not moved to a higher level of business sustainability, rather it is maintaining its position as a BST 1.0 company. The management of the company attributes much of its challenges to the unsustainable external environment of the country. The new CEO of the company stated the "ongoing turbulent political condition and continued energy shortages in Pakistan" as one of the biggest challenges for the company (ICI, 2014). So the most significant question that we can ask after analysing the sustainability journey of ICI Pakistan is: "Can a company progress on the path to true business sustainability in such adverse conditions?"

> "Can a company progress on the path to true business sustainability in such adverse conditions?"

In the World Economic Forum's meeting held in Davos (Switzerland) in 2012 it was suggested that:

Attention needs to be given not so much to what business has to do, but what governments need to do to get a business more firmly on the sustainability track. Governments are a crucial part of the implementing front line. Much can be done at the national level, all the more so given the manifest weaknesses of today's intergovernmental processes (Zadek, 2012).

The role of governments in creating and supporting business sustainability has also been discussed in various other studies. Peck and Gibson (2000) state:

Anticipating rising world demand for sustainable products, services and systems is also an obligation and an opportunity for governments. Indeed, there is a crucial role for governments in facilitating the transition to an economy that is much more efficient, much fairer and much less damaging. Governments that lead will be in a stronger position to set the agenda and establish advanced positions in their industries and their citizens. Countries that lag behind will inevitably face increasing competitive disadvantage and lost opportunity.

Further strengthening this argument is a study done by the Institute of Southern Studies on some of the American states. The research revealed a positive relationship between a state's economic and environmental performance. The states that were ranked the lowest for their official economic performance also showed the worst environmental performance by the businesses (Bell, 2002). The situation is even more critical in developing countries as a twin need for both economic development and sustainable development and implementation exists, making the task more challenging (Lifshitz, 2010). Furthermore, the socioeconomic environment in which the company is operating, and the development priorities in the respective region shape the structure of a firm's sustainability efforts. In Nigeria, which, according to the International Statistical Institution (2015), is a developing country like Pakistan, the socially responsible activities of businesses are oriented towards the socioeconomic development challenges of the country which include poverty reduction, healthcare provision, infrastructure development and education. However, in the Western, developed part of the world, the socioeconomic activities of most businesses are focused on consumer protection, fair trade, green marketing, climate-change concerns, or socially responsible investments. In developing countries, the government institutions are weak, resulting in poor political governance, so that the responsibility for socioeconomic development is often delegated to private actors, like relatives, neighbourhoods, religious bodies, non-profit organizations or increasingly business (Visser, 2008). The discussion shows that business sustainability is severely limited without the support of positive external factors. The role of governments in supporting businesses to pursue sustainability is being emphasized more and more. However, in most of the developing countries business is not getting support or motivation from the government.

Pakistan is also an example of a developing country that is struggling for its mere survival among numerous threats like terrorism, religious intolerance, severe resource scarcity, energy shortages, corruption, low economic growth, over-population and high rates of illiteracy. In 1997, Pakistan managed to draft

The situation is even more critical in developing countries as a twin need for both economic development and sustainable development and implementation exists, making the task more challenging

The discussion shows that business sustainability is severely limited without the support of positive external factors

Pakistan is also an example of a developing country that is struggling for its mere survival among numerous threats like terrorism, religious intolerance, severe resource scarcity, energy shortages, corruption, low economic growth, over-population and high rates of illiteracy

its Environment Protection Act and in 2011, drafted its first climate-change policy; much later than the developed part of the world (Dawn, 2012). Naseer Memon, the chairperson of Strengthening Participatory Organization (SPO) Pakistan said:

> Regrettably, there is a serious lack of political will on the part of the government to make development sustainable. Politically motivated decision-making in public sector development often compromises principles of sustainable development. Environmental sensitivities and community rights are flagrantly violated in public infrastructure projects. As a matter of fact, the recent flood disasters have exposed the country's vulnerability due to faulty development paradigms. It must be noted that although public policies make tall claims, bad governance and the absence of political will preclude meaningful actions.

At the start of the case study, we termed ICI Pakistan's journey of sustainability as "sustainability through adversity" because while analysing the challenges and milestones achieved by this company we cannot ignore the external factors, which are severely restricting the company. The journey of ICI Pakistan and its current position in terms of business sustainability can only be understood when analysed in context of the environment it is operating in. So while looking for an answer to the question raised at the start of this section we are reminded of the words of the Director General of the Pakistan Environment Protection Agency, Asif S. Khan, who in an interview with a national newspaper said:

Hope prevails within the employees of ICI Pakistan regarding the future of the company in terms of the new leadership role in taking ICI Pakistan to the next levels of business sustainability

> The requirements of Agenda 21 and the Rio Convention of 1992 for the eradication of poverty in order to increase production and sustainability so that "the needs of the majority of the people of our world" can be met, are dreams and part of a distant horizon for Pakistan. Is there any possibility of implementation of the measures discussed during the conference, in a country that has been ravaged by terrorism and whose government considers defense a greater priority than environmental protection and sustainability? And is it fair to strike parallels between Pakistan and developed nations of the world (Dawn, 2012)?

The same applies to organizations operating in Pakistan. ICI Pakistan is fighting the battle for sustainable development in an unsustainable environment. So can we expect it to travel from BST 1.0 to BST 2.0 and ultimately embody the spirit of true business sustainability among the prevailing conditions in Pakistan?

"After the change in the shareholders of the company, I wish the new local ownership will prioritize sustainability with the same passion as it was done when we were part of a large international group"

Hope prevails within the employees of ICI Pakistan regarding the future of the company in terms of the new leadership role in taking ICI Pakistan to the next levels of business sustainability; as one employee states: "After the change in the shareholders of the company, I wish the new local ownership will prioritize sustainability with the same passion as it was done when we were part of a large international group".

Bibliography

Ahmed, A. (2014, July 14). Pakistan's urban air pollution off the charts: World Bank. *Dawn*. Retrieved from http://www.dawn.com/news/1119031

Akhtar, R. (2011). Why we're failing to sustain—and how can we succeed, right now. *TBL Sustainability Advocacy*. Retrieved from http://www.tbl.com.pk/why-were-failing-to-sustain-and-how-can-we-succeed-right-now

AkzoNobel (2014, September 11). AkzoNobel ranked top of DJSI for third year running. Retrieved from AkzoNobel: https://www.akzonobel.com/news_center/news/news_and_press_releases/2014/akzonobel_ranked_top_of_djsi_for_third_year_running.aspx

Arifeen, M (2013). Need for massive CSR in Pakistan. *The Financial Daily*. Retrieved from http://thefinancialdaily.com/Articles/ViewArticleDetail.aspx?ArticleID=5418

Baig, M.A. (2013, November 7). YBG were cognisant of the value that the ICI brand would bring, particularly for diversification under the ICI umbrella. *Dawn*. Retrieved from aurora.dawn.com/.../ybg-were-cognisant-of-the-value-that-the-ici-brand-

Baloch, F. (2011, December 6). Explaining the spin-off: AkzoNobel gearing up to supply Middle East paint market from Pakistan. Retrieved from http://tribune.com.pk/story/302658/explaining-the-spin-off-akzonobel-gearing-up-to-supply-middle-east-paint-market-from-pakistan

Bell, D.V. (2002). The role of government in advancing corporate sustainability. *Sustainable Enterprise Academy*, York University (Canada).

CECP (2012). Giving in numbers. Retrieved from http://cecp.co/pdfs/giving_in_numbers/GIN2012_finalweb.pdf

CEFIC (2015). *About us.* Retrieved from http://www.cefic.org/About-us/Cefic

CIA World Fact Book (2014). Pakistan economy. Retrieved from: https://www.cia.gov/library/publications/the-world-factbook/geos/pk.html

Corporate Philanthropy (2015, March 8). In *Business Dictionary*: http://www.businessdictionary.com/definition/corporate-philanthropy.html

Dawn. (2012, May 27). Pakistan's sustainable development conundrum. Retrieved from: http://www.dawn.com/news/737641/pakistans-sustainable-development-conundrum

Dow Jones Sustainability Index (2014). Retrieved from: http://en.wikipedia.org/wiki/Dow_Jones_Sustainability_Index

Dyllick, T. & Muff, K. (2015). Clarifying the meaning of sustainable business: Introducing a typology from business-as-usual to true business sustainability. *Organization & Environment*, 1-9.

Fry, L.W. & Slocum, Jr., J.W. (2008). Maximizing the triple bottom line through spiritual leadership. *Organizational Dynamics*, 37 (1), 86-96.

Fullan, M. (2005). *Leadership & Sustainability: System Thinkers in Action*. Thousand Oaks: Corwin Press.

Gilani, S.R., Mahmood, Z., Hussain, M., Baig, Y., Abbas, Z., & Batool, S (2013). A study of drinking water of industrial area of Sheikhupura with special concern to arsenic, manganese and chromium. *Pakistan Journal of Engineering & Applied Science, 13*, 118-126.

Hamid, M. (2012, August 12). A history of ICI in Pakistan: Story of an icon. Retrieved from http://www.brecorder.com/articles-a-letters/626:/1226481:a-history-of-ici-in-pakistan-story-of-an-icon/?date=2012-08-12

Hargreaves, A., & Fink, D. (2003). The seven principles of sustainable leadership. *Educational Leadership*, 2-12.

Hils, K.M. (2011). The Pakistani perspective on sustainability reporting. Retrieved from http://www.tbl.com.pk/the-pakistani-perspective-on-sustainability-reporting

ICI Pakistan Limited. (2008). *ICI Pakistan Limited Annual Report*. Karachi: Corporate Communication & Public Affairs Department ICI.

ICI Pakistan Limited. (2009). *ICI Pakistan Limited Annual Report*. Karachi: Corporate Communication & Public Affairs Department ICI.

ICI Pakistan Limited (2010). *ICI Pakistan Limited Annual Report*. Karachi: Corporate Communication and Public Affairs Department.

ICI Pakistan Limited (2011). *ICI Pakistan Limited Annual Report*. Karachi: Corporate Communication & Public Affairs Department.

ICI Pakistan Limited (2012). *ICI Pakistan Limited Annual Report*. Karachi: Corporate Communication & Public Affairs Department.

ICI Pakistan Limited (2013). *ICI Pakistan Limited Annual Report*. Karachi: Corporate Communication & Public Affairs Department ICI.

ICI Pakistan Limited (2014). *ICI Pakistan Limited Annual Report*. Karachi: Corporate Communication and Public Affairs Department.

Imperial Chemical Industries (2015, February 13). Imperial chemical industries. Retrieved from: http://en.wikipedia.org/w/index.php?title=Imperial_Chemical_Industries&action=history

International Statistical Institute (2015). Developing countries. Retrieved from http://www.isi-web.org/component/content/article/5-root/root/81-developing

Jaspal, Z.N., & Haider, N. (2014). Management of chemicals in Pakistan: Concerns and challenges. *South Asian Studies*, 497-517.

Jensen, D. (2006). *Endgame, Vol. 1: The Problem of Civilization*. Reed Business Information.

Kazmi, Z. (2014, January 7). Pakistan's energy security. *The Express Tribune*. Retrieved: http://tribune.com.pk/story/655573/pakistans-energy-security.

Khwaja, M.A. (2012). Environmental challenges and constraints to policy issues for sustainable industrial development in Pakistan. *Sustainable Development Policy Institute*, p. 31.

Lifshitz, I. (2010). Balancing sustainability with economic development in developing countries: The case study of Indonesia. *Environmental Leader*, pp. 8-9.

Ministry Of Planning, Development & Reforms (2014). Retrieved from pc.gov.pk/mtdf/11-Environment/11-Environment.pdf

Peck, S., & Gibson, R. (2000). Pushing the revolution. *Alternatives Journal, 26* (1), 23-36.

Porter, M.E., & Kramer, M.R. (2011). Creating shared value. *Harvard Business Review*, 63-77.

Rehman, F. (2010, January 21). Industrial units causing pollution. *The Nation*, p. 3.

SCALA. (2014). *The Sustainability Culture and Leadership Assessment Survey*. Louisville, KY: Miller Consultants, Inc.

Siddiqui, H. (2009, December 28). Poor disclosure/poor rating for Pakistan in recent Asian sustainability report. Retrieved from http://www.cipe.org/blog/2009/12/28/poor-disclosure-poor-ratings-for-pakistan-in-recent-asian-sustainability-report/#.VQEqkI65gvw

The News (2011). Corporate philanthropy increases to Rs3.8bn despite economic challenges. Retrieved from: http://www.thenews.com.pk/Todays-News-3-148035-Corporate-philanthropy-increases-to-Rs38bn-despite-economic-challenges.

Tirmizi, F. (2012, July 31). Mergers and acquisitions: Lucky Cement led group buys ICI Pakistan for $152m. Retrieved from http://tribune.com.pk/story/415097/mergers-and-acquisitions-lucky-cement-led-group-buys-ici-pakistan-for-152m

UNDP. (2015). The Millennium Development Goals. Retrieved from http://www.pk.undp.org/content/pakistan/en/home/mdgoverview.html.

Visser, W. (2008). *Corporate Social Responsibility in Developing Countries*. Oxford: Oxford University Press.

Wilson, M. (2003). Corporate sustainability: what is it and where does it come from? *Ivey Business Journal*, March/April.

World Bank (2013). Pakistan. Retrieved from http://data.worldbank.org/country/pakistan.

World Business Council for Sustainable Development. (2015). 10 key messages. Retrieved from http://www.wbcsd.org/newsroom/key-messages.aspx

Zadek, S. (2012, January 31). Governments need to play a key role in aligning business and sustainability. *Guardian Sustainable Business*. Retrieved from http://www.theguardian.com/sustainable-business.

Zeeshan, M., & Ahmed, V. (2013). Energy, environment and growth nexus in South Asia. *Environ Dev Sustain*, pp. 1465–1475.

Appendix

Interviews with the company's top management and supply chain partners were conducted to gain a better understanding of the company's sustainability journey. The interviewees were selected in collaboration with the corporate HSE&S manager of the company, based on their level of experience and engagement in the sustainability initiatives. In order to give representation to all the business units of the company, the vice presidents of all the businesses were selected as interviewees. The interview protocol was shared with the respondent a few days before the interview in order to facilitate the generation of maximum information.

Table A1 Research Participants

Name	Title	Years of engagement with ICI Pakistan
Internal stakeholders		
Mr Iqbal Haider	GM Technical	35 years
Mr Sohail A. Khan	VP Soda Ash & Polyester	29 years
Mr Zafar Farid	Corporate HSE&S Manager	25 years
Mr Asif Malik	VP Life Sciences	15 years
External stakeholders		
Mr. Shakoor	Owner Shakoor & Co. (supply chain partners)	34 years

 Syeda Nazish Zahra Bukhari, Assistant Professor, Institute of Business & Information Technology (IBIT), Quaid-a-Azam Campus, University of the Punjab, Lahore, Pakistan.

📞 092-4299230826
💻 nazish.bukhari@bsl-lausanne.ch

For Product Safety Concerns and Information please contact our EU representative GPSR@taylorandfrancis.com Taylor & Francis Verlag GmbH, Kaufingerstraße 24, 80331 München, Germany

Batch number: 08153807

Printed by Printforce, the Netherlands